Oxford AQA History

A LEVEL AND AS — Component 1

Industrialisation and the People: Britain c1783–1885

Ailsa Fortune

SERIES EDITOR
Sally Waller

Great Clarendon Street, Oxford, OX2 6DP, United Kingdom

Oxford University Press is a department of the University of Oxford. It furthers the University's objective of excellence in research, scholarship, and education by publishing worldwide. Oxford is a registered trade mark of Oxford University Press in the UK and in certain other countries

© Oxford University Press 2015

The moral rights of the authors have been asserted

First published in 2015

All rights reserved. No part of this publication may be reproduced, stored in a retrieval system, or transmitted, in any form or by any means, without the prior permission in writing of Oxford University Press, or as expressly permitted by law, by licence or under terms agreed with the appropriate reprographics rights organization. Enquiries concerning reproduction outside the scope of the above should be sent to the Rights Department, Oxford University Press, at the address above.

You must not circulate this work in any other form and you must impose this same condition on any acquirer

British Library Cataloguing in Publication Data
Data available

978-019-835453-6

Kindle edition: 978-019-836394-1

10 9

Paper used in the production of this book is a natural, recyclable product made from wood grown in sustainable forests.
The manufacturing process conforms to the environmental regulations of the country of origin.

Printed and bound by CPI Group (UK) Ltd, Croydon, CR0 4YY

Approval message from AQA

This textbook has been approved by AQA for use with our qualification. This means that we have checked that it broadly covers the specification and we are satisfied with the overall quality. Full details of our approval process can be found on our website.

We approve textbooks because we know how important it is for teachers and students to have the right resources to support their teaching and learning. However, the publisher is ultimately responsible for the editorial control and quality of this book.

Please note that when teaching the AQA A Level History course, you must refer to AQA's specification as your definitive source of information. While this book has been written to match the specification, it does not provide complete coverage of every aspect of the course.

A wide range of other useful resources can be found on the relevant subject pages of our website: www.aqa.org.uk.

Please note that the Practice Questions in this book allow students a genuine attempt at practising exam skills, but they are not intended to replicate examination papers.

Contents

Introduction to features	v
AQA History specification overview	vi
Introduction to the *Oxford AQA History* series	viii
Timeline	x
Introduction to this book	xii

PART ONE: AS AND A LEVEL
THE IMPACT OF INDUSTRIALISATION: BRITAIN, c1783–1832

SECTION 1
Pressure for change, c1783–1812 — 1

1 The British political system c1783 — 1
- Government and representation — 1
- Democracy at national and local level — 6
- Whigs and Tories — 7
- Summary — 9

2 Government: Pitt the Younger as Prime Minister and his successors — 11
- Pitt's relationship with the King — 11
- The 1784 election — 13
- Reform of finance, trade and administration — 15
- William Pitt's successors — 18
- Summary — 19

3 Economic developments — 21
- Industrialisation — 21
- The growth of cotton and other industries — 23
- Changes in the source and use of power — 26
- Condition of agriculture — 27
- Summary — 28

4 Social developments — 31
- A changing class structure — 31
- Working conditions — 33
- Standards of living — 36
- The Combination Acts 1799 and 1800 — 38
- Summary — 39

5 Political pressures on government — 41
- The political influence of the French Revolution — 41
- Irish rebellion and union — 45
- Radicalism and opposition — 46
- Demands for parliamentary reform — 48
- Summary — 49

6 Wartime pressures on government — 51
- The political, economic and social impact of war 1802–1812 — 51
- The condition of Britain in 1812 — 57
- Summary — 60

SECTION 2
Government and a changing society 1812–1832 — 61

7 Government: Lord Liverpool as Prime Minister — 61
- Lord Liverpool's administration — 62
- The Corn Laws and other legislation — 64
- Attitudes to repression and reform — 67
- The economy — 68
- Summary — 69

8 Government: Canning, Goderich and Wellington as Prime Ministers — 71
- Canning, Goderich and Wellington — 71
- Legislation — 75
- Peel's Metropolitan Police Force — 76
- O'Connell and Catholic Emancipation — 77
- Summary — 78

9 Economic developments 1812–1832 — 81
- Continuing industrialisation — 81
- Developments in key industries — 83
- Agricultural change — 85
- Economic policies and Free Trade — 87
- Summary — 89

10 Social developments — 91
- The effects of industrialisation — 91
- Standards of living — 95
- Working class discontent — 97
- Summary — 99

11 Pressures for change — 101
- Luddism — 101
- Radical agitation — 104
- The anti-slavery movement — 105
- Methodism — 107
- Early socialism and Robert Owen — 108
- Summary — 109

12 Greater democracy — 111
- The election of the Whigs — 111
- Pressure for parliamentary reform — 113
- The Great Reform Act and its impact — 116
- The state of Britain politically, economically and socially by 1832 — 119
- Summary — 121

PART TWO: A LEVEL
THE AGE OF REFORM: BRITAIN, 1832–1885

SECTION 3
Political change and social reform, 1832–1846 — 123

13 Government: Grey and Melbourne as Prime Ministers — 123
- Grey, Melbourne and the ideas and ideology of the Whig Party — 124
- The Tories in opposition and government — 129
- Summary — 132

14 The Whig response to social change — 133
- Whig social reforms — 133
- Summary — 142

Contents (continued)

15 Pressure for change — 143
- Chartism — 143
- Irish Radicalism — 147
- The Anti-Poor Law League — 147
- The Anti-Corn Law League — 149
- Social reform campaigners, including Shaftesbury and Chadwick — 150
- Summary — 152

16 The Conservative response to change — 153
- Finance, administration and the economy — 153
- The Bank Charter Act, 1844 — 157
- Trade and Business Reform — 158
- Summary — 160

17 Economic developments — 161
- The railway 'revolution' and associated economic growth — 161
- Agriculture and the repeal of the Corn Laws — 165
- Summary — 169

18 Social developments (1832–1846) — 171
- Conditions in urban Britain — 171
- Changes in the lives of workers — 174
- Changes in the lives of the poor — 175
- Unions and other working-class movements — 176
- Other working class movements — 178
- Summary — 180

SECTION 4
Economy, society and politics 1846–1885 — 181

19 Government and developing political organisation — 181
- The development of the political system and party realignment — 181
- The emergence of the Liberal Party — 185
- Summary — 188

20 Government and democracy — 191
- Gladstone as Prime Minister; his ministries, ideas and policies — 191
- Disraeli, his ministries, ideas and policies — 195
- Increasing democracy — 198
- Summary — 201

21 Pressure for change (1846–1885) — 203
- Social campaigns — 203
- Public health reform — 205
- Chartism — 206
- Pressure for parliamentary reform — 207
- Irish nationalism — 210
- Summary — 213

22 Economic developments — 215
- The mid-Victorian boom — 215
- The 'golden age' of agriculture — 216
- Industrial and transport developments — 218
- Impact of increased trade — 222
- The Great Depression — 223
- Summary — 225

23 Social developments 1846–1885 — 227
- Prosperity and poverty in towns and countryside — 227
- Regional divisions — 231
- Influences shaping social developments, including Evangelicalism — 232
- 'Self-Help' — 234
- Trade unions and education — 235
- Education — 237
- Summary — 237

24 The political, economic and social condition of Britain by 1885 — 239
- The political condition of Britain – the extent of democracy — 239
- The economic and social condition of Britain by 1885 — 242
- Britain's industrial position — 243
- Summary — 246

Conclusion — 247
Glossary — 250
Bibliography — 253
Acknowledgements — 254
Index — 255

Introduction to features

The **Oxford AQA History** series has been developed by a team of expert history teachers and authors with examining experience. Written to match the new AQA specification, these new editions cover AS and A Level content together in each book.

How to use this book
The features in this book include:

TIMELINE
Key events are outlined at the beginning of the book to give you an overview of the chronology of this topic. Events are colour-coded so you can clearly see the categories of change.

LEARNING OBJECTIVES
At the beginning of each chapter, you will find a list of learning objectives linked to the requirements of the specification.

SOURCE   EXTRACT
Sources introduce you to material that is primary or contemporary to the period, and **Extracts** provides you with historical interpretations and the debate among historians on particular issues and developments. The accompanying activity questions support you in evaluating sources and extracts, analysing and assessing their value, and making judgements.

KEY QUESTION
The six key thematic questions in the specification for this topic are highlighted to help you understand and make connections between the themes.

 PRACTICE QUESTION
Focused questions to help you practise your history skills for both AS and A Level, including evaluating sources and extracts, and essay writing.

STUDY TIP
Hints to highlight key parts of **Practice Questions** or **Activities**.

ACTIVITY
Various activity types to provide you with opportunities to demonstrate both the content and skills you are learning. Some activities are designed to aid revision or to prompt further discussion; others are to stretch and challenge both your AS and A Level studies.

CROSS-REFERENCE
Links to related content within the book to offer you more detail on the subject in question.

A CLOSER LOOK
An in-depth look at a theme, event or development to deepen your understanding, or information to put further context around the subject under discussion.

KEY CHRONOLOGY
A short list of dates identifying key events to help you understand underlying developments.

KEY PROFILE
Details of a key person to extend your understanding and awareness of the individuals that have helped shape the period in question.

KEY TERM
A term that you will need to understand. The terms appear in bold, and they are also defined in the glossary.

AQA History specification overview

AS exam | **A Level exam**

Part One content
The Impact of Industrialisation: Britain, c1783–1885
1. Pressure for change, c1783–1812
2. Government and a changing society, 1812–1832

Part Two content
The Age of Reform: Britain, 1832–1885
3. Political change and social reform, 1832–1846
4. Economy, society and politics, 1846–1885

AS examination papers will cover content from Part One only (you will only need to know the content in the blue box). A Level examination papers will cover content from both Part One and Part Two.

The examination papers
The grade you receive at the end of your AQA AS History course is based entirely on your performance in two examination papers, covering Breadth (Paper 1) and Depth (Paper 2). For your AQA A Level History course, you will also have to complete an Historical Investigation (Non-examined assessment).

Paper 1 Breadth Study
This book covers the content of a Breadth Study (Paper 1). You are assessed on the study of significant historical developments over a period of around 100 years, and associated interpretations or extracts.

Exam paper	Questions and marks	Assessment Objective (AO)*	Timing	Marks
AS Paper 1: Breadth Study	**Section A: Evaluating historical extracts** One compulsory question linked to two historical interpretations (25 marks) • The compulsory question will ask you: 'with reference to these extracts and your understanding of the historical context, which of these extracts provides the more convincing interpretation of...'	AO3	Written exam: 1 hour 30 minutes	50 marks (50% of AS)
	Section B: Essay writing One from a choice of two essay questions (25 marks) • The essay questions will contain a quotation advancing a judgement, and will be followed by: 'explain why you agree or disagree with this view'.	AO1		
A Level Paper 1: Breadth Study	**Section A: Evaluating historical extracts** One compulsory question linked to three historical interpretations with different views (30 marks) • The compulsory question will ask you: 'using your understanding of the historical context, assess how convincing the arguments in these three extracts are, in relation to...'	AO3	Written exam: 2 hours 30 minutes	80 marks (40% of A Level)
	Section B: Essay writing Two from a choice of three essay questions (2 x 25 marks) • The essay questions require analysis and judgement, and could include: 'How successful...' or 'To what extent...' or 'How far...' or a quotation offering a judgement followed by 'Assess the validity of this view'.	AO1		

*AQA History examinations will test your ability to:

AO1: Demonstrate, organise and communicate **knowledge and understanding** to analyse and evaluate the key features related to the periods studied, **making substantiated judgements and exploring concepts**, as relevant, of cause, consequence, change, continuity, similarity, difference and significance.

AO2: **Analyse and evaluate** appropriate source material, primary and/or contemporary to the period, within the historical context.

AO3: **Analyse and evaluate**, in relation to the historical context, different ways in which aspects of the past have been interpreted.

Visit www.aqa.org.uk to help you prepare for your examinations. The website includes specimen examination papers and mark schemes.

Introduction to the *Oxford AQA History* series

Breadth Studies

The study of history concerns the study of change and continuity over time. Sometimes it is easy for you to over-concentrate on the former and forget that, for long periods throughout history, much remained the same. In undertaking a historical breadth study covering approximately 100 years of history, you will have the opportunity to reflect on the processes of change and continuity and, in so doing, come to appreciate what drives and hinders change and how historical development is a multi-faceted process.

The course of history brings together many different strands or themes, so, in order to understand any broad period as a whole, it is helpful to divide it into its various aspects or perspectives. This book reflects the AQA **Key Questions** which address a range of perspectives. These Key Questions are given at the beginning of the book and regularly through the text of the chapters. The most common themes in all the questions relate to the differing political, economic and social developments, but sometimes they highlight the place of religion, ideology or cultural movements across time.

Sometimes specific individuals colour history, changing the course of events or affecting others for good or ill, and the **Key Profile** features in this book will help you to identify the major influences on the period you are studying.

Practice questions help familiarise you with the new exam-style questions, while **Study Tips** highlight key parts of the Practice Questions and words to look out for

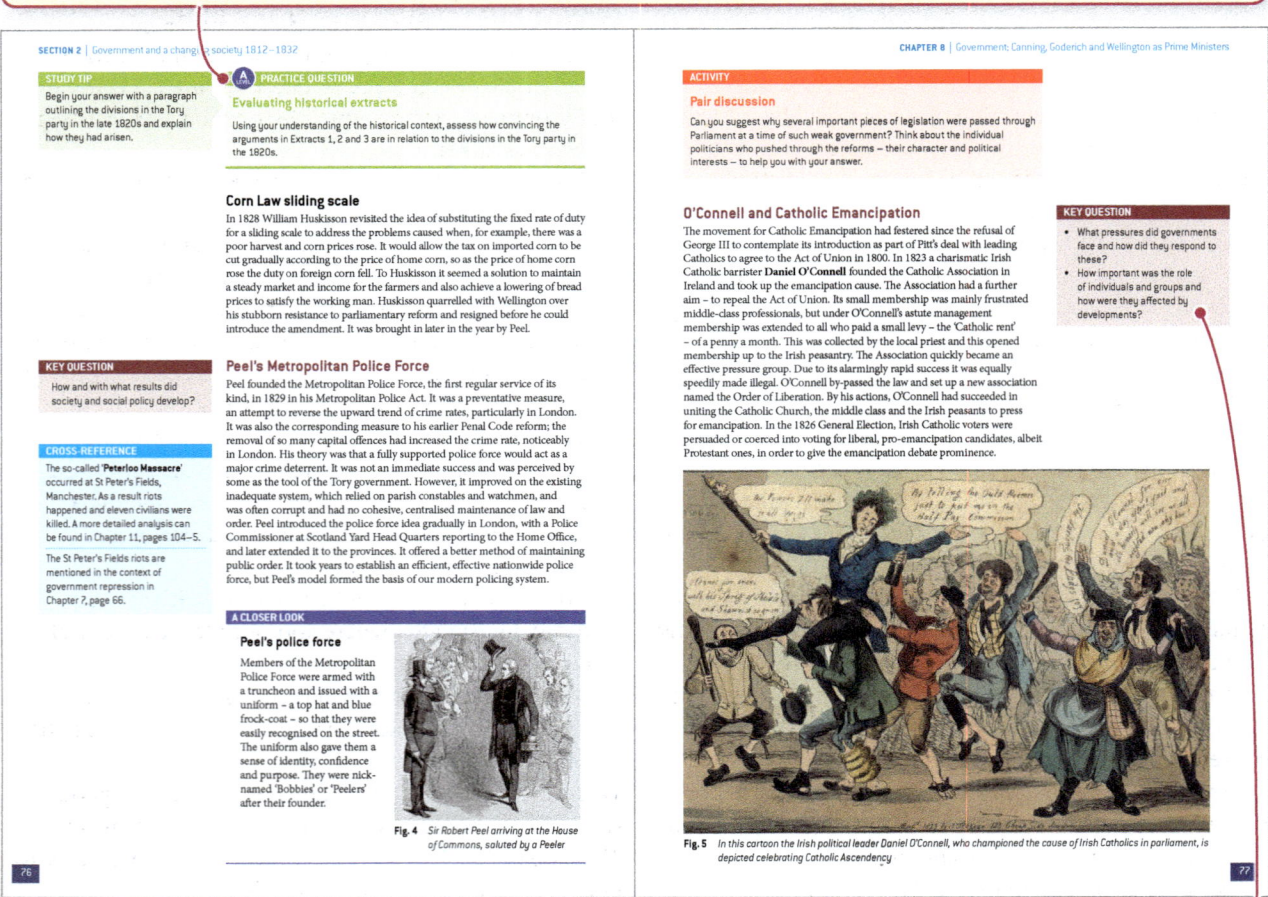

▲ Industrialisation and the People: Britain c1783–1885

Key Questions in each Breadth Study help you to understand and make connections between the key themes

While this book is designed to impart a full and lively awareness of a significant period in the history of one or more countries, far more is on offer from the pages that follow. With the help of the text and activities in this book, you will be encouraged to analyse past events, rather than merely learn to describe them. You will thus build up key historical skills that will increase your curiosity and prepare you, not only for A Level History examinations, but for any future study.

This book also incorporates passages of historical interpretation. These **Extract** features will encourage you to reflect on the way in which the past may be seen in different ways by academic historians and how the same factual evidence may support a variety of conclusions. The accompanying **Activity** features pose questions that are designed to stimulate debate on these interpretations. Suggestions for research also encourage you to read further and understand for yourself how history is a 'living' discipline and subject to constant revision.

The chapters which follow are laid out according to the content of the AQA specification, in four sections. Obviously, a secure chronological awareness and understanding of each section of content will be the first step in appreciating the historical period covered in this book. However, on reaching the end of each section, you should pause to reflect on the key questions posed and consider the 'big picture' which has emerged by that point, and the interpretations that have accompanied this. In this way, a broad and satisfying appreciation of history and historical processes will emerge.

Developing your study skills

You will need to be equipped with a paper file or electronic means of storing notes. Organised notes help to produce organised essays and sensible filing provides for efficient use of time. This book uses **Cross-References** to indicate where material in one chapter has relevance to that in another. By employing the same technique, you should find it easier to make the final leap towards piecing together your material to produce a broad historical picture. The exercises and research activities in this book are intended to guide you towards making selective and relevant notes with a specific purpose. Copying out sections of the book is to be discouraged, but selecting material with a particular theme or question in mind will considerably aid your understanding.

For students preparing for the AQA A Level examination, the essay questions posed in the examination will cover around 20–25 years of history or more. AS questions will also be broad, although there is no specific minimum timeframe for these. There are plenty of examples of such 'breadth' **Practice Questions** in these books, both at AS in Part One and A Level in Parts One and Two of this book, as well as **Study Tips** and activities to encourage you to think about change, continuity, historical perspectives and interpretations. You should also develop timelines, make charts and diagrams, for example, to illustrate causation and consequence, analyse interpretations of key events, dissect broader developments thematically and identify the significance of major issues.

It is particularly important for you to have opinions on and be able to make informed judgements about the material you have studied. Some of the activities in this book encourage pair discussion or class debate, and you should make the most of such opportunities to voice and refine your own ideas. The beauty of history is that there is rarely a right or wrong answer, so this supplementary oral work should enable you to share your own opinions.

Writing and planning your essays

At both AS and A Level, you will be required to write essays and, although A Level questions are likely to be more complex, the basic qualities of good essay writing remain the same:

- **read the question carefully** to identify the key words and dates
- **plan out a logical and organised answer** with a clear judgement or view (several views if there are a number of issues to consider). Your essay should advance this judgement in the introduction, while also acknowledging alternative views and clarifying terms of reference, including the time span
- use the opening sentences of your paragraphs as stepping stones to take an argument forward, which allows you to **develop an evolving and balanced argument** throughout the essay and also makes for good style
- **support your comment or analysis** with precise detail; using dates, where appropriate, helps logical organisation
- **write a conclusion** which matches the view of the introduction and flows naturally from what has gone before.

While these suggestions will help you develop a good style, essays should never be too rigid or mechanical. This book will have fulfilled its purposes if it produces, as intended, students who think for themselves!

Sally Waller
Series Editor

Timeline

The colours represent different types of event as follows:

- **Blue:** economic events
- **Yellow:** social events
- **Red:** political events
- **Black:** international events (including foreign policy)
- **Green:** religious events

1783
- William Pitt appointed Prime Minister aged 24

1786
- Pitt introduces his Sinking Fund, a saving scheme to be used to pay down the National Debt
- Pitt signs an Anglo-French trade treaty

1789
- Start of the French Revolution on 14 July in Paris, causes fear of unrest at home

1790
- Publication of *Reflections of the Revolution in France* by Edmund Burke condemning the revolutionaries

1800
- Act of Union with Ireland passed through parliament

1801
- First official census puts population of Great Britain and Ireland at over 15 million

1805
- Nelson's victory at Trafalgar

1806
- Death of Pitt

1819
- The Peterloo Massacre
- Lord Liverpool's government passes the repressive Six Acts

1823
- Reform of the Penal Code, cutting number of crimes punishable by death

1824
- Repeal of the Combination Acts

1828
- repeal of the Test and Corporation Acts

1834
- Trial of the Tolpuddle Martyrs
- Robert Peel's Tamworth Manifesto defines Conservatism
- Poor Law Amendment Act, established a workhouse system for poor relief

1835
- Municipal Corporations Act leads to a complete overhaul of local government

1836
- Registration of Births, Deaths and Marriages Act

1837
- Queen Victoria succeeds to the throne

1846
- Repeal of Corn Laws split the Conservative party

1847
- The Ten Hour Act regulating hours in factories

1848
- Public Health Act was a response to spread of disease in overcrowded towns and cities

1851
- The Great Exhibition showcased inventiveness of Britain's manufacturing industries

1872
- Criminal Law Amendment Act made it difficult for unions to enforce a strike by picketing
- Secret Ballot Act enabled men to vote without fear of reprisal

1873
- Start of period of depression in agriculture and industry

1875
- Artisans' Dwelling Act
- Conspiracy and Protection of Property Act replaced unpopular Criminal Law Amendment Act

1879
- Land League founded in Ireland by Michael Davitt to secure land reform for Irish tenants
- Charles Parnell emerges as leader of Irish Nationalists

Timeline

1791
- Publication of Tom Paine's *The Rights of Man* in support of the Revolution

1793
- Britain becomes involved in French Revolutionary wars

1798
- Irish Rebellion led by Wolfe Tone
- Introduction of income tax for the first time, as a war measure

1799/1800
- The Combination Acts to prevent groups of workers combining to demand better wages and conditions

1807
- William Wilberforce campaigning achieves abolition of slave trade by Britain

1811
- Prince of Wales made Regent, because of deteriorating mental health of George III

1811–12
- Luddite riots were an indication of textile workers' anger at low wages and social distress

1815
- Wellington's victory over Napoleon at Waterloo marked the end of the Napoleonic Wars
- Passing of the Corn Laws to protect home grown wheat against import of cheap foreign corn

1829
- Granting of Catholic Emancipation
- Introduction of the first Metropolitan Police Force

1830
- Opening of the Liverpool to Manchester railway line

1832
- The first Parliamentary Reform Act, challenges the political dominance of the landed aristocracy

1833
- Abolition of Slavery throughout the British Empire
- Factory Act limited hours children could work

1838
- Publication of the Six Points of the People's Charter and start of Chartist Movement

1842
- Prime Minister Robert Peel's budget introduces peacetime income tax
- Mines Act prohibits underground employment for women and children

1844
- Factory Act shortens working hours in textile factories
- Bank Charter Act to balance the issue of bank notes against the volume of gold reserves
- The Rochdale Pioneers started the Cooperative Movement

1845
- Start of Irish Famine in which a million Irish peasants died

1865
- Death of Lord Palmerston clears the way for parliamentary reform

1867
- Second Reform Act gives vote to some working-class men for the first time

1868
- Gladstone's first term as Prime Minister, in which he carries through a series of far-reaching administrative reforms

1871
- A unified Germany starts to compete against Britain in industrial output
- Trade Union Act gave unions certain legal rights

1882
- Construction of Forth Rail Bridge begun, linking north of Scotland to rest of Britain

1884
- Third Reform Act extends franchise to include unskilled labourers

1885
- Redistribution of Seats Act meant size of constituencies related to distribution of population

Introduction to this book

Fig. 1 *Newcastle Upon Tyne, 1877*

The years between 1783 and 1885 encompass a period during which Britain underwent some of the most dramatic and far-reaching changes in its history. At the beginning of the period the dull but dutiful George III (reigned 1760–1820) was a third of his way through a long and, in the latter years, difficult reign, which saw an important change in the role of the monarchy and a reduction in its political power and influence. After his reign came the short, tempestuous Regency and rule of his elder son George IV (reigned 1820–30), when the popularity of the monarchy was at a very low ebb. Following the rule of his brother William IV (reigned 1830–37), a young, eager but politically inexperienced Queen Victoria (reigned 1837–1901), a granddaughter of George III, ascended the throne. By 1885, Victoria had restored the prestige and dignity of the Crown and had increased its popularity. Any real political power of the monarch had gone, but instead Victoria fulfilled an important symbolic role as the titular head of Britain, the most powerful nation in the world.

In 1783, Britain was on the cusp of important changes in the economy, the structure of government and the organisation of society. The driving force of the changes was the rapid development of industry. This process of industrialisation transformed the lives of the British people, bringing great wealth to some and extending the misery of poverty to others. The population increased rapidly and many people moved from rural areas to the expanding industrial and urban centres, where there were jobs to be had. A key starting point of industrialisation was the increasing level of production of coal and iron, both natural resources in plentiful supply in Britain, and the related technology. This stimulated the economy, which in turn supported further advances in industry. Developments in this untried and untested territory brought new challenges and problems and tested the ingenuity of politicians and the imagination and resourcefulness of society. The initial impact of industrialisation is the subject of the first section of this book.

In 1783, Britain had suffered the humiliating loss of its American colonies in the American War of Independence (1776–83). William Pitt, the Prime Minister, lifted Britain out of its financial stagnation brought about by war and steered the country through the anxious period of French Revolution (1789–93) and the early years of the French/Napoleonic Wars that followed. After victory in 1815, successive governments had little involvement in foreign wars and Britain entered a period of unparalleled peace and prosperity. Britain's economic supremacy and world domination continued virtually unchallenged until the 1880s, when it was faced for the first time with competition from newly industrialised nations, principally Germany and the United States of America.

Threading through the narrative is the continuing rise in population, which hastened change on all levels. There was a great deal of discussion about whether or not the population was rising and whether this brought economic advantage. **Thomas Malthus** (1766–1834), a political economist, believed the population was growing and in his work 'An Essay on the Principal of Population' published in 1798, he forecast that population would outstrip the rate of production of food and cause massive social problems including an increase in poverty. Some years before Malthus' pessimistic predictions, the Bishop of Chester caused a stir in 1781, when he asserted in the House of Lords that there was an astonishing growth of population in his diocese. He linked the growth to the fact that it was occurring in the trading and manufacturing towns such as Manchester and Liverpool. In retrospect, he was linking population growth to economic growth and as the industrialisation process moved forward, the increasing population provided both an endless supply of cheap labour and a ready and growing market for manufactured goods. In 1801 the first official census was carried out, establishing the population of England, Wales and Scotland at 10.5 million. Ten years later a second census demonstrated that the population had increased to 12 million. This was indisputable confirmation that the population was indeed rising. It also provoked discussion on whether or not the level of poverty was rising at the same pace.

Poverty was an important social issue. Society was developing and undergoing massive changes. At the start of the period the population was more rural than urban, but by 1885 it had become a predominantly urban population. Industrialisation had created a new prosperous middle class, who lived mainly in the growing towns, and an industrial working class who supplied the labour. Although there is general agreement that the standard of living of most of those people rose in both town and country, there were large numbers of people living in poverty. Agricultural wages were low and in spite of the wealth of the nation there were periods of high unemployment in the factories. The concentration of people in the towns led to poor quality housing for the workers, overcrowding, urban squalor and the spread of disease. Working conditions in factories were also deplorable. Radical groups, reformers and protest groups put pressure on successive governments to introduce social reform to alleviate the worst effects of poverty. Social reforms were introduced on a limited scale in the 1820s, but increased in number and extent as the decades rolled on. Governments remained cautious about the extent of state interference in people's lives, maintaining as late as the 1870s that individuals should be responsible for their own well-being, but this attitude was beginning to change as more action was taken to deal with social problems.

At the same time, these groups, together with the voices of the prosperous middle-class industrialists and manufacturers, challenged the aristocratic monopoly of political power and pressed for political change. In 1783, political power was in the hands of a small, wealthy, aristocratic elite. General elections were held infrequently and less than ten per cent of the population had any involvement in the political process. Very few people had the right to vote and MPs tended to represent their own interests, rather than the interests of the people.

CROSS-REFERENCE

Malthus and his theory of population is covered in Chapter 3.

KEY PROFILE

Fig. 2 *Thomas Malthus*

Thomas Malthus (1766–1834) was a mathematician, clergyman and professor of political economy. In 1798 Malthus 'captured the mind of a generation' (Asa Briggs) in his *Essay on the Principle of Population*, proposing that, in a healthy society, population grows more quickly than food can ever be produced, so that if the population wasn't checked many would be condemned to a life of poverty. His ideas were disproved by the continuing rise in population alongside an increase in wealth.

By 1885 the political landscape had changed to such an extent that the political supremacy of the traditional ruling class was in decline and the franchise had been extended to include about two thirds of the male population. Britain's system of government could at last be described as moving towards democracy.

It was an era of outstanding political figures – Lord Liverpool, William Huskisson, Sir Robert Peel, Earl Grey, Lord John Russell, Benjamin Disraeli and William Gladstone – the ideas and ideologies of all of whom made significant contributions to the structure and reform of government, the economy and society. Reformers and philanthropists like William Wilberforce, Anthony Ashley Cooper and Edwin Chadwick instigated much-needed social improvements, urged on by popular protest, so that governments were obliged to respond in some measure to the pressure for change. Inventive entrepreneurs such as James Watt, Richard Arkwright, George Stephenson and Isambard Kingdom Brunel, to name a few of many, seized the initiative and took Britain on a forward path of industrialisation, at apparently break-neck speed.

This book is concerned with understanding and explaining the sweeping changes that took place across this hundred-year period of British history, fuelled by the process of industrialisation, and with identifying and accounting for those issues that remained the same. The following chapters will explore the developments and narrative of British political, social and economic history, and importantly, will consider the many varied influences that shaped the country's development. You will be taken on a journey through this era, considering the position of the monarch and Parliament, the vast growing population over whom they ruled and the impact of industrialisation that could not be ignored. On this journey you will come to understand for yourself how individuals, groups and ideas all played their part in the ongoing development of our democratic system of government and in promoting the health, welfare and prosperity of British society towards the beginning of the twentieth century.

As you study this period of British history, you are invited to consider the following Key Questions:
- How was Britain governed and how did democracy and political organisations change and develop?
- What pressures did governments face and how did they respond to these?
- How and with what results did the economy develop and change?
- How and with what results did society and social policy develop?
- How important were ideas and ideology?
- How important was the role of individuals and groups and how were they affected by developments?

Try to keep these questions in mind as you work through this book. They are highlighted in the text to help you. They are the 'big' questions that have occupied historians studying the period 1783 to 1885 and by reflecting on them you will come to appreciate more fully the changes and developments that occurred in Britain over this period. Remember too that political, economic and social developments go hand-in-hand, and to build up a full picture you will need to explore the links between them.

There is plenty to learn and much to think about in the following pages. If you approach your studies in a spirit of inquiry, keen to piece together past events and trace the development of key movements, you will enrich your understanding of the whole and will find much to enjoy in your study of Industrialisation and the People. You will also emerge with a greater understanding of the processes and influences that helped to shape our modern society.

Part One: The impact of industrialisation: Britain, c1783–1832

1 Pressure for change, c1783–1812

1 The British political system c1783

Government and representation

EXTRACT 1

Political power in Britain was shared between King, Lords and Commons, who together made up a 'supreme authority', but no single member held power in isolation. In the late eighteenth century, the King really was in the middle of the political picture and not above it. The King still chose his own **ministers**. He was, however, compelled to choose his ministers from inside Parliament and although they were not party leaders in any modern sense, dependent on the pressure of opinion outside Westminster, ministers could not afford to ignore parliamentary support. To control parliamentary support they had at their disposal a considerable amount of public patronage – rewards, honours and pensions – and they knew that the electorate which lay in the background was small, infrequently called on to vote and amenable to pressure. The ministers were agents of the King, yet they always had to pay careful attention to Parliament. Had not the main elements in this **mixed constitution** been glued together by patronage, the King's government could not have been carried on.

Adapted from Asa Briggs, *The Age of Improvement*, 1967

KEY QUESTION

As you read this chapter, consider the following Key Question:
How was Britain governed and how did democracy and political organisations change and develop?

ACTIVITY

Evaluating historical extracts

1. According to Extract 1 how was political power shared in eighteenth-century Britain?
2. What do you understand by the phrase 'the King was in the middle of the political picture and not above it'?
3. The King had the power to choose his own ministers. What were the limitations of that choice?

Political power was a fine balance between King and Parliament and depended on **patronage** to make it work. As you study the chapter think about the main elements of this mixed constitution (or **constitutional monarchy**, as it is generally known) and how successfully or not they worked together and depended on each other. Asa Briggs asserts that patronage was the key to holding them together and if the King had not been able to reward loyalty through handing out well-paid positions, annual pensions and honours (such as knighthoods) he would have lost control of government. Briggs

LEARNING OBJECTIVES

In this chapter you will learn about:

- key aspects of the British political system c1783
- the constitutional monarchy
- government and parliamentary representation
- national and local democracy in Britain
- the two main political parties, Whigs and Tories.

KEY TERM

ministers: politicians who hold significant public office in a national or regional government

mixed constitution: form of government in which a hereditary monarch is head of state, with powers limited by Parliament; it is sometimes referred to as a constitutional monarchy

A CLOSER LOOK

Patronage

Patronage means the right to give privileges or make appointments. The King had the power of patronage over many important appointments, which gave him considerable political influence. He could in theory fill Parliament with men who would support his policies. His ministers also had limited powers of patronage to build up their support in the Commons or in the country. Loyalty was expected in return.

SECTION 1 | Pressure for change, c1783–1812

CROSS-REFERENCE

The Commons was the elected part of Parliament. This is discussed later in the chapter, on page 3.

KEY TERM

statute: a written law

divine right: concept that a monarch rules by authority of God, not through the consent of the people

KEY PROFILE

Fig. 2 *George III*

George III (reigned 1760–1820), wished to be seen as a conscientious monarch and play an active role in political life. He accepted his limited role as constitutional monarch but he used his powers of patronage to influence Parliament on issues about which he felt strongly. He suffered from an increasingly debilitating mental illness and, in 1811, his eldest son George was appointed Prince Regent.

KEY TERM

civil list: a fixed annual sum, agreed by Parliament to meet the monarch's household expenses

veto: to reject a decision or proposal made by a Parliament

ACTIVITY

Draw up a list of key points that define Britain as a constitutional monarchy in 1783.

refers to ministers as 'agents of the King', yet they also had to 'pay attention to Parliament', in other words gain Parliament's support, to carry out the King's wishes. Briggs suggests patronage was vital to achieve this support.

A constitutional monarchy

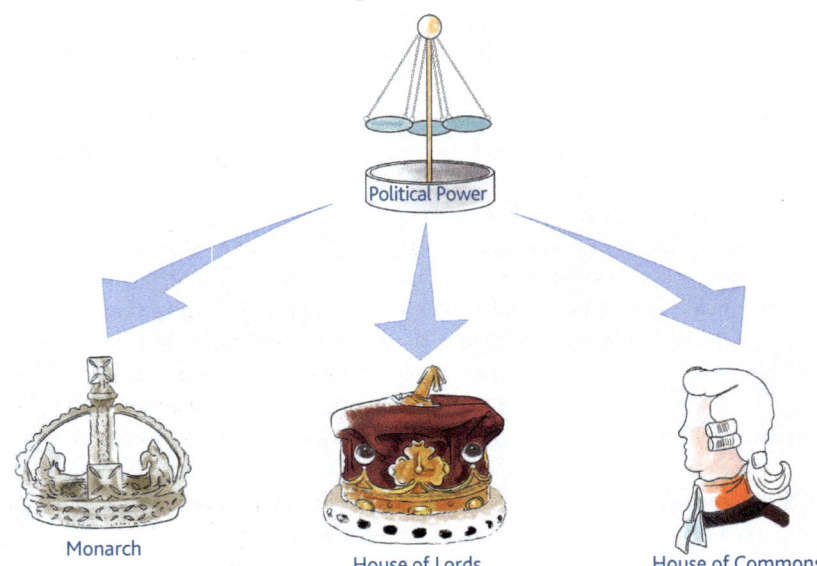

Fig. 1 *The perfect balance of the British constitution*

By 1783, Britain had a system of government based on a constitutional monarchy. Britain's monarch in that year was King George III. He was bound by oath to govern according to 'the **statutes** in Parliament agreed upon and the laws and customs of the same'. The principle of the supremacy of Parliament over the monarch was established in the Bill of Rights passed in 1689 after the 'Glorious Revolution', when the Stuart King James II, who persisted in his belief that he ruled by **divine right,** was forced to abdicate in favour of his daughter and son-in-law Mary II and William III. The Bill of Rights aimed to prevent any future monarch interfering with the law and restricted the power of the monarchy. It was Parliament that made laws, took decisions on taxation and spending and debated issues of national and local importance.

The monarch was not without power. He still influenced general policy and, as head of state, retained the power to choose and dismiss his ministers. The monarch also retained the right to summon and dissolve Parliament, but could not rule without it. If Parliament was dissolved, a general election had to be called immediately. The monarch was financially dependent upon Parliament, which would only grant funds to the monarch on an annual basis, through the **civil list**. The monarch still had the power to **veto** legislation, although was unlikely to do so if it jeopardised his income. In essence, by 1783, although the Bill of Rights of 1689 had established the principle of the supremacy of Parliament, political power was shared between the King and Parliament.

EXTRACT 2

During the period between the Glorious Revolution of 1689 and the Reform Act of 1832, the sovereign's powers were gradually diminished, despite a powerful rear-guard action fought by George III; and by the time of the Reform Act, the sovereign's power to determine policy had effectively been reduced to influence. In the eighteenth century, anyone who sought to become a minister would benefit by enjoying the sovereign's support, but such support was becoming neither sufficient nor necessary. The position of the prime minister came gradually to rest not so much on royal support, as upon the support of the Commons. Once it had become accepted that the prime minister owed his position, not only to royal favour, but also to parliamentary approval, the sovereign's role came inevitably to be limited.

Adapted from Vernon Bogdanor, *The Monarchy and Constitution*, 1995

ACTIVITY

Evaluating historical extracts

1. According to Extract 2, how did George III react to the gradual loss of the sovereign's powers?
2. Why was the position of the prime minister no longer so dependent on the power of the sovereign?
3. Why do you think the sovereign's power was diminishing?

A CLOSER LOOK

Society and social terms

Society was organised according to the rank in which a person was born. The minority made up the propertied classes, who had wealth, power and social superiority. They could be divided into (a) the aristocracy – the privileged, ruling elite, who were great land owners; (b) those with substantial property and local influence; (c) the gentry whose position in society was based on lesser land ownership. Yeoman farmers differed from gentry in that they farmed their own land. There was a small, prosperous, expanding middle class, the 'middling sort', among whom were the wealthy merchant class. The vast majority of the population belonged to the lower orders – the property-less labouring classes and the poor.

Fig. 3 *Pitt addressing the House of Commons*

Composition of Parliament

Parliament comprised the House of Lords (the upper house) and the House of Commons (the lower house). The Lords, made up of unelected hereditary peers, the ruling elite, had great political influence, including the power to block measures passed by the Commons. New peers could be created by the monarch if he wanted to reward loyalty. The House of Commons was an elected assembly, although not democratic, as few men had the right to vote. The MPs who sat in the Commons belonged to the gentry for the most part. Many MPs regarded a seat in Parliament as an opportunity for advantage and advancement. There were other MPs, who valued what they regarded as their independence. They represented the county seats and the interests of the landowners and gentry in their constituencies.

The system allowed the House of Lords to maintain influence in the Commons. However, the Commons controlled taxation and its main duty was to act as a check on the executive (ministers). Within the Commons there were several different factions and interest groups, which made it difficult to achieve control of a stable majority. The late eighteenth century saw the growth of parties and this strengthened the Commons.

The Prime Minister had to have the support of the majority of the Commons to carry on government. Although much political power within Parliament rested with the Lords, by the late eighteenth century, the influence of the House of Commons was increasing.

Role of the prime minister and Cabinet

Traditionally, the monarch had a group of advisers, known as the Privy Council, which acted as a bridge between the King and Parliament on policy decisions. Privy Council members were appointed for life and the council

SECTION 1 | Pressure for change, c1783–1812

> **KEY TERM**
>
> **Cabinet:** known today as the committee at the centre of the British political system responsible for making decisions in government; in 1783 its role was to offer advice to the King
>
> **First Lord of the Treasury:** one of the Lords Commissioners of the Treasury and by custom, which continues today, Prime Minister

> **CROSS-REFERENCE**
>
> The **Whigs and Tories** will be discussed on page 7.

> **CROSS-REFERENCE**
>
> This political crisis over the loss of the **American colonies** is dealt with in more detail in Chapter 2, page 12.

> **KEY TERM**
>
> **prerogative:** special right or privilege
>
> **coalition:** an alliance between two or more political groups of parties

> **KEY PROFILE**
>
> **William Pitt (1759–1806)**, styled 'the Younger' to differentiate him from his father William Pitt, the Elder, also a British statesman and prime minister, was the youngest holder of the office of prime minister at the age of 24 in 1783. His political career spanned his entire adult life and he died in office aged 46. His considerable financial and administrative skills were complemented by his great political skill, which helped him survive in office.

> **CROSS-REFERENCE**
>
> The **1784 election** is dealt with in detail in Chapter 2, page 13.

became too large to be manageable. One consequence was that the Cabinet gained more executive power. A smaller more manageable group of ministers, the **Cabinet**, emerged during the eighteenth century, in place of the unwieldy Privy Council, and gained more executive power holding weekly meetings and advising the monarch. From within the cabinet, the **First Lord of the Treasury** nominally became the monarch's chief or prime minister. It was important for the monarch to choose someone whom he could trust as his chief representative in Parliament. Most of George III's appointed ministers were peers of the realm and sat in the House of Lords, but it was vital that the prime minister enjoyed the confidence of the House of Commons in order to carry through the business of government. The monarch, therefore, tended to choose a prominent member from one of the two main political parties, **Whigs** or **Tories**, whichever had a majority in the Commons. The prime minister, whether in the Lords or Commons, was then able to use public patronage, handing out honours, positions and pensions, to cement essential parliamentary support.

King and constitution

It was assumed that it was the King's **prerogative** whether or not he accepted the advice of his ministers, who felt honour bound to abide by the King's decision and persuade Parliament to agree. George III's position was weakened, however, over the crisis surrounding the loss of the **American colonies**, when, in 1782, he was forced by an angry Parliament to accept the resignation of his Prime Minister, Lord North and accept in his place Lord Rockingham, whom he detested.

The main constitutional debate surrounding George III during his long reign (1760–1820) was whether or not he tried to restore a more politically active monarchy. Vernon Bogdanor suggests George III was fighting 'a powerful rear-guard action' to impose royal influence on policy decisions, and enjoying some success. By 1783, the most contentious period of his reign was almost behind him, but his determination to secure the position of 24-year-old **William Pitt**, his choice of prime minister, in the Commons, by undermining the existing **coalition** of Charles Fox and Lord North and forcing an election, was seen by many, such as historian G. M. Ditchfield, as 'ignoring constitutional priorities'.

William Pitt's success in the **1784 election** seemed to vindicate the King's interference, but ultimately hastened the reduction of the monarch's powers; the prime minister had become more accountable to the House of Commons that supported his majority. The result was the position of the prime minister assuming greater importance and, as Bogdanor suggests, coming 'gradually to rest not so much on royal support, as upon the support of the Commons'.

> **ACTIVITY**
>
> 1. Find an example from the text to support Vernon Bogdanor's assertion that George III fought a 'powerful rear-guard action' to preserve his royal power. Explain in your own words why George III's attempt to preserve royal power ultimately failed.
> 2. To what extent was Britain a state that was 'headed by a sovereign who reigns but does not rule'? Discuss this as a class. To prepare for the discussion look up definitions of 'reign' and 'rule' and research more details about George III. Later in the course it might be valuable to compare his powers in 1783 with those of Queen Victoria when she came to the throne in 1837.

Representation by the few

The British political system in the late eighteenth century was in need of reform. Parliament was dominated by wealthy and influential landowners and aristocrats, who saw little necessity for any change in the existing system. They were in Parliament principally to look after their own interests, to seek political advancement and to benefit from the system of patronage. There was a firm belief among them that the British constitution was close to perfection with power balanced nicely between King and Parliament and that 'Englishmen' enjoyed the benefits of a free and democratic nation. Within this 'perfect' system, however, only a small number of men could vote and the majority of the population was completely unrepresented. This situation was accentuated by the effects of industrialisation, which was changing the social and economic landscape and causing a movement of the population from the countryside to the rapidly expanding towns and cities. Many small market towns and boroughs, which served the surrounding rural areas, declined in size and importance, but still sent two representatives to Parliament. The new large urban areas lacked any representation.

An unrepresentative Parliament

Although the power and influence of Parliament as the instigator of government policy was strengthening and gradually replacing that of the monarch, Parliament was not more democratic, nor was it representative. In Britain, few of the governed were involved in the process of choosing who should govern them. The electorate was small, male, based on ownership of property and unrepresentative of the population as a whole. Whatever legislation was passed through Parliament it was not the will of the people. Two attempts by William Pitt, in 1792 and 1795, to reform Parliament and redistribute seats to the expanding, unrepresented industrial towns, were defeated in the Commons.

The members of the House of Lords had little interest in political reform as it would threaten their position. The right to sit in the Lords was based on holding a hereditary title (a peerage); there was no election. In 1783 about 220 peers sat in the House of Lords. They were a small, powerful, wealthy aristocracy, belonging to a relatively closed society and linked through blood, marriage and an interest in maintaining their political dominance. Their political power, wealth and social dominance came from their ownership of vast tracts of land, which enabled them to be able to control nominations for the majority of seats in the House of Commons.

The House of Commons comprised 558 elected members. They were landed gentry, or knights of the shires; gentlemen of independent means who could afford the privilege of being an MP, as MPs received no salary. Men of ordinary means were excluded from standing for Parliament; a **county member** had to have an annual income of £600 and a **borough member** an annual income of £300.

The franchise

In 1783, there were about 250,000 men in England and Wales who had the vote and, as the population was rising (about 9.4 million in 1801), the number of voters as a percentage of the population was falling. There was no uniform system of **franchise**. The county MPs were elected by men who held **freehold** land of a minimum rateable value of 40 shillings a year. They were known as the 40-shilling freeholders and were often swayed in their voting by the dominant landowner, who had nominated his own candidate.

There was no uniform system of franchise in the boroughs, but it usually depended on property ownership. The qualification to vote varied in the boroughs. There were 'potwalloper' boroughs, where ownership

> **KEY TERM**
>
> **county member:** each county was represented by two MPs, elected by the men whose freehold land had a rateable value of at least 40 shillings a year
>
> **borough member:** each borough was represented by two MPs, irrespective of size of population

> **KEY TERM**
>
> **franchise:** the right to vote, which was generally based on a property qualification
>
> **freehold:** if land was freehold it meant that the man who held it owned it

SECTION 1 | Pressure for change, c1783–1812

> **KEY TERM**
>
> **freemen:** people who had been given the freedom of a city or borough, meaning they enjoyed all the civil and political rights accorded to people under a free government

of your own hearth gave you the right to vote, and there were boroughs where only '**freemen**' could vote. In some boroughs the right to vote was based on payment of a local tax, the 'scot and lot'. In corporation boroughs, only the mayor and members of the corporation could vote, but in Preston anyone who stayed the night before the election could vote. The term 'pocket' boroughs described places entirely controlled by the landowner and 'rotten' boroughs, like Banbury, had few qualified voters yet still returned two MPs.

Scotland was even more severely under-represented than England; 45 Scottish MPs had a seat in the Commons and 16 'representative Scottish peers' sat in the Lords. The electorate numbered about 4500 out of a population of 1.6 million and electoral power was concentrated, as in England, in the hands of the large landowners, who had no interest in the social and economic issues of their constituents.

Parliament was corrupt in its electoral procedures. When elections were held, not all the seats were contested. In pocket boroughs, the landowner nominated the MP, who was returned unopposed. Where voting did take place it was carried out in public. This open system allowed widespread bribery and corruption.

> **ACTIVITY**
>
> **Summary**
>
> Summarise the main problems with the system of parliamentary representation in Britain in 1783.

> **KEY QUESTION**
>
> How was Britain governed and how did democracy and political organisations develop?

A CLOSER LOOK

Bribery and corruption – a normal feature of the voting system

Men regarded their vote as a piece of property, which could be sold to the highest bidder. In a closely-fought contest, the candidates' agents would be out buying votes. Candidates would pick up the bills run up by supporters and hold a lavish victory breakfast after results were announced. Threats were sometimes issued and dirty tricks employed, such as 'cooping' – keeping a voter drunk so he couldn't vote for the opposition.

> **KEY TERM**
>
> **liberal:** broad-minded, not constrained by generally accepted opinion; liberal views are in a political sense, those which support individual freedom and greater freedom in political institutions
>
> **democratic:** representative of, for and by the people; derived from the word democracy, which is a form of government in which people collectively hold political power

Democracy at national and local level

The nature of the constitutional monarchy in Britain in the early 1780s extended beyond the relationships between Monarch and Parliament. Contemporaries saw the defence of freedom and 'democracy' as based also on the Rule of Law (especially the Common Law), the independence of the judiciary, religious toleration (for dissenting protestants) and a free press. Most of these (the exception being a free press) had been specifically established in the 1689 Bill of Rights. Thus, the British Constitution was generally regarded as **liberal** and **democratic**, and admired by Britain's European neighbours, but, in fact, the majority of people had very limited opportunity to voice their opinions on matters of national or local importance. Engaging popular support for government policy was not seen as necessary or wise. The ruling elite held a belief that authority exercised by those of birth, rank, property and learning in order to maintain law and order, would preserve a stable and well-governed society. This applied equally at local level.

General elections to the House of Commons were held at least every seven years by law. Many seats were not contested – the upheaval and expense of elections encouraged 'compacts and compromises' between local landowning families to agree a nomination, and so the electorate often did not get the opportunity to use their vote. We may regard this as a denial of democratic right, but historian Jonathan Clark takes a different view:

A CLOSER LOOK

Elections every seven years

The Septennial Act was passed in 1716, to extend Parliament from three to seven years. In theory it created a more stable government and cut down on election expenses.

> **EXTRACT 3**
>
> The cry was not generally raised that electors were deprived of a right to participate by the absence of a contest. It is a modern assumption that there is, and ought to be, a contest in each constituency at each election in order that the system may function properly as a system of representative government.
>
> Jonathan Clark, *English Society 1688–1832*, 1985

The landed aristocracy and gentry dominated administrative arrangements for the counties and the towns. In the counties, the most important official was the Lord Lieutenant, whose position was decided by royal appointment. The Lord Lieutenant was almost always a member of the aristocracy and sat in the House of Lords and therefore supported the government and had access to crown patronage. He was responsible for maintenance of order and local defence. The Lord Lieutenant appointed Justices of the Peace (JPs) from among the local gentry and clergy. They symbolised authority. Their job was to administer the county and the parishes. They also administered justice, often serving harsh punishments for petty crimes, such as poaching on one of the local landowner's estates.

In the towns, power was shared by the gentry and the merchant class, whose common qualification was property, wealth and influence. Some towns were run by a Mayor and Corporation, which comprised the local elite, with the **alderman** as Justice of the Peace. Closed corporations like Edinburgh were self-electing and therefore self-perpetuating. There were calls for reform, not from among the **lower orders**, but from within the propertied class who themselves wished a share of power.

KEY TERM

alderman: a civic dignitary in the borough, next in rank to the Mayor and elected by fellow councillors

CROSS-REFERENCE

The '**lower orders**' are explained in the Closer Look on Society and social terms on page 3.

ACTIVITY

Below is a list of components of a modern interpretation of democracy. This differs in several respects from that of 1783. Consider this list, and as you work through the course, note any examples you find in this chapter under the headings. Add your own headings. This should help you to answer the question 'How did democracy change and develop between 1783 and 1885?'
- the right to vote – universal suffrage
- rights of representation – at Westminster and at local level
- religious toleration – the right to worship freely
- freedom of speech (including to express political views)
- freedom of the press
- fair justice system – right to a fair trial & to be treated equally by the law
- rights of association
- rights of land ownership and property
- the right of every man to be free (i.e. no slavery)

Whigs and Tories

'Whig' and 'Tory' were originally names of abuse that became attached to the two main groups of political opponents during the reign of Charles II (1660–85). In what was called the Exclusion Crisis, the Whigs tried to prevent Charles' brother, James Duke of York, succeeding to the throne because he was a Catholic. The Tories supported his claim and the right of the Stuart monarchs to the throne, without success. After the accession of Protestant William of Orange, the Tories lost political influence. For most of the eighteenth century,

SECTION 1 | Pressure for change, c1783–1812

> **A CLOSER LOOK**
>
> ### Where did 'Whig' and 'Tory' come from?
>
> The Whigs were one of the great English political parties, but the word 'whig' was in fact an insulting term for a Scottish Presbyterian. The Tories were the opposing political party, but the word 'tory' was a derogatory term for an Irish robber.

> **ACTIVITY**
>
> What is the message of the cartoon in Fig. 4?

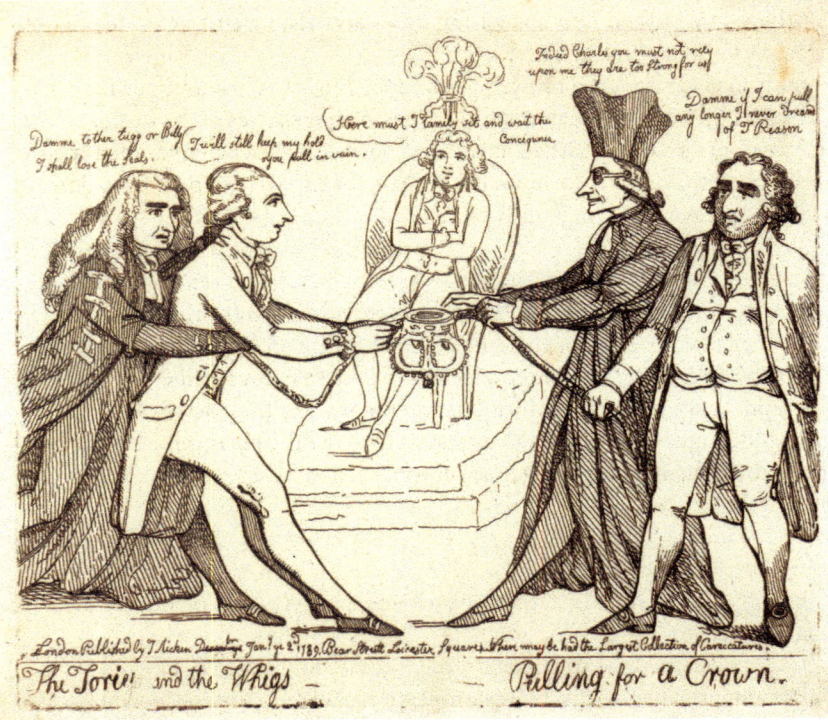

Fig. 4 'The Words [sic] Whig and Tory were originally names of contempt, which at times, when division ran high, the opposite parties in their spleen fix'd upon each other by way of reproach.' Mist's Weekly Journal, 7 October 1727

the great Whig Protestant families monopolised political power, while the Tories continued to suffer from association with their failed attempts to restore the Stuart monarchy.

Concepts of sovereignty and political power

By 1783, the connection with early eighteenth-century Whigs and Tories had almost disappeared. Although Whigs and Tories could be loosely identified by their political, economic and religious beliefs, there were **factions** and interests within both parties who often opposed each other in Parliament and were re-grouping constantly. The members of both parties came from the landed classes and the aristocracy. As such, both wished to maintain the **status quo**, the main issue being how to win political advantage over the other side. Both accepted royal patronage as part of the political system.

The Whigs' conception of political power was that it should be with the people (or more realistically with the people's representatives, i.e. Parliament); that the monarch should not interfere with the will of Parliament and that the power to appoint ministers and officials should come from within Parliament and not from the King. The late eighteenth-century Whigs believed in religious toleration for **Dissenters.**

The Tories believed that sovereignty belonged to the monarch and that the people were subjects whose duty it was to obey. They accepted the hereditary nature of monarchy and the authority of the established Church – the Anglican Church. They were hostile to **Radicals**, Dissenters and Catholics.

End of Whig supremacy: Tory ascendancy

By the end of the eighteenth century, the Whigs and Tories were emerging as two distinct political parties, though they lacked the unity and organisation of modern political parties. It was, however, the Whigs who led the way in making improvements in their organisation and creating a sharper identity,

> **KEY TERM**
>
> **factions:** small groups of politicians who disagreed with others
>
> **status quo:** the situation as it is; the existing condition
>
> **Dissenters:** Protestants who broke away from the established Anglican Church and adopted their own practices
>
> **Radicals:** politicians who argue for political and social change

after they were pushed into opposition by George III, when he gave his support to William Pitt in 1783.

Pitt initially positioned himself as an independent Whig, and he and his supporters preferred to be perceived as the representatives of the nation. Pitt, however, is often regarded as the first Tory although he never identified himself as such. He did, however, criticise the Whig party as being too narrow, with political power being tightly controlled by a Whig **oligarchy** serving only their own interests.

After Pitt's election success of 1784, there was a gradual redefinition of the term 'Tory' and by the close of Pitt's period in office in 1806, the supremacy of the Whigs had been broken. When the Whigs emerged again as a powerful political force in the 1830s, after decades of Tory dominance, they too had undergone a process of redefinition and reformation. They became more closely associated with liberal ideas and reform, while the Tories became regarded as reactionary and against reform.

> **KEY TERM**
>
> **oligarchy:** a government of a small elite group, in this context the ruling Whig families who dominated the political scene in the eighteenth century

Summary

- In 1783, Britain had a system of government based on a constitutional monarchy.
- Political power was shared between the King and Parliament.
- Parliament made laws, took decisions on taxation and spending and debated issues of national and local importance.
- The monarch was head of state and retained some important powers, but could not rule without Parliament and so his powers were limited.
- Within Parliament, most political power rested with the Lords, but the influence of the House of Commons was increasing.
- The position of prime minister was becoming more dependent on the support of Parliament than on the support of the monarch.
- Parliament did not represent the vast majority of the population; the electorate was small, male and based on ownership of property.
- Parliament was dominated by wealthy and influential landowners and aristocrats, who saw little necessity for any change in the existing system.
- The landed aristocracy and gentry (and the wealthy merchant class) also dominated local affairs in the counties and the towns.
- Industrialisation was changing the social and economic landscape and forcing the need for political reform onto the agenda.
- Whigs and Tories were emerging as two distinct political parties, though they lacked the unity and organisation of modern political parties and they remained unrepresentative of the people.
- The ruling elite were comfortable with the idea that Britain was a well-governed and democratic nation.

> **ACTIVITY**
>
> **Pair discussion**
>
> In pairs, summarise why there was a need for parliamentary reform in 1783 and produce some counter arguments that you think Members of Parliament might have put forward.

> **AS LEVEL PRACTICE QUESTION**
>
> 'Britain had become a democratic nation by the late eighteenth century.' Explain why you agree or disagree with this view.

> **STUDY TIP**
>
> In order to answer this question, you need to consider the ways in which Britain had evolved democratically by the late eighteenth century and the ways in which it had not. You may find it helpful to define 'democratic' in your introduction and don't forget to advance your own judgement and support it with evidence.

2 Government: Pitt the Younger as Prime Minister and his successors

EXTRACT 1

It is upon his solution of the problems caused by the American war that Pitt's reputation as a great peacetime minister rests. He simplified customs and reduced them drastically on consumption goods, especially tea, in order to check for ravages to the financial system caused by smuggling. Whenever he could, he abolished any measure which tended to check the flow of raw materials to British manufacturers or which impeded the export of finished articles. With finance he was less successful. He accepted the views of **Dr Price** on the **National Debt and Sinking Fund**. But Dr Price's views were based on a mistaken idea and, apart from an immediate gain in confidence, Pitt's operations with the Sinking Fund produced no benefits. Nevertheless, as the years passed, his reforms in the national economy and the lavish honours bestowed on his supporters by royalty, created for Pitt a very strong position.

Adapted from John H. Plumb, *England in the Eighteenth Century (1714–1815)*, 1964

A CLOSER LOOK

National Debt was a long-term debt set up in 1696 initially to meet the high cost of Britain's continental wars. The Bank of England organised loans to the government, with interest to be paid annually. Taxes had to be raised to pay the interest. The Debt kept increasing as further loans were sought by the government and it became an accepted feature of national finance and still exists today. A sudden increase in the Debt can cause national anxiety, as in 1783. The system has benefits for government financial planning and private investors.

Sinking Fund was a saving scheme to be used to pay off the National Debt. Money from taxation was paid into the fund and, with the interest gained, used to reduce the capital debt. Started in 1716, it was habitually raided by ministers for other purposes.

Pitt's relationship with the King

William Pitt entered the House of Commons as an MP in 1781, at the age of 21, and within three years was chosen by the King to be Prime Minister. It was a meteoric rise to power by any standards, even given Pitt's political pedigree (his father, the Earl of Chatham, had been prime minister and his mother was from a formidable Whig family, the Grenvilles). It is perhaps difficult to understand why the King should choose one so young and politically inexperienced as Pitt for the most important position in government.

William Pitt, precocious and clever with a fierce intellect, a passion for politics and a deep ambition for power, was a reserved and distant character, ill-at-ease in society. During his years of office it was these personality traits that informed his relationship with George III. There was mutual politeness and respect but their relationship lacked any warmth of feeling and remained guarded throughout. After Pitt became Prime Minister in 1783, he remained loyal to the King, who rewarded him with his continued support.

LEARNING OBJECTIVES

In this chapter you will learn about:

- Pitt's relationship with George III
- the issues surrounding the 1784 election
- the reforms of Pitt's first ministry in finance, administration and trade
- the successors to William Pitt.

KEY QUESTION

As you read this chapter, consider the following Key Questions:

- How important was the role of individuals and groups and how were they affected by developments?
- How was Britain governed and how did democracy and political organisations change and develop?

ACTIVITY

Evaluating historical extracts

1. What reasons does Extract 1 give for Pitt's reputation as a great peacetime prime minister?
2. Does this extract provide a favourable or negative interpretation of Pitt? Explain your answer.

KEY PROFILE

Dr Richard Price (1723–91) was a well-known philosopher, writer and political radical, some of whose financial ideas influenced Pitt. According to the Oxford Dictionary of National Biography, Price's reputation in financial matters 'suffered because of the failure of the attempt to reduce the national debt by sinking fund procedures'.

SECTION 1 | Pressure for change, c1783–1812

CROSS-REFERENCE
Pitt's management of Britain's war with France until 1806 is the subject of Chapter 5.

KEY CHRONOLOGY

1783	17 December	Fox–North coalition defeated
	19 December	Pitt appointed as Prime Minister by the King
1784	March	General election; Pitt wins majority support
1786		Pitt introduces his version of the Sinking Fund
1787		Pitt's Consolidation Act reformed collection and administration of revenue
1806		Death of Pitt

A CLOSER LOOK

Fox's India Bill, November 1783

India was an important and lucrative part of Britain's Empire. Fox introduced an India Bill, which was a serious attempt to resolve the problems of the British rule in India, but it also contained elements which would increase Fox's influence. The Bill passed through the Commons where Fox had support, but in the Lords, George III threatened to make a personal enemy of any peer who voted for it. The Bill was defeated and Fox and North dismissed. The King had successfully asserted his royal power.

The political crisis of 1782

After the loss of the American colonies, George III faced the most serious political crisis of his reign. His favourite Lord North had resigned and George was forced to accept a Whig ministry led by Lord Rockingham, whom he disliked, but who was capable of leading a majority in the Commons. When Rockingham died unexpectedly, his place was taken by **Lord Shelburne,** whose political motives were deeply distrusted because of his close friendship with the King. In agreement with Shelburne, the King appointed William Pitt as Chancellor of the Exchequer. William Hague suggests that the reason George made this appointment in the politically unusual circumstances of 1782, was that 'the system was literally running out of talented material'.

Shelburne's ministry was short-lived, as two opposing factions of Lord North and **Charles James Fox** had joined forces to bring him down. The unpalatable prospect of a coalition between Fox, whom George detested, and his former trusted Prime Minister Lord North was anathema to him, but one he was ultimately forced to accept. However, the King manoeuvred to destroy the Fox–North coalition and they were dismissed at the earliest opportunity.

KEY PROFILE

Lord Shelburne (1737–1805) was a leading Whig, closely connected to Pitt's father, and had considerable influence on Pitt. He believed in allegiance to the King rather than to a party or faction. He had a brilliant mind and ideas ahead of his time, was patron to radical thinkers like Dr Price and embraced Adam Smith's ideas. He was distrusted for his secrecy and political aloofness.

Fig. 1   Lord Shelburne

Charles James Fox (1749–1806) came from a prominent Whig family. Intellectually gifted, a brilliant speaker, champion of individual freedom, he could have enjoyed political success, but he was reckless and unpredictable, criticising the government and calling for a reduction in the King's powers. He was detested by George III who, probably with Pitt's connivance, kept him out of office. He became the leading opposition figure for the rest of his political life.

Fig. 2   Charles James Fox

The appointment of Pitt

George needed someone he could trust to restore national confidence, but he was to have difficulty as far as choice of minister was concerned. He refused to contemplate the Rockingham Whigs, who had a majority in the Commons, because they wanted to curb his powers, but the Shelburne Whigs who supported the King's position, did not have enough backing to hold together a government. George was determined to exercise his prerogative to choose his ministers and avoid political humiliation. He would never again trust his old friend Lord North for his betrayal. Pitt, in spite of his youth, had made a strong impression in Parliament as Chancellor, with his outstanding debating skills and logical arguments, and he was regarded as honest and conscientious. By appointing Pitt, George could keep the ambitious Fox out of office. George did not particularly like Pitt, but he trusted him enough to give him his confidence. In short, he preferred Pitt to any other Whigs.

EXTRACT 2

Pitt was never a royal toady [flatterer]; indeed he shared some of Rockingham's concerns about royal influence, though to a milder degree. He did, however, both recognise and respect the constitutional position of the sovereign and he was not inclined either to bluster or dictate to George. He respected the convention that he was genuinely taking office as 'the King's minister' with all that that phrase implied for royal choice.

William Pitt the Younger by Eric J. Evans

A CLOSER LOOK

Historiography of William Pitt the Younger

It is suggested by historian Derek Jarrett that, after the 1784 election, Pitt maintained good relations with George III because he generally told the King what he wanted to hear. The surviving letters George III wrote to Pitt give the impression that the King believed himself to be in charge of policy and have led historians such as Donald Barnes to suggest that the King was 'the senior partner in the firm'. Jarrett asserts, however, that as far as the all-important financial and administrative matters were concerned, it was Pitt who made the decisions, as there was no one else in the Cabinet who understood their complexities, and therefore the King was unable to take contrary advice from any other ministers, although he may have made a pretence at doing so.

The 1784 election

The mince-pie administration

In December 1783, the announcement that Pitt had accepted office as Prime Minister from the King caused his opponents alarm. Pitt had no following in the Commons and was faced with a large majority opposition. No member of the Commons would serve in his Cabinet, which he then made up of members of the Lords, leaving him isolated. It was almost impossible to pass any measures through Parliament. His position was very weak. Cartoonists nicknamed his government 'the mince-pie administration', anticipating it would not survive beyond Christmas.

Fox and his friends had a majority but the King ignored the accepted convention of inviting them to take office, maintaining his right to choose his ministers. Fox was furious and suggested this was proof of the King's contempt for Parliament and the electorate. His outspoken condemnation of the King's actions lost Fox vital support. When votes went against Pitt in the House of commons and calls were made for his resignation, Pitt stood his ground. He survived partly because he had the firm support of the King, partly because Pitt's personal ambition made him determined to cling on to power until he could gain the necessary majority, and partly because Fox gradually upset his own supporters.

EXTRACT 3

Pitt accepted the responsibility of office. The knowledge that, if he could hold on long enough, preparations would be made to ensure victory in a general election helped to bring him to a decision. He did not concern himself with the means by which Fox had been driven from office in November 1783. He was no party

Fig. 3 *William Pitt*

ACTIVITY

a) Why did George III choose Pitt as 'the King's minister' in December 1783?

b) Can you foresee any problems this choice might bring?

ACTIVITY

Class discussion

Pitt and the King did disagree on several important issues, such as parliamentary reform. They tended to pull back from open conflict or come to a compromise. Can you suggest why? Before you begin, you should read more about their disagreements on page 48.

ACTIVITY

Evaluating historical extracts

1. According to Extract 3, why did Pitt accept the responsibility of office in December 1783?

2. What does Extract 3 suggest to you about Pitt's character and political skill?

3. How convincing are the arguments in Extract 3 as to Pitt's motive for accepting office without the support of the House of Commons?

man. He thought of himself as a mediator between the King and the factions. He preferred to get into office and govern, rather than rot in pointless opposition. But his precious independence was a greater asset than ever; he could take office at the invitation of the King without betraying any principle or wounding any friend. If he succeeded he would be able to rule as he wished, within the usual conventions of constitutional practice; conventions, which unlike his rival, Fox, he did not question. Pitt did not doubt that a ministry led by himself was the solution to the dilemma, whatever the manoeuvres which had made it possible.

Adapted from John W. Derry, *William Pitt,* 1962

The 1784 election

As Pitt watched Fox's majority dwindle, he chose the moment there was a 'single vote' between them to ask the King to call an election in March 1784. Parliaments usually ran for seven years. It was clear that the King was dissolving this Parliament after three so that his chosen minister Pitt had a chance to gain a parliamentary majority: it could be argued that the King was again pushing the boundaries of his constitutional position. In the meantime, the King 'managed' the election. He used all influence possible in government-controlled boroughs, while Pitt used the sizable election fund at his disposal, provided by the King. In the county seats, however, where there was less opportunity to sway the electorate, they still demonstrated their support of Pitt and their disenchantment with Fox.

Pitt was elected for Cambridge, the seat he held for the rest of his life. Fox only just scraped in for Westminster, but about 160 of his followers lost their seats. The electorate had given Pitt and the King their vote of confidence and Pitt returned to the Commons with a large majority. Pitt drew his support from some of the Whigs (or Whig families) who had supported his father, from some of the moderate Tories, and from the group of politicians known as the 'King's Friends', whose votes depended on the King's wishes. The King used his **patronage** to create new peers in the Lords from the wealthy merchant class in **the City**, overwhelming the old Whig aristocracy, with the result that Pitt could also count on support from the **Upper House**. Pitt had increased the significance and influence of the office of Prime Minister, within the constitutional limits acceptable to the King.

> **KEY TERM**
>
> **the City:** the old centre of London where trading in goods and commodities took place, the home of the Bank of England and the centre of financial activities

> **CROSS-REFERENCE**
>
> The concept of **patronage** is covered in Chapter 1, page 1.
>
> The **Upper and Lower House** are explained on page 3.

> **A CLOSER LOOK**
>
> Another interesting political development came out of the 1784 election. Charles James Fox emerged as the leader of the remainder of the old Rockingham Whigs, who sat in the Commons and were now a more cohesive group. They began to be regarded as the party officially in opposition to the government. Organised opposition to His Majesty's government was a recent concept in politics and a further stage in highlighting political differences between Whig and Tory parties.

> **ACTIVITY**
>
> **Extension**
>
> What evidence is there that the King 'pushed the boundaries of his constitutional position' in order to get his chosen minister in office?

Fig. 4 *Pitt and Fox contending for power by George Moutard Woodward*

> **ACTIVITY**
>
> **Thinking point**
>
> What qualities/strengths might MPs and the electorate have seen in Pitt which would have persuaded them to prefer him over Fox? Can you identify any inconsistency or hypocrisy in Pitt's path to gaining a majority in Parliament?

Reform of finance, trade and administration

Once Pitt had emerged victorious from the election, it was easier to establish himself as Prime Minister. He had several pressing issues to tackle, most urgently to deal with the financial legacy of the war with the American colonies and to take control of the spiralling **National Debt** and restore confidence in the government. He was eager to introduce reforms to improve trade and establish more efficient procedures for government administration.

> **EXTRACT 4**
>
> Pitt had an aptitude for financial reform and enlightened politics. He was lucky to preside over a period of natural economic expansion as the Industrial Revolution took shape and his reforms were often based on the ideas of others who had gone before him. Even so his achievements in creating a simpler and more sustainable basis for the nation's finances and cutting through many of the complexities of regulation and administration were great. His confident exposition of the benefits of freer trade helped to create the climate in which later governments could go further, his struggle to produce a fair and productive method of taxation proved to be the basis of income tax, and his reforms of the financial system helped to keep Britain creditworthy through the wars with France that lasted until 1815. At the same time he ended much of the corruption with which that system had previously been associated. Such advances must always be immensely to his credit.
>
> Adapted from William Hague, *William Pitt the Younger*, 2004

Finance and trade

The National Debt

Britain's debts were especially high in times of war. Britain had fought a very expensive war against the American colonists that had been settled in 1783. The result was that the National Debt had reached an all-time high of £240 million. It meant that a large proportion of the annual government revenue was required simply to keep up with the interest payments, which were about £8 million a year. This didn't reduce the actual debt, which was approximately 16 times the Government's annual revenue. Pitt intended to tackle the debt by setting up a reformed and tightly managed **Sinking Fund**, into which he paid £1 million a year from taxation. It was a successful peacetime policy; it cut the debt by £10 million and helped restore national confidence, but was a failure as a war-time policy.

Trade reforms

Pitt was interested in adopting **Free Trade** as a policy, as he believed it would boost the economy. He was an early disciple of **Adam Smith** and attempted to put his theories of Free Trade into practice by reducing heavy customs duties. Britain had an outdated system of **tariffs,** which Pitt believed restricted the development of trade and industry. It was based on the historic assumption that it was a government's duty to regulate trade for the benefit of the nation. The system was known as **mercantilism.** More than three quarters of government

> **CROSS-REFERENCE**
>
> See the Closer Look on page 11 for more on the **National Debt**.

> **KEY QUESTION**
>
> - What pressures did governments face and how did they respond to these?
> - How and with what results did the economy develop and change?
> - How important was the role of individuals and groups and how were they affected by developments?

> **ACTIVITY**
>
> **Evaluating historical extracts**
>
> 1. What factors does Extract 4 identify as contributing to Pitt's great achievements in office?
> 2. Does this extract provide a favourable or negative interpretation of Pitt? Explain your answer.

> **CROSS-REFERENCE**
>
> See the Closer Look on page 11 for information on the **Sinking Fund**. Once Britain was at war with France in 1793, Pitt borrowed the money to pay into the Fund, rather than abandoning the system, and so lost money. This will be discussed in Chapter 6, page 55.

> **KEY TERM**
>
> **Free Trade:** the economic policy that involves a free exchange of commodities (goods) between nations without imposing duties or tariffs
>
> **tariff:** a set or list of customs duties on import or export of certain goods
>
> **mercantilism:** the accepted method of trade regulation which involved a complex system of tariffs levied on goods coming into and going out of the country

> **KEY QUESTION**
>
> How important were ideas and ideology?

> **KEY PROFILE**
>
> ### Adam Smith (1723–1790)
>
> In 1776, Adam Smith, a Glasgow University professor, known as 'the father of political economy', published *The Wealth of Nations*. He expounded the theory of Free Trade – which meant freedom from tariffs and other trade restrictions imposed on merchants and manufacturers by the Government to raise income – the opposite to the existing system of mercantilism. Pitt was greatly influenced by Smith's theories, which inspired nineteenth century free trade movement.

revenue came from indirect taxes – that is from customs and excise duties levied on every commodity possible. There was a duty on the import of French wine, which dated back to Parliament's rejection of the Stuart monarchy a century earlier and caused friction with the French. Tea was seen as a luxury and therefore a dangerous indulgence for the working classes, whom it was felt should stick to beer. As a result of the tariffs, smuggling flourished and government revenue was reduced. The loss of the American colonies impacted on trade as Britain lost beneficial trading rights and this highlighted the need for change.

Pitt lowered, simplified or removed the outdated and complex customs duties on both imports and exports under the umbrella of his Consolidation Act of 1787. Customs duties and excise duties were amalgamated, so that goods qualified for one tax instead of several. A Book of Rates published the rate of duty for each item. The changes made the collection of taxes easier and more efficient. The high taxes paid on tea, wine and tobacco were reduced and this lessened the attractiveness of smuggling. Smuggling was made more difficult by Pitt's Hovering Act, which enabled the authorities to confiscate ships discovered to be carrying smuggled goods within four miles of the shore. An Excise Bill allowed tobacco and spirits to enter the country untaxed and be stored in bonded warehouses and then re-exported tax free. A Board of Trade was set up to oversee this whole area. The result of these reforms was to increase the volume of legitimate trade although in the short term the overall income from taxation was reduced.

New taxes

The unsustainable reduction in the Government's revenue was halted by Pitt's extensive reform of the tariff system. Pitt recouped the losses from the reduction of duties by introducing new indirect taxes. He put taxes on horses, coaches, windows, bricks, hats, playing cards, maid servants, man servants, ribbons and candles – all commodities that the wealthy and aspiring classes used. Pitt's approach to increasing the revenue through taxation was seen as ingenious by some and was ridiculed by others. The window tax was seen as a poor decision as it was perceived as a penalty on light and air and limited the development of the glass industry.

Fig. 5 *Ladies dressing their ribbons, which formed part of ladies' headgear and became a taxable commodity*

> **ACTIVITY**
>
> ### Thinking point
>
> Can you suggest why Pitt would tax ribbons?

Commercial treaties

Pitt attempted to make a trade treaty with Ireland but was strongly opposed; British manufacturers feared competition as Irish wages were low. He was more successful in his dealings with France and made a successful free trade treaty in 1786, whereby both countries reduced duties on imports from the other country. The objective was to encourage a greater flow of trade between them. However, his success here was short-lived as any benefits were negated by the outbreak of the French Revolution in 1789.

Outcome of reforms

Pitt's financial and commercial policies were enlightened and to him seemed the prerequisite for the growth of trade and industry. By 1793, the annual government revenue had increased by £4 million through the introduction of new taxes, with the value of imports and exports doubling. Smuggling was hit hard and was becoming unprofitable. He succeeded in restoring national credit and public confidence. The end result was that he put Britain in a stronger position than France to face war when it came in 1793.

Administrative reorganisation

Administrative problems

To carry through his financial reforms it was necessary to reorganise the machinery of government, which was inefficient and in need of overhauling. There were no set procedures for carrying out the day to day business of government and this led to confusion and inefficiency. For example the roles of various ministries overlapped. MPs took advantage of privileges such as free post – a good 'perk' as postal costs were high – but more significant was the corruption among government ministers, who enriched themselves from public funds through accepting profitable **sinecure offices** and pensions. There was no proper system for checking government accounts. The government loans system was corrupt as ministers allowed their friends to raise loans at high rates of interest.

Administrative solutions

Pitt made some important changes in government structure. He abolished many of the hundreds of sinecure offices, mainly by allowing them to lapse, so as not to provoke opposition. He did set an example, however, by refusing the lucrative sinecure of Clerkship of the Pells, worth £3000 a year. He devised a new budgeting system by taking estimates of expenditure from each government department and drawing up parallel tax proposals – a system still in place today. He created a Consolidated Fund at the Bank of England into which revenue received from taxes was paid and out of which government payments were made. He established an Audit Office run by independent experts to oversee public expenditure and thus curb corruption. He abolished the system of free post for MPs. He set up a central stationery department to supply public departments instead of them purchasing high cost goods from 'friendly' suppliers. Government loans were raised by public tender and so were genuinely competitive. He reorganised the Cabinet and established the Prime Minister's office as being the most important.

The result of these measures was to create a much more efficient administration, cut duplication of labour, bring order and method into government business and cut unnecessary expenditure.

> **KEY TERM**
>
> **sinecure office:** position with salary, handed out to MPs to gain their support, but that required little or no work; the modern informal term is 'a cushy job'

> **ACTIVITY**
>
> **Pair discussion**
>
> Was it the King's patronage or political skill that gave Pitt a strong base after the 1784 election?

> **ACTIVITY**
>
> **Evaluating historical extracts**
>
> 1. Pitt's achievements as Prime Minister between 1783 and 1793 are almost universally praised. Look back at Extracts 1 and 4 and identify any reservations each of them makes about Pitt's successes.
> 2. Do you think the reservations expressed in the extracts are justified? Explain your answer.

SECTION 1 | Pressure for change, c1783–1812

KEY CHRONOLOGY

Terms of office of Pitt's successors

1801–04	Henry Addington
1804–06	Pitt returns to office
1806–07	Lord Grenville
1807–09	Duke of Portland
1811	Prince of Wales made Regent
1809–12	Spencer Perceval
1812	Assassination of Prime Minister Spencer Perceval

CROSS-REFERENCE

See Chapter 5, pages 45–6, for more on **Catholic Emancipation**.

The **Act of Union** (1800) brought Ireland into the British political system – see Chapter 5, page 46.

KEY PROFILE

Henry Addington, 1st Viscount Sidmouth, (1757–1844), son of the physician to Pitt's father, was William Pitt's childhood friend. He was strongly influenced by Pitt, but was more conservative and anti-reform. As prime minister (1801–04) his strengths went unrecognised as he was seen as being in Pitt's shadow. Later as Home Secretary (1812–22) he had a reputation for ruthless efficiency in repressing popular demonstrations.

A CLOSER LOOK

Addington and income tax

Although Addington was almost in awe of Pitt, he did not slavishly adhere to all Pitt's earlier measures. He briefly abolished income tax in 1802 during a spell of peace in the long French wars (1793–1815), but when he reinstated it in his war budget in 1804, he improved on Pitt's version by deducting tax before workers were paid – the basis of the modern system of direct taxation today.

ACTIVITY

Summary

Copy and complete the table below.
a) In small groups consider the problems facing Pitt when he came to office. List all these problems in the first column of the table.
b) Identify Pitt's solutions to each problem and add them to the second column.
c) Discuss the likely effects of Pitt's solutions and add them to the third column.
d) As a group draw a simple conclusion as to the overall value of Pitt's reforms and write it in the fourth column.

Problems	Solutions	Effects	Conclusion

William Pitt's successors

Pitt resigned in 1801, over George III's refusal to accept **Catholic Emancipation**, which Pitt had promised as part of the deal over the **Act of Union** with Ireland. Pitt had been in office for seventeen years. He recommended that **Henry Addington**, a politician he held in high regard, should take his place. Addington was always seen as second best, although, according to historian Boyd Hilton, he 'left Britain much stronger than he had found it'. Unfairly, this was not the view of his political contemporaries, nor the verdict of several later historians.

He introduced improvements in income tax collection and instigated several measures to attempt to win the war with France, but his ministry was weakened by his own lacklustre performance in Parliament and opposition schemes to bring him down. Many were convinced that the country needed Pitt and by May 1804, Addington's support had fallen away and he stood aside and Pitt became Prime Minister again.

Pitt attempted to form a broad coalition government, but interference from George III, who still refused to allow Pitt to include Fox, made that impossible. Pitt was seriously unwell and no longer had such a tight grip on government matters. He was probably heading for defeat in the Commons when he died on 23 January 1806 at the age of 46.

Pitt had dominated British politics for over twenty years and since 1793 Britain had been embroiled in war with France. There followed a succession of governments, led by politicians whose main focus had to be the conduct of the war and as a result there was little progress in domestic affairs. The next government was led by **Lord Grenville** and was optimistically referred to as the Ministry of All Talents. It included Pitt's old adversary Fox as Foreign Secretary, whose appointment George III finally had to accept. Within months Fox was dead and with him went a large slice of the government's 'talent'. One important measure achieved was the Abolition of the Slave Trade (1807), first attempted by Pitt in 1788, but destroyed by powerful commercial interests. When Grenville tried to raise the issue of Catholic Emancipation, to which he and Fox were committed, the King's absolute refusal to allow any concession to Catholics brought his resignation. Grenville was liberal-minded and principled, in the context of the period, but his lack of success as a war leader defined his short premiership.

> **KEY PROFILE**
>
> **Lord William Grenville (1754–1834)** was Pitt's cousin. He entered politics in 1782 and served in Pitt's government as Home Secretary in 1789 and Foreign Secretary in 1791. Grenville left office with Pitt in 1801 over the issue of Catholic Emancipation, but then threw in his lot with leading Whig, Charles James Fox, and did not return to office with Pitt. After his resignation in 1807, he continued in opposition for many years.

The elderly Duke of Portland, although a leading member of the Whig aristocracy, took office as prime minister of what was in essence a Tory administration in 1807. He had become an admirer of Pitt and, as his Home Secretary in the 1790s, had rigorously applied Pitt's repressive measures against radical agitators. His period as prime minister was marked by accusations of corruption and military ineptitude. He failed to direct policy and left his Cabinet to their own devices. Portland resigned through ill health in 1809 and died shortly afterwards. He was replaced by **Spencer Perceval** who, according to the modern historian Dick Leonard, was 'too rooted in the past and to the ideas of Pitt'. He was less open to reform than Pitt and continued the anti-Catholic stance of his predecessor, Portland. His most pressing business was dealing with the Regency issue, as George III's mental health deteriorated. He took a lead from Pitt's Regency bill prepared in 1788, which strictly limited the Regent's powers of patronage. The Regency Act came into force in 1811. He had the capacity to get on with the business of government, though not necessarily with success. He had to deal with a serious trade crisis, opposition to high taxation, popular unrest and try to hold together a Cabinet of the quarrelsome factions that had previously supported Pitt. Perceval's time in office was brief; he was assassinated by a deranged individual who shot him at point blank range in the House of Commons lobby in May 1812.

> **KEY PROFILE**
>
> **Spencer Perceval (1762–1812)** was a Tory MP who became prime minister in 1809, after holding office of Chancellor of the Exchequer during the previous ministry of the Duke of Portland. He is best remembered, possibly unfairly, because of the circumstances of his death – he was assassinated. Further details of his ministry are included in Chapter 2 on page 19.

> **CROSS-REFERENCE**
>
> Pitt's repressive measures introduced in the years immediately following the outbreak of the French Revolution are the subject of pages 43–44 in Chapter 5.

> **ACTIVITY**
>
> What reasons can you give for the apparent lack of success of Pitt's successors as prime minister between 1801 and 1812?

Summary

- In 1783 William Pitt was chosen by George III to become prime minister.
- There are several reasons why George III appointed Pitt, who was young and inexperienced:
  - He was impressed by Pitt's early performance in Parliament as a new MP.
  - He detested the alternatives, especially Fox who sought to curtail the King's power.
  - He needed someone he could trust to restore national confidence after the war with the American colonists.
- Pitt remained loyal to the King, who rewarded him with his continued support. Pitt was successful in gaining the confidence of country and Parliament in the 1784 election.
- Pitt increased the significance and influence of the office of prime minister, within the constitutional limits acceptable to the King.
- As Prime Minister, Pitt had several pressing issues to tackle: the financial legacy of the American war, control of the National Debt, and the introduction of reforms to improve trade and establish efficient procedures for government administration.
- Pitt's financial and commercial policies were enlightened and a prerequisite for the growth of trade and industry.
- Britain was in a stronger position than France to face war when it came in 1793.
- After Pitt's resignation in 1801, there were a series of short and largely unsuccessful ministries.

SECTION 1 | Pressure for change, c1783–1812

STUDY TIP

The first step in answering a question like this is to identify what interpretation each extract actually gives. Look back at your answers to the activities on these extracts and identify the view conveyed in each. You will need to use your own knowledge to evaluate these views and should provide a supported explanation of why you feel one is more convincing than the other.

 PRACTICE QUESTION

Evaluating historical extracts

Using Extracts 1 and 4 and your understanding of the historical context, which provides the more convincing interpretation of Pitt's achievements?

STUDY TIP

In this type of question always weigh up the evidence *for* and *against* the statement. You should examine each of the throw areas of reforms separately – i.e. finance, trade and administration – and draw mini conclusions for each, before drawing a final conclusion. Remember you will need to make it clear in your introductory paragraph what your criteria for assessing 'success' will be.

 PRACTICE QUESTION

'The reforms in finance, trade and administration 1783–1812 were remarkably successful in strengthening Britain.'
Assess the validity of this view.

3 Economic developments

EXTRACT 1

It would be wrong to imply that by 1800 most industry was organised in factories and large workshops. At least half the population of many villages were engaged in industrial pursuits and not only textile production; every county produced a wide range of manufactured goods. Much industry, even larger-scale industry, was still located in the countryside. Coal mining was a village activity. Pits were small and widely scattered. Rapidly industrialising areas, like the valleys of South Wales, comprised strings of industrial villages, each centred on the pit or ironworks. Innovations in textiles intensified this trend. The early spinning factories of the cotton industry were powered by water and so **entrepreneurs** turned to the countryside for power. The countryside became increasingly dependent on manufacturers, while remaining essentially rural. Changes did not occur until the application of steam power in the nineteenth century.

Adapted from Edward Royle, *Modern Britain, a Social History, 1750–1997*, 1997

ACTIVITY

Evaluating historical extracts

What interpretation on economic changes does Royle advance in Extract 1?

LEARNING OBJECTIVES

In this chapter you will learn about:

- the process of industrialisation between c1783 and 1812
- the growth of the cotton industry
- the growth of other industries – iron, coal and canals
- changes in the use and source of power
- the condition of agriculture.

KEY QUESTION

As you read this chapter, consider the following Key Question:
How and with what results did the economy develop and change?

CROSS-REFERENCE

Chapter 4 deals with the impact of industrialisation on society between 1783 and 1812.

KEY TERM

entrepreneur: a person who undertakes an enterprise, often involving financial risk

Industrial Revolution: a rapid development in industry which took place in Britain in the late eighteenth and early nineteenth centuries

Industrialisation

By 1783, Britain was in the process of industrialisation. It is generally accepted that rapid industrialisation occurred in Britain from around 1780 and continued well into the nineteenth century. Industries developed from small-scale production of goods, often in domestic surroundings, to large-scale production in factories and iron foundries. This period of change and development is often referred to as the **'Industrial Revolution'**. This was a phrase coined by economic historian Arnold Toynbee in his *Lectures on the Industrial Revolution in England* published in 1884, though more recently some historians have avoided using the term, arguing that the change was more gradual than revolutionary. Conflicting opinions persist among historians about various aspects of industrialisation, with little consensus as to whether or not it 'took off' at a specific period and if so, when that period was. Historian Ronald Hartwell comments that 1760 to 1830 is regarded as the 'most acceptable revolutionary period' and that 1780 marks the beginning of 'the sharp upward movement in industrial production'.

There was a sharp rise in both imports and exports in the decades of the 1780s and 90s, indicating a marked increase in economic activity. The annual growth of industrial output increased to three or four per cent from the long-term level of two per cent and this could indicate that the decade of the 1780s was a crucial turning point. Between 1780 and 1812, it appears that the rate of economic advance was rapid and several important industrial developments took place. Those developments, particularly in the production of iron, coal and cotton came to be associated with the process of industrialisation and brought in their wake far-reaching changes to the British economy and society.

There were already many well-established industries in Britain, which operated from small premises, as Royle suggests. Britain was renowned for the variety and quality of its manufacturing industries, such as small metal goods from

SECTION 1 | Pressure for change, c1783–1812

KEY CHRONOLOGY

1780s Mechanisation of spinning process in cotton industry established.

1784 Henry Cort invented a new process for the smelting of iron.

1789 Edward Cartwright invented the power loom.

1798 Malthus' *Principle of Population* published

1801 First official Census of the population

KEY TERM

The East India Company: the largest and most influential English trading company, formed in 1600. It enjoyed a trade monopoly in India and the Far East until the nineteenth century and large parts of India came under its political control

census: an official count or survey, especially of a population

CROSS-REFERENCE

Look back at the Key Profile for **Dr Price** in Chapter 2, page 11.

KEY PROFILE

Arthur Young (1741–1820) was best known as an agricultural reformer, but was also a political and social observer, writer and traveller. As he journeyed around England he formed the opinion that the population was rising, and made interesting observations on the signs of industrialisation. He was also an improving farmer, though not financially successful.

Birmingham and woollen cloth from Yorkshire. Tin was mined in Cornwall and used in the manufacture of many utensils. There were printing works, breweries, glass-making and leather-curing. The biggest market for these goods was London, with its ease of access to home and foreign markets through its sea port.

It is difficult to identify a single cause of industrial advance and why it occurred in Britain first. David Hume (1711–76), the eighteenth century philosopher, suggested greed was the spur of industry. While this is an interesting comment on human nature, it does not stand up to scrutiny. There were several likely preconditions for economic growth: development of trade, availability of capital, access to raw materials, improvements in agriculture, political stability, scientific and technological invention, and, within Britain, free movement of people and goods. Underlying these was a growth in population.

Shipbuilding, exploration, discovery of new overseas markets and colonisation had all brought a growth in trade and this in turn had stimulated the development of banking and finance. The **East India Company** was trading in spices, silk, cotton and tea and there was a thriving market in cotton, sugar, tobacco and slaves in the West Indies. As a result, there was capital available to borrow at low interest rates, to invest in the expansion of existing industries and to set up new enterprises. The rise in population meant that there was a large labour force available. It also led to an increased demand for food, clothing, housing and other commodities. This in turn led to increased production of manufactured goods, especially textiles, at low prices, and stimulated agricultural output. Political stability allowed more enlightened ideas to flourish. Scientific thought encouraged innovation and invention. In Britain's relatively liberal and democratic society, compared with their continental neighbours the people were free to move themselves and goods around the country and so there was little hindrance to new ventures.

In addition, Britain was endowed with natural resources to create power to drive the newly-invented industrial machines. Fast-flowing streams could be modified to harness water power. There were plentiful supplies of coal and iron ore was often found close by, providing vast amounts of raw materials for the manufacture of heavy machinery. As an island, even points inland were never too distant from the sea; there were navigable rivers and a new industry in canal building – all essential for the transport of raw materials and manufactured goods.

Population growth

The first official **census** to enumerate Britain's population was conducted in 1801. It was done partly to settle the conflicting views on whether or not the population was growing, and partly, if it was increasing, to address the anxiety about its sustainability. Fierce debates raged on all sides. **Dr Richard Price** argued that Britain was weak and that was causing a decline in the population. Thomas Malthus believed the population was growing, but forecast that it would outstrip the rate of production of food and cause massive social problems. There were supporters, like **Arthur Young**, of the common sense view that the population was increasing and he observed a healthy economy in 'the flourishing state of our agriculture, our manufactures and commerce (and) our general wealth'. The results of the first official census in 1801 put the population of Britain at 10.9 million, but by 1811 it had risen to 12.6 million. Although these results are not as reliable as the census returns from after 1841, they provide evidence of a strong growth in the overall population.

Knowledge that the population was growing led to lengthy discussions as to the causes. There was an increase in the birth rate and a fall in the death rate.

There are several possible explanations for this. Agricultural improvements meant an increase in food production, better quality food and low prices, which in turn led to a rise in living standards, better health, fewer infant deaths and increased longevity. Industrialisation created more jobs, and therefore more young men could afford to live independently, marry and have children earlier.

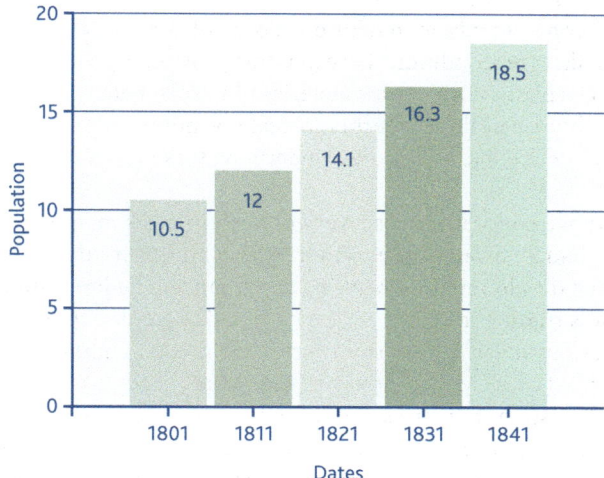

Fig. 1 *Population changes in Britain, 1760–1810*

The growth of cotton and other industries

The cotton industry

> **EXTRACT 2**
>
> The basis of industrial wealth in the late 1700s was the steady spread of the technological advances and the improved methods of industrial organisation. This was most obvious in the rapid development of the cotton industry in Lancashire, where the factory system and power-driven machinery were most commonly found. However even in Lancashire, pockets of old-fashioned industrial methods still lingered side by side with the new. Big mills and the great textile **magnates**, like the **Horrocks**, were exceptional. For one capitalist of this stature, there were fifty small masters, risen from the ranks of the workers themselves, or **yeomen** (small freeholder farmers) with a little capital, lured to Manchester and the boom towns by the prospect of quick wealth. The same is true of the light metal industries of Birmingham and the small-scale potters of the **Five Towns**. Great fortunes were already being made by those industrialists who adopted most completely the new methods and this was obvious to contemporaries.
>
> Adapted from John H. Plumb, *England in the Eighteenth Century (1714–1815)*, 1964

A CLOSER LOOK

The phrase '**Five Towns**' refers to the renowned pottery towns in Staffordshire. There were in fact Six Towns known for high-quality pottery – Burslem, Tunstall, Hanley, Stoke, Longton and Fenton (which amalgamated to form the city of Stoke-on-Trent in 1910), but the phrase 'Five Towns' came into popular usage after the publication of Arnold Bennett's novels, in the early twentieth century, based on the pottery towns.

ACTIVITY

1. a) Working in pairs can you suggest why people in Britain took advantage of their natural resources in the late eighteenth century, when their ancestors had ignored them? Draw up a list of factors that might explain this.
   b) Do you think any one factor was responsible or was it a combination of factors? Explain your answer.
2. Working in small groups, think of the ways in which the rise in population stimulated economic growth. Devise a diagram within the group to demonstrate your answer and present it to the class.

KEY QUESTION

- How and with what results did the economy develop and change?
- How important was the role of individuals and groups and how were they affected by developments?

ACTIVITY

Evaluating historical extracts

What does Extract 2 suggest about the extent and impact of industrial development, particularly in the cotton industry, during this period?

KEY TERM

magnate: a person of rank, wealth or power

A CLOSER LOOK

An enterprising Lancashire man, **John Horrocks** set up a spinning mill during the period of rapid growth in the cotton trade in the 1790s, and developed a remarkably successful business. He adopted Samuel Crompton's Mule, which spun high quality yarn. In 1803, Horrocks was responsible for introducing an all metal version of Cartwright's power loom, which led to its widespread use.

STUDY TIP

Consider Royle's view in Extract 1 and Plumb's in Extract 2 and note the similarities and differences. Use your own knowledge to decide which is the more convincing.

PRACTICE QUESTION

Evaluating historical extracts

Using Extracts 1 and 2 and your understanding of the historical context, which provides the more convincing interpretation of the state of British industry in the 1790s?

Fig. 2 *New Lanark Cotton Mills built on the Upper Clyde by David Dale in the 1780s. Can you explain why the Mills are in the countryside?*

A CLOSER LOOK

The slave trade

The increase in the production of cotton clothing was only possible due to the vast numbers of slaves, transported from Africa, who worked on cotton plantations in the British West Indies.

By 1783, Britain was in the midst of rapid growth in the cotton industry. Traditionally, wool and linen manufacturing were at the heart of cloth production, but they were small-scale operations, most of which were carried out in people's homes or small workshops, by means of a spinning wheel and a hand-loom. This was referred to as the domestic system of production, or **cottage industry**. Under this system, the processes were slow and lacked quality control, and production was limited, allowing little prospect of expansion. The industry changed with the increased import of raw cotton.

As the population rose, there was an increasing demand for clothing and textiles. A spate of technological innovations in cotton manufacturing and the subsequent reorganisation of the labour force to work in large factories helped to bring about this revolution in the textile industry. Cotton clothing had advantages over linen and wool garments; it was cheaper, more comfortable to wear and easier to wash. Cotton manufacturing was quickly established in two areas – in Lancashire in the north of England and in Lanarkshire in south-west Scotland – for two key reasons: fast-flowing rivers which could be harnessed to produce power to turn machines, and proximity to the major sea ports of Liverpool and Glasgow. An abundance of raw cotton was shipped across from the West Indies, where British merchants and traders had a dominating influence on both production and export. A canal system connected cotton factories to the ports and to other towns for redistribution.

The development of Arkwright's water frame in 1769, heralded the start of the factory system of production and revolutionised the industry. Samuel Crompton's 'Mule' (1779), a cross between the water frame and Hargreaves' 'Spinning Jenny', produced exceptionally high quality yarn that was both strong and fine. Once harnessed to water power, its use became widespread in factories and by the 1820s was acknowledged as the most import invention in spinning. The mechanisation of the **spinning** process was a great success, but it had left the **weaving** process behind. The industry could not function efficiently while this imbalance persisted. In 1789, Edmund Cartwright designed a power loom which was operated by steam power. Industrialisation had entered a new phase and by 1820, the cotton industry was fully mechanised and the balance set between spinning and weaving.

Iron and coal

During the 1780s the technological developments in the manufacture of cotton gave a vital boost to the iron industry. As new cotton mills were built to accommodate bigger and more sophisticated machines, and massive water wheels were designed to generate the power to run them, demand for iron increased. Output of **pig iron** rose from 68,000 tons in 1788 to 250,000 tons in 1804. Iron foundries were built on the edge of coal fields to access their essential source of fuel cheaply and easily. The industry became concentrated in four main areas where there were supplies of both coal and iron ore: the Black Country, South Wales, South Yorkshire and Clydeside. As a result, many small villages in those areas, like Merthyr Tydfil in South Wales, quickly developed into large industrial towns with growing populations. Several entrepreneurial ironmasters, such as **John Wilkinson**, built up large-scale ironworks to meet the increasing demands of industrialisation.

The growth of both the cotton and the iron industries depended on coal. Coal replaced wood as a fuel in iron smelting and was mined in huge quantities to provide fuel to power steam engines in the factories. Coal became essential to the progress of industrialisation as it provided cheap fuel for any manufacturing process that required heat. Output rose from an estimated seven million tons in the 1780s to around 14 million tons by 1812.

A CLOSER LOOK

Mechanical developments in the cotton industry

By the 1770s, James Hargreaves' 'Spinning Jenny' had speeded up the process of cotton spinning, with several spindles turning simultaneously. Richard Arkwright improved on the 'Jenny' with his water frame. These machines were large and water-powered so had to be housed in substantial buildings – 'manufactories'. These were erected close to fast-flowing water, which provided one central source of power to drive all the machinery.

KEY TERM

spinning: the process that converts raw cotton to yarn (thread)

weaving: the process of using the yarn to create cloth

A CLOSER LOOK

Pig iron

When iron is first extracted from the iron ore deposits that have been taken out of the ground, it is smelted (melted in a furnace fuelled by coke, a by-product of coal) and poured into moulds known as pigs, to form bars.

KEY PROFILE

John Wilkinson (1728–1808) pioneered the use and manufacture of cast iron. He had the foresight to commission a James Watt steam engine to improve the efficiency of his metal blasting. He combined his engineering skills with iron founding and built the first iron bridge across the Severn and the first floating iron boat. According to his wish he was buried in an iron coffin.

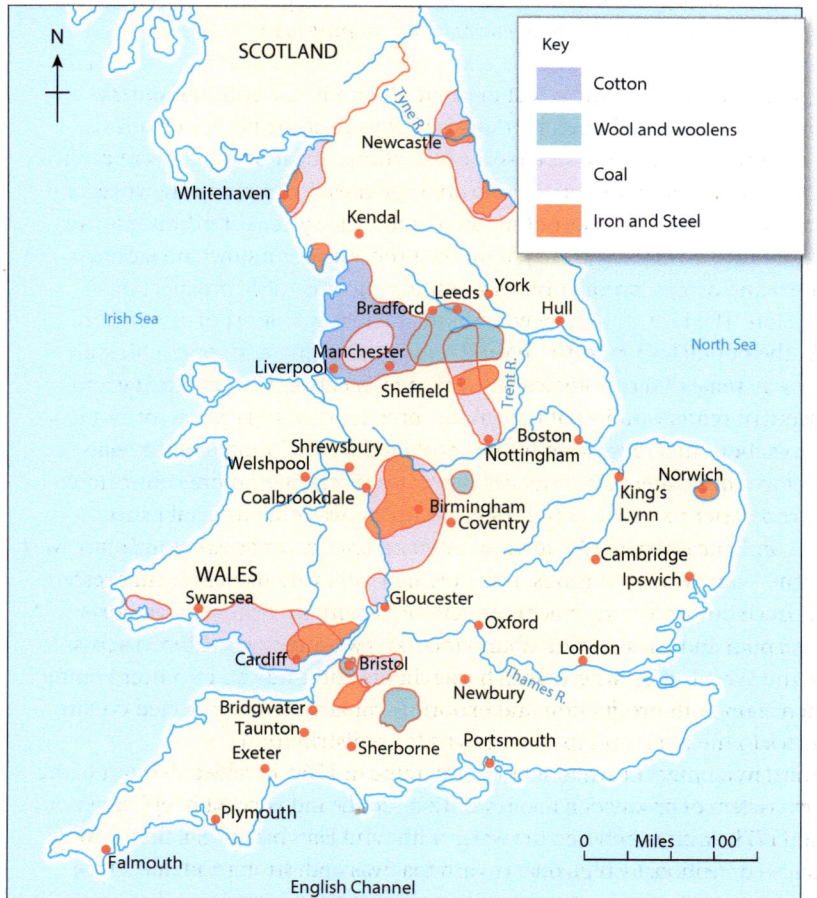

Fig. 3 *A map of Britain in 1800 showing the main areas of industrial activity*

> **ACTIVITY**
>
> **Extension**
>
> Try to discover more about the lives of the key inventors (Kay, Hargreaves, Arkwright, Crompton and Cartwright) of the technological innovations that transformed the cotton industry.

> **ACTIVITY**
>
> Devise a flow chart to show the ways in which the developing industries depended on each other.

Transport – canals

An efficient means of transporting raw materials to factories and manufactured goods to a wide market was essential for continuing industrial growth. The main development in transport was in the construction of a network of canals across the country and the 1780s saw the height of the canal era. Heavy and bulky goods could be transported more cheaply and easily than by road or river and new areas were opened up. Industrial centres were linked to sources of raw materials, such as coal fields, markets and sea ports. Fresh agricultural produce could be carried by canal to the newly-expanding towns and centres of population. Canal companies provided attractive investment opportunities. It was in the interests of entrepreneurial businessmen like the potter Josiah Wedgwood to invest as they needed canals to transport their own goods.

Canals were regarded as spectacular 'improvements', but they were bedevilled by their shortcomings: difficult and expensive to construct; could only follow limited routes; froze up in winter and were slow to operate. Canals facilitated the process of industrialisation at its most crucial period of development. However, the canal age, which spanned approximately seventy years from 1759 when the first canal was cut, was short-lived. It was superseded by the railway age in the early nineteenth century, which had its beginnings transporting coal a short distance from the pit-head often to the coast, for conveyance to the nearest factory or industrial town.

Changes in the source and use of power

Until the late eighteenth century the basic sources of power were man, horse, wind and water. While harnessing water power to machines speeded up production, particularly in the textile industry, there was one obvious limitation: the manufacturer had to build his factory close to the source of power; it wasn't transferable. It was not until the possibilities of steam power were realised that every aspect of manufacturing and transportation was revolutionised. Steam power allowed a massive increase in the volume of goods produced in almost every area of manufacture, and provided the technology to create the means of moving those goods almost anywhere in the country and across the world.

> **KEY QUESTION**
>
> How important was the role of individuals and groups and how were they affected by developments?

Development of steam power

The name **James Watt** is associated with the successful development of the steam engine, which enabled a range of machines to be harnessed to steam power. He did not invent the steam engine. The steam engine evolved largely to solve the earlier technical problems of haulage and flooding in coal mines, before Watt's time. Watt's genius in inventing a steam engine with a separate condenser – to cool the steam and make the engine more efficient – circumvented the defects of earlier attempts and made the concept commercially viable. His later invention of a rotary motion in 1781 allowed steam power to be used more effectively, initially in cotton manufacturing, with entire mills able to be driven by steam power. It was an important turning point as the steam engine became predominant in the production and use of industrial power.

> **KEY PROFILE**
>
> **James Watt (1736–1819)** was Scots born and stands out as one of the most brilliant technical innovators of the period. As a young man, he set up as a scientific instrument maker attached to Glasgow University. While working on a repair of an early steam engine, he developed his ideas for a completely innovative and efficient engine. It took twenty years and near bankruptcy before he found commercial success through his partnership with Boulton.

Watt, in common with many other inventors, was not able to exploit his discoveries. He lacked both the organising ability and access to sufficient resources. It wasn't until he teamed up with Matthew Boulton, a bold and far-sighted Birmingham businessman who financed the enterprise, that Watt was able to build his new steam engine. Their successful partnership, which brought together business ability and inventiveness to produce a major technical advance, was a key element in the process of industrialisation. By 1800, Boulton and Watt had hundreds of engines in operation in Britain. Less than a third of these were in the cotton industry – an indication that steam power was revolutionising several other industries. Watt's steam engines were used extensively in tin mines, coal mines, ironworks, breweries and distilleries and in the engineering of canals. Steam power completely altered the old patterns of life and, according to historian C.P. Hill, 'extended the range of man's economic activities'. In coal mines and ironworks the use of steam power brought cheap and plentiful iron and coal; in the textile industry it brought cheap and plentiful clothing; its application revolutionised the method, speed and accessibility of transport and, in the nineteenth century, brought about the development of the railway and the development of engineering as a highly-skilled industry.

ACTIVITY

Group discussion

What part do you think steam power played in the accelerating pace of industrial change during this period? Think about how it impacted on each of the industries mentioned in this chapter.

Fig. 4 *James Watt's steam engine revolutionised manufacturing and eventually transport*

Condition of agriculture

For centuries agriculture, the most traditional form of economic activity, had been the main source of income and employment in Britain. Although by 1800 there had been a steady increase in the number of people working on the land, in percentage terms it had fallen to less than half of the total labour force; proportionately, for the first time in Britain, more people were employed in industry than in farming. However, production levels in agriculture were rising and by 1800, one farm worker on average was producing enough to feed 2.5 people, whereas a century earlier the average was 1.7. The expanding population increased the demand for food, which drove up prices. This encouraged farmers to keep up levels of production in order to benefit as much as possible from the higher prices. Contemporary experience showed that **enclosure** of the land resulted in higher crop yields and healthier livestock, and this helps to explain the surge in enclosures at this time. Historians Williams and Ramsden are in no doubt that enclosure of the land 'quickened the pace of agricultural improvement'.

The old open-field system of farming was regarded as inefficient. With enclosure a system of crop rotation could be developed, ensuring that all the

KEY QUESTION

- How and with what results did the economy develop and change?
- How did society and social policy develop?

KEY TERM

enclosure: the new system of dividing agricultural land into compact fields closed in by fences, hedges or walls; it replaced the old open-field system, where the land was divided into strips

land was under cultivation every year, with a good selection of crops. Root crops, like turnips, were introduced to provide winter feed for cattle and as a bonus they put goodness back into the soil, which made it rich enough for wheat or corn the following year. In addition, spreading manure further improved the quality of the soil. Experiments in scientific stock-breeding improved the quality of farm animals and produced bigger quantities of meat. In spite of the overwhelming production of new machines in the textile and other industries, mechanical improvements came slowly to farming – there was a seed drill, a horse-drawn hoe, a lighter-weight plough, but nothing spectacular at this time to revolutionise farming methods.

> **ACTIVITY**
>
> **Evaluating historical extracts**
>
> Do Williams and Ramsden provide a favourable or unfavourable view of enclosure in Extract 3?

> **KEY TERM**
>
> **husbandry:** the cultivation and breeding of crops and animals

> **EXTRACT 3**
>
> In agriculture, the process of improvement was a gradual one. Enclosure by agreement was overtaken by the more contentious method of enclosure by Act of Parliament. The number of such Acts increased as grain prices rose, and reached a record level in the years after 1793. There can be no doubt that enclosures quickened the pace of agricultural improvement, and the rise in rents for enclosed acreages was a recognition of their enhanced productivity. The main innovations on the land came from a more imaginative rotation of crops. With a mix of arable and livestock farming, farmers gained in security as well as productivity – wet summers that meant poor grain harvests produced favourable conditions for livestock. Despite contemporary complaints, the most disruptive effect of the enclosures on village life was the shutting off of common land where customary grazing rights helped the domestic self-sufficiency of rural households. On balance the new enclosures, with their fencing and building activities, land reclamation and intensive methods of **husbandry**, needed more labour not less.
>
> Adapted from Glyn Williams and John Ramsden, *Ruling Britannia A Political History of Britain 1688–1988,* 1999

The outcome of enclosure was not all beneficial – there were losers as well as winners. In terms of the agricultural industry and the population at large, enclosure was an outstanding success. The landowners and farmers who bought up the land and created bigger farms increased overall production and tended to make healthy profits. The growing population in the growing industrial towns had the benefit of a greater variety of fresh food. However, enclosure emphasised inequality in the countryside, as more land was in the hands of fewer people and the once hard-working smallholding class virtually disappeared. This left the social structure of the landowner who rented out his land to several tenant farmers, who employed the landless agricultural labourers for a pitiful wage. Not all smallholders who sold land thrived. Some invested their capital in new industrial enterprises with mixed success, but many of them drifted to the northern industrial centres, where the population was already rising, and contributed to a shift in population. There was sufficient work on the new farms, but the poor wages led to demoralisation and many people were forced to fall back on poor relief.

> **ACTIVITY**
>
> **Thinking point**
>
> In what ways did the Enclosure Acts quicken the pace of agricultural improvement?

Summary

- By 1783, Britain was in the process of industrialisation. There were several preconditions for economic growth.
- There was a rapid growth in the cotton industry. The rise in population brought an increasing demand for clothing and textiles.

- A spate of technological innovations in cotton manufacturing and the reorganisation of the labour force to work in large factories revolutionised the textile industry.
- This brought to an end the domestic system of production and established a factory system.
- The iron industry was stimulated by mechanisation of the cotton industry.
- New techniques and technologies transformed the iron industry, as iron could be produced cheaply.
- Coal became essential to the progress of industrialisation as it provided cheap fuel for any manufacturing process that required heat.
- An efficient means of transporting raw materials to factories and manufactured goods to a wide market was essential for continuing industrial growth.
- Canals facilitated the process of industrialisation at its most crucial period of development.
- Steam revolutionised every aspect of manufacturing and transportation.
- Enclosure quickened the pace of agricultural improvement, and improved the productivity of the land, resulting in higher crop yields and healthier livestock, but it led to low wages and the demoralisation of many farm labourers.

ACTIVITY

Summary chart

Complete the following chart to show what changed and what remained the same in agriculture, industry and transport from 1783 to 1812.

	1783	1812
Cotton		
Other industries		
Transport		
Power		
Agriculture		

 ### PRACTICE QUESTION

'There was more continuity than change in the British economy in the years 1783 to 1812.'
Assess the validity of this view.

STUDY TIP

Your summary chart (in the activity above) will enable you to decide whether you want to agree with the statement in full or in part or argue against it, perhaps only to some degree. You may choose to look at continuity first and change secondly or vice versa but it is essential that you give full consideration to both.

 ### PRACTICE QUESTION

'The development of the cotton industry transformed the British economy in the years 1783 to 1812.'
Explain why you agree or disagree with this view.

STUDY TIP

As always, you need to address ways in which the cotton industry brought about an economic transformation and balance this against ways it did not OR other factors that were more important. Either approach is acceptable but the answer must show balanced evaluation.

4 Social developments

EXTRACT 1

The exploitation of workers was usually most intensive in the smaller factories where the desire to accumulate capital was most feverish. The vast bulk of the population fell within the contemporary category of 'labouring poor'. It is difficult to judge whether their lot grew better or worse with the intensification of industrialisation. It varied according to the trade, to the district, to the employer and to the nature and temperament of individual men. But working men today would have found the lives of their ancestors almost unbearable. The hours of work were 14, 15 or even 16 a day, six days a week throughout the year except for Christmas Day and Good Friday. That was the ideal timetable of the industrialists. It was rarely achieved because the human animal broke down under the burden, and he squandered his time in drink, promiscuous sexual behaviour and **blood sports**. Alternatively he burned down the factory, or broke up machinery in a pointless, industrial revolt. Riots were endemic in the industrial areas.

Adapted from J.H. Plumb, *England in the Eighteenth Century, 1714–1815*, 1964

ACTIVITY

Evaluating historical extracts

1. According to the extract, why is it difficult to 'judge' whether or not conditions for the 'labouring poor' improved with industrialisation?
2. What view does the extract give of the working conditions of the 'labouring poor'? Do you think it is a balanced view? Explain your answer.

A changing class structure

At the end of the eighteenth century, the old social order was changing. The traditional structure was based on a small, wealthy, landowning elite comprising the monarch and the aristocracy in authority over the rest of the population. This structure was becoming less relevant with the rapid developments in trade and industry. Industrialisation, the effects of agricultural change and the subsequent shift of the population to the growing urban centres disturbed the traditional bonds which had existed for centuries in rural communities and small towns, and created new social divisions or classes. The huge increase in population also blurred old social divisions.

The middle class and the industrial workforce

The middle class

Within the growing urban centres, a strong middle class emerged. A middle-class outlook already existed among comfortably off merchants, tradesmen and professional people, but industrialisation brought extensive opportunities for entrepreneurial men to invest and grow new businesses and increase their wealth. The new industrial world was organised and run by this emerging middle class. They started to question the wealth and privileges of the old order. They were competitive and hard-working – many became successful manufacturers – and were eager to enjoy the new wealth they had helped to create. They built and furnished substantial town houses and adopted a pattern of social behaviour that mimicked the upper classes. Together with the professional class (such as lawyers) who provided services for them, they formed the basis of the middle class which by 1800 made up approximately 25 per cent of the population.

LEARNING OBJECTIVES

In this chapter you will learn about:

- a changing class structure: middle class, industrial workforce, landowners, agricultural labourers and the poor
- working conditions
- standards of living
- the Combination Acts

KEY QUESTION

As you read this chapter, consider they following Key Question:
- How and with what results did society and social policy develop?
- How important was the role of individuals and groups and how were they affected by developments?

KEY TERM

blood sports: sports which involve the killing of animals, for example foxes; animal-baiting and cock-fighting events were a common form of entertainment in the past

KEY CHRONOLOGY

1793	Friendly Societies Act
1793–1815	Duration of the French Wars
1795–6	Series of poor harvests
1799/1800	The Combination Acts make it illegal for working men to meet together to demand better wages and conditions.
1798	Introduction of income tax for the first time
1800	Robert Owen takes charge of New Lanark Mills

Fig. 1 *A middle-class family at home, gathered round the piano in 1873*

The industrial workforce

The majority of the population in urban centres made up what came to be known as the working class. Most of them were employed in the new factories. This industrial workforce comprised skilled craftsmen and unskilled labourers and they received an hourly wage. This was higher than that of the agricultural labourers who had stayed on the land. As long as the economy was booming, they had a regular wage, but too often if there was an economic downturn, wages were lowered or they were temporarily 'laid off'. The majority of the urban, labouring class lived a hand to mouth existence, dependent on a job and wage from those in the middle class. The skilled craftsmen were able to protect themselves to some extent by subscribing to **Friendly Societies**, which paid out in hard times.

Social division

While the trading and manufacturing classes benefited from the expanding capitalist economy and became the new urban elite, the accompanying changes in urban development brought problems for the working population and caused deep divisions in society. There was, however, one disadvantage shared by all classes of this new urban society – **a lack of political rights**. As a result, new enlightened ideas flourished and provided the scope for radicalism, popular disturbances and demands for reform in the towns and cities. Both emerging classes questioned the privilege and monopoly of the political power of the ruling class, but it was some years before a real challenge was mounted. When it came, the working class demanded the overthrow of the existing political system, while the middle class sought to modify it in order to include them.

Landowners

The changes were less evident in the countryside than in the cities. For those who remained in rural areas, the landowning classes controlled most political, economic and social activity in the district. They had inherited title and land

---

CROSS-REFERENCE

For more information on the role of **Friendly Societies** see Chapter 4, page 38.

KEY QUESTION

How important were ideas and ideology?

CROSS-REFERENCE

When you come to read Chapter 12 Greater Democracy you should be able to follow how both classes eventually dealt with their **lack of political rights** and the outcome of their challenge to the government.

and had been made even wealthier by enclosure, agricultural improvements and excavation of mineral deposits (iron ore and coal) on their land. Their privileged, sheltered existence continued much as before, but with greater opportunities for **consumerism** from industrial production. Below them were the tenant farmers, now fewer in number but more prosperous and carrying some local and political status. The yeoman class were small independent farmers who farmed their own land. They were not wealthy and their numbers were dwindling. The generally-held view is that they were economic victims of the process of enclosure, as they were unable to meet the costs and sold out to the large landowners.

Agricultural labourers and the poor

The majority of the rural population, largely made up of landless agricultural workers, were the lowest paid. They were resentful of the privileges of their landed proprietors and the prosperity of the tenant farmers; they also resented their high rents, payment in kind and the restrictive Game Laws which prevented them from supplementing their basic diet. They were often forced to fall back on parish **poor relief**.

ACTIVITY

Group discussion

Working in small groups, discuss the advantages and disadvantages of the two newly emerging social classes in the industrial towns: the middle class and the industrial workforce. What would cause the deep divisions between them?

Working conditions

EXTRACT 2

Limited increases in industrial wages were secured only in return for novel modifications in the worker's way of life. The industrial town and the factory were new social institutions, which demanded new forms of behaviour and created new attitudes. Industrial workers had, above all else, to discover a new attitude to work itself. Seasonal, irregular work to which they were accustomed had to give way to far more regular and disciplined work, at least within the factory walls. Time, which had acquired a new significance for the employer, had to acquire a new significance for the employee too. A new and less natural industrial routine was imposed by long hours, the call of the factory hooter, the constant sight of the over-looker or foreman, the imposition of fines as penalties for breaching of working rules, and the relentless demands of the machines.

Adapted from Asa Briggs, *The Age of Improvement*, 1967

AS LEVEL PRACTICE QUESTION

Evaluating historical extracts

With reference to Extracts 1 and 2, and your understanding of the historical context, which of these two extracts provides the more convincing interpretation of the impact of the changing working conditions for the labouring classes during the period of industrialisation?

Industrialisation in Britain in the late eighteenth and early nineteenth centuries created new working conditions for many of the labouring classes.

A CLOSER LOOK

The Speenhamland system of poor relief

Poverty was so **endemic** among agricultural labourers that in 1795, the magistrates in Speenhamland, Berkshire, introduced a system to supplement wages with an allowance that varied according to the price of bread and the size of a labourer's family. It was widely adopted, but became an unacceptable burden on parish rates. It was an honest attempt to help the poor – its failure was related to an increasing population and continuing industrialisation.

KEY TERM

consumerism: in this context, a preoccupation with and an inclination towards spending money on goods, often luxury or non-essential items

endemic: something which is regularly found among a group of people

ACTIVITY

Evaluating historical extracts

1. What was the significance of *time* in the factory for both employer and employee?
2. Does this extract provide a negative or positive view of working conditions in a factory? Explain your answer.

STUDY TIP

A good approach to answering this type of question is first of all to identify and note down the arguments from each extract separately and then use your knowledge on how working conditions changed with industrialisation (e.g. from working at home to working in a factory) to comment on the extent to which each identified argument is convincing.

> **CROSS-REFERENCE**
>
> Read over Chapter 3, page 24, to refresh your memory on the **domestic system** of production.

> **ACTIVITY**
>
> **Thinking point**
>
> To what extent does the image of working in a factory support the view that conditions were harsh?

> **KEY TERM**
>
> **paternalistic:** taking on the role of a father, but in this context the attitude of a well-meaning boss, whose supervision could be regarded as too interfering

> **A CLOSER LOOK**
>
> **New Lanark Mills**
>
> David Dale built four large cotton mill buildings at New Lanark, powered by the Falls of Clyde. The workforce was treated well by the standards of the day. Many of the children were orphans. They were fed and clothed and by an enlightened initiative they were taught to read and write and given physical exercise. In 1800, Dale's son-in-law, Robert Owen, took over and made it an even better place to live and work, and hoped other factory owners would copy his ideas.

There are differing views among historians as to whether or not working conditions for ordinary people worsened with industrialisation or whether they had been just as hard under the **domestic system**. Most, like Asa Briggs, take the view that adaptation to the new and rigid regime was necessary, although it was harsh and unpalatable for most workers. He suggests that the higher wages paid in the factories than had been paid under the old domestic system helped to offset the tougher conditions.

Fig. 2 *A mill in the nineteenth century; men, women and children all worked there*

The higher wage could not compensate for the poor working conditions in many of the factories, which were built to accommodate machines and not men. The male workforce resented the machinery that was running their lives and they resented the factory owner, who even if he was **paternalistic** like Robert Owen (see below), was nevertheless making capital out of their labour. As Plumb highlights, some turned to attacking and destroying machinery, with consequences that were only terrible for themselves and their families.

The factories were several storeys high and took little account of the comfort of the work force. In cotton mills it was necessary to maintain a humid temperature to prevent the threads from snapping and so there was little ventilation. The result was that workers were prone to lung infections. There were no safety regulations in place and the machines had no safety guards. This resulted in terrible accidents if workers caught their fingers or hair in the machines. There was also a high risk of fire, as early machines had wooden frames. Discipline was harsh and workers were fined for lateness or slowness. The machines worked 24 hours a day in order to make maximum profit for the owner and so a system of shift work was in place. The shifts were usually twelve hours and sometimes longer and the working week was six days. The pace was relentless and the workforce had to keep to a strict timetable. Factory work lacked the freedom and flexibility of small domestic enterprises or working on the land.

This schedule was tough for an adult, but at least 20 per cent of the workforce were children, sometimes as young as six. Together women and children made up most of the workforce in the cotton factories, for the simple reason that they were cheaper to pay than men and easier to discipline. Whole families often worked in a factory – the man earning twice as much as his wife and ten times more than his children. There was no allowance for sickness and no compensation for personal injuries received at work. Pauper children were a useful source of labour and were often taken to work far from their home parish. The employment of children was not a new departure, as it was the norm for them to work under the old domestic system and on the land, where working conditions had as many drawbacks as those in the factories and the hours were just as long. Asa Briggs points out that what the factory system did was to 'spotlight the problem' of child labour, at a time when the number of children in the population was rising rapidly.

There were some notable exceptions to grim factories, for example **New Lanark Mills**, in Scotland, started up by a Scottish businessman, David Dale, in 1784.

Fig. 3   A schoolroom for child workers at the New Lanark Mills, 1825

> At least 1500 people live in the village, and about 1400 of them work in the cotton mills. The others are either too young, or too old to work. About 500 of the workers are children, who are given food and lodgings in the apprentice house in return for their work.
>
> In some other mills, there is a lot of disease, illness and bad behaviour, but not at New Lanark. Out of nearly 3,000 children who have been working at the mills for the last twelve years, from 1785–1797, only 14 have died. Not a single one has been in trouble with the law. What a wonderful man David Dale is! He has made so many people happy and comfortable.

Fig. 4   A letter written by Sir Thomas Garnett after a visit to New Lanark in 1798

ACTIVITY

Thinking point

Reviewing the evidence in the chapter so far, what is your opinion of working conditions in factories during this period? Give reasons to support your answer.

SECTION 1 | Pressure for change, c1783–1812

Standards of living

The standard of living debate

Historians have debated at length whether or not the standard of living rose following the mechanisation of industry, from the late eighteenth century onwards. There is no doubt from an economic point of view that Britain was 'getting richer' (Edward Royle), but while the statistics that are available indicate that industrial wages rose and were higher than those in the old domestic industries and agriculture, they are incomplete and therefore cannot be used as a measure of change. In spite of this, historian R.M. Hartwell, who takes the **optimist** view, has asserted that 'the standard of living of the mass of people was improving', as the '**indices**' on the cost of living and wages indicate an upward trend and 'unquestionably the amount and variety of food consumed increased between 1800 and 1850'.

There was an increase in the output of manufacturing industry, even when measured against the rise in population, which suggests there was greater availability of goods, and with new farming methods there was more food production. As the proportion of the total working population employed in manufacturing industry was rising, it meant that more people had a wage. It was not until later in the nineteenth century that there were more figures available to compare prices and wages and to consider the average consumption per head of basic food items.

Social historians such as E. J. Hobsbawm take the **pessimist** view, arguing against a rise, as once regional variations in wages and prices and the numbers of unemployed are taken into account, the picture is not so clear. Hobsbawm also makes the point that poor living and working conditions in the industrial towns negated any positive effect of the rise in wages. The regional variations are a problem as skilled workers did well in some areas and not in others. Handloom weavers for example began to suffer after the introduction of **Cartwright's power loom** in the cotton mills. The fluctuations in living standards from year to year, largely accounted for by poor harvests and the disruption of war, make a definitive analysis difficult. There are insufficient statistics to compare money wages against prices. Some historians, like Hobsbawm, factor in the loss of the gentle pace of rural life and compare it with the harsh inflexible factory system, although rural life in Britain before industrialisation was not so idyllic.

Table 1 *Average percentage in prices and wages 1788–1820*

	% price changes	% wage changes
From 1788–92 to 1809–15	+74.1	+63.1
From 1809–15 to 1820–26	−29.3	−10.6

> **KEY TERM**
>
> **standard of living:** a measure indicating the relative wealth and comfort in which people live
>
> **indices:** the indicators, or reference points showing the relative changes in the cost of living, wages etc., usually worked out from a predetermined base level

> **A CLOSER LOOK**
>
> **Optimist vs pessimist**
>
> The standard of living debate revolves around two views – the 'optimist', which is positive and sees a real rise in living standards, and the 'pessimist', tending to the worst, which sees a fall.

> **ACTIVITY**
>
> **Pair discussion**
>
> a) What factors indicate the optimist view that there was a rise in the standard of living after 1780?
>
> b) Can you put forward the pessimist side of the argument too?

> **CROSS-REFERENCE**
>
> **Cartwright's power loom** restored the balance between spinning and weaving processes in the factories, but it had a devastating effect on the skilled handloom weavers who were put out of work. For more information about Cartwright's power loom see Chapter 3, page 25.

> **KEY TERM**
>
> **real wages:** the spending value of the wage earned

> **ACTIVITY**
>
> **Statistical analysis**
>
> What conclusion, if any, can you draw from these figures about the standard of living, especially for the labouring classes, during this period? Remember, if prices fall and wages stay the same, the value of **real wages** rises. What other statistics would be useful to have to make a better assessment?

The impact of war on the standard of living

The economic disruption caused by the wars with France, which continued from 1793 to 1815, led to stagnation of average **real wages** and caused real hardship. A series of bad harvests in 1795–6 and 1799–1800 made the situation worse, as it was difficult to import grain from Europe. As grain became scarce, the price rose from approximately £2.70 a quarter in the early 1790s to an average price of £4.70 between 1811 and 1814. In 1812, it reached a peak of £6.30. This dramatically increased the price of bread, which was the staple food of most working families. Although wages rose at the same time, they rose more slowly than the prices of both food and manufactured goods and they were not distributed evenly among the population. Taxation increased between 1793 and 1815: it was a burden to the poorer classes where it was raised on consumer goods, but in 1798, a tax on incomes was introduced for the first time, which was unpopular with the wealthier classes.

It seems that living standards were starting to improve at the beginning of this period of study, but the progress was slowed by the interruption of Britain's involvement in the wars with France. The food shortages, price rises and unsteady job market created hardships particularly for the lower classes and nurtured discontent, which manifested itself in protests and riots. Industrialisation stimulated the growth of trade societies and later trade unions, whose object was to maintain a decent standard of living for their members.

CROSS-REFERENCE

There is more detail on the economic disruption of war in Chapter 6, pages 53–6.

ACTIVITY

Summary

Using the information in the preceding section, produce a diagram which demonstrates the impact of war on the standard of living for most ordinary people.

Fig. 5 *Poor harvests and disruption caused by the war pushed up the price of bread. When Pitt suggested people eat meat instead, which was beyond the ordinary labourer's means, it caused anger.*

SECTION 1 | Pressure for change, c1783–1812

KEY QUESTION

- What pressures did governments face and how did they respond to these?
- How important was the role of individuals and groups and how were they affected by developments?
- How important were ideas and ideology?

The Combination Acts 1799 and 1800

EXTRACT 3

Disputes became increasingly common during the latter part of the eighteenth century and the decade preceding the Combination Laws of 1799 and 1800 saw a renewed peak of activity. Undoubtedly, there are some special factors which must be borne in mind: we probably know more about the disputes in these years because of concern about popular movements and organisation among the lower classes, which were engendered by the fear of popular radicalism in the aftermath of the French Revolution. Nonetheless, the number of combinations and strikes seems to have gone beyond anything experienced before. Wartime conditions and high prices played an important part. The year 1789 witnessed trade depression and high prices; the winter of 1792–3 was one of shortage and growing trade depression; the war years after 1793 saw violent fluctuations in prices and trading conditions, providing the background to the disputes of 1795–6 and 1799–1800.

Adapted from John Stevenson, *Popular Disturbances in England, 1700–1832*, 1992

ACTIVITY

Evaluating historical extracts

What explanation does Extract 3 give for the increasing number of disputes and strikes in the latter part of the eighteenth century? How convincing are these arguments?

KEY TERM

combination in restraint of trade: a legal phrase to describe a form of strike action that aims to interfere with the normal course of trade

artisan: a skilled manual worker

journeyman: a man who has completed his apprenticeship and is competent at his trade

trade societies: the forerunners of **trade unions**; they represented the interests of skilled artisans, dealing with employers to ensure a fair wage and also to protect them from unskilled workers taking their jobs

A CLOSER LOOK

Friendly Societies had existed for centuries and were formed when a group of people (usually men) with a common interest, for example the same trade, contributed to a mutual fund that enabled them to receive benefits in times of need. There was no government welfare and in distressed circumstances they would otherwise have to depend on charity or poor relief.

Combination in restraint of trade, or strike action, was illegal in eighteenth century Britain, but it was a device used from time to time by tradesmen to persuade their masters to give them higher wages. These tradesmen, referred to as skilled **artisans** or **journeymen,** had started to organise themselves into **trade societies** or clubs within their particular occupation, for their mutual benefit. These were the forerunners of **trade unions**. The members paid a subscription; they were part of a network that kept them in touch with the job market and they received help in sickness and unemployment. They considered themselves superior to labourers and unskilled workers, who lacked any organisation. Similar to trade societies were **Friendly Societies**, made up of groups of workmen to provide insurance for themselves and their families against sickness, old age and death. In 1793, the Friendly Societies Act gave members legal rights to hold meetings and have their funds protected. According to historian Henry Pelling, 'the dividing line between friendly societies and combinations for wage-bargaining' was in doubt. There was such a narrow difference that the friendly societies were sometimes used as a cover for organising strike action.

One effect of industrialisation in the late eighteenth century was a steady movement of people from small market towns, villages and farms to the expanding industrial towns of Northern England, seeking employment in factories, potteries and ironworks. It meant that for the first time, large numbers of workers were employed in the same location, instead of in small scattered local industries. This gave working men a greater opportunity to exchange ideas, to air and share grievances. The new capitalist employers were less likely to know the workforce personally and were more interested in making profit than listening to grievances. The trade societies, in particular, started to adapt to the different working conditions and as a result they improved their efficiency and organisation and became less localised, bigger and more powerful.

Running parallel to the developing trade societies were the **Corresponding Societies** that sprung up in London and most large industrial towns in the wake of the **French Revolution** in 1789. They were akin to the working men's social clubs of a later era, but their meetings were alive with talk of events in France and exciting ideas of freedom and democracy. Artisans and journeymen were typical of the men who joined them. The government grew nervous of possible republican plots and made the corresponding societies illegal on the basis that they were 'unlawful combinations'.

A petition presented to the House of Commons in 1799 by the master millwrights of London, complaining about strike threats by their journeymen, pushed the government into further tough action. Legislation already on the statute books prohibiting the combination of workers acting 'in restraint of trade' was brought together and passed through parliament – as the Combination Acts – making all associations of working men illegal.

This particular action was directed at the trade societies and outlawed the normal practice of workers gathering together to bargain for better wages and conditions. Anyone caught on suspicion of breaking the law could be dealt with by magistrates without recourse to a trial by jury. Taken together with the series of repressive measures by the government in response to the outbreak of war with France in 1793, the passing of the Combination Acts was a comprehensive measure to put an end to any working men's organisations that the government chose to regard as potentially subversive. There was no opposition when the Bill came before parliament; Fox's Whigs who supported basic liberties also feared the new radicalism which had developed.

There was a parallel act to prevent combinations of **masters** acting against their workforces, but as there were no prosecutions, it appears the legislation was passed in order to give a semblance of **parity** between employer and employee. In fact there were few prosecutions under the new combination laws against the workers, as local magistrates turned a blind eye to meetings, as long as there was no violence. There is also evidence that new trade societies were formed in spite of the law. The message, however, was clear that the establishment supported capitalist interests, rather than adopting an even-handed approach.

Summary

- At the end of the eighteenth century, the old social order was changing and being challenged.
- As industrialisation occurred the traditional bonds of society were disturbed and a new society was created which started to question the wealth and privileges of the old order.
- Urban development brought prosperity for the newly emerging middle class and problems for the working population, and caused deep divisions in society.
- In the rural areas the principal landowner remained in control and little changed.
- Agricultural labourers were poorly paid and had poor living conditions.
- There are differing views among historians as to whether or not working conditions for ordinary people worsened with industrialisation.
- Historians debate whether or not the standard of living rose following the mechanisation of industry.

CROSS-REFERENCE

The **Corresponding Societies**, the **French Revolution** and the government's repressive measures are all dealt with in greater detail in Chapter 5, pages 43–4.

KEY TERM

master: the expression used to describe the owner of a workshop, foundry or factory

parity: equal status

ACTIVITY

Summary

Working in pairs, make two lists:
- one of the problems that faced the labouring classes during this period
- one of the benefits they enjoyed.

What conclusion can you draw from your findings? Explain the possible limitations of your conclusion.

- The economic disruption caused by the war led to stagnation of average real wages and caused hardship for the labouring classes.
- Industrial disputes became increasingly common during the years before the Combination Acts.
- Trade societies started to make their organisations more efficient and more powerful.
- The Combination Acts made all associations of working men illegal.
- It was clear that the establishment supported capitalist interests, rather than those of the working population.

STUDY TIP

Before you can assess the validity of this statement you must decide what the hardships of the labouring classes were. Consider whether or not the hardships that existed by 1812 were the result of industrialisation or whether they had always existed. You must argue a view in your essay.

PRACTICE QUESTION

'The hardships of the labouring classes in the years 1783–1812, as a result of industrialisation, have been overstated.'
Assess the validity of this view.

5 Political pressures on government

The political influence of the French Revolution

EXTRACT 1

So strong was the energy behind the radical ferment of 1792 and 1793 that it seemed as if the whole pace of British political argument and agitation would be speeded up. In fact it was soon to be slowed down. The main effect of the French Revolution was not to revitalise British politics at the base of society but to encourage repression from above. The change in approach can be accounted for in three ways. First the radical societies were minority societies and the feelings of the majority were easily stirred up by talk of the evils of the French. Second was the successful imitation of radical organisation by supporters of the **established order**, by setting up their own Society to convince the public that radical measures were against the interests of the country, and by publishing anti-reform tracts. Third, which made majority opinion swing away from reform ideas and the government turn towards repression, was the course of events in France. The trial and death of Louis XVI in January 1793 made many young reformers think again.

Adapted from Asa Briggs, *The Age of Improvement*, 1967

ACTIVITY

Evaluating historical extracts

1. What do you understand by the phrases 'politics at the base of society' and 'repression from above'?
2. What reasons does Extract 1 give to suggest the French Revolution 'encouraged repression from above'?
3. As you study this chapter think about why the government felt pressurised to introduce repressive measures.

LEARNING OBJECTIVES

In this chapter you will learn about:

- the political influence of the French Revolution on the British government
- Irish Rebellion and Union
- Radicalism and Opposition and party splits
- demands for Parliamentary reform.

KEY QUESTION

As you read this chapter, consider the following Key Questions:
- How was Britain governed and how did democracy and political organisations change and develop?
- How important was the role of individuals and groups and how were they affected by developments?
- How important were ideas and ideology?

KEY TERM

established order: the class that holds power, which is strengthened by social links, and that generally holds conservative and conventional views

Fig. 1 *This cartoon depicts the British reaction to the French Revolution*

SECTION 1 | Pressure for change, c1783–1812

KEY CHRONOLOGY

1789 French Revolution begins in Paris

1790 Publication of *Reflections of the Revolution in France* by Edmund Burke condemning the revolutionaries

1791 Publication of Tom Paine's *The Rights of Man* in support of the Revolution

1791 Formation of the Society of the Friends of the People by a group of reformists

1792 Formation of Thomas Hardy's London Corresponding Society

1794 Habeas Corpus suspended

1795 Treasonable Practices Act

1795 Seditious Meetings Act

1797 Naval mutinies an

c1801 Irish Union concludes

A CLOSER LOOK

The French Revolution

By 1789 the old absolute monarchy in France was economically bankrupt. When the French Parliament met in May 1789, the 'ancien regime' came under attack from the common people who forced change. Initially, they established a constitutional monarchy, as in Britain, but by 1792 the revolution had grown more extreme and in September 1792 a Republic was declared.

In the years immediately following the outbreak of the French revolution in 1789, there was a revival of political activity in Britain from middle class radicals, and it appeared that British politics was moving swiftly towards reform at the 'base of society'. Asa Briggs argues that in spite of the 'energy' expended by the radical element, the main effect of the French Revolution was for the government to take a step backwards from reform towards repression. Briggs identifies three main reasons why those agitating for reform failed to make any headway: the feelings of the majority outweighed the influence of the radical societies; 'supporters of the established order' were well organised and, working through their own societies, they were able to convince the public that radical activities went against the interests of the country; and the ugly events in France upset most decent-minded people and made them fear reform. Briggs suggests that it was these factors that persuaded the government that the dominant mood in the country wanted repressive policies, and that persuaded Pitt to take the lead from the prevailing anti-French sentiment in the country, rather than from his own views, which until that time had appeared to be more geared to reform than repression.

Fig. 2 *Government propaganda to persuade the public that British Liberty is superior to that of the French.*

CROSS-REFERENCE

Dissenters are explained in Chapter 1, page 8.

KEY PROFILE

Edmund Burke (1729–1797) was an Anglo-Irish politician renowned for his pronouncements on political events. He sympathised with the American colonists during the War of Independence; he supported limiting power and patronage of the King, but from 1789 spoke out vehemently against the French Revolution. His *Tract on the Popery Laws* became central to the debate on the poor treatment of Irish Catholics in the 1790s and 1800s.

British reactions to revolution in France 1789

When news reached Britain of the outbreak of Revolution in France, there was a mixed reaction. Initially Prime Minister Pitt believed that internal strife would preoccupy the French government to the extent that France would not disturb either Britain or European peace. His response was cautious but there was no sense of alarm. The opposition Whigs, led by Charles Fox, hailed the Revolution as a victory for democracy and freedom, viewing it as the French version of Britain's Glorious Revolution of 1688, curbing the power of an autocratic monarch and holding the Catholic Church to account. Protestant **Dissenters** welcomed the Revolution, believing it might open the way to more religious tolerance and end the discrimination against them. **Edmund Burke**, outspoken Whig politician and writer on many issues of the day, laid out his serious misgivings in *Reflections on the Revolution in France,* published in 1790, in which he warned that the revolution would end in bitter bloodshed. Some members of the aristocracy agreed with Burke and felt threatened by the possibility of an uprising from the 'mob', but they were in the minority and Burke was mocked for what was regarded as extreme overreaction. His views put him at odds with his friend and Whig leader in the Commons, Charles Fox.

Radical response

Tom Paine rebuffed Burke in *The Rights of Man,* published in 1791, in which he made clear he viewed the Revolution as a triumph for the ordinary man. He called for political reform including universal male suffrage and a reduction in the influence and privileges of the aristocracy. He envisaged a society in which advancement would be based on merit and government would take responsibility for welfare. Paine had a ready audience among the self-educated, skilled artisan class, who were eager to better themselves. They formed **Corresponding Societies** in most large towns and cities. The most influential was the London Corresponding Society set up in 1792 by a shoemaker, **Thomas Hardy**. The members wanted political reform and lower taxes and they exchanged ideas through 'corresponding' with each other and like-minded men in France, through meetings and distribution of pamphlets. When Hardy wrote 'The time is approaching when the Object for which we struggle is likely to come within our reach,' the government could be forgiven for thinking the society members had dangerous revolutionary ambitions, rather than their stated aims of political inclusion for the working man.

It is possible that government agents were behind an attack on a group in Birmingham, who called themselves the Friends of France. In July 1791, they were at a dinner to celebrate the anniversary of the fall of the Bastille when they were attacked by a local mob. The mob got out of control and attacked the homes of any known Dissenters. If government agents were involved, it suggests there was a move towards repression by the government, before the ugly events of late 1792 ever took place in France.

Government repression and war with France

A series of actions by the French Revolutionary government caused serious alarm to the British government. News of the **September Massacres** in 1792 was met with general revulsion in Britain, except among radicals and convinced reformers. The Edict of Fraternity, issued in November, which promised assistance to any nations rising against their sovereign, was followed by the French invasion of the Austrian Netherlands. In January 1793, the French King Louis XVI and his Queen Marie Antoinette were executed. Pitt began to fear a threat to British interests and declared war. The many liberal thinkers in Britain who had hailed the French Revolution as a success for freedom and democracy, began to turn against it as they witnessed the extremes of French politics.

Pitt's first act of repression in May 1792 came as the French Revolution grew more radical. The rapid spread of Corresponding Societies and the

> **KEY TERM**
>
> **Corresponding Society:** a predominantly working-class political society, set up to encourage discussion of political issues by corresponding with (i.e. writing to) members of similar associations and to advance the cause of democratic reform
>
> **seditious libel:** published writings directed against the state that are intended to cause disorder

> **KEY PROFILE**
>
> **Tom Paine (1737–1809)** was typical of the Dissenters who pressed for greater rights and freedoms for ordinary men. His proposals for the state to take responsibility for people's basic needs pre-empted twentieth century ideas of social reform. He was charged with **seditious libel** for his republican views expressed in *The Rights of Man,* and fled to France. His influence continued to spread among working class men.
>
> **Thomas Hardy (1752–1832)**, a Scot by birth, set up as a shoemaker in London. He was inspired by the writings of Richard Price, believing the political system was corrupt and that working men should be enfranchised. His London Corresponding Society welcomed all-comers and was more successful than he imagined but that led to his arrest and trial for high treason, at which he was acquitted.

> **KEY TERM**
>
> **September Massacres:** event of 1792 when revolutionary leaders sanctioned the deaths of thousands of French prisoners held in Paris goals as suspected counter-revolutionaries

SECTION 1 | Pressure for change, c1783–1812

> **KEY TERM**
>
> **habeas corpus:** preserves the right of the individual not to be detained illegally; it has occasionally been suspended by the government during social unrest
>
> **agents provocateurs:** government spies who went among workers deliberately stirring up trouble to flush out the ring leaders
>
> **republican:** supporter of a republic, which is a state in which power is invested in those elected by the people; a republic does not have a monarch

> **A CLOSER LOOK**
>
> ### Unrest in the 1780s and 90s
>
> Rioting occurred in many local areas mostly about food prices, causing government alarm, though it was more spontaneous than planned – a mob at Aylesbury market in Buckinghamshire seized the farmers' wheat and sold it at their own cheaper price.

> **ACTIVITY**
>
> ### Pair discussion
>
> Consider the following: 'The government's repressive reaction to the increasing violence in France was justified.' To what extent do you agree and disagree with this view? Explain your views to the rest of your group.

> **KEY TERM**
>
> **Jacobin:** a member of a group of more extreme French revolutionaries; the term became used to describe political radicals

various anti-government publications made Pitt nervous and an order against 'seditious writings' was issued to curb radical influence. More harsh restrictions followed: magistrates' powers were extended and reformers were arrested, prosecuted and given severe sentences. In May 1794, however, the most prominent leaders of radical reform societies including Thomas Hardy were tried for treason, but were acquitted. In the same year, **habeas corpus** was suspended; this enabled the authorities to arrest and detain a person without trial. It was justified on the grounds that firm measures had to be taken to guarantee safety of the King. In 1795, the Treasonable Practices Act made it an offence to speak against the King and the Seditious Meetings Act was passed to curb large gatherings, in order to avoid possible riots. An Aliens Act was passed to prevent French agents coming to Britain. **Agents provocateurs** went among working men deliberately stirring up trouble, in order to flush out radical ring leaders. The press was censored and forbidden to report on riots and unrest. Corresponding Societies and the Society of United Irishmen were banned in 1799. Pitt also took action to ban trade associations or unions, for fear they were simply a cover for political action, by passing the Combination Act.

1797 was a particular bad year. The predictions for the harvest were poor, which spelled potential unrest; the Government, facing a financial crisis, suspended cash payments and introduced a paper currency, and most crucially, the Navy, upon whom Britain's security depended, mutinied. The conditions for able seamen (i.e. non officers) were appalling, the pay was often months in arrears and punishments for minor misdemeanours were harsh. In the end, Pitt resorted to severe measures, hanging the ring leaders, to regain control of a basically loyal but undervalued and essential workforce.

There is a view that Pitt overreacted to the threat of incitement to revolution in Britain – British **republicans** were more noisy than dangerous. If Pitt genuinely feared revolution then it could be argued that it was a sensible precaution to extend the powers of magistrates. If he was interested in reform before, he certainly laid it aside after 1792. His measures were effective in curtailing the activities of the reform movement and led to the restriction of political freedom in Britain. He had been positive about the revolution in 1789, but it had got out of hand and he felt it was his duty to safeguard Britain from the possibility of revolution. He was encouraged by the support he received in Parliament and many of his measures were in step with public opinion. A lot of the unrest at home was because of a spate of bad harvests, high bread prices and a slump in trade, and not because of a desire to overthrow the British monarchy, though because the government feared the unrest was caused by radical agitators, the poor hungry worker got little sympathy or understanding of his plight.

A weak policy might have had serious consequences, but Pitt's actions can be seen as damaging to long-held beliefs in British liberties, and set a precedent for repressive governments for many years.

> **EXTRACT 2**
>
> Radical agitation and demonstrations for cheap bread and an end to the war had their origins in the sufferings of the common people. Dismal harvests played a greater part than **Jacobin** spies in instigating calls for reform. But ministers who were preoccupied with the French menace, and who had little knowledge and less experience of life in the industrial towns were ill-equipped to comprehend this blunt fact. Consequently repression was the order of the day, a policy born of fear and of the horror engendered by the example of the fall of the French monarchy. To recoil before this disorder was to be overcome by it, and Pitt and his colleagues never forgot this during those years of fortitude, hardship and disappointment. Throughout the last

months of uneasy peace, the government watched the growth of radical societies with baffled concern. After the outbreak of war the authorities went on the offensive.

Adapted from John W. Derry, *William Pitt*, 1962

Irish rebellion and union

> **KEY QUESTION**
> - How important was the role of individuals and groups?
> - How important were ideas and ideology?

Context of Irish problems

Ireland had been under English rule since before the seventeenth century. The majority of the Irish population were Catholics and the majority of these belonged to the peasant class. Most of Ireland's land was granted to English Protestant settlers, while most of the Irish became tenants of largely absentee landlords, who were members of the aristocracy. In 1782, after unrest in Ireland, the Irish Parliament was granted legislative independence. Parliament was still dominated by the Anglican ascendancy, the administration was still controlled by England through the Lord Lieutenant, and Catholics were still excluded and denied full civil rights. The small Irish **Presbyterian** manufacturing class, living in Belfast, who were mainly linen producers, were also denied civil rights. Their businesses were hampered by unfair trading restrictions and taxation.

> **AS LEVEL PRACTICE QUESTION**
>
> **Evaluating historical extracts**
>
> With reference to Extracts 1 and 2 and your understanding of the historical context, which of these two extracts provides the more convincing interpretation of the reason why the government introduced repressive measures against radical activity in Britain in the 1790s?

Wolfe Tone and the United Irishmen

News of the French Revolution encouraged the Irish Catholics and Presbyterians to demand reforms. In October 1791, the Society of United Irishmen was formed; their aim was to establish a democracy in Ireland through parliamentary reform and seek equal rights for all men of whatever religion. One of the founders was Wolfe Tone, a talented young Protestant barrister from Dublin. He believed that the ascendancy (who owed their position to Westminster support) would have to be ousted if the Presbyterians were to gain freedom to properly pursue their own interests. He proposed they worked together with the Catholics for political rights. His ultimate desire was for a complete separation from England.

Pitt attempted to dampen Catholic enthusiasm for the United Irishmen by persuading the Dublin Parliament to pass a Catholic Relief Act in 1793, allowing Catholics the right to vote, but not to become MPs. A half thought-through attempt in 1795 to introduce full **Catholic Emancipation** met with fierce opposition from George III and was dropped. This appeared to stoke up old tensions between Catholics and Protestants, while at the same time adding fuel to the determination of the United Irishmen for an independent Ireland.

> **ACTIVITY**
>
> **Evaluating historical extracts**
>
> According to Extract 2 what were the causes of radical agitation and disorder? How well did the government understand this? Explain your answer.

> **KEY TERM**
>
> **Presbyterians:** part of a broader group of Dissenters which was widespread in Scotland; there was also a small, strong community in Belfast

> **STUDY TIP**
>
> Understanding the historical context is important here, as it is quite complex. Take into account the influence of the Radical activity on the British public.

> **KEY CHRONOLOGY**
>
> | | |
> |---|---|
> | 1791 | Formation of the Society of United Irishmen in Belfast |
> | 1793 | Catholic Relief Act |
> | 1795 | Formation of the Orange Society |
> | 1798 | Irish Rebellion led by Wolfe Tone |
> | 1800 | Act of Union with Ireland passed through Parliament |

SECTION 1 | Pressure for change, c1783–1812

> **A CLOSER LOOK**
>
> **Catholic Emancipation**
>
> Restrictions existed on the rights and religious freedoms of Roman Catholics. These were imposed by the Test Act in 1673 and excluded both Catholics and Protestant Nonconformists from holding public office, voting or serving in Parliament. After 1800, agitation grew for repeal of the Test Acts against the Nonconformists, to formalise what was already normal practice, but there was an unwillingness to remove the disabilities from Catholics.
>
> There was a minority Catholic community in England and Scotland, but in Ireland, where 90 per cent of the population was Catholic, discrimination against the Catholics was a cause of growing resentment, particularly after the Act of Union in 1800.

During 1797–8, Wolfe Tone was involved in plotting French landings in Ireland, to overthrow the government. The attacks failed and Tone was captured; on shore the poorly organised, poorly armed rebellion by United Irishmen, supported by the peasantry, was overwhelmed by government troops. It was clear to Pitt that the Protestant-dominated Irish Parliament could no longer maintain stability, and this was the catalyst to carry through his plan for union with Ireland. Wolfe Tone cut his throat in prison before his trial and died a few days later.

The Act of Union 1800

There were two main issues for Pitt to consider if he was to bring Ireland into the British political system: he would have to persuade the Dublin Parliament to accept fewer seats in the Westminster Parliament (the 300 Dublin MPs would be reduced to 100 Irish Westminster MPs) and he would have to bribe the Catholics with a promise of emancipation, to avoid danger of a further uprising.

> **EXTRACT 3**
>
> If union was to be acceptable to the majority in Ireland then it must, argued Pitt, be accompanied by Catholic Emancipation. After much persuasion and patronage in Dublin, the Act of Union was passed by both Parliaments, but its most immediate defect was the failure to include any measure of Catholic Emancipation. Leading Catholics thought they had received an assurance from Pitt that they would be able to sit at Westminster. As Pitt's policy became known half the cabinet were opposed and then finally and fatally George III got wind of the proposal.
>
> Adapted from Glyn Williams and John Ramsden, *Ruling Britannia*, 1990

> **ACTIVITY**
>
> **Evaluating historical extracts**
>
> In what ways do Extracts 3 and 4 differ in their interpretation of the failure to introduce Catholic Emancipation with the Act of Union? Are there any areas in which they agree?

> **EXTRACT 4**
>
> The British government undermined Catholic opposition by dishonestly promising that the Union would be followed by Catholic Emancipation, which would allow Catholics to sit in Parliament. The government refused, however, to include these pledges in the terms of the Union, because this would make it impossible to persuade the ascendancy class to agree to the Union. Having failed to persuade, Pitt and his associates intimidated the general populace by sending extra troops to Ireland. They also offered money, jobs and peerages to many Irish MPs.
>
> Adapted from Liz Curtis, *The Cause of Ireland*, 1995

> **CROSS-REFERENCE**
>
> The interference of **George III** over Catholic Emancipation was a reminder of the power still held by the monarch, explained in Chapter 2, page 18.

As both extracts suggest, the Protestant ascendancy were eventually persuaded with honours, appointments and pensions. The small Presbyterian population in the north were easily satisfied with the promise of concessions for their linen trade. Intervention from **George III** prevented the promised relief to the Catholics, particularly the right to sit in Parliament. As a matter of principle, Pitt felt obliged to resign after 17 years in office.

Radicalism and opposition

There was a growing movement of radical opinion in the late eighteenth century. It was centred round a number of high-profile individuals who spoke out on issues which concerned them regarding the political and social system of the day. They were for the most part intellectual radicals: Dissenters, like

Richard Price, expressing criticism of the established church, the political establishment and the influence and values of the aristocracy who dominated politics and society.

There were active radical groups in London, but outspoken and extreme in their views as some of these men were, they largely belonged to the 'respectable classes' and were not perceived as posing any real threat to the government. They were excited at the advent of the French Revolution, imagining it would spur on the government at home to extend civil and religious rights and freedoms. When the later extreme violence of the revolutionaries became known in Britain, many of them changed their position.

The 1790s saw the rise of a new radical element – popular radicalism. Groups of artisans from London and the industrial towns and cities of Scotland and the north of England were inspired by Tom Paine's *Rights of Man* to join radical societies. This development caused alarm as there had never been any consideration that the lower orders could possibly have any right to a political existence, and it was instrumental in bringing about the change in government policy from one of 'gradual reform' to the introduction of repressive measures.

The radical movement was strong in Scotland and in 1793, a series of trials took place in Edinburgh against a group of prominent reformers for writing and circulating seditious literature. Much of the material was on the need for Parliamentary reform. The leaders, among them Thomas Muir, were sentenced to transportation to Australia, an unnecessarily severe punishment.

> **KEY QUESTION**
> - How was Britain governed and how did democracy and political organisations change and develop?
> - How important were ideas and ideology?

Fig. 3 *Satirical cartoon of Tom Paine, holding a scroll on which is written his 'Rights of Man',*

26 December 1791

The Whig opposition

Within Parliament, the French Revolution split Whig opinion – on one side were the pro-revolution Whigs led by Fox and on the other the anti-Revolution Whigs, who gradually moved their support to Pitt as reports of 'The Terror' filtered through from Paris and war was declared. Edmund Burke was the first of the leading Whigs to desert to Pitt. The rest were led by the Duke of Portland, who was rewarded with the post of home secretary, while other positions were bestowed on a handful of his followers, giving Pitt's government the flavour of a coalition war cabinet. Fox hung on in opposition, with a much reduced following, insisting that 'Pitt was a greater menace to English liberties' than the French revolutionaries.

It meant the end of the Whig party that had dominated politics during most of the eighteenth century. Differences of opinion and a strong peacetime government under Pitt had weakened it. The substantial Whig defection to Pitt made one observer inquire, 'Are you not afraid that you might be outvoted in your own cabinet?' to which Pitt answered, 'I am under no anxiety on that account. I place much dependence on my new colleagues; and I place still more dependence on myself.' The reply was a measure of Pitt's continuing confidence. However, as historian John Derry points out, he 'could not overlook the inflexibility which the Portland Whigs showed towards the republican regime in France and their vociferous demands for stern measures to stamp out defection at home.' This interpretation offers another reason why Pitt reverted to a policy of repression in 1793.

The disintegration of the Whig party as a result of insurmountable differences of opinion over the potential danger to Britain of the influence of the French Revolution was a critical moment in British parliamentary politics and cleared the way for Tory ascendancy in the early nineteenth century.

Demands for parliamentary reform

Early in his political career, Pitt had believed some redistribution of Parliamentary seats was desirable to redress imbalance between the over-represented south of England and the under-represented northern industrial areas. In 1785, he proposed a Bill to redistribute seats from several rotten boroughs, with few voters, to the more densely populated northern counties and London. It was defeated and when the King expressed his disapproval, Pitt dropped any notion of reform. The political elite, the aristocracy, were not interested in supporting change which would disturb their dominance of power.

Although Pitt's passing interest in reform did not show any commitment to the idea of extending the franchise beyond the propertied classes, and there was no intention to create a democratically elected Parliament that was representative of the people, it was an opportunity lost for a gradual reform of Parliament.

A moderate movement for Parliamentary reform emerged in the 1780s, calling for universal male suffrage and annual Parliaments, run largely by middle-class, intellectual radicals. Ironically its progress was both given a boost and damaged by the advent of the French Revolution. On one hand there was a surge of interest and support from a wider group of middle-class men, skilled artisans and shopkeepers, who rushed to join the many new societies set up to further the cause of reform and on the other hand, the

---

ACTIVITY

Group work

Divide into four groups to consider the impact of the French revolution in Britain on:
- Edmund Burke and the aristocracy
- the Whig opposition led by Fox
- radical leaders like Tom Paine
- the skilled workers/artisans.

Write a speech to deliver to your group on your hopes and fears for the future.

ACTIVITY

Extension

The question is often asked whether Pitt deliberately exaggerated the threat of a 'British Revolution' in order to cause division among the Whigs, or whether the division in the party simply reflected the mood change in the country. Which of these views is more valid? Explain your answer.

KEY QUESTION

How was Britain governed and how did democracy and political organisations change and develop?

violence of the Revolution made the government suspicious of the reformers' motives, seeing threats of republicanism in all their activities and clamping down heavily on them. Also the range of interests of radical groups – extension of religious freedoms for Dissenters, the abolition of the slave trade, etc. – diluted the effectiveness of the campaign for Parliamentary reform. The republican views of some groups like the Society for Constitutional Information lost the sympathy of moderate opinion.

Charles Grey, a young aristocratic Whig supporter of Fox, formed the Society of the Friends of the People to promote equal representation, but when he put forward a motion for Parliamentary reform in 1793, it was defeated by 282 votes to 41. Reaction seemed more popular than reform even among the Whigs. Anxiety and fear about what was happening in France put paid to any further serious attempts at reform.

Working-class disturbances 1800–1812

There was little activity from the main radical groups after 1800, but working-class discontent continued, albeit sporadically, despite Pitt's repressive measures. There were the usual food riots, which were more a response to distress than stirred up by radical influence. A group calling themselves United Englishmen threatened insurrection, but in reality were of little consequence. The short peace calmed nerves on all sides. The industrial disputes of the period between 1800 and 1812, in spite of the Combination Laws, were an indication of the hardships caused by wartime fluctuations and the adverse impact of technological changes. The introduction of the power loom in factories threatened the livelihood of the handloom weavers, especially in Lancashire. When they failed to secure a Minimum Wages Bill in 1808, they rioted and sabotaged the new machines. Their actions became part of wider machine-breaking disturbances, which by 1811 had become associated with **Luddism**. These outbreaks of unrest were early indications of the potential strength of workers to negotiate for improved conditions. It was more likely they were seeking improved conditions than contemplating revolution. The outbreaks were sporadic and the Government was in fact preoccupied with the progress of the war.

> **CROSS-REFERENCE**
>
> **Luddism** is the subject of Chapters 6 and 11.

Summary

- The French Revolution set the direction of British politics for the following two decades.
- Initially, there was a mixed reaction to the outbreak of the Revolution – notably Pitt was not alarmed by early events.
- Edmund Burke spoke out against the Revolution, believing it would descend into violence.
- The Revolution marked the rise of popular radicalism in Britain with men like Tom Paine calling for political reform.
- There were outbreaks of unrest and protests from a number of groups, with demands for religious toleration and Parliamentary reform.
- The September massacres in 1792 and the execution of the French King in January 1793 shocked Britain and quietened some reformers.
- Pitt's government acted swiftly to suppress any attempts to speak against government policy or to call for reforms.
- There was a rebellion in Ireland in 1798. It convinced Pitt to push through the Act of Union with Ireland in 1800.
- There is a view that Pitt overreacted to the threat of revolution spreading to Britain – but his views were widely shared at the time.
- A weak policy might have had serious consequences, but Pitt's actions can be seen as damaging to long-held beliefs in British liberties and set

> **ACTIVITY**
>
> **Summary**
>
> What were the pressures on Pitt's government between 1789 and 1800 and how were these dealt with? Draw up a list of the pressures and in a separate column indicate how each was dealt with. Was Pitt justified in adopting such harsh measures? Draw your own conclusion.

> **ACTIVITY**
>
> Using your knowledge from this chapter, and the historical context, how convincing do you think the poster in Fig. 3, on page 47, would have been? Give reasons for your answer.

a precedent for repressive governments for many years. Demands for Parliamentary reform were ignored.

> **STUDY TIP**
>
> Look back to Chapter 1 to remind yourself of political developments in the years 1784 to 1812 and combine that knowledge with what you have learned in this chapter to provide a balanced answer. Remember that you need to consider not only the changes brought about by the French Revolution but also other influences on political change.

> **PRACTICE QUESTION**
>
> To what extent did the French Revolution affect Great Britain in the years 1789 to 1812?

6 Wartime pressures on government

The political, economic and social impact of war 1802–1812

EXTRACT 1

By 1812, the war effort seemed to be marked by retreat and disappointment. There was criticism not only of the ministry but of the whole political system, which divided the country. Military incompetence, bureaucratic scandal, interference with trade and the alarming growth of the National Debt all came under attack. There were calls for a reduction in the power of the Government; **William Cobbett's** *Political Register* denounced the growth of government patronage through war; the philosopher and reformer **Jeremy Bentham** argued that a more representative electoral system was essential. The protests were more impressive in variety than in coherence for the critics were separated by generation and political outlook. In practical terms the critics were weakened by their distance from the Parliamentary Whigs.

Adapted from Williams and Ramsden, *Ruling Britannia, A Political History of Britain*, 1990

LEARNING OBJECTIVES

In this chapter you will learn about:

- the political, economic and social impact of war with France on Britain
- the condition of Britain in 1812.

KEY QUESTION

As you read this chapter, consider the following Key Questions:

- What pressures did governments face and how did they respond to these?
- How important was the role of individuals and groups and how were they affected by developments?

ACTIVITY

Evaluating historical extracts

According to Extract 1, what criticisms were made against the government? Can you identify the reasons why the government was able to ignore the criticisms?

KEY PROFILE

William Cobbett (1762–1835) was the son of a smallholder from Farnham, Surrey, who became an outstanding political journalist. Pitt sought him out, but Cobbett wished to retain his independence. In 1802 he launched his weekly *Political Register*, using it to expose the government's mishandling of the war and to speak out against corruption in Parliamentary elections in 1806. An individualistic radical, he championed the poor and believed unrest was caused by unemployment and starvation.

Jeremy Bentham (1748–1832) was an influential Radical with a strong following for his philosophy of Utilitarianism – a belief in the organisation of society to benefit the greatest number. Ideally he sought a balance between individual freedom and what was in society's best interest. The impact of the French wars made him aware of the need for political and social improvement. He called for wide-ranging reform in law, politics and administration. He was progressive but never extreme.

Fig. 1 *Painting of Napoleon crossing the Alps on 20 May 1800 by Jacques Louis David*

SECTION 1 | Pressure for change, c1783–1812

KEY CHRONOLOGY

1793	First Coalition against France between Britain, Prussia, Austria, Holland and Spain
1795	Collapse of First Coalition
1799	Second Coalition between Britain, Russia, Austria, Turkey, Portugal, Naples
1801	Collapse of Second Coalition
1802	Treaty of Amiens halts war with France
1803	Resumption of war through distrust of Napoleon
1804	Third Coalition between Britain, Russia and Austria
1805	Collapse of Third Coalition
1805	Nelson's victory at Trafalgar
1806	Napoleon issues the Berlin and Milan Decrees, preventing British trade with continental Europe
1807	Britain retaliates with the Orders in Council, boycotting French trade
1808/9	Start of the Peninsular War; Wellington fights the French here
1812	United States declares war on Britain

KEY TERM

Continental System: a blockade of Britain inaugurated by Napoleon in the Berlin Decrees issued in November 1806

KEY TERM

coalition allies: partners of different parties or countries (in this instance, Britain formed four coalitions with various European countries over the duration of the French wars; the third and fourth coalitions were between Britain, Russia and Prussia)

The political impact of the war

The first phase of the war with France (1793–1801) was brought to a close by the Treaty of Amiens, signed in March 1802. By this time Pitt, who had led Britain through eight years of war against the French Revolutionary armies, was no longer Prime Minister. His successor Henry Addington was criticised for hesitating before declaring war in May 1803 after Napoleon, who was now First Consul, breached the peace terms, and was then further criticised for indecisive action. In fact, he took the initiative in building up a home guard in preparation for a possible attack by Napoleon. The *Levee en Masse Act* was swiftly introduced, in July 1803, listing all men between 17 and 55, who were to be trained, armed and ready to fight. It was the biggest armed mobilisation attempted in Britain until this date and cut across all social classes, although so many men came forward it was impossible to train them properly. It is estimated there were 800,000 men under arms.

A CLOSER LOOK

Napoleon and Europe

Napoleon Bonaparte (1769–1821) established his military reputation during the French Revolutionary Wars. He overthrew the Directory government in 1799 and made himself First Consul of France for life. He won remarkable victories over his European enemies, but his inability to invade Britain and the failure of his **Continental System** dented his power. His overriding ambition to dominate Europe collapsed and finally ended at the Battle of Waterloo in 1815, in which he was defeated by a coalition of Britain and Prussia.

Addington introduced efficiencies in income tax to boost the war funds: he believed it was important to defeat Napoleon at sea and ordered a clean-up of corruption within the Navy Board, and he understood the importance of attacking France's trading ability and ordered a blockade of French ports. Yet, in spite of these achievements, Addington's ministry was criticised. By contrast, Pitt was making rousing patriotic speeches reminding the nation what was at stake: 'It is for our property, it is for our liberty, it is for our independence, nay for our existence as a nation.' In May 1804, Addington stood aside and Pitt became Prime Minister once again.

Pitt's government was weak from the start and his health was poor, but he received a huge psychological boost after **Horatio Nelson's** defeat of the French at Trafalgar, in October 1805. Meanwhile, the conduct of the war on the continent continued to go Napoleon's way and Britain's **coalition allies** were soon in disarray. Asa Briggs comments that 'time had not made [Pitt] a great war minister. He was an ineffective analyst of the continental political situation and lacked boldness of imagination to frame a comprehensive war strategy.'

ACTIVITY

1. Write an explanation of what is shown in Fig. 2. (Note: Addington was the son of Pitt's family doctor and was looked down on by the other aristocratic ministers, because of his middle-class origins.)
2. Using your understanding of the historical context do you agree with the cartoonist's portrayal of Addington? Explain your answer.

Fig. 2 *Pitt kicking Addington out of Britannia's sickroom.*

After Pitt's death in 1806, Lord Grenville's government failed to establish a clear strategy for dealing with the war and the Third Coalition crumbled as Britain's former ally Russia signed the Treaty of Tilsit with Napoleon. It was the issue of Catholic Emancipation, not the war that brought down Grenville. Britain continued its war against Napoleon making further futile coalitions with its allies. It was left to Spencer Perceval to pick up the pieces of a disastrous military expedition at Walcheren on the Dutch coast, in 1809, which had resulted in another failure to secure a viable continental coalition against France. Although Perceval's ministry was regarded as weak, some historians have given a positive assessment of his conduct of the war. According to Dick Leonard, he 'pursued the war against France more fruitfully than any of his predecessors' and Asa Briggs maintains his ministry 'provided the nucleus of the administration which won the war'.

The fact remains, though, that not one of Addington, Pitt, **Grenville, Portland or Perceval** succeeded in bringing an end to the war. None adopted a clear overall strategy against Napoleon and they were continually let down by their continental allies. However, by 1812, Napoleon's ambition was overstretching his resources and Britain was in a strong enough position to take advantage when the opportunity came.

The economic impact of war

Napoleon's failure to invade Britain by sea, in 1804, led him to attempt to destroy Britain's trade through economic warfare. Britain was not self-sufficient and so if Napoleon could prevent Britain from importing raw materials and food as well as exporting manufactured goods, the country would be starved into surrender. He planned to achieve this through his domination of the European ports and in November 1806 issued the Berlin

KEY PROFILE

Horatio Nelson (1758–1805) joined the navy aged 12 and received rapid promotion because of his distinguished record in naval action, during the French Revolutionary Wars. His greatest victory was the defeat of the French at Trafalgar in 1805, in which he lost his life.

CROSS-REFERENCE

See page 19 in Chapter 2 for more on **Grenville, Portland and Perceval**, and their domestic policies.

KEY QUESTION

- How and with what results did the economy develop and change?
- How important were ideas and ideologies?

Decrees, in which he proclaimed Britain to be in a state of blockade and forbade European trade with Britain. The Milan Decrees extended the initial declaration and threatened that any ships that entered British ports could subsequently be seized by the French.

Britain retaliated with **Orders in Council** in January 1807, which stated that all countries that excluded British ships would be subjected to a British blockade and imposed restrictions on neutral ships trading with blockaded ports. The Prime Minister, Grenville, who believed in Free Trade, had been against retaliation but was overruled. The Orders were extended after much political disagreement.

There followed months of tit-for-tat by Britain and France, each one ramping up the stakes. It seemed both countries were intent on mutual destruction. As long as Napoleon prevented French wheat from entering Britain he was harming his own farmers; consequently during the harvest shortages of 1808–10 he allowed the export of French wheat under licence and sabotaged his own blockade.

> **KEY TERM**
>
> **Orders in Council:** orders issued by the British government to blockade France in retaliation

Fig. 3 The cartoon suggests that Britain was confident it would get the better of Napoleon (nicknamed 'Boney' for Bonaparte) in its counter-blockade, because of its naval supremacy and ability to feed itself

Napoleon couldn't successfully seal off the entire European coast from British ships, and they continued to trade through certain ports. In 1808 Napoleon marched his troops through Spain and into Portugal, in order to plug the gap. On the way, he turned the once compliant Spaniards against him with his bullying tactics. This marked the start of the Peninsular War, in which Britain intervened to attack Napoleon on land. According to historian

Boyd Hilton, in retrospect it can be seen as a decisive move as it drained France of men and material, although Portland's government 'received no credit'.

Historian Richard Brown asserts there were major flaws in Napoleon's policy, pointing out that 'Napoleon had no control over Britain's trade with the rest of the world and it was to this Britain increasingly looked'. He continues, 'Napoleon failed to achieve an economic stranglehold because he did not have naval supremacy and because Britain's economic expansion was directed at non-European markets. The British blockade inflicted more harm on France than exclusion from Europe ever did to Britain'.

War finance

Wars have a high economic cost. It was imperative that the government had the ability to raise money at short notice. Pitt had decided to pay for the war by raising loans. Money was borrowed in such large quantities at the start of the war that the price of government stock fell and in 1797 the Bank of England had to suspend payments in gold, i.e. cash payments, to stem the fall in gold reserves and instead issue a paper currency to avert a serious financial crisis.

By 1801 the National Debt stood at £456 million, having risen from about £228 million at the start of the war. Pitt had continued the sinking fund to pay down the capital of the older debt. Successful in peacetime, it was disastrous in war, as the price of borrowing money had risen, but Pitt would not **renege** on the Debt. The National Debt continued to rise to £876 million in 1815 and the interest was a continuing burden on taxpayers.

In 1798 Pitt introduced **income tax** for the first time, as an alternative to raising loans. Money was needed constantly to pay for armaments and for subsidies to Britain's allies, to keep them in the field. The tax was raised on all incomes over £60 with a maximum rate of 10 per cent. It was made more efficient by Addington in 1803, and in 1805 Pitt raised income tax on all incomes over £150. It was intended purely as a wartime measure and although initially less successful than anticipated, by 1806 it began to offset some of the high costs of the war and helped the country's financial recovery. There were accusations that it was 'iniquitous' and allowed state interference in what should be men's private affairs, but although the measure was highly unpopular among the middle classes, it had the virtue of excluding the labouring classes.

The economy and the people

The strength of the British economy was a key factor in the country's ability to continue the long wars with France. Industrialisation continued at an increasing rate in spite of the war, which stimulated certain areas of the economy. The huge demand for armaments increased the demand for coal and iron. Factories, ironworks and coalmines ordered **Watt's steam engine**, to improve the efficiency and speed of manufacture. The army and navy required uniforms and this stimulated the textile industry. It was given a further boost by orders for uniforms and blankets from both Britain's continental allies and enemies including France. Napoleon was obliged to lift his blockade from time to time for much-needed supplies of British greatcoats and boots for his armies.

However, there was a serious economic and political crisis in 1810 and 1811 caused by the government's insistence on continuing to issue Orders in Council. Merchants and manufacturers regarded the Orders as unnecessary government interference. When the neutral United States closed its ports

ACTIVITY

Pair discussion

1. What do you understand by the term 'economic warfare'?
2. Why did Napoleon's attempt at economic warfare against Britain fail?
3. What were the repercussions for Britain?

KEY QUESTION

How and with what results did the economy change and develop?

KEY TERM

renege: to go back on one's word

income tax: a form of direct taxation raised on a person's earnings; it has become an integral part of the British taxation system and an important source of government income since being introduced by Pitt over 200 years ago

CROSS-REFERENCE

See Chapter 3 for a reminder of industrialisation and **Watt's steam engine**.

to both British and French shipping, they clamoured for the Orders to be removed. However, British merchants saw an opportunity to switch their trading to newly emerging South American countries eager for British goods. Boosted by instant success, manufacturers over-produced and within months faced the consequences of an economic collapse. Added to this, two consecutive harvests failed, several banks collapsed, there was a shortage of cash, an over-production of banknotes and inflation.

Fig. 4 *Life was particularly hard for the labouring classes as many of the menfolk were away fighting; children worked long hours to make ends meet*

KEY QUESTION
- How and with what results did society and social policy develop?
- How important was the role of individuals and groups and how were they affected by developments?

The social impact of war

William Alexander Mackinnon (1784–1870), a Tory politician, commented, in a treatise written in 1828 looking back on the war, that 'the mass of people did not suffer as severely as would seem probable. The country was not overrun by a hostile force; industry and commercial activity were not checked, but rather increased, and, although taxation was high, the produce of land and of every article of manufacture being paid for in proportion, the war, except to fixed incomes, made a trifling difference.' Other contemporary commentators such as Joseph Lowe drew similar conclusions, that continuing economic growth minimised the strain of war and that many of those who would have been out of work in peacetime, 'were brought by the war into situations attended with income'. These views did not take into account the 'distress' suffered by many of the labouring classes; people on fixed incomes and the poor, in both the new industrial towns and the countryside, could not afford basic necessities and many were starving.

EXTRACT 2

'Distress' was the most effective catalyst of discontent. During the war when bad harvests and high food prices coincided with business depression and urban unemployment, morale tended to fall and ideas to spread. The threat to business prosperity from the 'Orders-in-Council' made businessmen more receptive to ideas of reform. The new business prosperity of the last years of the war reduced middle-class discontent, but the new working classes, helpless victims of distress, were less easily contented. In the bad years earlier in the war [1795 and 1800–1] they had been driven to riot and disturbance; in 1811 the Luddites set about machine-breaking and disturbing the peace. The continuity of working-class discontent suggests that changes in the industrial structure of the country and fluctuations in the means of livelihood were more important than the war itself in stirring both hand and machine workers. Such workers might have little sympathy with the French or with Napoleon, but there was a limit to their passivity.

Adapted from Asa Briggs, *The Age of Improvement*, 1967

An economic crisis in 1810–11 caused by 'bad harvests and high food prices coincided with business depression and urban unemployment' brought more distress to the labouring population, already hard hit by the effects of the war. The earlier high demand for uniforms and weapons stimulated the development of more productive machinery, particularly in the textile industry, and led to unemployment among hand-workers. Stocking-knitting machines could make stockings for the army faster than hand-knitters, and power looms started to destroy the trade of the skilled handloom weavers. Consequently there were outbreaks of unrest in the manufacturing districts in Yorkshire, Lancashire, Nottingham and Derby and some workers started breaking the machines, which they perceived as taking away their livelihood. After 1811, this unrest was associated with the **Luddites** who 'set about machine-breaking and disturbing the peace' (Briggs). The fluctuating demand and the subsequent reductions in their pay had already led the handloom weavers to petition Parliament for a Minimum Wage Bill. When it was rejected in 1808 there was serious rioting, followed by a strike which only ended when the employers, desperate to fulfil new orders, agreed to a wage rise for the weavers.

There was another phase of price rises in 1811, which lasted until 1814 and rose to a higher level than at any time in the nineteenth century. There were several reasons: the Bank of England failed to agree to a resumption of cash payments, suspended by Pitt in 1797, and it continued issuing too many bank notes, which caused inflation; the commercial speculation and poor harvests also contributed to price rises. Wages had fallen behind prices, making life hard for those on fixed incomes, but the urban and rural poor who had no fixed income were starving. Evidence from the period suggests diets were less varied than previously. There was a drop in the purchase of non-food items and the economic historian Peter Mathias has argued that living standards may well have been lower than at any other time since the beginning of the eighteenth century. Landowners and farmers benefited from the high prices as rents and profits rose. The impact of the period of high price rises was felt most by those who could least afford it and could do nothing to offset its consequences.

The condition of Britain in 1812

EXTRACT 3

After twenty years of war Britain was emerging as the strongest, richest and most powerful country in the world. But the war and the Continental System had aggravated the confusions and social disasters of rapid industrial change. Britain seemed on the edge of bankruptcy and social revolution. Starvation was driving the poor to wreck the machinery which seemed to them to be the cause of misery, and the government, without wisdom and

ACTIVITY

Evaluating historical extracts

According to Extract 2 and your understanding of the historical context, what arguments does Asa Briggs put forward to support his statement that 'distress was the most effective catalyst of discontent'?

CROSS-REFERENCE

The **Luddites** are the subject of a section in Chapter 11.

A CLOSER LOOK

Wheat prices

Wheat prices were a good indicator of the price of bread, the staple diet of the labouring classes. Before the wars in 1793 the average price of wheat was around 47 shillings a quarter. Between 1803 and 1813, it averaged 92 shillings and in 1812 rose to its highest level of 126 shillings.

ACTIVITY

In pairs make a list of the problems faced by the labouring classes during the war. From your reading of this chapter what do you regard as the main causes of those problems? Was the hardship limited to the labouring classes? Explain your answer.

STUDY TIP

You should first identify the interpretation put forward in each extract and support or criticise it from your own knowledge. Decide which interpretation you find most convincing and write an argued response.

CROSS-REFERENCE

Lord Liverpool's long period as Prime Minister is the subject of Chapter 7.

without foresight, repressed brutally what in its turn it could not comprehend. To thinking men the horizon was dark and foreboding. France was on the verge of defeat in the struggle for commercial empire and the ports of the New World were opening to Britain. But what a racked and distracted Britain might make of these long-sought opportunities was hidden in the future. Towards the end of the long endurance of war, there was fear, and envy, and greed, but little hope.

Adapted from J. H. Plumb, *England in the Eighteenth Century, 1714–1815*, 1964

 PRACTICE QUESTION

Evaluating historical extracts

With reference to Extracts 2 and 3 and your understanding of the historical context, which of these two extracts provides the more convincing interpretation of the economic and social impact of the Napoleonic wars on Britain?

In 1812 Britain was in crisis. The country had been at war for almost 20 years and there was no resolution yet in sight – it was still reeling from the repercussions of a disastrous economic collapse; there was real poverty, distress and starvation in both town and countryside; many of the labouring classes grew resentful as they could see others profiting from the war. All these problems and perceptions were producing considerable social unrest and outbreaks of violence. The assassination of Spencer Perceval in May 1812 created turmoil in government circles and necessitated the appointment of the sixth prime minister in just over a decade. The Tory, Lord Liverpool, leader of the House of Lords, had already been a member of the Cabinet for that length of time as Foreign Secretary, Home Secretary and Secretary of War and the Colonies. He seemed a sensible choice in the circumstances. He chose as his Home Secretary former Prime Minister Henry Addington, 1st Viscount Sidmouth, who developed a reputation for his ruthless and efficient crackdown on dissent.

There were positive aspects of Britain's condition in 1812. None of **Lord Liverpool**'s five predecessors had had any notable success in managing the war, but it could be argued that each had made some contribution to strengthening Britain's position *vis-à-vis* Napoleon. By 1812 a combination of Britain's sea power, military efforts in the Spanish Peninsular and economic blockade, however unpopular, were effectively weakening Napoleon and ultimately helped to lead to his defeat, although in 1812, a decisive victory had to be put on hold until the following year.

In spite of Napoleon's continental system, Britain's export and re-export trade increased as it had a virtual monopoly in shipping goods across the world. Pressure, however, was maintained on the government to rescind the damaging Orders in Council, but by the time the decision was made and relayed across the Atlantic to the United States, that country had already declared war on Britain in June 1812. This caused further stress on the already heavy burden of the National Debt.

In demographic terms, Britain was changing rapidly. As a more capitalist system of agriculture developed with fewer but larger farms, there was considerable rural depopulation to the centres of industry. At the same time the total population was rising – it had increased from 10.5 million in the

1801 census to 12 million in the 1811 census. It was a youthful population and therefore possibly looking towards change.

Parliamentary elections had continued to be held at intervals during the war years, but there was no strong movement for Parliamentary reform, as yet, and Parliament remained unrepresentative of the vast majority of the people. There were a handful of Radicals in Parliament, (the best known among them was **Sir Francis Burdett**), but they tended to be more concerned with establishing individual rights and liberties such as the rights of Dissenters to hold public office, rather than an extension of the Parliamentary franchise.

The nature of radicalism, however, was changing. It was greatly influenced by Jeremy Bentham's ideas of political reform, which he believed must come before all other reform. His conversion to democracy influenced a broad spectrum of politicians and administrators and gave 'an impetus to all ideas of practical improvement' (Briggs). Some radical reformers attempted to make the most of popular support but were cautious about encouraging violent action, which would give an excuse for government repression and could alienate 'respectable' opinion. In 1812, the Hampden Club was formed by a group of leading radicals and 'pointed the way to the Whig-radical politics of the post-war world', but it had little impact as a force for real political change.

The exercise of political power was much the same in 1812 as it had been in the 1780s – the aristocratic landed interest was still predominant. There was a growing awareness of the importance of commercial and manufacturing interests and a greater willingness to listen to their opinion, but not to share political power. The opinions of the labouring classes counted for nothing.

Industrial growth, urban development and the consequent social changes that had started to accelerate in the 1780s continued and ran parallel to the war. Industrialisation permanently changed the face of Britain. But war too was changing Britain and as naval and military successes began to stack up, Britain was on the threshold of emerging from the war stronger and wealthier and, as the nineteenth century progressed, the most powerful country in the world.

To many of the labouring classes in 1812, the picture seemed a little different. The war had made worse the hardships suffered as a result of industrialisation, particularly in the textile industry. The Continental System contributed to increasing those problems. There was unrest, distress and all sorts of protest, which the government, either careless of the real plight of the workers, or through fear of serious disorder continued to repress with brutality. When parliament removed centuries old protective legislation for domestic textile manufacturers, it provoked an attack on textile machinery Luddism. The workers would take any measures to protect their property – their labour. It was the politicisation of the newly emergent industrial working class. Britain, on the brink of victory also seemed, in 1812, to be on the edge of a political, social and economic revolution.

> **KEY PROFILE**
>
> **Sir Francis Burdett (1770–1844)** – a popular champion of the radicals – was elected MP in 1807. He kept up pressure on the government on the subject of fair and free elections. He got into conflict with the government by criticising the House of Commons in fellow radical William Cobbett's *Political Register*. After a brief imprisonment in the Tower, he stepped back for fear of stirring up the mob and risking more serious charges being brought against him.

ACTIVITY

Summary

Look back over the chapter. In groups, draw up separate lists under the headings political, economic and social impact of the French war. Review your lists as a group and discuss which factor would be likely to have the most lasting impact on Britain and why.

Summary

- Britain resumed war with France in 1803 after a brief period of peace.
- Britain had a succession of wartime prime ministers, including Pitt, in his second term of office.
- Britain had a succession of coalition partners in the fight against Napoleon, to whom Britain paid large subsidies to little effect.
- From 1806, Britain and France fought a damaging economic war against each other, after Napoleon inaugurated a continental blockade.
- Britain maintained the upper hand through its superior sea power while Napoleon made errors in his execution of the blockade.
- Britain's Orders in Council were blamed for the serious economic collapse in 1810.
- Britain was able to recover partly because of a strong underlying economy and a continuing industrial growth.
- The labouring classes and the poor suffered distress and starvation because of the war and the continuing effects of mechanisation in industry.
- The labouring poor had no political voice and although radical elements called for reforms they were not sufficiently united to have any impact.
- By 1812, Britain was facing a variety of problems which were causing social unrest, the government's policy was still repressive and the war had not yet drawn to a conclusion.

STUDY TIP

This is a comparative question so you might begin with your findings from the summary activity on page 61. Use these to create a plan which balances the effects of the wars on the economy and society against those on British politics. Decide whether you will agree with the view or not and argue accordingly, looking at each area in turn.

PRACTICE QUESTION

'The wars with France in the years 1793 to 1812 had a greater effect on British society and the economy than they did on British politics.'
Assess the validity of this view.

STUDY TIP

Make a list of the economic effects of the wars, both positive and negative. You then need to prioritise these so you can see how important each was. Decide whether you feel these were 'major' effects or not, and argue accordingly in your answer.

PRACTICE QUESTION

'The Revolutionary and Napoleonic Wars in the years 1793 to 1815 had a major economic impact on Britain.'
Explain why you agree or disagree with this view.

2 Government and a changing society 1812–1832

7 Government: Lord Liverpool as Prime Minister

EXTRACT 1

It was once customary to divide **Lord Liverpool**'s administration into two distinct halves. The first consisted of the prolonged Cabinet reshuffle of 1821–23, a period of disorder in the country and robust official repression; the second of a liberal awakening in which Peel amended the criminal law, **William Huskisson** and Robinson freed up the economy and Canning asserted British interests abroad. This is no longer an acceptable view. There was actually continuity and many of the new policy directions preceded the reshuffle. The ministers promoted in 1821–23 had held influential positions before they took up front-line Cabinet posts and that two of the ministers most associated with the earlier period (Sidmouth, Vansittart) continued to serve in Cabinet following their demotion from office. There was no great discontinuity between the two phases of Liverpool's Government.

Adapted from Boyd Hilton, *A Mad, Bad, and Dangerous People? England 1783–1846*, 2006

KEY QUESTION

As you read this chapter, consider the following Key Questions:
- How was Britain governed and how did democracy and political organisations change and develop?
- What pressures did governments face and how did they respond to these?
- How important were ideas and ideologies?

ACTIVITY

Evaluating historical extracts

As you study this chapter reflect on how convincing the interpretation in Extract 1 is. At the end of the chapter you will be asked to compare Hilton's view with that of Brock in Extract 2.

KEY PROFILE

Robert Jenkinson – Lord Liverpool (1770–1828) entered Parliament in 1790 and held the three great offices of state, Foreign Secretary, Home Secretary and Secretary for War and the Colonies, before becoming Prime Minister in 1812. He admired Pitt and his balanced system of government. He was often regarded as mediocre, but he exercised firm control over major decisions. He was patient, pragmatic and fair-minded. He resigned in 1827.

LEARNING OBJECTIVES

In this chapter you will learn about:
- Lord Liverpool's administration
- the Corn Laws and other legislation
- attitudes to repression and reform
- Liverpool, government and the economy.

KEY PROFILE

George Canning (1770–1827) was a brilliant and ambitious politician. As Foreign Secretary (1807–09) he was irritated by the overlap of his role with that of Secretary for War Lord Castlereagh, whose decisions he believed were inept. Their quarrel erupted in a duel, after which Canning was in the political wilderness for a time. In 1822, he was again appointed Foreign Secretary. He was Prime Minister for five months in 1827.

William Huskisson (1770–1830) gained the confidence of Pitt, who nurtured his beliefs in a system of Free Trade. Appointed President of the Board of Trade in 1823, Liverpool sought his advice on matters of finance, commerce and trade. He pushed for the amendment of the Corn Laws. He was the first railway passenger fatality at the opening of the Liverpool–Manchester line.

Fig. 1   *Lord Liverpool (1770–1828)*

Lord Liverpool's administration

Lord Liverpool formed a Tory government after the assassination of Spencer Perceval in May 1812. Liverpool was not the first choice of the Prince Regent, but after several failed attempts to appoint a Whig administration, the Prince Regent had to accept him. Liverpool was an uninspiring character, but he was conscientious, morally sound and regarded as 'a safe pair of hands'; above all, he proved himself able to 'coordinate the forces of order', as the modern historian Asa Briggs has written, and bring a victory against Napoleon, in 1815. In office, he tended to rely on a small inner cabinet whom he could trust. Lord Sidmouth, formerly Prime Minister Addington, was the **reactionary** hard-line Home Secretary; Lord Eldon, son of a Newcastle merchant, also a reactionary Tory was Lord Chancellor; Nicholas Vansittart was the rather unimaginative Chancellor of the Exchequer and J. F. Robinson was President of the Board of Trade. Liverpool would have included the talented and flamboyant George Canning, but for Canning's refusal to work alongside his political arch-enemy Lord Castlereagh, who held the positions of Foreign Secretary and Leader of the Commons.

> **KEY TERM**
>
> **reactionary:** a person who tends to oppose reform or political change

Political difficulties

Liverpool faced several political difficulties and had to apply his skills as mediator to bring together the strongly differing views and personalities among his ministers, and to make a constant effort to overcome Whig opposition in the Commons. The few Government ministers who sat in the Commons were out-matched in debating skills by a group of articulate and forceful Radicals and Whigs and it proved difficult to hold a majority in the Commons; Liverpool was caught mid-way between the declining system of patronage and a new disciplined party machinery coming into force. Fortunately for Liverpool, the opposition lacked unity and leadership.

The opposition made much of the situation that developed over the 'Queen's affair' in 1820, but failed to unseat Liverpool. The popularity of the monarchy was low, as a result of the extravagant behaviour and lax moral standards of the Prince Regent, who on the death of his father, George III, in 1820 became George IV. To many he was a profligate, moral bankrupt and earned the contempt of many of his subjects. He dragged down the Government through a scandalous attempt to divorce his wife, Caroline of Brunswick, and then Liverpool had to deal with the unsavoury attempt by George to exclude her from the throne. This tarnished Liverpool's own reputation, increased the Government's unpopularity and roused popular demonstrations for Caroline, which created a serious threat to constitutional stability.

> **A CLOSER LOOK**

The decline in political patronage

Pitt had begun reducing **sinecures** as a money-saving device after 1783 and the process continued so that appointments to key administrative posts were related to duties and not to influence. Liverpool got rid of approximately 1800 sinecure offices between 1815 and 1822. The decline in patronage led to a decline in royal influence and stimulated the development of party politics.

> **CROSS-REFERENCE**
>
> **Sinecure offices** were defined in Chapter 2, page 17.

The 'new look' Tories

EXTRACT 2

The change that took place in 1822 was very marked. With the return of prosperity there was a change in the whole tone of government; within a few years the very suspicion of revolution had vanished and the broad outline of Victorian England had been sketched by a government that has some claim to be called the first of the great improving ministries of the nineteenth century and one of the mainsprings of later political thought and action. Parliament was still unreformed, the Catholics still hampered by **restrictive legislation**, but in its economic policy, the Government was winning the approval of thinking men and had gained the admiration of posterity. This is the period which may be called that of 'Liberal Toryism'. The name is artificial, but because some **High Tories** accused the Government of 'liberalism' – which was then a suspect and dangerous thing – it is not inappropriate to speak of Liberal Toryism.

Adapted from William R. Brock, *Lord Liverpool and Liverpool Toryism 1820 to 1827*, 1941

CROSS-REFERENCE

For a reminder on **restrictive legislation** against Catholics look back to Chapter 5, pages 45–6.

A CLOSER LOOK

The **High Tories** (also referred to as Ultra Tories) arose in the 1820s; they were reactionary and anti-reform Tory MPs, particularly with regard to Catholic Emancipation (see Chapter 8, page 77) and parliamentary reform.

ACTIVITY

Evaluating historical extracts

1. In Extract 2, what does Brock claim to be the key to the 'change in the whole tone of government'?
2. What arguments does Brock put forward for using the phrase 'Liberal Toryism'?
3. What counter arguments to this claim can you find in the extract?

KEY PROFILE

Fig. 2 Robert Peel (1788–1850)

Robert Peel (1788–1850) was the son of a wealthy cotton manufacturer, and was academically brilliant. As Home Secretary in the years 1822–27 and 1828–30, he achieved penal code and prison reform and established the Metropolitan Police Force. Controversially, he guided Catholic Emancipation through the Commons. His 'Tamworth Manifesto' in 1834 heralded a new conservatism, by accepting the principle of reform. As Prime Minister from 1841 to 1846 he introduced a dazzling number of free trade and financial measures, but split his party over the repeal of the Corn Laws in 1846.

Between 1821 and 1823, there was a 'new look' to Liverpool's Cabinet and a new mood began to emerge. The Government had survived the various challenges of the **post-war economic slump** and deep **social unrest**, against the odds, and was strengthened by self-reliance, rather than royal favour. In fact, it completely won over several opposition groups, including the influential Grenville Whigs. The hero of Waterloo, the Duke of Wellington, came into the Cabinet; younger promising political talent such as that of **Robert Peel** and William Huskisson was encouraged; in 1822, after the shocking suicide of Castlereagh, Canning, with his liberal beliefs, stepped up as Foreign Secretary. The Government seemed to re-invent itself – moving from a tendency to be reactionary to a more liberal approach, but no single new appointment brought a break with earlier policies. It may have followed a different direction in economic policy and in its approach to social problems, but for example when Peel became Home Secretary, 'the pattern of reform in criminal law' was 'already set' (Briggs) and when Robinson became Chancellor the Government was already moving to a change in fiscal policy and a reduction in taxes on consumption. There has been much debate among historians about the nature of the Government after this 'reshuffle' and its cause. W. R. Brock, writing in the 1940s, was the great exponent of the doctrine of Liberal Toryism and the idea of a dramatic 'sea-change'. More recently, historian Boyd Hilton gives a new twist to the now more generally accepted idea of continuity in Liverpool's government, by suggesting that continuity does not exclude any 'ideological division between the ministers'.

Lord Liverpool's tenure of office ended in 1827 when he suffered a paralysing stroke, and he died the following year.

SECTION 2 | Government and a changing society 1812–1832

KEY TERM

corn: in this context, a generic word for the wheat, barley, oats, rye and bean crops; wheat and barley were used in nineteenth-century Britain principally for two main household commodities: bread and beer; the term 'grain' is sometimes used to describe wheat, barley, oats and rye

CROSS-REFERENCE

Details of the post-war economic slump and the deep social unrest can be found in Chapter 6, pages 58–9.

ACTIVITY

Evaluating historical extracts

Note down the main arguments mentioned in Extract 3 in favour of Parliament passing the Corn Law in 1815.

The Corn Laws and other legislation

The Corn Law of 1815

> **EXTRACT 3**
>
> Although the 1815 **Corn** Law had its origins in pressure from landed interest, it was taken over by ministers as official policy and reflected their concerns about subsistence. Defying widespread popular protests, Parliament enacted that no foreign corn could be imported until the home price of wheat had reached an average of 80 shillings a quarter. Opponents objected that wheat would never fall below 80 shillings again, but on closer inspection the Law was much less of a capitulation to the landed interest than it appears at first sight. Wheat from British overseas territory was to be admissible at 67 shillings, a form of colonial preference. The cut-off point for chosen foreign wheat (80 shillings), was much below the price of the previous five years (107 shillings in 1808–13) and very much less than the agriculturists were demanding. It is clear that the Government was anxious, not to maintain the price permanently, but merely to avoid such a sudden fall from bloated wartime levels as would lead to capital being withdrawn from agriculture.
>
> Adapted from Boyd Hilton, *A Mad, Bad, and Dangerous People? England 1783–1846*, 2006

In 1815, Parliament passed a Corn Law that stipulated no foreign corn could be imported until the home price reached 80 shillings a quarter. The landowning classes dominated both Houses of Parliament and land was their main source of income. Therefore, the passing of the Corn Law has generally

Fig. 3 *A cartoon commenting on the Corn Law; four landlords stand on the shore, sternly dismissing French sailors in a small vessel filled with sacks of corn. A man in the boat holds open a sack, inscribed 50 s [50 shillings], displaying a bunch of wheat-ears, saying, 'here is de best for 50 s.' One landlord replies, 'We won't have it at any price. We are determined to keep up our own to 80 s. and if the poor can't buy at that price, why they must starve, we love money too well to lower our rents again, tho the Income Tax is taken off.'*

ACTIVITY

Pair discussion

The cartoon in Fig. 3 appeared in the press at the time the Corn Law was being debated in Parliament. Which side of the argument does the cartoonist support? Explain your answer.

been regarded as the dominant landed interest in Parliament protecting themselves. Landowners and farmers had done well during the war as demand was high, but suffered from the result of a bumper harvest in 1813, which caused a dramatic fall in prices and, in the following year, from a poor harvest, which led to the import of foreign corn to make up the shortfall. The problem was that foreign corn was cheap and undercut the price sought by the English farmers. After the trading blockade was lifted at the end of the French wars, foreign corn flooded the market. The landed interest wanted protection from foreign competition, so that they could rely on demand for their grain, whatever the price. Boyd Hilton acknowledges the pressure from the landed interest, but suggests that the Corn Law was 'taken over by ministers as official policy'. He suggests that ministers were concerned to ensure sufficient food supply for a rapidly growing population and wanted to allay their 'concerns about subsistence'. He supports his theory by presenting evidence that the Government was not, in fact, acting solely in the interests of the landowners and farmers. He also suggests the Corn Law of 1815 was never intended to be a permanent solution, but was introduced to avoid the worst effects of a post-war slump in prices. The Government appears to have been able to ignore the popular protests, believing perhaps that it was acting in the longer term interests of the population.

Consequences of the 1815 Corn Law

The Corn Law pushed up the price of bread, the staple diet of the labouring poor. It seemed the Government ignored the adverse impact of the policy on the majority of the population. There was a huge public outcry against the Corn Law, petitions were presented to Parliament and serious rioting broke out. This contributed to a period of unparalleled **civil unrest** to which the

> **KEY QUESTION**
> - What pressures did governments face and how did they respond to these?
> - How and with what effects did the economy develop?

> **KEY CHRONOLOGY**
> | 1815 | The Corn Law |
> | 1816 | Repeal of Income Tax |
> | 1819 | Truck Act |
> | 1819 | Relief Acts and Toleration Act |
> | 1819 | Factory Act |
> | 1819 | Six Acts |
> | 1819 | Return to Bank of England cash payments |
> | 1824 | Penal code reform |
> | 1824 | Repeal of the Combination Act |
> | 1825 | Amending Act |
> | 1827 | End of Liverpool's tenure of office |

> **CROSS-REFERENCE**
> **Civil unrest** and the government responses to these are covered in Chapter 11, pages 105–5.

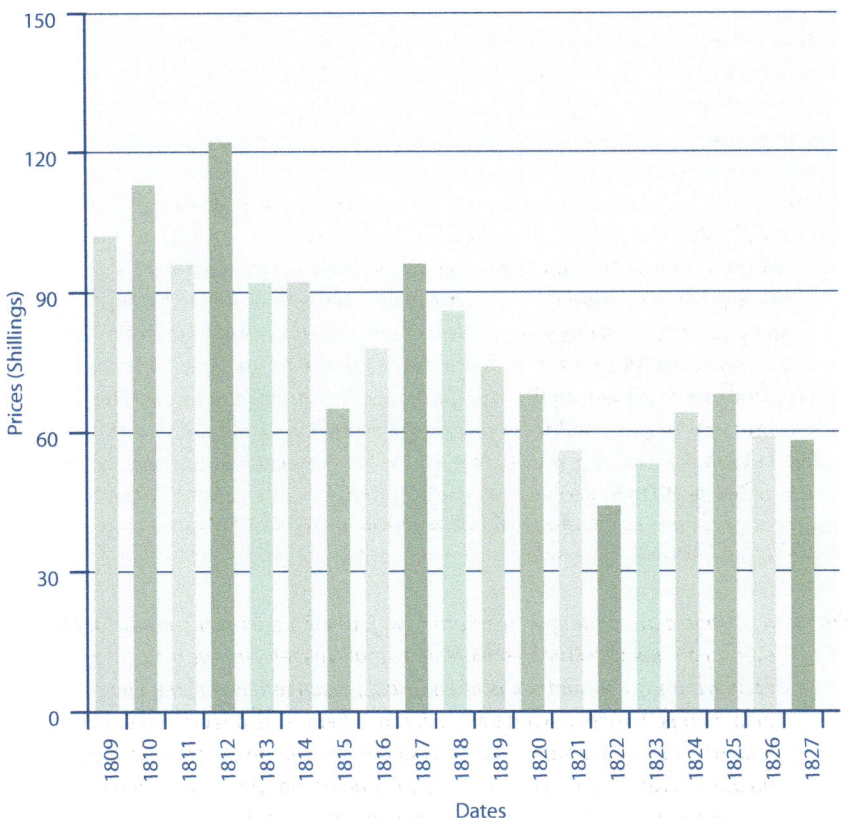

Fig. 4 *The average yearly price of wheat 1809–27*

> **ACTIVITY**
>
> **Group work**
>
> Divide into three groups to consider the impact of the Corn Law on:
> a) landowners and farmers
> b) manufacturers and industrialists
> c) the labouring population and the poor.
>
> Write a petition to Parliament arguing your point of view. As a group decide which argument is the most convincing and why.

Government responded with harsh measures. The fury against the Corn Law extended to powerful commercial and industrial interests, who complained they would have to raise wages and curtail further investment and expansion into new markets.

Landowners claimed to represent all agricultural interests, but with less ground under cultivation, as it was no longer viable, many agricultural labourers were made redundant. In fact, many small farmers struggled in spite of the Corn Law; corn prices stayed high but never reached the prices obtained during the war and poor harvests continued to plague producers and interfere with their profits. The price of wheat fell from 71 shillings 6 pence in March 1815 to 52 shillings 10 pence in January 1816.

Other legislation

A wide range of legislation was introduced across the period of the Liverpool government. It has been traditionally categorised by historians as repressive until the reshuffle in 1821–23 and then largely reformist. In 1816, income tax was abolished, as a result of pressure from MPs, who argued successfully against the Government that it was a special measure for war and had no place in peacetime. However, this resulted in the Government raising indirect taxes on commodities, such as candles, beer, sugar and salt, which adversely affected the 'lower orders'. The poor were reduced to supplementing their diet by poaching, but in 1816, the Government tightened up the already severe penalties for breaking the Game Laws. In 1817, the habeas corpus was suspended after a worrying attack by the mob on the Prince Regent's coach. In 1819, a series of tough repressive measures, collectively known as the Six Acts, was passed to deal with the exceptionally high level of unrest, which led to demonstrations such as at **St Peter's Fields** in Manchester. These outlawed unofficial military training, seditious meetings, seditious libel; introduced stamp duties on newspapers to put them out of the reach of most working men; gave magistrates special powers to search homes for weapons; and sped up the judicial process in the law courts. The authorities aimed to silence public opinion and the Six Acts were introduced to safeguard the position and authority of the ruling classes.

> **CROSS-REFERENCE**
>
> The so-called 'Peterloo Massacre' occurred at **St Peter's Fields**, Manchester, when a mass meeting for reform got out of hand and 11 civilians were killed. There is a more detailed analysis in Chapter 11, pages 104–5.

However, there were other measures in the early years of Liverpool's government that sent out a different message. There were Relief Acts for Dissenters and a Toleration Act for Unitarians that permitted greater religious freedoms; the Poor Employment Act made money available for local corporations to develop public works; a Truck Act attempted to curtail the underhand practice of employers paying wages in kind to factory workers; and in 1819, a Factory Act was introduced which intervened in conditions of employment. It legislated against the employment of children under nine in cotton factories and restricted working hours to 12 hours a day for young people. It was an important early step in state intervention and caused resentment among factory owners.

Repeal of the Combination Acts

> **KEY PROFILE**
>
> **Francis Place (1771–1854)** set up a library at the back of his tailor's shop in London, with free access to books and pamphlets. He worked closely with Radicals such as Francis Burdett, Robert Owen, Jeremy Bentham and Joseph Hume. After the repeal of the Combination Acts he turned his attention towards parliamentary reform, believing it essential working men had the vote.

After 1822, there were a number of important pieces of legislation. In 1824, the Combination Acts were repealed after pressure from the skilled artisan class led by **Francis Place**, a leading Radical journeyman. Trade was expanding and unemployment had fallen and Place's argument to the government commission was that by allowing trade unions to have legal status, members would reject violence and work towards greater productivity and thereby their own prosperity. Ironically, the short trade boom between 1822 and 1824 led to a rise in living costs, followed by recession, creating hardship again. There was a subsequent burst of strike action and the Government pulled back on their reforming position and passed an Amending Act in 1825, which put obstacles in the way of further strikes by making it illegal to 'molest' or 'obstruct' other workers.

As Home Secretary from 1822, Robert Peel re-codified the English criminal law with the aim to simplify and consolidate the existing system. This included the removal from the statute book of many relatively minor offences which carried the death penalty, such as pick-pocketing. Gaol Acts attempted to regularise and standardise the provision of gaols across the country. There were some important advances in the treatment of convicted women. A classification and separation of prisoners was introduced and female prisoners were to be looked after by female wardens. The reforms introduced a degree of humanity, but also a greater degree of efficiency. Juries had become reluctant to return a guilty verdict for a crime where they knew the penalty was death. The result of Peel's reform was to secure more convictions for lesser crimes.

Attitudes to repression and reform

Part of the Liverpool government's reputation rested on the repressive legislation that it adopted early on in the ministry, in response to the unprecedented social unrest that erupted in the wake of the **Napoleonic Wars**. It could be argued that they were responding to the long legacy of fear of the French Revolution and the multiplicity of post-war problems that they faced. The passing of the Corn Law in 1815 brought further economic hardship for the majority of the population, but the Government's economic policy appeared to be organised to suit the interests of the landowning political class, rather than the ordinary people. If the mob was restive because they had no work or their wage was too low to feed their family, it seemed sufficient justification for the ruling elite to pursue a policy of repression, rather than deal with the primary causes. Disorderly or criminal conduct could be swiftly dealt with through application of a brutal penal code that too often **transported minor offenders** to the other side of the world for life.

In a letter Peel wrote in March 1820 to a political friend, he asked the question: 'Do you not think that there is a feeling in favour of some undefined change in the mode of governing the country?' This could be interpreted as a reference to the attitude developing in the nineteenth century that it was the duty of Parliament to pass reforms to improve the lives of the less fortunate in society. Radicals and reformers both inside and outside Parliament became involved in leading campaigns to press for some measures of social and political reform.

A CLOSER LOOK

Changing attitudes to Catholic Emancipation

By 1821, Liverpool could sense a change in attitude towards Catholic Emancipation and informed George IV that 'there is an increasing spirit in favour of Roman Catholics'. The modern historian Asa Briggs explains that Liverpool believed the 'Catholic question was correlated with general interest in improvement and reform'. In spite of Liverpool's apparent insight, an Emancipation Bill was defeated by the Lords in 1825, as Liverpool failed to get consensus from his party, though his cabinet supported it.

ACTIVITY

a) In pairs, list and date reactionary government measures and reforming government measures.

b) From your lists, can you make a judgement as to whether or not there was any continuity in policy direction across the Government's legislative programme?

c) When you have worked through the rest of the chapter, re-visit your judgement and decide whether or not it still stands.

KEY QUESTION

What pressures did governments face and how did they respond to these?

CROSS-REFERENCE

Details of the unrest that happened after the **Napoleonic Wars** appear in Chapter 10, pages 97 and 98, and also in Chapter 11.

Fig. 5 *A nineteenth-century engraving of Newgate prison*

Liverpool's government, however, is not generally characterised as a reforming government. It did not address the two main issues on the minds of most reformers, Parliamentary Reform and **Catholic Emancipation**, although there was a little headway on both. In 1819, the worst of the rotten boroughs, Grampound, lost both its seats; these were reassigned to the county of Yorkshire, which had a population of 20,000, but not to an unrepresented industrial city like Manchester. This was hardly a precursor to reform.

Peel took up a reforming mantle as Home Secretary, with his overhaul of the penal code in 1824, making it in the first instance more efficient, but also more humane. This was motivated more by a sense of responsibility and fair-mindedness than an enthusiasm for social reform, an attitude typical of the Liverpool government. This **pragmatism** was also present in the repeal of the Combination Acts, which had the support of Huskisson – the new President of the Board of Trade – and was an indication of a willingness to put faith in the skilled artisan class, who contributed to the country's industrial prosperity. Overall, Liverpool's administration was conservative in any approach to reform.

> **KEY TERM**
>
> **pragmatism:** taking a practical approach rather than a theoretical one

> **KEY QUESTION**
>
> How and with what effects did the economy develop?

> **CROSS-REFERENCE**
>
> The economy during this period is discussed in more detail in Chapter 9.

The economy

After a brief post-war boom in 1815, in which there was a high demand for goods not available during the war, a deep post-war depression set in. The sharp fall in prices was particularly damaging to Britain's industry and for a time slowed down the rate of expansion and caused a reduction in wages, but not across the board.

The slow improvement in Britain's economy after 1819 appeared to coincide with the 'general interest in reform'. The Government made a crucial decision, with the approval of Parliament, in favour of the Bank of England resuming cash payments – the value of British currency rose and the amount of gold reserves increased. The depression began to lift with an increase in export trade, a run of good harvests, a stabilising in the price of wheat, reduction in the price of bread and an increase in demand for other commodities.

Summary

Lord Liverpool's Tory government was often regarded as mediocre, but Liverpool – patient, pragmatic and fair-minded – exercised firm control over major decisions. He brought together the strongly differing views (there were deep divisions in the Tory party over the issue of Catholic Emancipation) and personalities among his ministers without patronage or party machinery in place.

In 1815, Parliament passed a Corn Law stipulating that no foreign corn could be imported till the home price reached eighty shillings a quarter. The Corn Law pushed up the price of bread, the staple diet of the labouring poor, and there was a huge public outcry that led to unparalleled civil unrest. The Government responded with harsh measures. The passing of the Corn Law has generally been regarded as the dominant landed interest in Parliament protecting themselves.

A wide range of legislation was introduced by Liverpool's government, in response to post war unrest, some of which was repressive. Further legislation was introduced after a major Cabinet 'reshuffle' in 1821–23. Modern historical consensus is that there was continuity rather than a break with earlier policies. Overall, Liverpool's administration was conservative in its approach to reform. However, the Government's resumption of cash payments was a decisive move in outlining the nature of its economic policy, pursuing commercial and manufacturing support, and the later budgets were important in establishing the principles of Free Trade.

A CLOSER LOOK

Resumption of cash payments

In 1797, the Bank of England suspended cash payments (in gold coins) because of heavy borrowing by the Government and cash withdrawals by private investors, who felt nervous about their money. The policy resulted in an increase in the amount of paper money in circulation and this led to inflation. After the war, there were mixed feelings about a return to gold but the support of respected economists like David Ricardo satisfied many of the doubters.

ACTIVITY

Evaluating historical extracts

With reference to Extracts 1 and 2 and using the information provided in this chapter, which of these two extracts provides the more convincing interpretation of Liverpool's administration? Explain your answer.

 PRACTICE QUESTION

Evaluating historical extracts

With reference to Extracts 1 and 2 and your understanding of the historical context, which of these two extracts provides the more convincing interpretation of Lord Liverpool's government?

STUDY TIP

First, you should identify the interpretation put forward in each extract, then decide which interpretation you find most convincing and write a well-argued response.

 PRACTICE QUESTION

'The years 1812 to 1827 were a time of reform.'
Explain why you agree or disagree with this view.

STUDY TIP

You need to balance evidence which supports the idea of reform against that which suggests otherwise. Don't forget to offer a well-supported personal judgement giving your own view.

8 Government: Canning, Goderich and Wellington as Prime Ministers

EXTRACT 1

All those who refused to serve under Canning, except Peel, opposed **Liberal Toryism**. Peel was in a difficult position. On the Catholic question his position was ambiguous, since two years earlier (in 1825) he had offered to resign to permit emancipation. In stepping down in 1827 Peel almost certainly hoped, not that Canning would *fail* to carry a Catholic Relief Bill (as everyone supposed), but that he would carry it swiftly and decisively, while Peel enjoyed being hidden on the back benches. If this was Peel's calculation, Canning's death on 8 August 1827 must have been a severe blow. If Peel had stayed in office he would have been in line for the succession. Moreover, when the time came to concede the Catholic claims, he might have been able to persuade his followers he was acting in considerably good faith. What was to weigh against him so strongly, when he finally proposed emancipation in 1829, was that only two years earlier he had helped to split the party in order (apparently) to prevent the policy.

Adapted from Boyd Hilton, *A Mad, Bad, and Dangerous People? England 1783–1846*, 2008

KEY CHRONOLOGY

1827 April	Canning becomes Prime Minister
1827 August	Death of Canning; Goderich becomes Prime Minister
1828 January	Wellington becomes Prime Minister
1828	Repeal of the Test and Corporation Acts
1828	Sliding scale of duties for Corn Law
1829	Metropolitan Police Improvement Act
1829	Catholic Emancipation Act
1830 July	Death of George IV, accession of William IV
1830 September	Death of Huskisson
1830 October	Fall of Wellington's government

LEARNING OBJECTIVES

In this chapter you will learn about:

- the ministries of Canning, Goderich and Wellington
- legislation passed, including the repeal of the Test and Corporation Acts
- the creation of the Metropolitan Police Force
- O'Connell and Catholic Emancipation.

ACTIVITY

Evaluating historical extracts

How revealing of Peel's character is Extract 1?

CROSS-REFERENCE

Look back to Chapter 7 for an explanation of **Liberal Toryism**.

ACTIVITY

Robert Peel was one of the nineteenth century's outstanding political (Tory) leaders, yet he was accused by some of being a traitor to his own party and he was blamed for ultimately causing its break-up. As you work through this chapter, make notes on Peel's contribution to the Tory Party (both positive and negative).

KEY QUESTION

How was Britain governed and how did democracy and political organisations change and develop?

CROSS-REFERENCE

See Chapter 7 page 61 for **Canning**'s Key Profile.

Canning, Goderich and Wellington

Canning as Prime Minister

George Canning became Prime Minister on Liverpool's resignation in April 1827. The politician and essayist John Wilson Croker remarked on Canning at the time, 'his genius is a bright flame'. He had been a great political favourite of Liverpool, although he was in and out of office on so many occasions, his long-term influence is hard to pinpoint. He was able and experienced but for many Tories he was too advanced in his ideas, too flamboyant in his manner and some doubted whether he could be trusted. The result was that half the Cabinet, including Wellington, who detested him, and Peel, refused to serve under him. They declared that the issue was Canning's support of Catholic Emancipation. They were also critical of his liberal, populist conduct of foreign policy during the Liverpool years and aristocrats in both main parties looked down on his humble origins – his mother was an impoverished actress. Undeterred by the significant number of ministers and junior ministers who refused a government position, Canning invited four Whigs into his Cabinet. The Whigs saw him as a

KEY PROFILE

Fig. 1　Frederick Robinson, 1st Viscount Goderich

Lord Goderich (1782–1859)
Goderich's entry into politics was secured by a relation, who found him a seat in Parliament in 1806. His political career advanced with the encouragement of Lord Castereagh, and he became Vice President of the Board of Trade in Liverpool's government. His affable nature and moderate views made him seem a safe compromise as Prime Minister in 1827. Goderich's lack of control over the different political factions and difficulties with the King quickly forced him out of office.

CROSS-REFERENCE

The **County Clare** by-election is explained in detail on pages 77–8, later in this chapter.

A CLOSER LOOK

The **Ultra Tories** (the 'Ultras') believed it was their duty to preserve the status quo, the 'Protestant Constitution', in Church and state. Their agricultural interests made them concerned to retain the Corn Laws (explained in Chapter 7, page 64) and uneasy about the concept of Free Trade. They were suspicious of Canning's liberal views.

'natural ally', liberal-minded and flexible, and the majority gave him their support in the Commons, in a coalition with the majority moderate Tories, including Huskisson. George IV accepted Canning as he could command the Commons and was popular in the country. There was little achieved: George IV insisted Catholic Emancipation remained an 'open' question and, in the Lords, Wellington annihilated Canning's attempt to reform the Corn Laws, by introducing a sliding scale of duties. Canning died in August 1827, after a short spell of illness, and was replaced by the former Chancellor Robinson, now Viscount Goderich.

Goderich as Prime Minister

Lord Goderich had had a successful political career as Chancellor of the Exchequer in Liverpool's government. When Canning became Prime Minister in 1827 he appointed Viscount Goderich as Leader of the House of Lords. It was a thankless task as most of the Lords were Tories and refused to cooperate with anything Canning attempted to do, and the Whigs led by Earl Grey wished to replace Canning's administration with a purely Whig Cabinet. Lord Goderich was impotent in his role and showed few qualities of leadership. He accepted the position of Prime Minister conferred upon him on Canning's death by a reluctant monarch George IV. He was miserable in a role for which he was clearly unsuited and resigned four months later before ever meeting Parliament.

Wellington as Prime Minister

A new Tory government in 1828 had the **Duke of Wellington** at its head. With his authoritarian manner, Wellington was not as adept at holding together his cabinet as Liverpool had been. Peel was appointed Home Secretary and agreed to lead the Commons as long as the Canningites (also supporters of Huskisson) were included, because their liberal ideas were popular with the people. Wellington excluded Lord Eldon, the previous Lord Chancellor, and therefore fell foul of the **Ultra Tories**. He appeared to lack resolution over the Government's legislative programme, giving way when he felt threatened by the opposition and at other times digging in his heels and often showing a lack of judgement in his decisions. For example, he accepted the resignation of Huskisson, one of his strongest ministers, over the proposed disfranchisement of two corrupt boroughs, causing further resignations. As a result of his clumsy leadership, he lost the confidence of several groups in Parliament and had no steady majority in the Commons. His cabinet reshuffle in 1828 brought the question of Catholic Emancipation to a head. Wellington had offered a Cabinet position to an Irish Protestant landowner, Vesey Fitzgerald, member for **County Clare**. It was customary for new Cabinet members to stand again for Parliament, necessitating a by-election. The result was almost always a foregone conclusion. On this occasion it was not. The by-election was won by an Irish Catholic lawyer, Daniel O'Connell. The repercussions of the result altered the political landscape forever.

KEY PROFILE

The Duke of Wellington

Arthur Wellesley (1769–1852) was renowned as a great military leader. He led a successful campaign against the French in the Peninsular War and defeated Napoleon at Waterloo. He took up politics, joining Liverpool's Cabinet in 1822, and became Prime Minister in 1828. He fought hard against parliamentary reform, but introduced Catholic Emancipation in the face of possible civil war in Ireland. He was later respected as an elder statesman and war hero.

Fig. 2　The Duke of Wellington (1769–1852)

Tory divisions

The withdrawal from political life of Lord Liverpool in 1827 created unfamiliar anxieties for the Tory party. He had been Prime Minister, without a break, for almost fifteen years. Liverpool may have been criticised for his dullness and lack of charisma, but his expertise in holding together his precocious Cabinet, full of diverse and strong personalities, was very soon missed. Without Liverpool's skilful leadership, divisions appeared among the Tory hierarchy and the party began to disintegrate.

Canning's brief time as Prime Minister highlighted one of the major difficulties within the party, successfully smoothed over by Liverpool: the existence of a number of contending factions.

- There was a pro-Corn Law faction – the agriculturalists who were concerned Huskisson's proposal of a sliding scale would not offer them the protection for their home-grown produce that they demanded as their right.
- There were a group of Tories, Huskisson among them, who recognised the importance of industrial growth and the need to encourage its expansion through free trade measures.
- There were traditional Tories, who would consider economic and administrative reform, but not anything that disturbed the integrity of the constitution or the preservation of Church and state, such as Catholic Emancipation and parliamentary reform.
- The Ultra Tories were an extreme version of the former, intolerant of any measure that would disturb their **patrimony,** and were prepared to vote themselves out of office to uphold their rigid anti-reform principles.

Some of the Ultras had attempted tactical voting over the repeal of the Test and Corporation Acts in 1828 (see below) as they realised they were swimming against the tide, but they hung onto the belief that once repealed, the Protestant Dissenters would turn against the Catholics in sufficient numbers and dissuade the Government from pursuing emancipation. However, by this stage emancipation was unstoppable.

EXTRACT 2

> The revolt against Canning in 1827 was not only an expression of dislike for an individual but also the result of fears among sections of the Tory party. Canning believed in the desirability of Catholic Emancipation, the need to restructure the Corn Laws and the enhancement of Britain's global trading position. Each of these positions exposed fundamental divisions between the Tories. Through the 1820s Tory Protestants and agriculturalists had been unable to persuade the Commons to boost the economy, draw back from Free Trade or reinforce agricultural protection. The success of the O'Connell Catholic Association in Ireland meant the Catholic question could no longer be avoided. The most common reason given by those who resigned was that Canning was a supporter of Catholic Emancipation, but this ignores the fact that he had no intention of promoting it as a government measure. Catholic Emancipation remained an 'open' question in his cabinet.

Adapted from Richard Brown, *Church and State in Modern Britain 1700–1850,* 1991

The passing of the Catholic Emancipation Act in 1829 divided the Tory party further. It also led to the final break-up of Pitt's coalition, which had governed Britain, first under Pitt during the French wars, then through the post-war years under Liverpool, until it disintegrated under Wellington. The accession of William IV after George IV's death in June 1830 prompted a general election, the results of which favoured the Whigs and the Canningite Tories, but left Wellington in office. Wellington had few options

KEY QUESTION

How important was the role of individuals and groups and how were they affected by developments?

A CLOSER LOOK

Huskisson's resignation

There was no dispute over the corruption during elections in Penryn (Cornwall) and East Retford (Norfolk). The issue for Huskisson was that the seats should be transferred to Leeds and Manchester, two unrepresented and expanding towns. It was an indication to Huskisson that Wellington remained opposed to any notion of parliamentary reform.

KEY TERM

patrimony: one's inheritance from a father or ancestors; in this context it means political inheritance – an elite and privileged position

ACTIVITY

Evaluating historical extracts

Read Extract 2 and then answer the following questions:
1. What does Richard Brown suggest were the fundamental divisions between the Tories?
2. What do you understand by the phrase 'Catholic Emancipation remained an 'open' question'?
3. Why do you think Canning 'had no intention of promoting Emancipation as a government measure'?

open to him. He had already cut adrift Huskisson and the liberal-minded Tories with his refusal to contemplate parliamentary reform in 1828, but there are suggestions that he was about to invite Huskisson back into the Cabinet. These are difficult to verify as Huskisson was accidently killed by a locomotive as he was climbing into Wellington's railway carriage, possibly to exchange pleasantries with him, in September 1830 at the opening of the Liverpool to Manchester railway line. Huskisson's death robbed the Tories of a prodigiously talented politician.

Fig. 3 *A twentieth-century portrayal of Huskisson's fatal accident*

Wellington's government was looking weak and indecisive as outbreaks of violence spread across England in response to a bleak harvest and an economic recession. There was a renewed interest in parliamentary reform, supported by the Whigs, who sensed deepening unrest if the question was ignored. Wellington's blunder of a major reactionary speech against reform, in November 1830, in which he praised the existing system as near-perfect, upset all sides and hastened the end of his term of office. His supporters believed he should have produced a moderate reform, instead of playing into the hands of the opposition, whose chance of introducing a more radical parliamentary reform had been enhanced. Wellington resigned over a defeat on a minor issue, with apparent relief. Ironically, his government had introduced several important, long-lasting reforms. The Whigs returned to power, for the first time in 50 years, under Lord Grey.

ACTIVITY

Group work

Working in small groups, identify the causes of the divisions within the Tory party. What do you think was the main cause, or were there several equally important causes? Present an argument to the group to justify your view. Once you have listened to everyone's point of view, try to reach a consensus.

Legislation

The repeal of the Test and Corporation Acts

Pressure from Protestant Dissenters mounted on the Government to remove the **disabilities** of the Test and Corporation Acts, which were seen to be outdated. Furthermore, some Dissenting groups believed that toleration should extend to Catholics, but others remained strongly anti-Catholic. The pro-repeal group was led by a young rising Whig, Lord John Russell, who put forward a motion for repeal in the Commons, with little warning. Peel was caught off-guard and tried to play for time when the 'motion was carried', but apart from a small concession on the final wording, the will of the Commons remained firm. The repeal of the Test and Corporation Acts in 1828 finally lifted the legal restrictions on Nonconformists holding public office.

> **KEY QUESTION**
>
> What pressures did governments face and how did they respond to these?

> **CROSS-REFERENCE**
>
> For an explanation of the **disabilities**, see the Closer Look for Catholic Emancipation in Chapter 5, page 46.

> **A CLOSER LOOK**
>
> **The Test and Corporation Acts**
>
> The Corporation Act was passed in 1661 to ensure that anyone who held a position in a municipal office, e.g. the mayor, had to be confirmed into the Anglican Church and take Holy Communion. The Test Act of 1673 was the equivalent Act for anyone who held a civil or military office under the Crown. The Acts were designed primarily to exclude Roman Catholics and to a lesser extent Nonconformists. They were passed after the restoration of Charles II to secure the monarchy and the established church.

SOURCE 1

Lord John Russell was jubilant, as illustrated by his own correspondence, first published in 1913, which suggests he was confident the repeal would have the desired impact on the 'Catholic question':

It is really a gratifying thing to force the enemy to give up his first line that none but Churchmen are worthy to serve the state, and I think we shall soon make him give up the second, that none but Protestants are. Peel is a very pretty hand at hauling down his colours.

> **KEY TERM**
>
> **Oath of Supremacy:** swearing allegiance to the monarch as Supreme Governor of the Church of England; Catholics' allegiance was to the Pope and so their religious beliefs would preclude them from taking the oath

ACTIVITY

Evaluating primary sources

What did Russell mean by his comments in Source 1? What appears to be his view of Peel's position regarding his willingness to accept the repeal? Does this tie in with any conclusions you may have drawn about Peel from Extract 1?

EXTRACT 3

The debates on the Test and Corporation Acts were important, not so much in their own right but because they impacted on the Catholic question. Supporters of repeal argued that the latter issue would be unaffected, since the **Oath of Supremacy** would remain in place, but few were deceived. Many who voted for Test and Corporation Act repeal explicitly did so because it would prise open the door for Catholics. Others opposed it for the same reason. But some (including Huskisson) voted against a measure they approved in principle because it might make emancipation *more* difficult to achieve, their fear being if Protestant Dissenters were relieved first, many of them would then turn against their Catholic 'allies'. Finally there were 20 to 30 Ultra Tory MPs who disliked Dissenters but disliked Papists even more, and who voted to repeal the Test and Corporation Acts in the hope it would actually stymie Catholic Emancipation. The result of these conflicting prejudices was that Russell's repeal motion was carried by 45 votes.

Adapted from Boyd Hilton, *A Mad, Bad, and Dangerous People? England 1783–1846*, 2008

> **ACTIVITY**
>
> **Evaluating historical extracts**
>
> In what ways does Boyd Hilton in Extract 3 suggest the repeal of the Test and Corporation Acts affected 'the Catholic question'? What do you understand by 'conflicting prejudices'? Can you explain how all the differing views/prejudices led to the repeal of the Test and Corporation Acts?

STUDY TIP

Begin your answer with a paragraph outlining the divisions in the Tory party in the late 1820s and explain how they had arisen.

PRACTICE QUESTION

Evaluating historical extracts

Using your understanding of the historical context, assess how convincing the arguments in Extracts 1, 2 and 3 are in relation to the divisions in the Tory party in the 1820s.

Corn Law sliding scale

In 1828 William Huskisson revisited the idea of substituting the fixed rate of duty for a sliding scale to address the problems caused when, for example, there was a poor harvest and corn prices rose. It would allow the tax on imported corn to be cut gradually according to the price of home corn, so as the price of home corn rose the duty on foreign corn fell. To Huskisson it seemed a solution to maintain a steady market and income for the farmers and also achieve a lowering of bread prices to satisfy the working man. Huskisson quarrelled with Wellington over his stubborn resistance to parliamentary reform and resigned before he could introduce the amendment. It was brought in later in the year by Peel.

KEY QUESTION

How and with what results did society and social policy develop?

CROSS-REFERENCE

The so-called '**Peterloo Massacre**' occurred at St Peter's Fields, Manchester. As a result riots happened and eleven civilians were killed. A more detailed analysis can be found in Chapter 11, pages 104–5.

The St Peter's Fields riots are mentioned in the context of government repression in Chapter 7, page 66.

Peel's Metropolitan Police Force

Peel founded the Metropolitan Police Force, the first regular service of its kind, in 1829 in his Metropolitan Police Act. It was a preventative measure, an attempt to reverse the upward trend of crime rates, particularly in London. It was also the corresponding measure to his earlier Penal Code reform; the removal of so many capital offences had increased the crime rate, noticeably in London. His theory was that a fully supported police force would act as a major crime deterrent. It was not an immediate success and was perceived by some as the tool of the Tory government. However, it improved on the existing inadequate system, which relied on parish constables and watchmen, and was often corrupt and had no cohesive, centralised maintenance of law and order. Peel introduced the police force idea gradually in London, with a Police Commissioner at Scotland Yard Head Quarters reporting to the Home Office, and later extended it to the provinces. It offered a better method of maintaining public order. It took years to establish an efficient, effective nationwide police force, but Peel's model formed the basis of our modern policing system.

A CLOSER LOOK

Peel's police force

Members of the Metropolitan Police Force were armed with a truncheon and issued with a uniform – a top hat and blue frock-coat – so that they were easily recognised on the street. The uniform also gave them a sense of identity, confidence and purpose. They were nick-named 'Bobbies' or 'Peelers' after their founder.

Fig. 4 *Sir Robert Peel arriving at the House of Commons, saluted by a Peeler*

ACTIVITY

Pair discussion

Can you suggest why several important pieces of legislation were passed through Parliament at a time of such weak government? Think about the individual politicians who pushed through the reforms – their character and political interests – to help you with your answer.

O'Connell and Catholic Emancipation

The movement for Catholic Emancipation had festered since the refusal of George III to contemplate its introduction as part of Pitt's deal with leading Catholics to agree to the Act of Union in 1800. In 1823 a charismatic Irish Catholic barrister **Daniel O'Connell** founded the Catholic Association in Ireland and took up the emancipation cause. The Association had a further aim – to repeal the Act of Union. Its small membership was mainly frustrated middle-class professionals, but under O'Connell's astute management membership was extended to all who paid a small levy – the 'Catholic rent' – of a penny a month. This was collected by the local priest and this opened membership up to the Irish peasantry. The Association quickly became an effective pressure group. Due to its alarmingly rapid success it was equally speedily made illegal. O'Connell by-passed the law and set up a new association named the Order of Liberation. By his actions, O'Connell had succeeded in uniting the Catholic Church, the middle class and the Irish peasants to press for emancipation. In the 1826 General Election, Irish Catholic voters were persuaded or coerced into voting for liberal, pro-emancipation candidates, albeit Protestant ones, in order to give the emancipation debate prominence.

KEY QUESTION

- What pressures did governments face and how did they respond to these?
- How important was the role of individuals and groups and how were they affected by developments?

Fig. 5 *In this cartoon the Irish political leader Daniel O'Connell, who championed the cause of Irish Catholics in parliament, is depicted celebrating Catholic Ascendency*

SECTION 2 | Government and a changing society 1812–1832

> **ACTIVITY**
>
> **Evaluating historical extracts**
>
> In pairs discuss what you think Paul Bew suggests are the implications of the 'collapse of proprietorial control over Catholic voters' in Extract 4.

The County Clare election

> **EXTRACT 4**
>
> The priests played a highly visible role in mobilising – some said coercing – support amongst the peasantry for O'Connell. Sir Edward O'Brien, an Irish Protestant Tory landlord, assembled his tenants in a body to march to the hustings and vote for Fitzgerald. Father Murphy of Corofin, the local parish priest, dramatically called upon the tenants 'to vote O'Connell in the name of their country and their religion'. O'Connell's overwhelming victory over Vesey Fitzgerald in the County Clare by-election on 5 July 1828 confirmed the collapse of proprietorial control over Catholic voters; both Wellington and Peel, now in power, were convinced that emancipation had to be conceded.
>
> Adapted from Paul Bew, *Ireland: The Politics of Enmity, 1789–2006*, 2009

In 1828, a by-election in County Clare was called to enable Irish Protestant landlord Vesey Fitzgerald to take up a position in Wellington's cabinet. With the resources and support of the Catholic Association, O'Connell stood for Parliament. Small farmers with land worth 40 shillings had the right to vote and O'Connell won the election by a ratio of two votes to one. The result threw Wellington's government into a quandary. It was entirely possible at the next general election that Catholics would stand for every Irish seat and be elected. The situation was tense and there was a real fear of civil unrest in Ireland. It would be difficult to refuse O'Connell his seat in Parliament without a violent reaction. Wellington and Peel acted in the only way left open to them to preserve law and order in Ireland and avoid the possible scenario of a break-up of the Union – in February 1829, they capitulated and agreed to introduce a Catholic Emancipation Bill. It was a bitter moment for Wellington, but he stood by his word, persuaded a loudly protesting George IV that it was in the country's interest and bullied the Lords into fearful submission. The Act was passed with the support of the Whigs but 142 Tories voted against it.

The Catholic Emancipation Act made Roman Catholics eligible for all offices of state bar Regent, Lord Chancellor and Lord Lieutenant General. No oath of supremacy was required to take a seat in either the Lords or the Commons. As a response to O'Connell and his campaign, the Catholic Association was banned and the 40 shilling franchise in the Irish counties was raised to £10, taking away the right to vote from the Catholic smallholders who had handed victory to O'Connell. Wellington's final needling action was to insist that O'Connell stood again for election, as the previous election was illegal as it took place before the Act was passed. This tit-for-tat soured Irish opinion for the future.

> **ACTIVITY**
>
> **Thinking point**
>
> What factors finally convinced both Wellington and Peel that 'emancipation had to be conceded'?

The aftermath was disastrous for the Tory party, most of whom felt betrayed by their leader. Wellington was challenged to a duel by one of his most vociferous critics in the Lords, Lord Winchelsea, and Peel resigned from his Oxford seat among taunts of cowardice and betrayal from his party colleagues: 'Oh! Member for Oxford! You shuffle and wheel! You have altered your name from R. Peel to Repeal.'

Summary

- There was no clear Tory successor to Lord Liverpool.
- Canning's appointment as Prime Minister split the Tories, as he was regarded as too liberal.
- Goderich was too weak to form a viable administration.

- Wellington was authoritarian and anti-reform and failed to hold together the differing party factions.
- Peel wanted to include Huskisson and the Canningites, as their liberal ideas were in tune with popular feeling.
- The repeal of the Test and Corporation Acts caused further division among the Tories.
- As Home Secretary, Peel was responsible for the establishment of the Metropolitan Police Force.
- The issue of Catholic Emancipation was extremely contentious.
- Daniel O'Connell and the Catholic Association raised the problems of the Irish Catholics.
- The County Clare election forced the issue of Catholic Emancipation.
- The passing of Catholic Emancipation finally destroyed the Tories.
- There was a renewed interest in the country in parliamentary reform, supported by the Whigs, who sensed deepening unrest if the question was ignored.
- Wellington resigned and the Whigs returned to power under Lord Grey.
- Ironically Wellington's administration had introduced several important, long-lasting reforms.

ACTIVITY

Group debate

The Tory party collapsed in the years after Liverpool's administration, but there were several lasting achievements for which they were not given much credit at the time. Split into two groups. One group should put together a defence of Tory achievements and the other group make an analysis of their failures. Discuss which view makes a stronger case.

PRACTICE QUESTION

'The Tories were divided in the years 1812 to 1830 because of their different attitudes to Catholic Emancipation.'
Explain why you agree or disagree with this view.

STUDY TIP

Try to identify several factors that split the Tory government. Assess the importance of each factor before you begin. In your answer you should balance the importance of Catholic Emancipation against these other factors and show whether you agree or disagree with the quotation, explaining why.

9 Economic developments 1812–1832

EXTRACT 1

Although there was agricultural improvement, the process was patchy in the years 1812 to 1832. The north-east of England provided a celebrated example of improved farming techniques and the success of men like **John Grey of Dilston** earned them national reputations. In 1815, Scotland, Wales and Ireland possessed wide areas that were still little affected by improved farming techniques. Scotland provided an example of both cases — the rapid improvement with agriculture in the lowlands being admired for its efficiency, in sharp contrast to the north and west where many farms provided bare subsistence and only large-scale sheep-farming prospered. Yet enough British landowners and farmers were gripped by enthusiasm for innovation to ensure big increases in the production of food and fodder. This played a crucial role in feeding the growing population and facilitating the expansion of industry and commerce. Most of the food supply of an increased population was provided by home production. Improvement took place, however unevenly, in the quality of cultivated crops, the breeding of cattle, sheep and other livestock and the application of fertilisers and machinery.

Adapted from Norman McCord, *British History 1815–1914*, 2007

Continuing industrialisation

After a sustained period of growth in the late eighteenth century, the British economy continued to flourish in the early years of the nineteenth century, in spite of the long and costly wars with France. Although historians are in broad agreement that economic growth continued between 1780 and 1800, some argue that there was a slow-down in growth, while prices fell. One of the problems is that change occurred slowly in most industries and rapidly in a few. Industrialisation was regional not national and so changes occurred in some places and not in others.

The growth in Britain's economy can be measured to an extent by looking at the production figures for the three main industries: cotton, iron and coal. Coal was the main source of energy for industry, therefore it would seem to follow that if coal production was rising then industry was expanding. Between 1815 and 1830, coal production rose from around 16 million to just under 30 million tons, according to one set of figures. In another, coal production was said to rise to almost 23 million tons by 1830. Whichever set of figures is taken, the overall picture is the same — coal production was rising. About half the coal produced was used in the iron industry. Between 1815 and 1830, most figures suggest the production of pig iron doubled. At the beginning of the century it took 8 tons of coal to produce 1 ton of pig iron; by 1830 this figure was down to 3.5 tons. This would suggest that the methods of production in the iron industry were becoming more efficient.

In spite of figures suggesting a slow-down, there was still remarkable growth in the production of cotton goods between 1815 and 1830, as imports of raw cotton increased two- or threefold and the export of manufactured cotton also increased. According to Williams and Ramsden, by the 1830s, an estimated 30 per cent of the industrial workforce was engaged in the cotton industry; 70 per cent of all British exports were textiles (mostly cotton), and raw cotton accounted for almost one fifth of Britain's imports.

LEARNING OBJECTIVES

In this chapter you will learn about:

- continuing industrialisation and developments in key industries
- agricultural change
- economic policies and Free Trade.

KEY QUESTION

As you read this chapter, consider the following Key Question:
How and with what results did the economy develop and change?

ACTIVITY

Evaluating historical extracts

In what way does Extract 1 suggest that agricultural improvement affected 'the expansion of industry and commerce'? Do you think this is a valid interpretation? Explain your answer.

KEY PROFILE

John Grey of Dilston (1785–1868) was an improving farmer from north Northumberland, an agriculturalist and a political commentator. He made interesting observations on the state of agriculture, providing evidence that there were many regional differences in the rate of progress of agricultural improvements. He defended the integrity of agricultural labourers, urging recognition of their right to be respected as decent human beings.

KEY CHRONOLOGY

1823	Reciprocity Treaty
1824–5	Free trade budgets
1825	Commercial crisis
1826	Bank Act

The growth of the export market was also reflected in the development of the shipbuilding industry. Shipping was still under sail at this point – the first steamship was not launched until 1838. In 1820, the tonnage of ships built and registered in Britain was 66,700 and by 1830 this had increased to 75,500.

The overall increase in production was also due to the continuing development of steam power. More factories were powered by steam rather than the water power of the earlier period and there was an increasing variety of products available for home markets and for export to expanding markets abroad. Pottery and china were in increasing demand in the domestic market, particularly among the new middle classes, who had disposable income and new homes in the outskirts of the towns to furnish and equip. It was the start of the age of **consumerism**. By 1832 there were new fast-growing industries, services and technologies mainly associated with the early development of the railway. There were further developments in steam power and more sophisticated machine tools and other machinery. These innovations meant that industrialisation spread to parts of the country previously untouched by the process, more hand-operated industries became mechanised, and increased productivity occurred in existing industries. However in 1832, these developments had not yet reached their full industrial or economic potential.

> **KEY TERM**
>
> **consumerism**: the trend of wanting to acquire more goods and services

> **CROSS-REFERENCE**
>
> The rapid pre-1793 growth of the **cotton and iron** industries is covered in Chapter 3, pages 23–6.

Table 1 *Production figures of coal in Britain, 1800–1835*

Year	Tons of coal (millions)	% exported
1800	11.0	2.0
1816	15.9	2.5
1820	17.4	1.4
1825	21.9	1.4
1830	22.4	2.2
1835	27.7	2.7

Table 2 *Coal output in Britain*

Year	Coal (tons)
1820	450,000
1832	1,000,000

Table 3 *Import as raw cotton and export as finished cotton goods*

Year	Raw cotton imported (lbs)	Export of cotton goods (yards)
1810–19	96,000,000	227,000,000
1820–29	173,000,000	320,000,000

> **ACTIVITY**
>
> **Group work**
>
> Divide into groups to research the development of the cotton, iron, coal and railway industries to 1832. Each group should create an informative poster and explain their findings to the rest of the class.

Whatever figures are produced to support theories of rate of growth, extent of growth, and areas of growth, the key element remains that industrialisation was a continuing process and continued for the best part of a century from about 1780. But industrialisation went beyond technical innovation and the effects of its output on the economy. It had a direct effect on trading. Putting aside the fluctuations in the market, trade expanded rapidly after the Napoleonic Wars and the lifting of sanctions. During the 1820s, trade received an impetus from Huskisson's free trade measures. Population growth contributed to carrying the industrialising process forward. In 1811 the population of the UK (excluding Ireland) was 12 million. By 1821 it had increased to over 14 million and in 1831 stood at 16.3 million. The rate of growth was higher in industrial areas than in the rural areas. This was the result of migration to the industrial towns for work and the higher incidence of earlier marriages and births in the crowded urban areas.

The industrialisation process after 1815 continued to encourage new thought, it brought new political pressures, it continued to emphasise the distinctions between the emerging industrial workforce and middle classes; it brought continuing working-class discontent and from it emerged new social groupings and a new concept of society. It was difficult to be objective about its effects at the time the changes were occurring, and it continues to invite many interpretations from the generations who have been able to look back and reassess its impact and its extent.

Developments in key industries

The most far-reaching development in the cotton industry was the wider use of the power loom. Cartwright's steam-driven wooden invention of 1789 was clumsy and inefficient, although its importance lay in its potential application for producing large quantities of cloth under one factory roof. Various modifications were applied to Cartwright's original ideas, first by the great Stockport cotton manufacturer, William Horrocks, in 1803 and 1813, and in the 1820s by Richard Roberts, who devised a reliable, cast-iron power loom in 1822. This popular version was extensively used in textile factories across the country and revolutionised cloth production. It was reckoned the number of power looms in operation rose from a modest 2,400 in 1803 to about 100,000 30 years later.

> **KEY QUESTION**
>
> How important were ideas and ideology?

> **CROSS-REFERENCE**
>
> Political and Social developments are the subject of Chapter 10.

Fig. 1 *Power looms being used in textile manufacturing in the nineteenth century*

The most important technical improvement in the iron industry during this period was the introduction of the hot-air blast furnace, developed by **James Beaumont Neilson** by 1828. By heating the blast of air between the steam engine and the furnace to a specific temperature, a better quality of iron could be obtained and raw coal could be used instead of coke, making the process cheaper and more efficient. It was hailed at the time as 'as great an advantage in the iron trade as Arkwright's machinery was in the cotton trade'. The invention was first described in the Encyclopaedia Britannica as having 'effected an entire revolution in the iron industry of Great Britain'.

> **KEY PROFILE**
>
> **James Beaumont Neilson (1792–1865)** was the son of a mill-wright. He left school at 13 and worked as a 'gin boy' (engine boy) operating a winding engine at Govan colliery. He learnt the trade of an engine-wright and was taken on as foreman of the first Glasgow Gasworks. He studied at night school and developed improvements in the manufacture of gas, before working on his revolutionary ideas for the iron industry.

Fig. 2 *The Nantyglo Ironworks in Wales, c1829*

ACTIVITY

Evaluating primary sources

What view does the Statistical Account of Scotland (1841) in Source 1 give of the impact of industrialisation in this part of Scotland?

SOURCE 1

In the Statistical Account of Scotland (1841) the entry for the parish of Old Monkland in Lanarkshire reads as follows:

The population of this parish is at present advancing at an amazing rate and this prosperity is entirely owing to the local coal and iron trade, stimulated by the discovery of the black band of ironstone and the method of fusing iron by hot blast.

Although there was a massive increase in the output of coal, there was surprisingly little innovation in the coal-mining industry in the early years of the nineteenth century. Coal was cut from the coal seams by manual labour with pickaxes. Coal mines were still relatively small and dangerous places to work. The biggest killer in the mines was methane gas. A safety lamp devised by Sir Humphrey Davy in 1813 inserted gauze around the naked flame and prevented explosion. An air pump was devised to help ventilation, but little else was done to improve safety. It appears there was sufficient human labour – men, women and children – to meet the increasing demands for coal.

KEY PROFILE

George Stephenson (1781–1848) was born in Wylam, Northumberland, and had no formal education. He became an engine-wright at Killingworth colliery. He built his first locomotive in 1814, which carried coals from the pit head at Killingworth to the River Tyne, a distance of nine kilometres. This established his reputation and he went on to design the famous Stockton to Darlington line in 1825, mainly to carry coal.

Early railways

During the post war years, the efficiency of the steam engine was improved by a series of refinements and within a short time was applied successfully to a new transport system – the railway. More efficient methods were needed for moving coal from the pit head to foundries, factories and other markets. Experiments in steam traction (a stationary steam engine powering trucks along the railway) developed into experiments in steam locomotion. By 1812, William Hedley's *The Puffing Billy* was operating in a Tyneside colliery. **George Stephenson**, however, is regarded as the genius who conceived and delivered the beginning of a modern railway system. The Stockton to Darlington railway line opened in 1825. Stephenson was the engineer for the first passenger railway using steam locomotives – the Liverpool to Manchester line, which was opened in 1830.

This marked the beginning of large-scale public railways in Britain, as its immediate success prompted a rash of railway companies building railway lines across the country. The railway was one of the key developments of the industrial age; the railway got the economy moving, transporting people and goods at speed and low cost. There was an immediate positive economic effect in the increased levels of employment. Railway work required a labour force of thousands. It gave a great boost to the iron and coal industries.

Fig. 3 At the Rainhill Trial, 1829, for the best locomotive to run on the new Liverpool to Manchester line, Stephenson's Rocket won first prize; it reached a speed of 30 mph (48 km/h)

EXTRACT 2

In 1833 Edward Gibbon Wakefield sketched a beguiling prospect for his fellow countrymen: 'The whole world is before you; let the English buy bread from every people that has bread to sell cheap. Make England for all that is produced by steam, the workshop of the world.' In these sentences Wakefield touched on much that was central to both the political and economic developments of the decades after Waterloo (1815). These were the years in which Britain's economic strength, naval power and far-flung empire gave her a global supremacy not approached before or since. The period was a unique one that appeared to the later Victorians as a golden age, one to which the term 'Pax Britannica' could be applied without undue extravagance. A longer retrospect would reveal weaknesses in Britain's position, but while it lasted the achievement was impressive and many-sided. At the heart of this dominance lay Britain's industrial supremacy.

Adapted from Glynn Williams and John Ramsden, *Ruling Britannia, a Political History of Britain 1688–1988*, 1990

ACTIVITY

Evaluating historical extracts

With reference to your understanding of the historical context, how convincing is Williams' and Ramsden's interpretation in Extract 2 of Britain's continuing success as an industrialising nation between 1812 and 1832?

KEY QUESTION

How and with what results did the economy develop and change?

Agricultural change

By 1812, agriculture was transforming into an industry, with large tenant farms set up as businesses and well-organised tenant farmers hiring agricultural labourers for seasonal work and producing goods for a commercial market. This was facilitated by the reorganisation of farm land by the Enclosure Acts, many of which were passed during the wars with France, and this continued through the 1820s. Enclosure quickened the pace of agricultural change. Rent for enclosed land was charged at a higher rate – it was more valuable as the crops in enclosed fields gave a higher yield; there was less wastage of land, more control over soil fertilisation

> **CROSS-REFERENCE**
>
> The policy of **enclosure** to bring more land into agricultural use was introduced in Chapter 3.

and more protection from hedging. **Enclosure** also encouraged improved systems of crop rotation. This in turn allowed more mixed farming – arable and livestock on the same farm – as a greater variety of cattle fodder could be produced, including winter feed. All this gave farmers greater security – when heavy rain spoilt the harvest, the cattle thrived – and therefore gave them higher profits for expansion and confidence to invest in the latest farming techniques and experiments.

Agriculture was stimulated by the war as wheat prices rose and, to seek as much financial advantage as possible, many farmers planted even their less fertile land with crops. The disruption of war and the rising population kept the demand for wheat high at a time when Britain was still largely self-sufficient in food production. When the war ended the demand fell, the price of wheat dropped and the cultivation of so much land no longer made economic sense. In addition the war-time trade restrictions ended, allowing cheap foreign corn into the British market. Tenant farmers who had taken on long leases during the war when rents were high saw their profits fall and responded by cutting wages and the jobs of their hired hands.

Although the demands of the landowners and the tenant farmers for protection against their losses culminated with the passing of the Corn Law, this measure did not necessarily shield them from the effects of the depression in agriculture in the years after the war. There were constant fluctuations in prices, even in the seasons of good harvests. Landowners who had borrowed large sums to pay for enclosures, new farm buildings and drainage schemes, partly to keep up with their wealthier 'improving' friends, found themselves overwhelmed with debt repayments. There were many farming bankruptcies during the 1820s. The plight of the agricultural labourer was much worse, but although there were concerns about rural depopulation, as many labourers moved to the industrial centres, the general increase in population meant there was never a shortage of labour on the land, no matter how low the wage.

Lack of uniformity in agricultural change

Agricultural improvements that had started in the early eighteenth century continued into the nineteenth century. Progress was very slow: innovation would occur in one region, but it might be years before it was taken up in another.

> **EXTRACT 3**
>
> What seems clear in the national story of agriculture in the early nineteenth century is that relatively small local improvements produced immediate results long before the new technical devices of ploughing, sowing, reaping and threshing were generally adopted. The slow movement of new ideas, the lack of basic techniques and the often unsatisfactory system of **leases** and **tenures** held back 'revolutionary advances'. Potatoes were produced in large quantities only near new towns; turnips were not grown in Devonshire; inferior livestock were still being bred in many distant parts of the country; and it was not until improved methods of drainage were evolved after the 1830s that the 'Norfolk system' of farming with its elimination of wasteful fodder and its 'scientific' rotation could be fully adopted on the intractable clay soils of the Midland counties.
>
> Adapted from Asa Briggs, *The Age of Improvement 1783–1867*, 1967

> **KEY TERM**
>
> **lease:** the contract letting or renting a farm for a given period
>
> **tenure:** the rights under that contract

> **ACTIVITY**
>
> **Evaluating historical extracts**
>
> To what extent does Briggs' interpretation in Extract 3 agree with that of Extract 1 regarding the pattern of agricultural improvement during this period? Explain your answers with examples from both extracts.

The invention of the threshing machine is a good example of this lack of uniformity in agricultural developments across the country. The threshing machine, which separated the husk from the grain mechanically, was first

Fig. 4 *A threshing machine in action*

invented in 1778 by **Andrew Meikle** at Houston Mill, near Dunbar in East Lothian. Meikle was a humble millwright and depended on the local landowners to use their influence to promote his product. It was not until the 1820s that threshing machines came into general use throughout the country. Meikle was dead by then and made no money from his endeavours. When the machines were brought onto farms, labourers fearful of their jobs attacked and destroyed them.

By the 1820s various systems of crop rotation developed in the eighteenth century were applied on many farms. The most popular was a variation of the Norfolk system of crop rotation adopted early on by landowner and MP Thomas Coke of Holkham Hall. The rotation of crops alternated clover and turnips with barley and wheat, and was soon widespread on the Holkham farms. Clover and turnip returned goodness to the soil and so overcame the problem of soil exhaustion and leaving the land fallow.

Coke, who inherited the estate in 1776 when improvement was the height of fashion, enthusiastically promoted the idea of rotation: 'No two white straw crops one after the other'. There were rotations designed to suit the various soils on the estate – every four, five or six years. At the time it was assumed that improvement was associated only with large estates, but by the nineteenth century they had become an important spur to development and change in agriculture.

Economic policies and Free Trade

Alongside the developments in technology and innovation in industry and agriculture, there were also government policies which helped to increase trade and prosperity. Lord Liverpool's government worked on **laissez faire** principles, believing that it was not the role of Government to regulate wages or prices; they would naturally settle at a level that was most efficient for the market, in other words the economy would function by the law of supply and demand and not by state interference. There was a lack of consistency in this approach as, for example, the Government was willing to intervene to prevent the fall in the price of corn to protect their own interest, but as part of a larger nineteenth-century development, this translated into an active economic policy of Free Trade in the 1820s and a rejection of mercantilism.

KEY PROFILE

Andrew Meikle (1719–1811) is credited with inventing the threshing machine, though it was a clever adaptation of an earlier model patented in 1734. Meikle's machine was trialled to a group of East Lothian farmers and was featured in Wright's *Present state of Agriculture in Scotland*. In spite of the publicity the machine was largely ignored.

ACTIVITY

Create a flow chart to show how Free Trade became an established government policy.

KEY QUESTION

- How and with what results did the economy develop and change?
- How important were ideas and ideologies?

KEY TERM

laissez faire: the doctrine that the state should not interfere in the workings of the market economy; the idea came from the teachings of the great political economists Adam Smith (1723–90) and David Ricardo (1772–1823)

The budgets of 1824 and 1825 were important in the history of economic policy as they were the first to apply the principles of free trade. They were principally the work of William Huskisson, President of the Board of Trade in Liverpool's Government and J. F. Robinson, Liverpool's Chancellor of the Exchequer, who introduced measures which led to a freeing of trade from tariffs and regulations and encouraged an expansion of trade. Customs duties were lowered on raw materials used in the textile and metal industries. Prohibitions on manufactured goods entering Britain were abolished and protective duties reduced. The most contentious of these was the prohibition of the import of silk goods, which was substituted for a 30 per cent duty, and which threatened the continuing existence of the fragile English silk industry. Raw wool could be exported for the first time. In 1823, a Reciprocity Act encouraged trade treaties with other countries on the basis of mutual tariff reductions. Preferential duties were set up for raw materials from Britain's colonies, for example silk from India and wool from Australia. Huskisson modified the Navigation Code, getting rid of anachronistic restrictions on trading in foreign ships, but retaining the condition that trade within the British Empire was to be carried out in British ships.

These measures stimulated industry and trade, bringing lower prices in manufactured goods and an increase in the volume of British exports and shipping. They reduced smuggling, which according to Boyd Hilton was a 'highly organised big business connived in by society at large'. They signified a comprehensive economic policy conceived largely by Huskisson and took Britain decisively in the direction of Free Trade.

A CLOSER LOOK

Free Trade versus mercantilism

Mercantilism as an economic policy weakened towards the end of the eighteenth century. Mercantile regulations were being largely ignored: for example, smuggling had become big business. A free trade policy removed many of those regulations, making smuggling unprofitable. Free trade policy also proved more successful and appropriate in the new age of economic expansion: as Britain's export trade grew and became more varied, it became more difficult to control through complex tariffs.

CROSS-REFERENCE

Mercantilism is explained in Chapter 2.

KEY TERM

speculation: the forming of a theory or conjecture without firm evidence

joint-stock bank: a limited liability company, engaged in banking as its trade, founded by subscribers or 'shareholders', whose liability is limited to the amount of money they subscribe; if the bank fails, they lose their subscription, but no more

However, when the 'commercial upturn' ended in 1825, there was heavy criticism of Huskisson's free trade theories and of the Liverpool Government's economic policies. The optimism of the previous years vanished, banks failed, businesses went bankrupt and there followed the usual distress among the labouring classes whose wages were reduced or worse who found themselves without a job. Liverpool was quick to blame the 'spirit of **speculation**', which he had warned the previous year was 'going beyond all bounds and likely to bring the greatest mischief on numerous individuals'. Problems occurred when speculators, confidant in the buoyant economy, bought assets at home and abroad that fell in value, partly because of over-subscription or over-production. Once the worst of the crisis was over, the Government responded with the Bank Act (1826) which made it legal for banks other than the Bank of England to operate as **joint-stock banks.** These could issue notes and had a more robust foundation than the small private banks, which had quickly gone to the wall in a crisis.

EXTRACT 4

Once the commercial upturn of 1822–25 began to deliver healthy revenues, it became possible to reduce indirect taxes, starting with duties on foreign timber in 1821. Excise taxes on windows, servants, horses and carriages were abolished or reduced in 1823, as were import duties on wool, coal, rum, silk, cotton, linen, paper, glass, earthenware and metals in 1824–25. Many export duties were done away with, but significantly not those on machinery, while the Reciprocity Treaty (1823) allowed ships of any country that responded in kind to carry goods to the United Kingdom on the same terms as British ships. So long as prosperity lasted, these measures were welcomed by a mainly landed House of Commons. Because Free Trade later assumed much importance, Huskisson and Robinson have often been seen as far-sighted, but in fact theirs was largely a tidying-up operation, in much the same way as Peel codified the criminal law.

Adapted from Boyd Hilton, *A Mad, Bad, and Dangerous People? England 1783–1846*, 2006

ACTIVITY

Evaluating historical extracts

1. Who would benefit from the reduction of the indirect taxes mentioned in Extract 4?
2. Why have Huskisson and Robinson been praised as 'far-sighted'?
3. What overall interpretation does Boyd Hilton put forward in this source?

Summary

- The British economy continued to flourish in the early years of the nineteenth century, in spite of the long and costly wars with France. The growth can be measured by looking at the production figures for cotton, iron and coal. There was an overall increase in production that was largely due to the increasing use of steam power.
- Industrialisation spread to parts of the country previously untouched by the process and more industries became mechanised.
- By 1812, agriculture was transforming into an industry and flourished during the later years of the Napoleonic wars, but entered a difficult period when the war ended.
- The process of enclosure, longer leases, the legacy of the eighteenth-century improvers and the inventions of gifted farm employees contributed to the changes in farming and foreshadowed agricultural advances later in the nineteenth century.
- In politics, the Government pursued an active economic policy of Free Trade in the 1820s.

ACTIVITY

Complete the following chart to show what changed and what remained the same in agriculture, industry and transport 1812–32.

	1812	1832
Agriculture		
Industry		
Transport		

SECTION 2 | Government and a changing society 1812–1832

STUDY TIP
Think about what the question is asking. You need to find a connection between the results of agricultural improvements and the expansion of industry and commerce. Look back at Chapter 3 to help you. You may conclude that the link was stronger in certain periods than in others.

A LEVEL PRACTICE QUESTION
Improvements in agriculture played a crucial role in facilitating the expansion of industry and commerce in Britain by 1832.
Assess the validity of this view.

STUDY TIP
When tackling an extract question, try to conclude your answer with a judgement, that is to say your opinion on the value of the extract.

AS LEVEL PRACTICE QUESTION

Evaluating historical extracts

With reference to Extracts 1 and 3 and your understanding of the historical context, which of these two extracts provides the more convincing interpretation of agricultural change in the years 1812 to 1832?

10 Social developments

The effects of industrialisation

EXTRACT 1

It is difficult to exaggerate the extent to which urbanisation affected British society in the nineteenth century. Indeed, the growth of towns and cities, and the radical overhaul of the balance of population between rural and urban worlds that this indicates, is one of the most sensitive indicators there is of a modern industrial state. The scale and nature of Britain's economic development during the nineteenth century suggests that urban growth was fundamental to it. If any single social experience can be said to have typified the living arrangements and new working experiences of the majority of the British people, then it was urbanisation. Although growth rates were uneven, varying by region, several key centres experienced rapid growth in the early industrial period. Big towns or cities such as Glasgow, Liverpool and Manchester doubled in size between 1811 and 1831. By the 1830s, Glasgow, Liverpool and Manchester each had more than 200,000 inhabitants. All epitomise the enormous effects of urban development.

Adapted from Jeremy Black and Donald M. Macraild, *Nineteenth Century Britain*, 2002

Population growth and urban development

Although industrialisation brought rapid **economic growth** in Britain during the early years of the nineteenth century, it also brought social turmoil and widespread unemployment. The huge growth in population and migration towards the northern industrial towns disturbed traditional habits and customs in the small rural communities. Some rural areas were transformed into industrial landscapes, with large smoking chimneys and blast furnaces creating an 'alien' skyline, and the constant noise of machinery disturbed the familiar tranquillity of the countryside. Towns developed into sprawling urban areas, situated close to the industrial activity with row after row of hastily-constructed houses and tenement blocks built to provide accommodation for the industrial workforce. These became the slum dwellings of the future.

Fig. 1 *Row after row of hastily constructed houses and tenement blocks were built to provide accommodation for the industrial workforce*

LEARNING OBJECTIVES

In this chapter you will learn about:

- the effects of industrialisation
- standards of living
- working class discontent.

KEY QUESTION

As you read this chapter, consider the following Key Questions:

- How and with what results did society and social policy develop?
- How important was the role of individuals and groups and how were they affected by developments?

ACTIVITY

Evaluating historical extracts

1. According to Extract 1 what was the importance of urbanisation on British society?
2. What do you think is meant by the 'new working experiences of the majority of the British people'?

CROSS-REFERENCE

For more context on the **economic situation** during this period, see Chapter 9, pages 81–3.

SECTION 2 | Government and a changing society 1812–1832

Table 1 Population figures (millions) between 1801 and 1831, with annual average percentage increase

	Population figure			Percentage growth
	Eng & Wales	Scotland	Ireland	Annual average increase (%)
1801	8.9	1.6	5.2	1.10
1811	10.2	1.8	6.0	1.43
1821	12.0	2.1	6.8	1.81
1831	13.9	2.4	7.8	1.58

Table 2 Population growth in major UK cities (%)

Year	Liverpool	% increase	Manchester	% increase	Glasgow	% increase
1801	82,000		75,000		77,000	
1811	104,000	26.8	89,000	18.6	101,000	31.6
1821	138,000	32.7	126,000	44.9	147,000	45.5
1831	202,000	46.4	182,000	44.4	202,000	37.4

> **CROSS-REFERENCE**
>
> For more information on **population growth** see Chapter 3, page 22.

In 1801, only London and Dublin had populations of more than 100,000, but by 1831 Edinburgh, Glasgow, Manchester, Birmingham, Bristol and Leeds had all exceeded that size. Manchester, Liverpool and Glasgow relied on differing economic bases – Manchester on textile mills and factories, Liverpool on commercial traffic through its docks and Glasgow, a commercial port, also had textile, shipbuilding and engineering industries – yet their patterns of growth in population terms was very similar. Some of the population increase in these three towns was the result of jobless unskilled labourers moving from the surrounding rural areas – from Cheshire to Manchester, from Lancashire to Liverpool and from the Scottish highlands to Glasgow. Another feature of migration to these towns was the influx of poverty-stricken landless Irish peasants, looking for a better life.

The modern historian Eric Hobsbawm denounced the impact of urbanisation on the labouring classes and the lack of welfare that accompanied it. The working hours were so long, and wages so low, that most workers had no life beyond the factory and their squalid tenement homes.

> **ACTIVITY**
>
> 1. What does Hobsbawm say about urban life in Extract 2?
> 2. What do you understand by 'the city was a volcano'?

> **EXTRACT 2**
>
> The city destroyed society. 'There is not a town in the world where the distance between the rich and the poor is so great or the barrier so difficult to be crossed', wrote Canon Parkinson, a nineteenth-century clergyman about Manchester. 'There is far less personal communication between the master cotton spinner and his workman, or the calico printer and his blue-handed boys [boys with hands dyed blue] from the calico [a type of cotton], than there is between the Duke of Wellington and the humblest labourer on his estate.' The city was a volcano, to whose rumblings the rich and powerful listened with fear, and whose eruptions they dreaded. But for its poor inhabitants it was not merely a standing reminder of their exclusion from human society. It was a stony desert that they had to make habitable by their own efforts.
>
> Adapted from Eric Hobsbawm, *Industry and Empire: From 1750 to the Present Day*, 1969

Social problems

The social problems that were created by economic growth and continuing industrialisation in the years between 1812 and 1832 were manifold and made worse by the failure of Government initially to recognise them and then to address them. It was unfamiliar territory; the towns were expanding so quickly that when problems of public health and maintaining social order arose there were no mechanisms in place to deal with them.

Population growth and urbanisation meant the crowding together of large numbers of people in towns and cities. While the wealthy middle classes segregated themselves from the rest in large houses in leafy suburbs, and the respectable middling ranks, such as trades and crafts people, lived in neat terraced houses not too far from the town centre, the rest – the vast majority – lived in overcrowded cramped tenement dwellings. These often housed an entire family in one room, with few basic facilities, a limited water supply and primitive sanitation. The poor living conditions caused numerous health problems and allowed disease to spread.

An absence of a system of local government meant a continuation or worsening of social problems. With urbanisation, many old boroughs had either declined or expanded into large industrial towns, but were still run by a mayor and corporation. These bodies had become corrupt; they largely acted in self-interest and did little to introduce any improvements, for example in lighting, drainage, water supply, sanitation or transport. There was no town planning to control the quality and direction of development. Sometimes the corporation would commission grand buildings in the town centres but these were of little value to the socially disadvantaged population.

Conditions in the workplace were equally detrimental to general health as men, women and children were enclosed in poorly-ventilated factories for up to 16 hours a day, six days a week, for little pay. The absence of safety regulations meant a high incidence of accidents. Much of the work in factories was done by women and children; they were easier to manage and cheaper to pay. Small children were used to clear jams in working machines, risking serious injury. There was a widespread use of orphan children, who were shamefully exploited. Child labour, however, was not a phenomenon of the industrial age and had existed for centuries. Humanitarian attention was drawn to the sight of so many small children crowding through the factory gates every morning and evening, and a long campaign to improve their conditions began.

Lack of education disadvantaged the working classes further. There was no state provision for children's schooling, indeed education was considered by many upper-and middle-class people to be socially dangerous among the poorer classes as it was thought to encourage revolutionary thinking. Others thought that an elementary level of education could be given, enough to remove the worst ignorance and teach children about the scriptures, but 'keep them in their place'. **Sunday schools** existed for this purpose, but there was no compunction or obligation to attend.

For those who could not find jobs, or lost their jobs through sickness, disability or old age, there was the prospect of endless grinding poverty. The system of poor relief was unable to cope with large-scale urbanisation, the flood of unemployed farm labourers into the towns and the high levels of unemployment among workers whose skills had been overtaken by machines. Relief came from the parish, but many rural parishes were swallowed up in the expanding cities and, over-burdened by demand, were unable to operate the relief system. As a result the anonymous poor were left to beg on the streets or turn to **crime**.

A CLOSER LOOK

Sunday School

In the nineteenth century, most Sunday schools took place on a Sunday afternoon, after the main act of worship usually in the morning. Religious instruction was given and bible reading encouraged.

CROSS-REFERENCE

The Metropolitan Police Force was formed in 1829 to deal with the increase in **crime**, especially in London and other large cities and towns. See Chapter 8 for details.

Fig. 2 *British emigrants departing for Canada*

Emigration as a response to economic forces

According to historian Christopher P. Hill, the rise in population stimulated the migration of the British overseas and was a powerful force in the extension of the British Empire. Historian Edward Royle asserts that it was peace at the end of the Napoleonic wars and 'renewed depression' that lay behind the sudden increase in emigration after 1815. There was a lull in population growth in the early 1820s, and then numbers began to rise again in the late 1820s. In 1832, almost 10,000 Scots emigrated, mostly to Canada. There were motives other than economic – some were social, personal or religious – but many went in a spirit of adventure as well as in the hope of a better life. In 1815 the first year records were kept of passengers leaving the country for non-European destinations, but they are incomplete.

Table 3 *Emigration figures for the whole of Britain, 1816–32*

Year	Total of British Emigrants
1816	13,000
1819	35,000
1830	55,000
1832	103,000

> **ACTIVITY**
>
> 1. Using Tables 1 and 3 and the information in this chapter, approximately what percentage of the total population of Britain emigrated in 1832? Use the 1831 census figures to calculate your answer. What percentage of the population of Scotland left Britain in 1832? Is the Scottish figure consistent with that of the whole of Britain?
> 2. What do you think were the most likely causes of the surge in emigration from Britain between 1815 and 1832?

Positive impacts of industrialisation

The positive aspect of the industrial revolution was that greater wealth was created and a larger population was sustained. The new middle classes, among them entrepreneurs, industrialists, merchants and financiers, all prospered as a result. It could be argued that the effect of industrialisation brought about a rise in the standard of living. Clearly it did for some. The main historical debate centres round the extent to which the population as a whole benefited and whether or not the living standards of the majority of working people declined or improved.

One other effect of industrialisation was that it facilitated the growth of trade unions, in that large numbers of men now worked together in close proximity and this gave them the opportunity to share their dissatisfaction over pay and conditions, exchange information more easily and fight against the effects of the recurrent economic fluctuations.

> **ACTIVITY**
>
> ### Thinking point
>
> Do you think that industrialisation could be regarded as beneficial or detrimental to society as a whole? Give examples from the text to support your answer.

Standards of living

Standards of living were affected by the continuing upheaval of industrialisation. It created wealth and employment for many, but undoubtedly a proportion of the population suffered deprivation and were possibly worse off as a result. There are widely differing views as to the extent to which living standards declined for the labouring classes. In his *Lectures on the Industrial Revolution*, the historian Arnold Toynbee regarded the Industrial Revolution as 'a period as disastrous and as terrible as any through which a nation ever passed; disastrous and terrible, because side by side with a great increase of wealth was seen an enormous increase of pauperism'. If Toynbee's view was correct and there was an 'enormous increase of pauperism', it would suggest a fall in the standards of living during this period.

> **KEY QUESTION**
>
> How and with what results did the economy change and develop?

> **CROSS-REFERENCE**
>
> The **standard of living** debate is introduced in Chapter 4. Refer back to this for further details.

A CLOSER LOOK

Interpreting historical data

Setting wages against prices, or income against expenditure, to draw conclusions about living standards can be helpful but ignores many of the problems of this approach:

- Data about wages can be unreliable as many labourers, e.g. farm labourers, were paid in kind with subsidised rent, wood fuel and produce.
- Wage data excludes the unemployed (this view is challenged as unemployment would have to be on a massive scale to cancel out the considerable rise in real wages).
- Wage data doesn't take into account under-employment, for example seasonal workers in agriculture, or textile workers paid off when orders declined.
- Regional differences in the rate of industrialisation affected wage levels.
- Some industries like cotton grew faster than others, so wages rose higher and faster.
- Wage data tends to consider adult male wages but not women or children, who often contributed to the household economy but were paid less than men.
- Wage data doesn't take into account environmental differences – for example, miners were paid higher wages but were more vulnerable to fatal diseases and accidents.

CROSS-REFERENCE

For more information on **Malthus** and his predictions, refer to his Key Profile in the Introduction to this book, page xiii.

Subsequently the anecdotal and statistical evidence to support this point is incomplete. In recent years, however, most historians have agreed that real wages rose considerably after the end of the Napoleonic wars, up to 1850, and possibly doubled, but that much of this increase was the result of falling prices rather than a rise in wages. If real wages had risen, it could be argued that living standards had improved. In the following extracts both Boyd Hilton and Peter Kirby raise the importance of taking into account other aspects, i.e. non-wage evidence, rather than just wage levels, in order to assess an individual's standard of living, for example size of family and cost of 'essential consumables'. Both acknowledge the generally accepted judgement that standards of living rose after 1815 and that is as far as Kirby goes, but Hilton introduces reservations. Hilton also draws attention to the question of what effect the move from the countryside to the town would have had on the quality of people's lives. This needs to be seen in the context of unprecedented social upheaval.

EXTRACT 3

In calculating trends in living standards, it is obviously not enough to divide gross national income by the size of population. An individual's circumstances depended on many things: his or her wages, patterns of consumption, the cost of essential consumables, family size and the number of dependants, the frequency of unemployment and short-time working, the availability of community support or charitable funds, and access to payments in kind and to customary rights such as raw materials, timber and grazing facilities. Between 1783 and 1846 there was probably a modest increase in people's material standards, although the quality of life often deteriorated with the move from the countryside to the town. Between 1825 and 1850, there was no overall improvement in real wages, while those of agricultural workers declined. The most successful workers were in leading-edge factory industries like textiles, but they were also the ones who suffered the worst assault in terms of gruelling conditions, disease, deformity and early death.

Adapted from Boyd Hilton *A Mad, Bad, and Dangerous People? England 1783–1846*, 2006

EXTRACT 4

The substantial increase in population affected poverty levels during the Industrial Revolution. Much of the 'hidden' rural poverty of the period resulted from rapid population growth coupled with declining employment opportunities. The proportion of children (aged 0–14) in society increased from 31.8 per cent in 1731 to 39.6 per cent in 1831. Thus, even if the income of a breadwinner rose, its real value would fall if the number of household members dependent upon that income increased at a faster rate. Contemporaries feared that an increase in the working-class birth rate might lead to a subsistence crisis similar to that predicted by **Malthus**. Such a crisis, however, failed to develop: though the period 1780 to 1850 saw unprecedented rates of population growth, it also witnessed comparable increases in the consumption of food. The productivity of the agricultural sector increased and food supply became more abundant in the early nineteenth century. The non-wage evidence supports an optimistic view of living standards in the post-Napoleonic War period.

Adapted from Peter Kirby, *The Standard of Living Debate and the Industrial Revolution*, 1997

According to research carried out by Peter Lindert and Jeffrey Williamson, who looked at a range of occupations and a greater range of items of expenditure, the real wages of clerical, non-manual workers rose more than those of unskilled labourers, especially farm labourers. The conclusion they drew was that the living standards of the middle classes improved to a greater extent than those of the majority of the labouring classes, but all labouring classes weren't necessarily less well off. The class system was becoming more complicated; for example, there were widening divisions within the working class itself. There was a growth of a large underclass, the labouring poor, who seemed unable to raise themselves above poverty and were harbouring resentment at their conditions.

ACTIVITY

Group discussion

Working in small groups, consider whether material possessions and wages or living conditions and leisure opportunities would have been more important to a worker in the early nineteenth century. Share thoughts in your class group and explain what you think mattered to workers and why.

PRACTICE QUESTION

Evaluating historical extracts

With reference to Extracts 3 and 4 and your understanding of the historical context, which of the extracts provides the more convincing interpretation of the standard of living experienced by the labouring population in the early nineteenth century?

STUDY TIP

You should first identify the interpretation put forward in each extract and support or criticise it from information in this chapter, as well as your own knowledge. Decide which interpretation you find most convincing and write an argued response.

Working-class discontent

In the early decades of the nineteenth century, working-class discontent arose from the demoralising effects of the revolution in agriculture and the continuing process of industrialisation. Enclosure had destroyed the livelihood of many small farmers and created a class of landless labourers, who were forced to rely on poor relief in the parish of their birth or make their way to the nearest large town and hope to find work in a factory. Industrialisation had brought into being a new industrial labour force who had to adapt to a harsher and more disciplined system of working within the factory. Even if wages were higher in the towns, the 'gruelling conditions' and the often unsatisfactory living arrangements caused underlying resentment. The developing pattern of social segregation in the towns, with the wealthier and middle-class families in large comfortable houses on the outskirts and the labouring poor in the over-crowded dingy back streets, was very different from the traditional rural existence where there was 'personal communication' between the village squire and the farm-hand, no matter how lowly, and a mutual respect, even though it may have been grudging. In the separation of the classes in the manufacturing towns, that deference began to disappear and there was, as the historian Briggs described, 'more opportunity for restlessness and organised discontent.'

CROSS-REFERENCE

For the decline in the standard of living of **hand-loom** weavers see Chapter 4. Before mechanisation their average earnings were about 20 shillings (£1) a week – a comfortable wage. In 1830, the average wage was 6 shillings (30p) a week. The power loom had made their skill redundant.

Working-class discontent was closely related to the state of the economy. Industry did not progress at a steady pace and every few years there were trade cycles of boom and bust. During an economic slump, trade and industry declined, employers cut back on production and either lowered wages or dismissed the workforce. Periodic bad harvests made the situation worse, as in addition to the hardships, the price of bread – a major element of the labourer's staple diet – rose. There was hunger and unemployment.

The existing system of poor relief was unsatisfactory. It was still based on the old **Speenhamland System**, which was completely inadequate to cope with the huge increase in population. In the countryside, the farmers simply reduced wages to the level at which an agricultural labourer could qualify for poor relief. In the large towns it had ceased to function effectively.

Discontent manifested itself most often in spontaneous outbreaks of disorder, which sometimes turned into serious rioting where the local militia were called out and arrests were made. The brutal punishments of capital punishment or transportation for life handed out by the courts further demoralised the struggling labouring poor, but did not halt the protests. Radical agitators who had their own reform agendas often stirred up the disaffected working classes. Examples of working-class discontent and disorder include Luddism and Luddite riots; the 1816 political demonstration at Spa Fields; the Blanketeers and the Peterloo Massacre.

> **CROSS-REFERENCE**
> The **Speenhamland System** of poor relief is outlined in Chapter 4, page 33.

> **ACTIVITY**
> Draw a spider diagram to show how the working class was affected by economic change 1812–32.

Fig. 3 *The Peterloo Massacre, 16 August 1819*

Summary

- Continuing industrialisation brought rapid economic growth but also social turmoil and widespread unemployment.
- Some rural communities were swallowed up into new industrial landscapes.
- The growth in population and movement towards the industrial north created large urban centres.
- Rapid urbanisation resulted in bad, overcrowded living conditions particularly for the labouring classes. The poor living conditions created social problems, which the Government failed to recognise or tackle.
- There was no duty of care for the workforce and working conditions were often appalling.
- There was no social safety net for the unemployed or low paid and the system of poor relief was unable to cope.
- There were several positive impacts of industrialisation such as a growth in wealth and an ability to sustain the growing population. It is generally accepted that the standard of living rose for many but a large underclass of labouring poor emerged.
- Aspects of industrial and agricultural change caused discontent among the working (labouring) classes that manifested itself in protests, which sometimes turned violent.
- Unrest decreased as the economy improved during the 1820s.

PRACTICE QUESTION

To what extent did urbanisation have an adverse effect on British society in the early nineteenth century?

STUDY TIP

To answer this question you must first define what is meant by 'urbanisation' and 'British society' in this context and make the point that there are huge variations within society. To be able to make a judgement you must find examples of the ways in which people's lives were changed by urbanisation. Remember this includes changes for the better as well as for the worse.

11 Pressures for change

EXTRACT 1

Although related to the tradition of industrial vandalism, the *Luddite movement* must be distinguished from it, first, by its high degree of organisation, second, by the political context within which it flourished. These differences may be summed up follows: while finding its origin in particular industrial grievances, Luddism continually trembled on the edge of revolutionary objectives. This is not to say that it was a wholly conscious revolutionary movement, but, on the other hand, it had a tendency towards becoming such a movement, and it is this tendency which is most often understated.

Adapted from Edward Palmer Thompson, *The Making of the English Working Class*, 1963

Luddism

The years after 1811 were a period of immense social and economic distress. Britain was struggling with the effects of the continuing changes in agriculture and industry, the high prices and increased taxation introduced because of the Napoleonic Wars, and the lack of an efficient system of poor relief to deal with the hardships faced by the growing labouring population. With low wages and high unemployment, the distress of the labouring classes often manifested itself in outbreaks of violence, while the Government, under pressure, adopted the repressive model of the Pitt government of the years after 1793 to deal with it.

Luddite riots

Outbursts of machine-breaking began in Nottinghamshire in 1811, carried out by groups of men who believed that machinery being used in the textile factories was depriving them of their livelihood. Initially, the problem was among the stocking-frame knitters who were angered by the use of a wide frame machine, which produced poorer quality 'cut-up' stockings faster and more cheaply than the traditional narrow frame used by skilled knitters. They accused the factory owners of underhand practices, which undervalued their skill, reduced their wages or put them out of work. Frustrated at the lack of resolution to the dispute, the stocking knitters turned to violent action and there followed a wave of machine-breaking, intimidation and rioting. The machine-breakers operated at night-time and rumour spread that they were organised by a mysterious figure, **Ned Ludd**.

The events caused Government real alarm. This was heightened by the apparent spread of machine-breaking to Yorkshire, Lancashire and Cheshire, which was also attributed to the Luddites. There were reports of 'quasi-military discipline, oath-taking and the use of numbers not names' (Briggs). The Yorkshire protests were directed against new technology rather than the unfair work practices of their employers. The skilled **croppers** in the woollen industry protested against the introduction of the shearing frame, which threatened to make their skill obsolete. In the Lancashire cotton mills, power looms were attacked and smashed by hand-loom weavers who had similar concerns about the future need for their expertise.

LEARNING OBJECTIVES

In this chapter you will learn about:
- Luddism
- Radical agitation
- the anti-slavery movement
- Methodism
- early Socialism and the ideas of Robert Owen.

CROSS-REFERENCE

An outline of the economic and social impact of war can be found in Chapter 6. It would be helpful to re-read this section to fill in the background to the Luddite riots.

KEY QUESTION

As you read this chapter, consider the following Key Questions:
- What pressures did governments face and how did they respond to these?
- How important was the role of individuals and groups and how were they affected by developments?

A CLOSER LOOK

Ned Ludd, legendary Luddite leader

Ned Ludd gave his name to the Luddites. He was rumoured to have his headquarters in Sherwood Forest and was most probably a mythical figure.

KEY TERM

cropper: (cloth-dresser) a well-paid, highly skilled job in the woollen industry; the cropper finished off the cloth, smoothing the surface by cutting any raised areas with special long heavy shears

Fig. 1 *Cloth croppers (cloth dressers) smoothing the surface the woven cloth with special hand shears*

The Yorkshire croppers initially tried the democratic process and petitioned Parliament to ask for help to safeguard their livelihoods. It was only when this failed that, in 1812, they turned to machine-breaking. In April, the violence became more than machine-breaking and a prominent woollen manufacturer, William Horsfall, was murdered by a group of four 'Luddites' in cold blood on his way home from market. Some months later 60 men stood trial for Luddite offences and three were hanged for Horsfall's killing.

As further instances of machine-breaking occurred, soldiers were drafted in to keep order. After a spate of arrests, trials, transportations and hangings, the resistance ended. Within a few years, the skilled croppers could no longer find work in the woollen industry and the hand-loom weavers in the cotton industry suffered years of falling wages as their skill was gradually taken over by the power loom. The stocking knitters were more successful, as the superior quality of their produce was still in demand and their wages rose once the unrest died down.

> **ACTIVITY**
>
> **Thinking point**
>
> What were the main causes of the Luddite disturbances? Why do you think Luddite activity had ceased by about 1813?

A CLOSER LOOK

The Luddite debate

One of the historical debates surrounding the Luddites is their motivation. The traditional view of historians like Frank Ongley Darvall is that the unrest was the response of uneducated men who saw the machines as a threat to their jobs. Their wages were low and employment variable and machine-breaking was an instinctive reaction to the anger and frustration at their inability to rely on a basic standard of living. This view rejects any idea that there was any attempt by the Luddites to form an 'insurrectionist movement' across various regions. Darvall claims that even the government spies couldn't find any evidence of treason or plan of revolution. The unrest was limited to local reasons in the places where it occurred and the Luddites were a small, largely ineffective movement which Darvall strongly asserts had no wider political motives.

On the other hand, Edward Palmer Thompson argues that the Luddites 'had a tendency towards becoming [a revolutionary] movement'. He argues that they were highly organised and the target of their protests was not the machines but the laissez faire system of the Government. Their wider objectives, therefore, were potentially dangerous to the status quo. This goes much further than the industrial vandalism of Darvall's view. Thompson also suggests that it would be highly unlikely that there would be no connection between the ringleaders, given the geographical proximity of the Luddite disturbances.

One of the problems in understanding the Luddite motives is the absence of reliable evidence. There is virtually no documentation from the Luddites themselves and the evidence produced at their trials came from 'alarmist local magistrates' (Brown) or spies and informants, who were interested in suggesting a conspiracy between the defenders.

ACTIVITY

Pair discussion

To what extent was Luddism motivated by self-interest or a sense of political injustice? Before starting your discussion, bear in mind that our twenty-first-century views of equal opportunities and social justice were not present in the early nineteenth century, when people tended to accept their position in society and there was little social mobility.

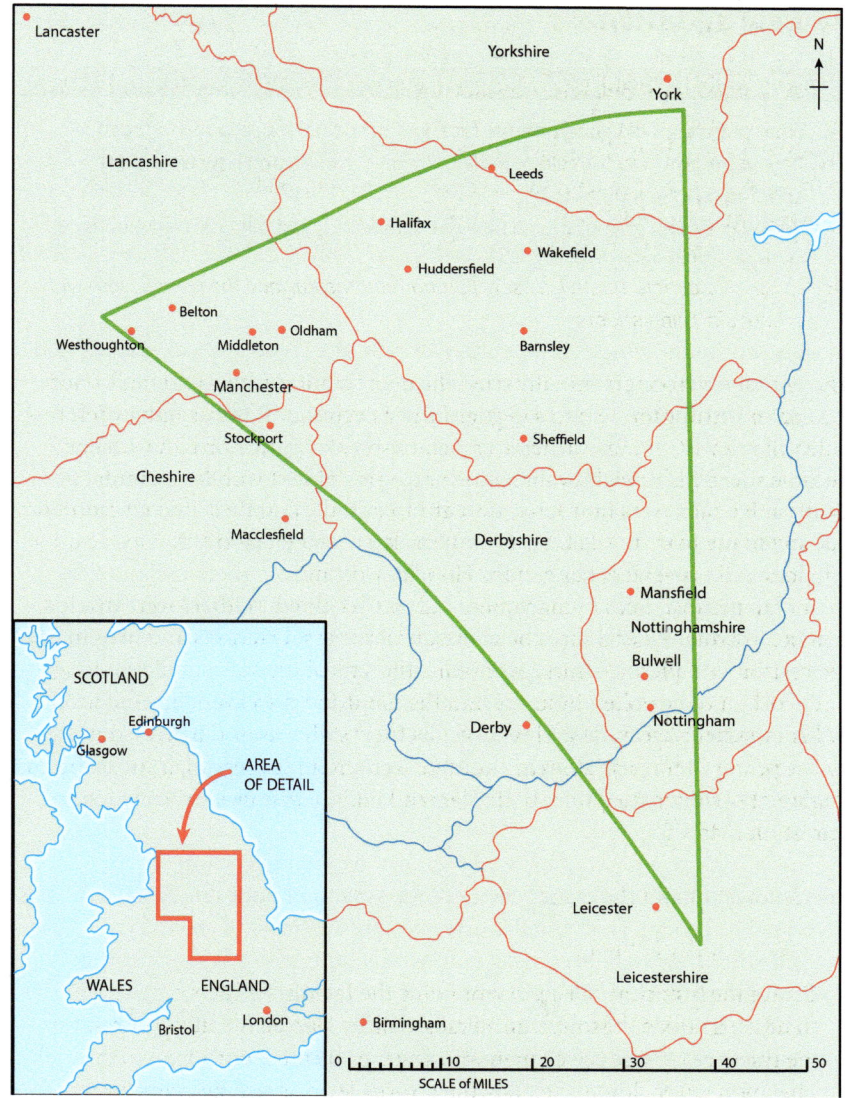

Fig. 2 *The location of the Luddite disturbances*

EXTRACT 2

There is no evidence whatever of any political motives on the part of the Luddites. There is not one single instance in which it can be proved that a Luddite attack was directed toward anything deeper than disputes between masters and men, between workmen and their employers. There was not a single Luddite and hardly a single riot of any kind against whom a charge of treason was advanced. There is no sign, despite the great efforts of the **spies** to prove such motives, that the Luddites, or indeed any but a few unimportant, unrepresentative, irresponsible agitators, had any large or political designs.

Adapted from Frank Ongley Darvall, *Popular Disturbances and Public Order in Regency England*, 1934

CROSS-REFERENCE

Look back to Chapter 5, page 44, to refresh your memory of **spies** and the role they played in British government.

SECTION 2 | Government and a changing society 1812–1832

STUDY TIP

When dealing with an extract question, always remember that the extracts express a particular point of view. Start by identifying the view expressed in each extract and then evaluate it using your contextual knowledge.

AS LEVEL PRACTICE QUESTION

Evaluating historical extracts

With reference to Extracts 1 and 2 and your understanding of the historical context, which of these two extracts provides the more convincing interpretation of Luddism in the early nineteenth century?

Radical agitation

CROSS-REFERENCE

Reasons and causes of **working-class discontent** are covered in Chapter 10.

KEY QUESTION

- What pressures did governments face and how did they respond to these?
- How important was the role of individuals and groups and how were they affected by developments?
- How was Britain governed and how did democracy and political organisations change and develop?

KEY PROFILE

Fig. 3   William Wilberforce

William Wilberforce (1759–1833) played a significant role in the evangelical revival, a spiritual movement within the Anglican Church that encouraged righteousness. The heart of the movement was the Clapham Sect, of which Wilberforce was a key member. He was an enlightened, rationalist, philanthropic reformer, but a traditionalist who believed in maintaining class distinctions.

CROSS-REFERENCE

Benthamite refers to those who followed the beliefs of Jeremy Bentham, who features in Chapter 6, page 51.

In eighteenth- and nineteenth-century Britain, the term 'Radical' was applied to any individual or group who wanted to see change or reform in an existing system or institution. After 1815 there was a revival of Radical agitation for political reform, which was more focused and determined than the earlier phase under Pitt. Radicals were usually from middle-class backgrounds. The Hampden Clubs were first formed in 1811 by Radical MP Sir Francis Burdett and made popular through the oratory of men like Henry Hunt.

There were several Radical MPs, but they were independent and pursued their own interest, rather than acting together. **William Wilberforce** used his seat in Parliament to fight for the abolition of slavery. David Ricardo was mainly concerned with protecting the economic interests of the industrial classes.

In 1821, the newspaper the *Manchester Guardian* was founded, and acted as a mouthpiece for middle-class manufacturers who started to press for parliamentary representation in the large unrepresented towns of the north of England. **Benthamite** Radicals, like James Mill, pressed more vocally for an extension of the franchise.

The working classes had focused their discontent on low wages, unemployment and the inadequacies of the system of poor relief, and expressed it through riots and disturbances during times of economic hardship, but they were becoming politicised and interested in achieving political influence through an extension of the franchise.

In 1816, a political demonstration was held at Spa Fields in London, at which the speaker was the charismatic Radical 'orator' Henry Hunt. Poor organisation led to fighting among the crowds, arrests and dispersal by the local militia. The following year a group of cotton workers planned to march from Manchester to London to present petitions to the Prince Regent (later George IV) for relief of distress. The Blanketeers, so-called as they were carrying bedding for their long march, were dispersed at the outset. Government spies also played a part in encouraging disorder among the discounted workers, ostensibly to catch the ring leaders. This was the case in the Derbyshire Insurrection the same year, which ended in the hanging of three poor unemployed framework knitters.

More serious was the meeting at St Peter's Field in Manchester in 1819. It stemmed from the grievances of the Lancashire weavers that their employers refused to agree to a legal minimum wage. Unable to make progress through negotiation, the weavers looked to a political solution and were in the forefront of the radical campaign to hold a public meeting to press for reform. **Henry Hunt**, a strong supporter of political reform, was to speak to the large assembled crowd and the Radical leaders insisted that it was to be a peaceful demonstration. The unnerved local magistrates, despatched the Manchester Yeomanry, who appeared armed and on horseback. Halfway through Hunt's speech, the magistrates gave orders for the constables to arrest Hunt. The Yeomanry went in to support the constables and in the ensuing charge through the crowd they killed eleven people and injured hundreds more. The government congratulated the magistrates on their prompt action: the press took up the story and it was dubbed the Peterloo Massacre, a contemptuous comparison with the victory over the French at Waterloo in 1815.

The aftermath was mishandled by a government more anxious to keep the local magistracy on side than to consider tackling the causes of the people's discontent. Even middle-class opinion was shocked by the unnecessary carnage. However, the government, keen to show their zero tolerance of public disorder, tightened up existing legislation to increase magistrates' powers and deter further public gatherings: these **Six Acts** were seen as a direct attack on the Radical movement.

> **KEY PROFILE**
>
> **Henry Hunt (1773–1835)**, Radical agitator and scourge of the Whigs, was a popular speaker at public protest meetings held during the period of widespread discontent after the Napoleonic wars. He was a flamboyant and controversial character. He agitated for political representation for the working classes, firmly rejecting violence. He was however, imprisoned for his part in Peterloo. He became a Radical MP for Preston in 1830.

The working-class agitation subsided with the economic recovery of the 1820s. William Cobbett, the eighteenth-century Radical political journalist summed up the cause of the unrest with the apt comment, 'I defy you to agitate a fellow with a full stomach!'. However, another sudden slump in the economy in the late 1820s led to outbreaks of violence among agricultural labourers in rural south of England. It was initially sparked off by rural changes and existing impositions: the introduction onto farms of threshing machines which threatened employment, and the continuation of the tithe – a tax in cash or kind, charged at one tenth of annual income and payable to the parish church. Farm machinery was smashed and hay-ricks set ablaze. In June 1830 the disturbances took an uglier turn, when a series of letters appeared, issuing threats against local landowners and farmers. They were signed 'Captain Swing', a reference to a flailing stick used in hand threshing, and became known as the Swing Riots. The Government acted swiftly and firmly, hanging troublemakers and gaoling or transporting several hundred more.

While both the middle-class and working-class agitators shared a goal of bringing an end to aristocratic dominance of the political system, the middle-class Radicals became wary of being too closely associated with the more violent tactics of working-class Radicalism, preferring to agitate for change through persuasion and rational argument.

The anti-slavery movement

The shipping of black slaves from the African continent in English vessels to the American colonies and the West Indies, where they were sold to work on sugar, and later cotton and tobacco plantations, had gone on for years without raising any moral issues. It was a lucrative trade and merchants in the

> **CROSS-REFERENCE**
>
> The **Six Acts** are detailed in Chapter 7, page 66.

> **ACTIVITY**
>
> Make a chart listing examples of Radical activity 1812–32, giving their causes and consequences.

> **KEY QUESTION**
>
> - How and with what results did society and social policy develop?
> - How important was the role of individual and groups and how were they affected by developments?

trading ports of London, Glasgow, Bristol and Liverpool became immensely wealthy. The wealth of many British families was based on their ownership of plantations in the British West Indies and was dependent on slavery.

By the early nineteenth century, it had become easier and more acceptable for people in Britain to express their opinions and make their views felt in opposition to the Government, as long as it was through peaceful channels. As a result there grew up reform societies and voluntary organisations that focused on a particular cause or interest. One of these was the anti-slavery movement, and early on it began to put pressure on Government to bring an end to the trading in African slaves. Supporters of this movement published pamphlets to shock a mainly middle-class and increasingly literate audience about the inhuman conditions suffered by trafficked black African slaves. In this way, the anti-slavery movement began to raise public consciousness.

Fig. 4 *The Abolition Campaign motif*

A CLOSER LOOK

Why was the Abolition of Slavery Act passed in 1807?

The West Indies' sugar production was no longer as important to the British economy, because industrialisation was producing greater sources of wealth. Also attitudes were changing and the middle and upper classes were developing a stronger moral outlook, influenced by humanitarian sentiments and evangelicalism. The Scottish academic James Beattie wrote in 1790 that slavery was 'utterly repugnant to every principle of reason, religion, humanity and conscience'.

The leading anti-slavery campaigner was William Wilberforce, a Yorkshire MP and close friend of William Pitt. Wilberforce was an evangelical and member of a group known as the 'Clapham Sect', whose primary aim was to 'save souls through the medium of political action' (Briggs). They were not democratic in any true sense as they upheld class differences and the distinctions between rich and poor. Their business was to encourage righteousness and to promote the idea of a society seeking to improve personal standards of morality. They encouraged more regular reading of the Bible. They took advantage of new trends in printing and publishing, by launching a propaganda campaign of morally improving literature aimed principally at the middle and upper-middle classes.

The 'Claphamites', as they were known, had a deep and genuine concern for groups of people who could not help themselves, for example, children subjected to cruelty and abuse, but also slaves. From its early days the anti-slavery movement had the support of some political 'heavyweights' like Pitt, Fox, Grey, Grenville and Canning, although Pitt had pulled back from abolition in the 1780s when conflicting interests surfaced within Parliament.

In 1807 the Abolition of Slavery Act passed through Parliament without much fuss. It formerly ended the trading in slaves, but did nothing to help those already enslaved in plantations in British colonies.

The issue of slavery resurfaced after the end of the Napoleonic Wars in 1815, during peace negotiations among the European powers. If Britain were to hand back some of its African and Caribbean spoils of war to their former European 'owners', the anti-slavery lobby was anxious for reassurance that the slave trade would not build up again as a result. They pressurised Liverpool's Government by bombarding it with petitions. Agreement in principle was reached, which included provision for British naval squadrons patrolling the West African coastline. Its effectiveness is another matter, but the discussions stimulated a new interest in tackling the continued use of slaves in British territories and also within Britain.

In 1823, Wilberforce and philanthropist MP **Thomas Buxton** formed the Anti-Slavery Society, which co-ordinated the wider campaign to outlaw slavery throughout the British Colonies. In 1825, Buxton took over leadership of the Anti-Slavery Party in Parliament from an ageing Wilberforce and kept the campaign alive. Canning, always pro the anti-slavery lobby, faltered over taking up the challenge to support Buxton's motion to allow children born to slaves to be born free, fearing too much opposition from MPs with 'interests' in the West Indies.

The plantation owners argued that a healthy slave had a value of about 50 pounds; they claimed that they would be overwhelmed by competition from rival slave owners in the southern states of America and that if they started giving freedom to slaves it would cause serious unrest. In any case, they argued, the slaves were so institutionalised that it was unlikely they would be able to deal with their freedom.

It wasn't however until the Whigs finally returned to power in 1830 under Lord Grey, that Wilberforce, with Buxton's help, was again able to press for an end to slavery. The **Abolition of Slavery Act** was passed in 1833, giving slaves within the British territories their freedom.

KEY PROFILE

Thomas Buxton (1786–1845) was an evangelical from a Quaker background who became interested in social reform. His wife Hannah was sister of Elizabeth Fry, and he supported her in her drive for prison reform in the 1820s. Buxton was an MP from 1818 to 1837 but he cared little for party politics and voted on the issues that interested him, such as slavery. He campaigned vigorously for the abolition of slavery in British colonies, working closely with Wilberforce.

ACTIVITY

Pair discussion

Pressure was put on the Government from two sides — the anti-slavery movement and those with interests in continuing the slave trade and slavery. Working in pairs, put forward the arguments for each side. Compare your notes. Can you find a convincing argument to explain the success of the anti-slavery movement against the 'slave interests'?

Methodism

Methodism as an alternative to the established Anglican Church took roots in England and Wales in the earlier part of the eighteenth century. Its autocratic leader, John Wesley, travelled around the countryside, exhorting people to find their own will and sense of purpose in life. He was suggesting in modern terminology that people could empower themselves – and once empowered could contribute something good to society. There was an emphasis on respectability, thrift, discipline, a strong work ethic and a belief in social equality. Some of the early Methodists who applied the principles of Wesleyan preaching very literally became wealthy industrialists and manufacturers, like Sir Josiah Guest who became the first MP for Methyr Tydfill in 1832.

After 1790 the Methodist movement took off and the numbers grew rapidly, with some estimates of membership as high as 350,000 by 1812, though in reality the membership was closer to half that number. Their expansion was regarded with suspicion among the establishment, and because of the Wesleyan view of a basic level of equality among all men in the sight of God, they were regarded as potentially dangerous and having

Fig. 5 *The founder of Methodism, John Wesley*

KEY QUESTION

- How and with what results did society and social policy develop?
- How important was the role of individuals and groups and how were they affected by developments?

radical tendencies. They put a great deal of effort into trying to convince the establishment that they were loyal subjects.

A CLOSER LOOK

Methodism

The Methodist movement was founded by John Wesley (1703–1791). It was initially a movement within the Anglican Church for soul-searching and seeking salvation from sin through Christ, leading to spiritual re-birth. Wesley finally broke with the Anglicans because of their hostility to him and his ideas, particularly the ordination of Methodist priests. Eventually Methodism developed into a social force for good works due to its followers leading active, selfless Christian lives.

In 1811 Home Secretary Lord Sidmouth had attempted to introduce a Bill requiring Dissenting (including Methodist) preachers to be licensed only if their respectability could be vouched for. There was so much uproar that the Bill was hastily withdrawn. **Jabez Bunting**, a leading Methodist minister, argued fiercely for the extension of Methodist rights. In 1812, the newly appointed Liverpool Government repealed two outdated pieces of seventeenth-century anti-Dissenter legislation, which forbade them meeting within five miles of a town – and Methodist preachers were accorded the same rights as Anglican clergy. A Toleration Act gave Methodists legal protection to worship and confirmed that they were not a destabilising influence on society. The Methodist leaders circulated literature giving assurance that they were loyal to the established order. In fact, they worked positively towards tackling the discontent of the industrial workforce and their firm belief was in 'peace and good order'.

KEY PROFILE

Jabez Bunting (1779–1858) was born in Manchester to a Radical tailor father and a Wesleyan Methodist mother. He started preaching at the age of 19 and became one of the most influential Methodist ministers. He was a conservative Methodist and opposed the actions of the Luddites. He exerted great control over the Methodist movement, making it independent of the Anglican Church.

KEY TERM

socialism: the sharing of wealth between all members of the community

KEY PROFILE

Robert Owen (1771–1858) was the son of a Welsh saddler and a self-made man, a prominent social reformer and an early influence in modern British Socialism. He was given a share of David Dale's New Lanark cotton mills on his marriage to Dale's daughter Caroline. Here he put into practice many of his ideas to improve living and working conditions for the labouring classes.

David Ricardo (1772–1823), a well-respected economist, made a personal fortune on the London Stock Exchange and wrote widely on economic issues. His most influential work was *Principles of Political Economy and Taxation* in 1817. He was an MP from 1819 until his death.

Early socialism and Robert Owen

KEY QUESTION

- How important were ideas and ideology?
- How important was the role of individuals and groups and how were they affected by developments?

In 1812, ideas of Socialism were starting to emerge in some sections of society. **Robert Owen** and **David Ricardo** were important figures in establishing the concept and applying socialist principles to their lives. Both Ricardo and Owen, who came from differing viewpoints, could see that the value of a product should bear some relation to the amount of labour that had gone into creating it. Owen applied this idea to the workforce. To Owen the industrial workforce had a great value and if properly treated and nurtured, people would work harder and the result would be increased productivity. His idea was to run the enterprise on benevolent lines to make the workforce feel valued and to encourage good behaviour and a good work ethic. There was to be no exploitation of the workforce and there were limits on the age at which children were employed and on their hours of work. Owen believed that organised recreation was essential for the workers' well-being. Dancing and singing classes were held after work, Owen ignoring the possibility that the operatives might feel exhausted after a 10- or 12-hour working day.

CHAPTER 11 | Pressures for change

EXTRACT 3

Socialism was very much in its infancy and can hardly be considered an important factor in 1815. The Radicals were the opposite of Socialists; yet David Ricardo, a Radical economist, produced a theory of value that was later seized upon by socialist writers such as Karl Marx. The theory was that the value of a commodity depended on the amount of labour that had been expended upon it. The first move in practical socialism was made by a successful business man, Robert Owen. He intended that his mills at New Lanark should be an example to the world of how good living conditions for the workers would in fact produce the greatest profits. He sounds more of a benevolent capitalist than a Socialist, but took his ideas further; his scheme was for industry to be organised in small integrated communities in which the producers would own the means of production and would exchange products on the basis of the labour value of the commodity. He went to America to set up his communities there and lost £40,000 in the endeavour.

Adapted from Anthony Wood, *Nineteenth-Century Britain,* 1969

CROSS-REFERENCE

Robert Owen and New Lanark mills are mentioned in Chapter 4, page 34.

ACTIVITY

What does Wood mean in Extract 3, by saying that Owen 'sounds more of a benevolent capitalist than a Socialist'?

A CLOSER LOOK

Historiography of Robert Owen

Despite arguing that Owen's idea was '**paternalist** rather than Socialist' at this stage, the historian Boyd Hilton also asserts that in the early nineteenth century, 'the only effective brand of socialism was Owenism'.

Owen wrote about his New Lanark experiment in *A New View of Society: Essays on the Principle of the Formation of the Human Character.* He believed that character was formed by circumstances, but it might be possible to develop and improve a person's character through controlling their environment. He tried to put this into practice in his school, where children started very young as their mothers were working in the mill. There was no corporal punishment. The publication of Owen's essays brought hundreds of visitors to **New Lanark and Robert Owen** became famous.

In 1824, Owen went to the United States to put into practice his ideas about small, integrated, self-sufficient communities in which 'the producers would own the means of production themselves and would exchange products on the basis of the labour value of the commodity'. The first was New Harmony in Indiana and the idea spread to Britain. Measuring their success is difficult as Owen lost a fortune setting them up.

After he returned to Britain he played a significant role in the establishment of the **Trade Union and Cooperative Movements**.

CROSS-REFERENCE

Robert Owen's political activities with regard to **Trade Union and Cooperative movements** are dealt with in Chapter 18.

ACTIVITY

Summary

Working in small groups, create a wall poster to illustrate one of the following and show how it put pressure on the Government:
- Luddites
- Radical agitators
- Anti-slavery campaigners
- Methodists
- Robert Owen and his ideas on Socialism

ACTIVITY

Pair discussion

Why do you think Robert Owen's ideas would be more acceptable to a twenty-first century generation than his own?

STUDY TIP

In order to answer this question it will be helpful to look back to Chapter 7 as well as reflecting on the material in this chapter. Make a list of 'pressures for change' and note the government reaction. This should help you to decide what you will argue.

 PRACTICE QUESTION

'Governments ignored working-class pressure for change in the years 1812 to 1830.'
Explain why you agree or disagree with this view.

STUDY TIP

As with the AS question it will be helpful to look at Chapter 7 as well as this chapter to help you answer this question. Again, make a list of 'pressures for change' and note government reaction to each. You will also need to consider whether pressures were ignored because of 'prejudices' or for other reasons.

PRACTICE QUESTION

'In the years 1812 to 1830 governments continually ignored pressures for change because of their own prejudices.'
Assess the validity of this view.

12 Greater democracy

EXTRACT 1

Middle-class reformers such as **James Mill** and Francis Place had no wish to see a revolution unless there was no possible alternative. They hoped an impression of overwhelming and irresistible force would be sufficient to bring about parliamentary reform without the risks of defeat or chaos that a genuine rising of the ordinary people could bring. This meant that popular demonstrations had to be orderly and well-conducted, for men who remembered the 'Six Acts' knew only too well that the wild displays of popular violence could rebound on the reform movement by providing the Government with an opportunity to rally support among propertied opinion and middle-class reformers and justify repressive legislation. It was in this frame of mind that many Radicals viewed the accession of Grey's administration in November 1830. In an atmosphere already excited by the **July Revolution** in France and the mounting wave of industrial and agricultural reactions to distress, the middle-class reformers intended to spur the Whigs to implement their pledge to reform quickly.

Adapted from John Stevenson, *Popular Disturbances in England, 1700–1832*, 1992

LEARNING OBJECTIVES

In this chapter you will learn about:

- the election of the Whigs
- pressure for parliamentary reform
- the Great Reform Act and its impact
- the state of Britain politically, economically and socially by 1832.

KEY QUESTION

As you read this chapter, consider the following Key Question:
How was Britain governed and how did democracy and political organisations change and develop?

ACTIVITY

Evaluating historical extracts

According to the extract what was the view of 'middle-class reformers'? How did they expect to achieve parliamentary reform?

A CLOSER LOOK

The July Revolution 1830

A rising in France in July 1830 deposed the French King Charles X, who had tried to adopt unpopular repressive measures, in favour of Louis Phillipe (1773–1850), a progressive French aristocrat. It sparked off a revolution in neighbouring Belgium. The British government recognised the new King and obtained his agreement not to interfere in Belgium.

KEY PROFILE

James Mill (1773–1836) was an outstanding political theorist, who attacked the predominance in Parliament of an aristocratic elite and argued that the rights of ordinary people were threatened by repressive laws and unfair taxation. He believed that political power should be extended to the middle classes, as they were best placed to act in the interests of the majority.

KEY CHRONOLOGY

1829		Thomas Attwood founds the Birmingham Political Union
1830		Death of George IV; accession of William IV
1830	November	Whig government takes office under Lord Grey
1831		Swing Riots subdued
1832		Great Reform Act

CROSS-REFERENCE

The Whigs' return to power is mentioned in connection with the Tory defeat in Chapter 8.

The election of the Whigs

The 1830 election gave the Whigs a sufficient majority to form a government. They had been out of office for most of the previous 50 years, except for a brief spell in 1806–07. This meant that the leading Whigs had plenty of experience in opposition but not in government.

SECTION 2 | Government and a changing society 1812–1832

KEY PROFILE

Fig. 1 Charles Grey

Charles Grey (1764–1845) was a supporter of the Whig Charles James Fox, and a consistent supporter of parliamentary reform. Foreign Secretary under Grenville (1806–7), he was out of office till 1830, but campaigned for Catholic Emancipation. George IV was his sworn enemy, but on the accession of William IV he was invited to form a government.

KEY TERM

universal suffrage: the concept of giving every adult the power of right to exercise the vote

CROSS-REFERENCE

See page 105 in Chapter 11 for information on the **Swing Riots**.

EXTRACT 2

In 1792, **Charles Grey** had first proposed a parliamentary motion in favour of reform, and his views had changed little in the intervening period. Then and now, he had been a moderate reformer, anxious to remove the anomalies in the existing system rather than to develop it radically in a democratic direction. An aristocrat to his finger-tips, he believed that the landed interest should be the predominant influence in Parliament and had no patience with those who were advocating **universal (or even male) suffrage**, annual parliaments or secret ballots. Yet he was convinced that it was dangerous to leave the rising manufacturing, trading and professional classes without an effective voice, fearing this would drive them to make common cause with Radical or even revolutionary forces. A cautious extension of the franchise, and the removal of the more indefensible and corrupt features of the electoral process, would on the contrary, effectively co-opt them to the governing class of, as he saw it, enlightened aristocrats.

Adapted from Dick Leonard, *Nineteenth Century British Premiers*, 2008

ACTIVITY

Evaluating historical extracts

According to Extract 2, what were Grey's views on parliamentary reform?

The new Whig government

The new Whig government that came to power in November 1830 was led by Charles Grey, who had championed reform for decades. The defeat of the Tories removed an obstruction to parliamentary reform. Grey was easily the most politically experienced of the Whigs and the one they looked to as their natural leader. In the dying days of Wellington's government, Grey had announced his intention of introducing a measure of parliamentary reform. Reform, therefore, was regarded as one of the main priorities of the new government and there was an expectation among many of the younger Whigs that it would be introduced without delay. The Cabinet was drawn almost entirely from the House of Lords, reflecting the continuing aristocratic dominance of the Whig party, and this influence was apparent in the nature and extent of reform that they were ultimately willing to support.

Grey's cabinet included several Canningites, a necessary compromise to ensure a majority following in the Commons. Viscount Palmerston, a Canningite Tory, with moderate reforming views, was appointed Foreign Secretary. Grey also made appointments among his relatives – still a common practice – including his son, and son-in-law, Lord Durham, 'Radical Jack'. Grey wished to employ the talents of Henry Brougham, the brilliant lawyer and orator, but also contain his Radicalism; he therefore created him a peer and appointed him Lord Chancellor. Grey's Home Secretary was Lord Melbourne, later Prime Minister, who was responsible for the tough line taken with rioters, whose activities caused the Government immediate concern.

Dealing with unrest

In the face of an economic downturn in the late 1820s, there had been serious unrest in the country, particularly with regard to the '**Swing Riots**', and although these had nothing to do with the reform movement, their ferocity had unnerved the authorities. Grey had already adjusted his priorities to focus on relieving distress, but realised firm action was first required to stem the upsurge of disorder and possible rebellion. The Government's response of immediately setting up special commissions to deal with rioters, who were handed down heavy sentences of death or transportation, was as repressive as any previous government under Pitt or Liverpool. The reforming Whigs had established their credentials. Grey now turned his attention to reform.

KEY CHRONOLOGY

1831 March	Reform Bill introduced and defeated in the Commons; Parliament dissolved
1831 June	Whigs return after election; another Reform Bill introduced
1831 October	Reform Bill rejected by the Lords; serious rioting breaks out across country
1832 May	Government defeated over latest Reform Bill in the Lords and resigns; Wellington fails to form a new government; Grey returns on the promise that the King will create sufficient new peers to get the Bill through the House of Lords
1832 June	Parliamentary Reform Bill becomes law

Pressure for parliamentary reform

Throughout the early decades of the nineteenth century there had been a gradual build-up of pressure on succeeding governments to radically change the outdated system of parliamentary elections. There were a variety of demands from various radical groups and individuals: for universal male suffrage, equal electoral districts, the secret ballot, payment of MPs, abolition of property qualifications to stand as an MP, and for annual elections. There were popular individuals like Henry Hunt, self-styled 'champion of Liberty', and William Cobbett who viciously attacked the 'Old Corruption' in his *Political Register*. By 1830 that pressure had to find a release. Opportunity for change came with the defeat of Wellington's Tory government in November 1830, which removed a stubborn obstruction and allowed Grey's more open-minded government to come to power.

There was a belief among many Whigs that some measure of political innovation was necessary, otherwise uncontrollable change might overwhelm the existing social order. Most Tories continued to regard parliamentary reform as a recipe for future disaster. The Whigs and moderate Radicals saw a perfect solution in moderate reform – getting rid of the worst of the rotten boroughs and giving representation to the larger industrial towns. When the majority Tory House of Lords flexed its muscles and rejected the reform bill in October 1831, over-stepping the mark, the prospect of a small aristocratic elite holding back the forces of progress and democracy was unacceptable to the reformers, even among the Whigs who held political power.

KEY QUESTION
- What pressures did governments face and how did they respond to these?
- How important was the role of individuals and groups and how were they affected by developments?
- How important were ideas and ideologies?

A CLOSER LOOK

Unequal distribution of seats
Wiltshire and Cornwall had as many seats as the eight densely populated northern counties of England and more than Scotland. Half of all the English boroughs were in the coastal counties of the south of England. Out of 658 seats in the Commons, 276 were controlled by landed patrons.

EXTRACT 3

In the climate of expectation – or dread – that followed the formation of the Whig government in mid-November 1830, disturbances in the country grew, rather than diminished. Aggression was expressed in many different ways. For the political unions in their infancy, it took the form of meetings. There

SECTION 2 | Government and a changing society 1812–1832

> **ACTIVITY**
>
> **Evaluating historical extracts**
>
> How convincing is Extract 3 in explaining the attitude of the political unions towards campaigning for reform?

was nothing straightforward nor indeed programmed about their growth. The Birmingham Political Union was obviously a formative influence and there would be many copies. At the same time the early unions – whatever their detractors might say – were essentially non-violent, this being a central tenet of Attwood's creed. Open-air banquets, open-air meetings, speeches, declamatory speeches – all these were symptoms of popular discontent rather than revolutionary calls to arms. Lord Grey complained about 'the large assemblages' near the new 'great town' of Manchester, under the direction of the local trade union, to protest against the low rate of wages offered by the master manufacturers, but he did not suggest that their methods were crudely violent.

Adapted from Antonia Fraser, *Perilous Question, the Drama of the Great Reform Bill 1832*, 2013

Fig. 2 *Announcing general policy statements before the election, 1830*

Several important influences had been brought to bear on Grey's Whig government that persuaded it to press ahead with reform. From the time the Bill was first announced in Parliament the pressure from outside Parliament was unrelenting. **Thomas Attwood's** Birmingham Political Union inspired other similar groups to form in places as diverse as Manchester and Worcester, and Francis Place founded the National Political Union. They were not all as socially well-integrated as the BPU, with its membership drawn from several social groups, and some like the Leeds Radical Political Union were anti-capitalist, but through petitions, mass meetings, demonstrations and sometimes rioting, they all demanded reform – 'the Bill, the whole Bill and nothing but the Bill'.

Although men like Attwood spoke out against violence, there were subtly threatening undertones that Britain could be on the edge of revolution if the people's demands were ignored. Historians disagree as to the likelihood of revolution. According to Hilton 'for a brief period control passed out of the hands of the parliamentary classes and into those of Radicals', whereas Antonia Fraser sees the massive demonstrations as 'symptoms of popular discontent rather than revolutionary calls to arms'.

Before the effects of industrialisation had brought economic benefits to them, the relatively small middle class had been willing to accept that political power and authority rested in the hands of the landed aristocracy. However, as the middle classes grew in number and more of their members enjoyed new wealth and prosperity, they believed they had a right as responsible, contributing, educated citizens to take a real share in that power. The industrial and commercial middle classes complained that they were not best served by the landed aristocracy whom they believed acted in their own selfish interests and made poorly-judged economic decisions.

KEY PROFILE

Thomas Attwood (1783–1856) ran his family's banking business in Birmingham. He felt strongly that Parliament needed more experienced businessmen who had an understanding of the economic needs of the country. He formed the Birmingham Political Union of the 'Lower and Middle Classes of the People', believing the movement would be strengthened by class cooperation. The Union put non-violent pressure on the Government to carry through reform.

ACTIVITY

Identify the groups who supported political reform and explain their motives for doing so.

Fig. 3 *The Meeting of the Unions on Newhall Hill, Birmingham, 16 May 1832*

The middle classes were influenced by the work of men like James Mill and Jeremy Bentham, both Radical thinkers, who wrote extensively about democracy and reform. In Mill's *Essays on Government (1825)* he was critical of the predominance of the aristocracy in government. Bentham, who applied his philosophy of utilitarianism to institutions and organisations, criticised Parliament for failing to achieve the 'greatest happiness of the greatest number', as its role was to take responsibility for governing the entire country and it only satisfied the needs of a minority and therefore needed to be reformed.

The working classes were more politically aware and had responded to Radical influence in the post-war years, but their interest fell away as the economy improved. They were often dismissed by the middle classes, most of whom believed they were not educated enough to vote. Radical journalist William Cobbett identified that much of the working-class interest in reform was about it bringing them tangible social and economic benefits. According to Cobbett, what the labouring man wanted was to be able to afford 'a cow, or a pig' for self-sufficiency, 'bread and cheese in his satchel' when he went to work and 'a bottle of beer to quench his thirst' instead of having to 'lie down on his belly to drink out of the brook'.

CROSS-REFERENCE

The system of representation and franchise in Parliament before the 1832 Reform Act is fully discussed in Chapter 1, pages 5–7.

STUDY TIP

Assess the overall argument of each extract. Decide which interpretation you find most convincing and write an argued response. Your evaluation will need to be supported by contextual knowledge.

A LEVEL PRACTICE QUESTION

Evaluating historical extracts

Using your understanding of the historical context, assess how convincing the arguments in Extracts 1, 2 and 3 are in relation to the reasons for parliamentary reform by 1832.

The Great Reform Act and its impact

Until 1832, Parliament was in essence a small, self-selecting, aristocratic, land-owning elite. The vast majority of the population had no freedom of choice to decide by whom or how they were governed. The Great Reform Act brought change to Britain's political system.

KEY PROFILE

Fig. 4 Lord John Russell (1792–1878)

Lord John Russell (1792–1878) was son of the Duke of Bedford and was elected Whig MP in 1813. He fought for religious equality and parliamentary reform. He is credited with drawing up the first Reform Bill as a backbencher. He joined the Cabinet in 1831 and, as Home Secretary, carried out reform of the penal code. He was Prime Minister twice in the years 1846–52 and 1865–66.

KEY QUESTION

- How was Britain governed and how did democracy and political organisations change and develop?
- How and with what results did the economy develop and change?
- How and with what results did society and social policy develop?

Drawing up a bill for reform

A Government committee of four pro-reformers, comprising **Lord John Russell**, Lord Durham, Lord Althorp, Leader of the Commons, and Lord Brougham, drew up detailed proposals for a far-reaching redistribution of seats and an extension and consolidation of the various franchises. It was put before the House in March 1831. When the bill was wrecked by Commons opposition at the Committee stage, Grey resigned and a general election was called, which resulted in a Tory **rout** and the return of the Whigs with a comfortable following.

KEY TERM

rout: an overwhelming defeat

CHAPTER 12 | Greater democracy

A CLOSER LOOK

Making a bill an Act of Parliament
Before any bill is made law it has to pass through three readings and a Committee stage in both the House of Commons and the House of Lords before it is passed to the monarch for royal assent. After each reading a vote is taken, which must be in favour of the bill before it continues to the next stage.

A slightly amended bill was reintroduced and passed through the Commons. In October 1831, the Tory majority in the House of Lords threw it out. In effect the Lords were turning their backs on any measure of parliamentary reform, denying middle-class interests and working-class aspirations for a fairer system of representation. This provoked an immediate and strong reaction across the country: high profile anti-reformists such as the Dukes of Wellington and Newcastle had their houses attacked by the mob; ugly riots occurred; worst of all was the destruction of the centre of Bristol by a crowd that was out of control. With the majority of the dependable, law-abiding middle classes roused to a fury by the intransigence of the aristocratic elite, the Government (many of whose members also supported reform) was not able to apply the usual heavy-handed response to the vociferous protests. Parliament had reached an impasse.

SOURCE 1

The Whig Prime Minister, Lord Grey, wrote in a letter to Princess Lieven, wife of the Russian Ambassador to London, on 9 November 1830:

In these times of democracy and foreign revolutions, it is possible to find real capacity in the high aristocracy – not that I wish to exclude merit if I should meet with it in the commonality; but given equal merit, I admit I should choose the aristocrat, for that class is the guarantee for the safety of the state and of the throne.

Days of May
In May 1832, after months of protest and unrest in the country, the Government faced its worst crisis. Another revised bill was introduced and rejected by the Lords again. Grey asked the King to create 50 new peers to get the bill through. When he refused, Grey resigned and Wellington was asked to form a ministry. To some, Britain seemed on the verge of revolution. There were mass demonstrations in Birmingham, Manchester and London. Wellington failed to find support, Grey returned as Prime Minister and King William agreed to create peers if the Lords refused to pass the Bill once more. However, in June 1832 the Reform Bill became Law. Bells rang out, the public rallied and there were great celebrations.

Terms of the Great Reform Bill
There was a significant redistribution of seats so that boroughs with small populations lost their MPs and these were transferred to the large centres of population that were now represented in Parliament for the first time. The franchise was extended and made more uniform, particularly in the boroughs, with the result that many middle-class men formed the new electorate. Approximately one sixth of the adult male population were enfranchised.

ACTIVITY
Evaluating primary sources
1. To what extent does Source 1 show Grey's attitude to reform? Explain your answer.
2. What is the value of Source 1 to an historian studying the motives behind Grey's desire to carry through parliamentary reform?

ACTIVITY
Thinking point
From what you have read so far in this book, how likely does it seem that the Whigs would introduce a truly democratic reform bill? Explain your answer.

> **A CLOSER LOOK**
>
> Terms of the Reform Act of 1832:
> 1. Voting qualifications
>   - the county franchise: the old 40 shilling freehold qualification remained and was extended to include £10 copyholders and £50 tenants-at-will.
>   - the borough franchise was made uniform by giving the vote to all (male) £10 householders.
> 2. Redistribution of seats
>   - 56 (rotten) boroughs lost both MPs; 30 boroughs lost one of their two MPs.
>   - 22 new boroughs such as Birmingham were created, each with two MPs.
>   - 20 smaller new boroughs like Gateshead were given one MP.
>   - Scotland was given 12 MPs and Wales 5.
>   - Larger counties gained extra seats.

Many problems and anomalies still existed. Voting still took place in public at the hustings and so bribery and corruption continued. The counties were still dominated by the landed gentry, and their position had been strengthened by redistribution of some of the seats to the counties, leaving many large industrial centres still under represented. The class composition of the Commons did not alter a great deal. A decade later 70 per cent of MPs came from the landed classes. The vast majority of the population still had no vote and the working classes who had frightened Parliament into bringing about reform were totally excluded.

The impact of the Reform Act

The Great Reform Act of 1832 proved an important landmark in parliamentary reform, as it pinpointed the start of Britain's move towards becoming a democratic society. This was not the intention of the Whig government that passed the act. The Whigs had argued for reform that made the House of Commons more representative of the industrial society that Britain had become. However, the Whigs wished to maintain the principle that owning land or property was an essential qualification for political power, and they continued to believe that the landed aristocracy played a part in maintaining stability and social order. Although the Whigs were the reforming party, many of them sat in the Lords and did not wish to threaten their own position.

They defended their position by involving commercial and industrial interests alongside landed interests. They increased county representation by sleight of hand and thus limited the power of the new forces of industrialisation, although the creation of the new industrial constituencies allowed the Commons to attend to the problems of a changing society. The Whigs had deliberately courted the middle classes and kept the working classes out of the system. They had gone as far as they could in terms of their outlook and traditions.

The Radicals were dissatisfied, arguing that reform had not gone far enough. The absence of a secret ballot meant bribery and corruption could continue unchecked and it allowed landlords to continue to exercise control at the hustings. The franchise was still too narrow and excluded the working classes. The size of the electorate increased from about 435,000 voters to about 652,000. This meant approximately one in five/six men (and no women) had the franchise. A Register of Electors was introduced but many wouldn't pay the one shilling registration fee and there were no properly-paid officials to organise the list.

The reform meant that the landed aristocracy lost their monopoly of political power and were forced to share it with the newly-enfranchised middle-class merchants, manufacturers and professional classes, in the rapidly expanding and previously unrepresented industrial towns. A steadily increasing number of them became MPs in the ensuing parliaments, including Thomas Attwood in Birmingham. They represented the new industrial wealth of Britain. The majority of this new entry voted with the Whigs and this enabled the Whigs to form majority governments for most of the following three decades. Ultimately the reform strengthened the Commons and it was gradually able to impose its will on the Lords and the monarch as it opened the way for further parliamentary reform. In 1832, however, the Whigs felt they had done enough to satisfy demand and that reform was complete.

In retrospect, parliamentary reform could be seen to have stimulated further social reforms and in the 1830s and 40s, legislation was passed to improve conditions in factories and mines, to improve public health, to abolish slavery, to reform municipal corporations and to amend the Poor Law.

The state of Britain politically, economically and socially by 1832

By 1832, Britain was a very different country from the Britain of 1783, which marks the beginning of this period of study. The early decades of the nineteenth century experienced significant political, social and economic change. The process of industrialisation and the accompanying increase in population had stimulated many of these changes. The economy was growing rapidly as a result of the new technologies based around the development of coal and iron. These natural resources were being used with great efficiency, stimulating trade and bringing new wealth into the country.

The economy was at the early stages of efficiencies of scale and so for example the long production runs achieved on the steam-driven power looms in the Manchester cotton mills were far more productive than the wife and husband team in a Pennine cottage, one spinning yarn and the other weaving the cloth on a wooden hand-loom. The widespread application of new technology altered the way in which people lived and so society changed with the growing economy.

There was greater material wealth, but there were increased social tensions caused by the disparity of wealth. The men, women and children who laboured long hours in the industrial factories and mills for a low wage, and went home to poor quality dwellings set in an urban sprawl, could not derive much pleasure from the country's increasing prosperity. They did have the benefit of better food however, as a result of the agricultural improvements that brought greater efficiency in food production. The irony here was that the main advance in farming had been enclosure, which had thrown many of them off the land, to find work in the industrial towns. The agrarian/domestic-based economy of the eighteenth century was being replaced by a manufacturing and trading economy.

The changes in the economy and society gave the impetus for the emerging manufacturing classes to challenge the unrepresentative, aristocratic system of government. They were forced to close ranks and put their collective heads in the sand or embrace the new small step towards greater democracy. The achievements of the reform of Parliament were immense and though it was not the intention of the Whigs, there was no going back once the Reform Act established the principle of electoral reform. In 1832, the urban middle classes were involved in the political process for the first time and this gave them the opportunity to inject society with their values of improvement, humanitarian

> **ACTIVITY**
>
> **Pair discussion**
>
> 'The Great Reform Act altered the reality of political power.' Do you agree or disagree with this statement? Working in pairs, one of you should draw up an argument that agrees with the statement and the other an argument that disagrees. Listen to both sides of the argument and draw a conclusion as to which is more convincing.

SECTION 2 | Government and a changing society 1812–1832

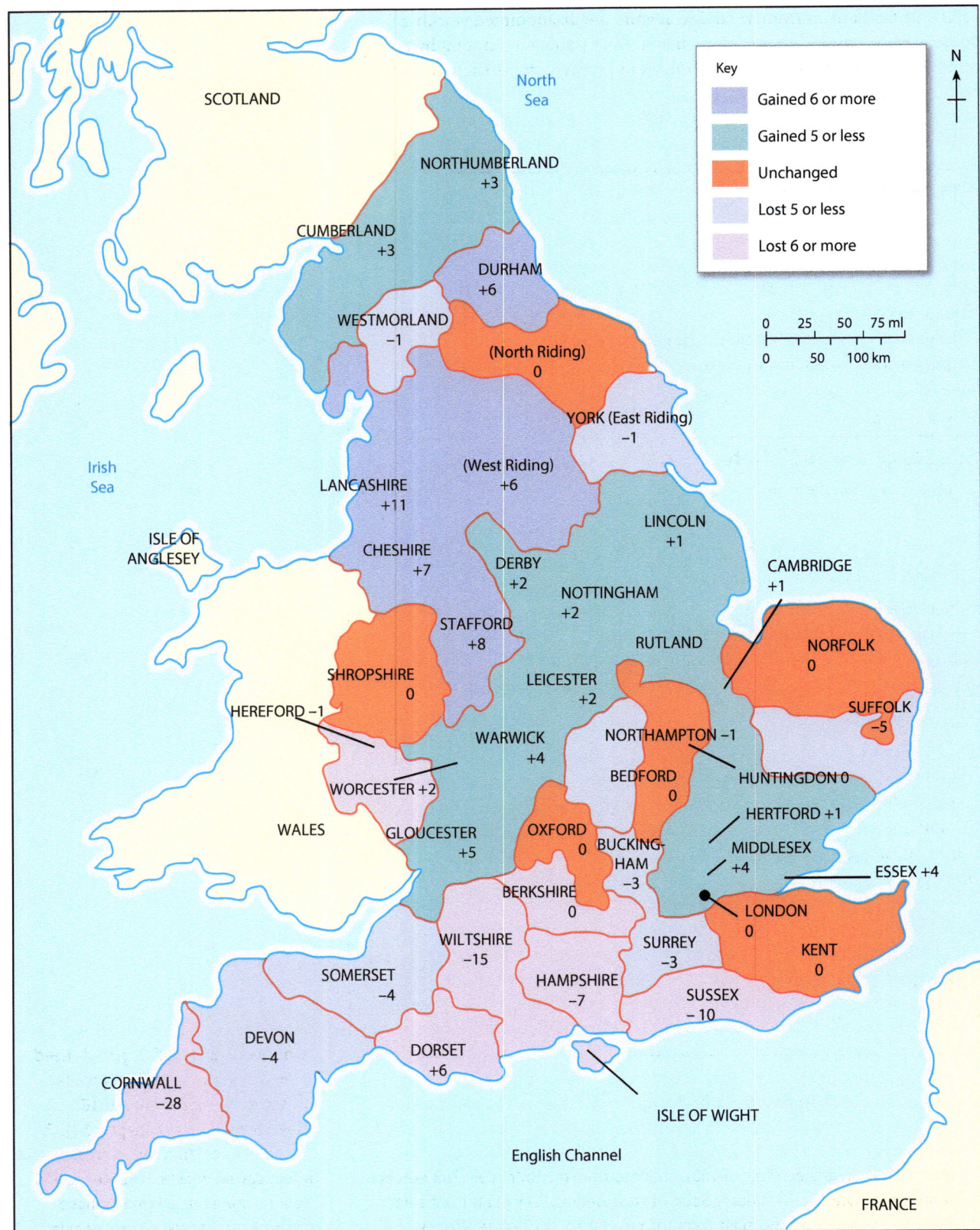

Fig. 5 *Changes to the distribution of parliamentary seats after the Great Reform Act*

ideals and rampant consumerism. Meanwhile the disappointed working classes were looking at ways of influencing society and government by acting together, assisted and inspired by middle-class philanthropists like Robert Owen with his brand of Socialism.

Summary

The need for reform

The electoral system was out of date:
- The population was rising
- Political power was in the hands of the landowning aristocracy
- Very few people had the vote
- Large areas of population had no representation in parliament
- Ownership of property was an essential qualification for political participation
- The middle and working classes who produced the wealth of the nation had no political power or influence

Effects of the 1832 Reform Act

1. Increase in size of electorate
   - Pre 1832   435,000
   - Post 1832   + 217,000 = 652,000 (figures are approximate)
2. Register of electors introduced after 1832 but excluded many eligible voters because:
   - people didn't bother to check
   - people wouldn't pay registration fee
3. Bribery and corruption continued through lack of secret ballot
4. Polling Day was reduced from a maximum of 15 days to 2
5. Redistribution of seats to the unrepresented industrial north, by abolishing most rotten boroughs
   - But rural south still over-represented
   - Industrial north still under-represented
6. Political Power
   - End of monopoly of political power of landed aristocracy
   - Urban middle classes had a share in political power
   - No working-class men got the vote
   - No women could vote

Significance of the Act

Great changes had occurred, but it was only a beginning – it ultimately opened the way to modern democracy.

ACTIVITY

Summary

In what respects had the Britain of 1832 changed from the Britain of 1783? Create a chart with the headings 'Political', 'Social' and 'Economic'. Do you think life had changed for the better for the majority of the population? Explain your answers.

PRACTICE QUESTION

'The Great Reform Act was the result of popular pressure.'
Assess the validity of this view of the years 1816–1832.

STUDY TIP

To answer this question you will need to reflect on the build-up of popular pressure for reform since 1816 (it will help to look at Chapter 11). To what extent did this earlier pressure affect developments in 1830–32 and was the pressure exerted in those years of any consequence? Decide what you will argue and try to offer a well-supported judgement – maybe suggesting that an alternative factor was of equal or even greater importance.

Part Two: The age of reform: Britain, 1832–1885

3 Political change and social reform, 1832–1846

13 Government: Grey and Melbourne as Prime Ministers

EXTRACT 1

Peel determined to make a fight of the election (of 1834). His preparation included the composition of one of the most celebrated political documents of the century, the Tamworth Manifesto. In theory this was Peel's address to the electors of Tamworth. It was in reality an early example of a party manifesto – a rallying call to Peel's followers, who were now to be given the designation of Conservatives rather than the somewhat tarnished Tory label. The new name expressed the core of the party's philosophy. Peel's case was that there were two main forces at work in British society, the Conservative and the Destructive. The former, under reliable leaders like Peel and Wellington, were concerned to conserve all that was essential and useful, while the Destructive faction, exemplified by extreme Radicals and Irish nationalists, comprised dangerous foes to the established order. It was not easy to portray men like the Whig Lord Melbourne as militant Radicals. It was easier to portray the Whigs, who had become dependent for their Commons majority on Irish and Radical votes, as the unwitting tools of more dangerous men.

Adapted from Norman McCord and Bill Purdue, *British History, 1815–1914*, (Short Oxford History of the Modern World), 2007

LEARNING OBJECTIVES

In this chapter you will learn about:

- Grey, Melbourne and the ideas and ideology of the Whig Party
- the Tories in opposition and Government
- Peel and the transformation of the Conservative Party.

KEY QUESTION

As you read this chapter, consider the following Key Question:
How was Britain governed and how did democracy and political organisations change and develop?

ACTIVITY

Evaluating historical extracts

Note the key points in McCord and Purdue's argument in Extract 1. What interpretation of Peel's contribution to the Tory Party is put forward?

KEY CHRONOLOGY

1832	December	Lord Grey and Whigs triumph in general election
1834	July	Lord Melbourne accepts office of Prime Minister
	November	William IV dismisses the Melbourne Government
	December	Sir Robert Peel becomes Prime Minister
		Peel issues the Tamworth Manifesto and establishes the Conservative Party
1835	February	Lichfield House Pact formed to undermine Peel
	April	Lord Melbourne replaces Peel as Prime Minister
1841		Election gives Conservatives a majority and Sir Robert Peel forms a new government
1846		Corn Laws repealed, Peel resigns

SECTION 3 | Political change and social reform, 1832–1846

KEY TERM

Foxite Whig: a Whig politician who admired Charles Fox

Canningite Tory: a Tory politician who admired Prime Minister George Canning

CROSS-REFERENCE

A Key Profile of **Canning** appears in Chapter 7, page 61, and a Key Profile of **Charles Fox** is in Chapter 2, page 12.

The **Whig reforms** are discussed in detail in Chapter 14.

KEY QUESTION

How important was the role of individuals and groups and how were they affected by developments?

KEY PROFILE

John Arthur Roebuck (1802–1879) was an advanced Radical, particularly in his views on political reform. He was elected MP for Bath in 1832 and challenged the Whigs at every turn, earning the nickname 'Tear 'em'. He advocated a reduction in the power of the Lords, the abolition of sinecures and a secret ballot.

CROSS-REFERENCE

A Key Profile of **Thomas Attwood** appears in Chapter 12.

John Stuart Mill's Key Profile is in Chapter 19.

A Key Profile of **William Cobbett** appears in Chapter 6.

Grey, Melbourne and the ideas and ideology of the Whig Party

KEY PROFILE

Lord Melbourne (1779–1848)

William Lamb, 2nd Lord Melbourne, was first a **Foxite Whig** and later as a **Canningite Tory** he resigned with Huskisson from Wellington's Government. He reverted to Whig principles and became Grey's Home Secretary in 1830, dealing harshly with Swing rioters. As Whig leader he was criticised for being too easy-going and had difficulty holding his Cabinet together. He was, however, a great favourite of the young Queen Victoria, to whom he acted as mentor.

Grey as Prime Minister

Once the Reform Act was passed in 1832, Lord Charles Grey called a general election in December 1832. The newly-enfranchised middle classes gave Grey a vote of confidence with a considerable majority in the Commons. Together with the support of the majority of Irish MPs and the Radicals, the Whigs could command 479 seats, while the Tories had 179. Grey's Government introduced a series of important social and administrative reforms, including factory reform, the abolition of slavery, reform of the Poor Law and reform of the banking system.

There were three major difficulties that faced the Whigs after carrying through their triumphant political and social reform: the fierce disagreements between the Whigs and the Radicals, the problems in Ireland, and the loss through resignation or retirement of several influential Whig leaders.

Fig. 1 *Howick Hall, Northumberland, which was Grey's home*

The Radicals were either men who had come into Parliament as a result of the Reform Act, such as **Thomas Attwood**, **John Arthur Roebuck** (a friend of **John Stuart Mill**) or older Radicals such as **William Cobbett**. Their effectiveness was reduced as they were divided amongst themselves as to what issues were most important, apart from further political reform, which most Whigs believed had been finally settled in 1832. They queried every institution and every tax and their enthusiasm to push for extensive reform was met with irritation from the Whig Government.

The privileged position of the Anglican Church in Catholic-dominated Ireland caused problems. There was continuing rural unrest in Ireland and calls for the repeal of the Act of Union. The Whigs differed in how to deal with the problem. Lord John Russell believed in concessions and Lord Stanley, Chief Secretary for Ireland, in **coercion**. In 1833–34 Church and education reforms were enacted, abolishing a church tax and effectively reducing the dominance of the Anglican Church of Ireland over the Catholic population. When this failed to settle the discontented population (and with a staggering lack of sensitivity), the Whigs followed their reforms with a Coercion Act. Russell reacted by proposing 'appropriation', the using of surplus Irish Church funds for educational and social benefits for the largely poor, uneducated Catholic population. This challenge from Lord John Russell split the Whigs further, caused the resignation of Stanley and other leading Whigs from the Government and helped to bring down Earl Grey's government in 1834.

Historian Dick Leonard suggests that after overseeing such an extensive programme of reforms Grey, who reached his seventieth birthday in March 1834, seemed exhausted: 'He no longer possessed the energy or patience to deal with awkward and quarrelsome ministers and was particularly vexed by disagreements on how to deal with Irish problems, which were still high on the political agenda, despite the granting of Catholic Emancipation in 1829.' Most Whigs were in favour of renewing the existing Coercion Act to deal with the continuing disorder in Ireland, but when Grey realised moves were afoot behind his back to dilute the Coercion Act, prompted by O'Connell, he stood down as Prime Minister and Whig leader. In August 1834 he was replaced by Lord Melbourne. After this, Grey appeared disillusioned and gave up politics altogether in 1839.

Melbourne as Prime Minister

When William IV invited Lord Melbourne to form an administration in August 1834, it was with the object of safeguarding himself against policies he disliked. Although a Whig supporter, Melbourne was known for his conservative approach to reform (he was for a brief time a member of the Canningite Tory administration) and is reported to have stated that 'change is of itself a great danger and a great evil'. After the passing of the 1832 Reform Act, he did not see the necessity for more reform. His critics interpreted this as either the lack of a clear plan or simply laziness.

When he formed a government in August 1834, he was immediately met with discord from all sides of the political spectrum. He refused the King's request to include Peel and Wellington, to achieve a moderate coalition. In his attempt to then appease the King and tread a middle ground he upset the Radical Whigs, such as Henry Brougham, by excluding them from his Cabinet. This was a huge mistake as Brougham would not sit back in silence. Melbourne believed that Lord Althorp, the Chancellor of the Exchequer, was the key to achieving cooperation and stability in the Commons, but when Althorp's father Earl Spencer died that year, Althorp succeeded to the Earldom and was obliged to take up his seat in the Lords. To replace him, Melbourne insisted on promoting Lord John Russell to the position of Chancellor and Leader of the Commons. The King, who disliked Russell's radical tendencies, refused and dismissed the Government even though it held a majority in the Commons. It has been suggested that 'Whig ineptitude' (Briggs) gave William IV the opportunity to ask the Tory Sir Robert Peel to take office, and had Melbourne been more assertive, William would have been unable to act in what was regarded as an unconstitutional manner. Historians McCord and Purdue suggest that Melbourne was relieved and 'made no serious effort to resist this royal decision'.

A CLOSER LOOK

Coercion Act of 1833

To overcome the rural unrest in Ireland and the on-going refusal of Catholic tenants to pay the tithe (taxes collected by Anglican clergy), the Whigs passed the stringent Coercion Act in 1833. It gives wide powers to the authorities in Ireland including curfew impositions and suppression of disturbances.

SECTION 3 | Political change and social reform, 1832–1846

A CLOSER LOOK

The Lichfield House Compact, 1835

Lord John Russell reacted to King William's unconstitutional behaviour by forming a pact with Daniel O'Connell, leader of the Irish MPs. This pact promised Irish support for the Whigs in Parliament and a Whig commitment to carry through Irish reforms when the Whigs returned to power. The Radicals were divided over making any pact with the Irish MPs.

CROSS-REFERENCE

Chapter 8 contains a section on **Daniel O'Connell** and his political support of the Irish issues.

CROSS-REFERENCE

The progress of the **Chartist Movement** and the **Anti-Corn Law League** form the basis of Chapter 15.

The King's interference angered the Whigs and the Radicals and a concerted effort was made to bring down Peel. When Peel's ministry failed a few months later, Melbourne returned to office, but with fewer Whig supporters and an increased reliance on the Radicals and the Irish MPs. **The Lichfield House Compact** that Lord John Russell had made in order to defeat the Tories, now came back to bite the Whigs as they had promised Irish reforms in exchange for Irish support. The Irish MPs were led by **Daniel O'Connell**.

The Irish MPs took the opportunity to call for an end to the Act of Union and this seriously discredited the Whig government. Peel played a clever waiting game while Whigs and Radicals quarrelled amongst themselves over their waning support. The Whigs lost the initiative over various Church reforms, failing to get a reasonable measure through the Lords to abolish the system of church rates, which imposed a burden on the Nonconformists.

Fig. 2 *Lord Melbourne instructing a young Queen Victoria in 1837*

In the general election held in August 1837, on the death of William IV, the Whigs again lost ground to the Tories (who became known as Conservatives after 1834; see below). The succession to the throne of Queen Victoria gave Melbourne an unexpected personal boost, as the young, politically inexperienced Queen demonstrated her preference for him over his political rival Peel. Melbourne resigned briefly over what he regarded as a vote of no confidence in Parliament, but returned when Peel refused to form a government. Melbourne limped on as Prime Minister for another two years, in the face of an economic crisis for which he had no solution. There was high unemployment and discontent and no further reform programme. There were two new sources of Radical agitation, the **Chartist Movement** and the **Anti-Corn Law League**, neither of which was well-handled by the Government. From 1837, budgets were in deficit, taxes – direct and indirect – had been raised and when Lord John Russell attempted a free trade budget in 1841, it was too late to convince the electorate. In the election of July 1841, support drained away from the Whigs, leaving the Conservatives victorious.

ACTIVITY

Pair discussion

Consider the strengths and weaknesses of the Whig leadership of Grey and Melbourne between 1830 and 1841. Draw up a table based on the one below. Once you have completed it, make a brief assessment of their competence as leaders.

The Whig Leadership 1830–41		
Leader	Strengths	Weaknesses
Grey		
Melbourne		

The ideas and ideology of the Whig Party

Traditionally, the Whigs differed from their political opponents, the Tories, in that they believed in a constitutional monarchy, in which the monarch's powers of patronage were limited. After the Reform Act it became clear that 'royal favour could no longer sustain in office a ministry which could not win from the electorate the support of a Commons majority' (McCord & Purdue). During the political machinations of the 1830s, when William IV attempted to manipulate who should run the Government, it became clear that it was no longer sufficient for a government to hold the confidence of the king, but it must seek the approval of the electorate. This was in line with Whig principles.

The Whigs had been instrumental in passing the Great Reform Act. Although the general election of December 1832 (the first after the passing of the Reform Act) gave the Whigs a resounding majority in the Commons and brought in more middle-class and radical elements among their number, the majority of Whigs still belonged to powerful aristocratic landowning families, many of whom had regarded the political concessions of the Reform Act as a final settlement. The leading Whigs still sat in the House of Lords and wielded enough influence for the junior branches of their families to be assured of seats in the House of Commons. The Whigs, like the Tories, were still essentially a party of self-interest. These aristocratic Whigs had come to the conclusion that parliamentary reform was 'both necessary and advantageous' (Richard Brown):

- they recognised it was necessary to give expression to middle-class opinion
- they realised they would gain political advantage by getting rid of the Tory-dominated rotten and pocket boroughs and thus strengthen their position in Parliament.

Once they had achieved these objectives, the Whigs did not then set out to pursue a programme of further reform. They were not a great reforming party *per se*, and believed they had gone far enough by dealing with revolutionary threats and revitalising the political system. In the event there was little further political reform for 30 years.

The Whigs passed several ground-breaking social reforms in the wake of the Great Reform Act, such as the Factory Act (1833), the Abolition of Slavery (1833) and the Municipal Corporations Act (1835). There were a number of progressive Whigs who were motivated by the Humanitarian movement that sought to improve the living and working conditions of the labouring poor and by **Bentham's** doctrine of **Utilitarianism** that promoted the necessity of efficiency and usefulness in laws and institutions. The Whig reforms reflected these influences.

> **KEY QUESTION**
>
> How important were ideas and ideology?

SECTION 3 | Political change and social reform, 1832–1846

A CLOSER LOOK

Early nineteenth-century ideologies

The ideologies of the early nineteenth century influenced the political thinking of progressive Whigs and to a degree the political reform and the social policies of the Whig governments of the 1830s:

Jeremy Bentham's theory of Utilitarianism was based on a view that minimal interference in the lives of people would bring 'the greatest happiness to the greatest number'. He saw it as the duty of government to try to achieve this by imposing as few restrictions as possible. His ideas chimed with the views of leading Whigs.

Evangelicalism was a spiritual movement within the Anglican Church, which encouraged righteousness (or goodness), adherence to the Bible's message and to seek salvation through faith (the idea that you could only be saved from sin through belief in God). Followers promoted a new morality centred on their faith, which relied on decency and a well-ordered and stable society. This appealed to Whig ideals.

Humanitarianism was a belief in the worthiness of human beings, in behaving decently and benevolently to fellow men, and in **philanthropy** and a love of mankind, demonstrated by contributing to general welfare. It steered politicians towards adopting a sense of duty to the poorer members of society.

KEY TERM

philanthropy: a love of mankind, demonstrated by contributing to general welfare; a philanthropist is someone who tries to benefit mankind and could be described as a humanitarian

In spite of their earlier confidence, the Whigs lost ground with each ensuing election. This was a cause of constant dissension between the Whigs and the Radicals, who made up their numbers in Parliament. The Whigs blamed the Radicals for frightening off moderate support, while the Radicals criticised the Whigs for failing to keep up the momentum for reform. Grey was coming to the end of his political career and had lost his reforming zeal. Melbourne did not see there were any pressing issues to be resolved. Lord John Russell, Brougham and Durham, the most outspoken Whig reformers, were dropped from the Cabinet in 1835.

One of the weaknesses of the Whigs was that they were not a party in a formal sense, but more of a coalition. This was because of their inclusion of the Radicals (largely associated with the middle class) who wanted further reforms, and their dependence on the fragile support of the Irish MPs, whose immediate agenda was to press for Irish concessions, but ultimately, it was suspected, the break-up of the Union.

The Whigs also lacked effective organisation, which was becoming increasingly relevant for retaining their political power and was something to which their main political opponents, the Conservatives, were paying particular attention.

ACTIVITY

The Whig governments of 1830–41 are best remembered for their extensive and ground-breaking programme of political, social and administrative reforms, which are detailed in Chapter 14, but there was internal discord and external criticism and eventually their 'support drained away'.

Write a post-election analysis in the style of today's media explaining what led them to lose the 1841 election.

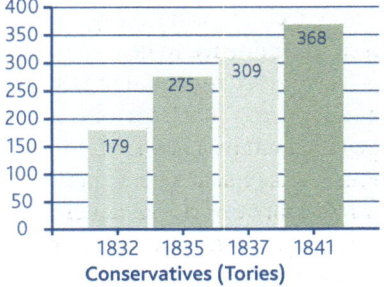
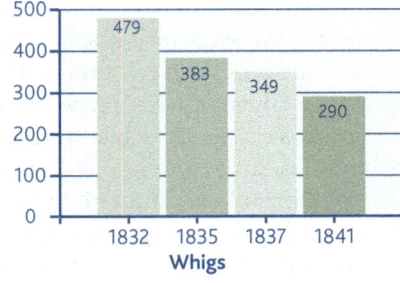

Fig. 3 *Election results from December 1832 to August 1841*

The Tories in opposition and government

Tories in opposition

The Tories remained in opposition for most of the decade between 1832 and 1841, but after 1834 started to recover their position. There were several reasons for this. According to Richard Brown, an important contributing factor to their recovery from virtual annihilation after the 1832 election was their 'cohesiveness in opposition', which was in sharp contrast to the 'problems which beset the Whigs'. Although Peel did not get involved directly with party management, he influenced its direction. The improved organisation of the party was the work of Francis Bonham (1785–1863), Tory election manager in 1832, appointed by Peel in 1834. The Tories made better and more efficient use of the system of parliamentary **whips**, up until that time more often used by the party in government. More frequent meetings of party members 'helped to raise levels of party consciousness' and instil a greater sense of loyalty to party and leader. This 'Party solidarity' was reflected in the springing up of local Conservative Party organisations, which encouraged the registration of possible Conservative electors and organised electoral campaigns. Bonham's initiatives led to the formation of a Tory network across the areas of the country where support became strong.

KEY QUESTION

- How important were ideas and ideology?
- How important was the role of individuals and groups and how were they affected by developments?

A CLOSER LOOK

Whips

Governments often functioned with a small majority and so employed 'whippers-in' from among their members to maximise the party's voting strength by making sure members attended crucial debates; the term comes from eighteenth-century hunting terminology, where a 'whipper-in' was a man who drove straying hounds back to the main pack using a whip

EXTRACT 2

> The Conservative recovery after 1834 and its cohesiveness in opposition can be compared with the problems that beset the Whigs. Belief in principles and policies, as the Whigs discovered, were, without effective organisation, insufficient to either retain or gain political power. The transformation of the Conservatives was largely, though not exclusively, the result of better organisation. Inside Parliament there were regular party meetings and an improved system of whipping. This helped raise levels of 'party consciousness' and reduced the occasions when substantial numbers of MPs voted against the wishes of the leadership. Increased party solidarity in the House of Commons was paralleled by the emergence of Conservative party organisations in the constituencies. The registration clauses of the Reform Act acted as an important stimulus to this development. By the beginning of 1837, there were several hundred Conservative associations demonstrating that the Conservative revival had a popular base and was something more than just the reassertion of influence by Conservative landowners and borough patrons.

Adapted from Richard Brown, *Church and State in Modern Britain, 1700–1850*, 1991

ACTIVITY

Evaluating historical extracts

According to Extract 2 how did the Conservatives make a political recovery after 1834? What evidence is there in the extract that supports this idea?

The Tories had a strong opposition leader in Robert Peel, who quickly established his authority over Tory MPs in the Commons. 'Peel's willingness to lead the party after two years' (Hilton) was a key factor in their recovery. He kept his distance from the Ultra Tories who had not forgiven him over his support of Catholic Emancipation. Instead of opposing every Government measure for the sake of it, he used his influence to get certain Whig bills through Parliament. It has been referred to by some as 'constructive opposition' – a clever tactic that unnerved the Whigs and strengthened his position, but by others as 'government in opposition' – a 'tacit alliance' between the Whigs and Peel. Peel also had his eye on encouraging moderate Whigs into the Tory ranks, particularly Sir James Graham and Lord Stanley. These men were both high-profile members of the Grey and Melbourne governments, who were uncomfortable with the Radical influences in the Whig party and in particular with the proposed

KEY TERM

appropriation: refers (in this context) to the Whig attempt to reform the established Irish Church, whose dominant position was resented by the Irish peasantry, by taking the surplus of Church income and redistributing it for secular purposes, e.g. education

'appropriation', a reform that would weaken the position of the Anglican Church in Ireland. The Lichfield House Pact organised by Lord John Russell increased Whig dependency on the Radicals and the Irish MPs and further alienated Stanley and Graham, both of whom later accepted posts in Peel's Government in 1841.

Peel and the transformation of the Conservative Party

The idea of the transformation of the Conservative Party centres round Peel's Tamworth Manifesto, which he delivered in December 1834 at the start of his tenure of office, after the dismissal of Melbourne by the King. It was clear to Peel that for the Tory Party to deny the 1832 Reform Act would be counter-productive and he accepted it as a 'final and irrevocable settlement of a great constitutional question' although he underlined the need to preserve Britain's institutions. His message was that moderate reform was the way to safeguard the traditional institutions of Church and state. It was, however, necessary to embrace the changes that had occurred with industrialisation – a developing urban society, a changing economy and new political demands. He thought it wiser to appeal to a broader electorate rather than deny their existence, particularly the new property-owning middle classes, who wanted stability, good government and recognition of their national contribution and influence. The Manifesto broke previous political conventions. It was a policy statement delivered to the Cabinet, but it was made public through the press and intended for a national audience. Around this time, the Tory party started to refer to itself as the Conservative Party. It was an important political turning point.

Fig. 4 Sir Robert Peel

EXTRACT 3

Far from being lazy and lacking direction, the Whigs governed in **tacit** alliance with Peel in order to weaken the pull of Radicalism. Thus, it is necessary to suggest a redefined position for Peel in his own party. Peel's ethic of 'governing in opposition' was not so much a **partisan** approach to the problems of governing a nation threatened by disruption and division, as it was Peel's method (by no means wholly successful) of strengthening his position within the party and with the electorate at the expense of the Ultra Tories. Peel had only limited success in controlling his party and influencing its principles; his inability to convince his followers of the need for moderation forced him into fighting the 1841 election as the defender of existing upper-class privilege. What triumphed in those elections were not Peel's Conservative principles, but those aspects of Toryism that he sought to subvert in his Tamworth Manifesto.

Adapted from Ian Newbould, 'Sir Robert Peel and the Conservatives 1832–1841: A Study in Failure?', *English Historical Review*, 1983

KEY TERM

tacit: something that is understand of implied without being directly said

partisan: prejudiced in favour of a particular cause

STUDY TIP

Your response should form a judgement on the validity of the arguments raised in each extract. You need to understand the context well and should be able to relate what is suggested in the extracts to your own knowledge. It will be helpful to read the historiography Closer Look before answering this question.

PRACTICE QUESTION

Evaluating historical extracts

Using your understanding of the historical context, assess how convincing the arguments in Extracts 1, 2 and 3 are in relation to Robert Peel as leader of the Conservatives in the years 1834 to 1841.

A CLOSER LOOK

Historiography on Peel

Ian Newbould is one of several historians who has in recent years challenged the accepted view of Peel and his new Conservatism. For Newbould, the view has been accepted for too long that the Whigs under Melbourne's negative leadership were desperately hanging on to power, courting the young, impressionable Queen Victoria, while the Conservatives, full of dynamism and energy, were steadily regaining confidence. Newbould's view is at odds with McCord and Purdue that the Whigs were a 'Destructive faction', and suggests on the one hand that it was the moderate Whigs who accepted a 'tacit alliance' with Peel in order to contain the Radicals within their party and that Peel's motive was more about getting the better of the Ultra Tories within his own party. Therefore, according to Newbould, his principles did not achieve the 1841 election victory; 'he set out to build a party and instead split one'.

Tories in government

Peel took office as Tory Prime Minister for the first time on 10 December 1834. He was in power for about 100 days until 8 April, when he was forced out by the constant opposition of the Whigs, angry at William IV's unconstitutional behaviour in dismissing Melbourne's majority government on a whim. In spite of this short tenure, Peel's admirers, including historian Norman Gash, have commented favourably on his achievement.

EXTRACT 4

> To a large number of his fellow countrymen Peel had presented a fresh and welcome political leadership, dissociated from the anti-reform image of old Toryism and yet different from the propensities of the new Whiggery… One thing at least was clear, Peel had emerged as a national leader.

Norman Gash, *Sir Robert Peel, The Life of Sir Robert Peel after 1830,* 1972

The single real achievement of Peel's brief ministry was the setting up of the Ecclesiastical Commission, whose recommendations were adopted by the Whigs when they returned to office. These ironed out anomalies and abuses in the Anglican Church, strengthening it against Radical and Nonconformist challenges for its disestablishment.

By 1841, the Whigs were a spent force and Peel's Conservative Party won a decisive election victory. Historians differ in their views as to what swung the vote in favour of the Conservatives. Newbould's view of a victory for the Ultras is given credence, if it is accepted that the agricultural and ecclesiastical interests adamant about protecting the Corn Laws and the Established Church, made a difference to the outcome. Gash would have it that the victory came about through the new urban voters, the industrial, commercial and professional classes, who put their faith in Peel's new forward-looking Conservatism.

Wherever the truth lies, Peel immediately faced problems with unrest at home from the Chartists; difficulties in Ireland with O'Connell and the National Repeal Association; financial concerns to balance the budget and make good the Whig deficits, and responsibility to maintain and develop the Whig social reforms. Peel had to deal early on in his government with the social effects of the economic slump that occurred in 1841 and 1842. The

SECTION 3 | Political change and social reform, 1832–1846

CROSS-REFERENCE
Chartism and difficulties in Ireland are the subject of Chapter 15, and the Repeal of the Corn Laws is the subject of Chapter 17.

ACTIVITY
When Peel took over leadership of the Tories the party was in crisis. Identify the steps Peel took to restore the Party's strength and credibility by 1841. Create a step diagram to illustrate the main points.

high unemployment, wage reductions and general distress brought about a widespread revival of **Chartism** and a spate of violent strikes and riots in the North. Peel took a firm line, arresting troublemakers and bringing an end to the agitation. His overall strategy was not to introduce reforms, but to stimulate trade and increase prosperity in which the working classes could take a share. There were those in his party that believed in active reform to improve conditions for the working classes. Peel went along with them to a degree with the Mines Act (1844) which halted underground labour for women and children, but believed that reducing adult working hours would injure the economy.

Peel's financial reforms met with the approval of the majority of his party, and although Peel tackled the major issues facing the government, there remained underlying tensions within the party about the extent to which members were expected to 'toe the party line'. Peel's Repeal of the Corn Laws in 1846, in the face of the crisis of the Irish Famine, tested the Conservative members' loyalty to the limits. Peel maintained that he was acting in the interests of the majority of the people and upon the 'principles of equity and justice'. It split the party. Peel was defeated shortly afterwards in June 1846, and resigned.

Peel may have alienated his followers and lost their support, but he managed to persuade Parliament to agree to a decision he had made as a matter of principle. In spite of founding the Conservative Party in 1834, he was poor at managing his party members, although he maintained the loyalty of several members of his Cabinet, who left the party with him.

ACTIVITY

Summary
Working in small groups, split into Whigs and Tories. Each side should make a summary of the strengths and the weaknesses of the other group. The points must be valid and able to be supported with evidence. Share your findings and come to a conclusion as to which side was stronger. Does your conclusion tie in with the statement in the essay question below?

STUDY TIP
Quotation questions such as this one ask you to weigh up the evidence for and against the statement – did Peel strengthen the Tories during this period, or did he not? You will need to identify the strengths and weaknesses of Peel's initiatives during this period, and also evaluate the strengths and weaknesses of the Tories versus the Whigs. Decide on your argument, and then use supporting evidence to write your essay.

PRACTICE QUESTION
'Peel strengthened the Tories between 1829 and 1846.'
Assess the validity of this view.

14 The Whig response to social change

LEARNING OBJECTIVES

In this chapter you will learn about:

- Whig Social reforms:
  1. Education
  2. Factory legislation
  3. Abolition of slavery
  4. The Poor Law Amendment Act
  5. The Municipal Corporations Act

EXTRACT 1

The 1830s saw the beginnings of policies that aimed to deal with the specific needs, abuses and problems of an industrialising society. It has been said that social policy in industrialising Britain did not really begin until the reformed parliament was elected in 1832. Though passed by a Whig parliament these policies can only be called 'Whig' to a limited extent. In fact most of the measures cannot be seen, except perhaps in retrospect, as grounded in any particular ideology, but rather as the product of interplay between general ideology (the presence of **Evangelicalism, humanitarianism, philanthropy** and **Benthamite Utilitarianism**) and the apparently fortunate appearance of dedicated individuals. The enhanced role of state intervention was largely the result of actions by the middle classes. This is not to deny the existence of pressure from the labouring population and the emerging trade unions, but is merely a recognition that the focus of sustained initiatives came from the middle classes.

Adapted from Richard Brown, *Church and state in Modern Britain, 1700–1850*, 1991

KEY QUESTION

As you read this chapter, consider the following Key Question:
How and with what results did society and social policy develop?

ACTIVITY

Evaluating historical extracts

What influences does the extract suggest are behind the beginnings of Government implementation of 'social policy'?

CROSS-REFERENCE

Bentham and **Utilitarianism** are discussed in Chapters 6 and 13.

Evangelicalism, humanitarianism and **philanthropy** are discussed in Chapter 13.

Whig social reforms

Pressure for reform did not end with the 1832 Parliamentary Reform Act. A period of legislation followed in the 1830s, under Grey and Melbourne, partly as a result of the continuing influence of reform agitation. Pressure came from a wide range of radical and religious groups, seeking social and administrative reforms in a variety of areas: the application of the Poor Law; working hours and conditions in factories; local government organisation; and the establishment of provision for education and the end of slavery in the British Colonies. Although the Whigs had not promised a reform programme, the achievement of a measure of political reform prompted expectation of improvement and changes in other areas. The various interests, such as factory bosses in this country and plantation owners within the British Empire, were eventually persuaded, however reluctantly, to come to an accommodation with new legislation.

Preparation for the introduction of any reform was usually preceded by the findings of a Select Committee of the House of Commons. This system was improved by the greater use of **Royal Commissions**, whose members included 'experts' as well as MPs and so opinion outside Parliament was taken into consideration in making legislative decisions. In this way, the opportunities for philanthropic, humanitarian and evangelical ideas (in other words the 'general ideology') to influence social reforms were increased. By 1846 it was becoming the norm for proposals on key social issues to be considered by a Royal Commission before being finalised.

The Whig social reforms were in the key areas of education, factories, slavery, the Poor Law and Municipal Corporations.

KEY CHRONOLOGY

1833	Government provision of £20,000 for voluntary societies to provide schools
1833	Factory Act
1833	Abolition of Slavery
1834	Poor Law Amendment Act
1835	Municipal Corporations Act

KEY TERM

Royal Commission of Inquiry: a body set up by government to look into a specific issue, e.g. the workings of the Poor Law; it includes 'experts' who make proposals and recommendations to Parliament to help them pass relevant legislation

> **KEY QUESTION**
>
> - What pressures did governments face and how did they respond to these?
> - How important were ideas and ideology?

> **A CLOSER LOOK**
>
> ### Education provision before 1830
>
> Until the nineteenth century, education was the preserve of the wealthy. Sons (and daughters to a lesser extent) of the aristocracy and upper classes were educated at home by private tutor. Sons then went on to 'public schools' such as Eton. Industrialisation created a new ambitious middle class who were prosperous enough and willing to pay fees for their sons to be educated either at public school or at a grammar school, where a smaller fee was charged and emphasis was placed on academic excellence. The syllabus was largely classical, but in a society where there was rapid technological development and innovation, there were demands for the schools to teach science and mathematics.

> **KEY CHRONOLOGY**
>
> ### Whig educational reforms
>
> | | |
> |---|---|
> | 1811 | Founding of National Society and British and Foreign Society |
> | 1833 | First government grant (£20,000) to provide more schools |
> | 1839 | Grant increased to £30,000 |
> | 1843 | Factory Education Bill |
> | 1846 | Failed attempt to establish national system of teacher training |

> **KEY TERM**
>
> **catechism:** a system of teaching based on question and answer, usually referring to the Christian faith

Education

The main concern for reformers was the lack of any real educational provision for working-class and poor children. An industrialised society required a more literate workforce. Sunday Schools were started up by Methodist Chapels and by 1830 over a million working-class children were attending Bible classes on Sundays – the one day in the week they didn't work – and they learned to read. Sunday Schools were financed by voluntary contributions from the congregations or interested benefactors. The most successful early school system for less well-off children was the **Monitorial schools**, in which one teacher instructed older pupils who were appointed as monitors to teach the younger children. Two different organisations, the National Society and the British and Foreign Society, both founded in 1811, promoted this system.

Fig. 1 *An example of a Monitorial school*

> **A CLOSER LOOK**
>
> ### Early beginnings of the Monitorial system
>
> The National Society, a Church of England foundation, ran schools in which children were taught reading, writing and arithmetic (known as 'the three Rs') and the Anglican **catechism**. The British and Foreign Society schools, led by the Quaker, Joseph Lancaster, taught 'the three Rs' without reference to Anglicanism. Consequently the British and Foreign schools were preferred by the Nonconformists and disapproved of by the Anglicans. Both were funded by voluntary subscriptions and benefactors.

These voluntary schools were overwhelmed by rapid urban development and the growing population and so in 1833 the Government made a grant of £20,000 to be shared between the two societies to help them open more schools. It was the start of official government activity in national education. The idea of using public funding to allow working-class children to spend time learning to read, when they could be more usefully employed on the factory floor, was strongly opposed by the traditional political classes. Regular accounts were to be submitted to the treasury, but the system was not rigorously administered. Attempts were made to improve accountability by appointing salaried inspectors. In 1839, the grant was increased to £30,000 and a Cabinet committee was set up to supervise how the money was spent. The Whigs, already struggling against party division and challenges from the opposition, put forward proposals to establish non-denominational colleges for teacher training and to place responsibility for education in the hands of a Privy Council Committee, without clergy representation. There was an outcry from the Anglicans and the Whigs dropped most of the scheme. However, the Committee was set up under **James Kay-Shuttleworth**, a philanthropist and champion of the poor, who devoted himself to establishing a state-funded system of popular education.

In 1843 the Factory Education Bill was introduced by James Graham, the Home Secretary. It attempted to make schooling under Anglican direction compulsory for child labourers, but was soundly defeated. The Whigs had miscalculated the joint Nonconformist and Catholic opposition to the scheme. In 1846, Kay-Shuttleworth's Committee attempted to establish a national system of teacher training to standardise the quality of teaching in grant-aided schools. The scheme required additional funding and met with so much criticism over the cost that it was abandoned.

The importance of these early grants and attempts to educate working-class children and 'impart such an amount of information as may fit them to discharge the duties of their station' (Kay-Shuttleworth), was that it was the beginning of state intervention and the responsibility to establish a compulsory comprehensive education system for all children, whatever their status or means.

> **KEY QUESTION**
>
> How important was the role of individuals and groups and how were they affected by developments?

> **KEY PROFILE**
>
> **James Kay-Shuttleworth (1804–1877)** was a philanthropist who trained as a doctor and developed a great concern for condition of the poor. He used his influence not only in the field of education but also to improve the living conditions and health of the working classes in Manchester. He was appointed Poor Law Commissioner and he set up the first teacher-training college from his own resources in 1839–40.

> **CROSS-REFERENCE**
>
> More information on the development of education appears in Chapters 20 and 23.

ACTIVITY

Thinking point

In what ways did religious concerns and denominational differences affect the progress of establishing a national system of education? Can you identify other attitudes or problems which made progress difficult?

> **KEY TERM**
>
> **free-marketeers:** those who believe in an economic system in which prices are allowed to fluctuate in accordance with supply and demand; it is a form of capitalism

Factory legislation

EXTRACT 2

On factory reform the Government confirmed its refusal to interfere with adult labour, but went one better than the ten-hour day, which **Lord Ashley** and other reformers were demanding for 9–12 year-olds, by legislating a maximum of eight hours. It looked like a remarkably generous gesture, but the beauty of the plan from the point of view of **free-marketeers**, like Lord Althorp at the Treasury and Charles Thomson at the Board of Trade, who 'did not apprehend that 69 hours work in the course of the week would be found injurious for 12–13 year-olds in any way', was that it enabled children to be used in relays, and so allowed adults to be worked up to 16 or 17 hours a day. Obviously it would be necessary to employ many more children overall, but Chadwick, a member of the Royal Commission of Inquiry, was confident that these could be supplied from the workhouses that were likely to be built as a result of his Poor Law Reform, already being planned.

Adapted from Boyd Hilton, *A Mad, Bad, and Dangerous People? England 1783–1846*, 2006

> ### ACTIVITY
>
> #### Evaluating historical extracts
>
> What reasons are put forward in Extract 2 to explain the Government's refusal to reduce adults' working hours in the factories?

> **CROSS-REFERENCE**
>
> The social reform campaigns of **Lord Ashley** and **Edwin Chadwick** are expanded upon in Chapter 15.

SECTION 3 | Political change and social reform, 1832–1846

Fig. 2 *Anthony Ashley Cooper, later Lord Shaftesbury, (1801–1885)*

CROSS-REFERENCE
Factory conditions are discussed in detail in Chapter 4.

KEY QUESTION
What pressures did governments face and how did they respond to these?

KEY PROFILE
Michael Sadler (1780–1835) was a Leeds merchant and Tory MP. He was an early leader of the Ten Hour Movement, and was renowned for his 'eloquent reasoning' about the need to introduce regulation into working conditions for children. One of his concerns was the adverse effects on children's health of long working hours. He lost his seat in the December 1832 elections over his support of factory reform.

Richard Oastler (1789–1861), was once a Leeds cloth merchant. He was an outspoken, Anglican, Tory **protectionist**. He was also a paternalist. In 1830 his letter to the *Leeds Mercury* on 'British Infantile Slavery', concerning the plight of child factory workers being no better than slaves, captured the headlines and increased awareness of the problem. Oastler organised vigorous campaigns for shorter working hours and continued to seek further factory reform after the 1833 Factory Act.

KEY PROFILE
Lord Anthony Ashley Cooper (1801–1885), later the 7th Earl of Shaftesbury, and then **Lord Shaftesbury** following the death of his father, was a leading evangelical social reformer, although he was a traditional Tory who voted against parliamentary reform. He became an ardent campaigner for improvement in children's working conditions, particularly in factories and in mines.

Edwin Chadwick (1800–1890), a lawyer, was a single-minded, self-educated reformer who was appointed President of the Royal Commission into factory conditions. He played a significant role in the Poor Law Report of 1834 and was appointed Secretary of the Poor Law Commission, though he lacked any real empathy with the poor. His work on Public Health reform is discussed in Chapter 15.

By the 1830s the industrial town with its factories producing goods for an expanding market had become an established part of the British landscape. For many thousands of people living in the industrial towns their daily routine involved working long hours in a factory, where the tasks were repetitive and the system harsh, disciplined and inflexible. Working hours were set in accordance with the requirements of the owner and not for the well-being of the labour force. It meant that entire families, including children, were working up to 16 hours a day, although employment of very young children was becoming less frequent. Employers liked to employ children and women as they could pay them less. Orphan children were often exploited by factory owners.

The campaign to persuade the Government to address the lack of regulation of conditions in factories, some of which were appalling, gathered momentum with the passing of the Reform Act. Lord Ashley, a Tory evangelical, led the Ten Hour Movement, a campaign to shorten working hours. He was supported inside and out of Parliament by other social reformers like **Michael Sadler**, a Tory MP, who had led the call for 'ten hours' before losing his seat in 1832. Additionally, **Richard Oastler** was quick to point out the uncomfortable comparison between the treatment of factory workers, especially children, in Britain, with that of slaves on plantations in the West Indies. Humanitarians and evangelicals joined forces with working-class groups and attended public meetings to pressurise the Government to reform.

SOURCE 1

Richard Oastler wrote this letter to the *Leeds Mercury*, 16 October 1830, in which he accused Britons of being complicit in slavery – meaning children in the Yorkshire town of Bradford who worked in the worst mills:

Let truth speak out, appalling as the statement may appear. The very streets which receive the droppings of an 'Anti-Slavery Society' are every morning wet by the tears of innocent victims! Thousands of little children, both male and female, but principally female, from seven to fourteen years of age, are daily compelled to labour from six o'clock in the morning to seven in the evening, with only – Britons, blush while you read it! – thirty minutes allowed for eating and recreation.

If I have succeeded in calling the attention of your readers to the horrid and abominable system on which the Worsted Mills in and near Bradford is conducted, I have done some good. Why should not children working in them be protected by legislative enactments, as well as those who work in cotton mills?

Your most excellent servant
A. Briton

Ashley's Ten Hour Bill (1846) failed. The Government was reluctant to interfere in the working hours of adults, and the voices of opposition were able to argue that if children's hours were shortened, adults would be compelled to work a shorter time too, because of the way the shift system operated. It was a firmly-held view among manufacturers that government intervention in market forces would bring economic disaster. The report of the Royal Commission, led by Edwin Chadwick, recommended legislation only in respect of children's working hours, on the grounds that they needed protection. It was this Benthamite approach, seeking an efficient solution to an emotive subject, that persuaded Parliament to pass the Factory Act in 1833.

> **KEY TERM**
>
> **protectionist:** believing in guarding the country's domestic industries from foreign competition by taxing imports

Fig. 4 *Richard Oastler (1789–1861)*

A CLOSER LOOK

The terms of the Factory Act 1833 (in respect of textile factories)

- No child under 9 could be employed in a factory.
- Children aged between 9 and 12 to work 8 hours a day with a maximum of 9 hours a day and 48 hours per week.
- Young people aged between 13 and 18 to work a maximum of 12 hours a day and 69 hours a week and no night-time work.
- Children to have 2 hours of compulsory schooling every day.
- Four factory inspectors were appointed as regulators of the new legislation.

The legislation 'went one better than the ten-hour day' proposal and restricted the working hours of children aged between 9 and 12 to eight hours. It was not a gesture of philanthropic concern; according to Boyd Hilton in Extract 2 the beauty of the plan from the point of view of free-marketeers was that it enabled children to be used in relays, and so allowed adults to be worked up to 16 or 17 hours a day. The new legislation would mean an increase in the numbers of child workers, but Chadwick factored in to the proposals that they could be drawn from the workhouses set up after the introduction of the Poor Law Amendment Act, which followed in 1834.

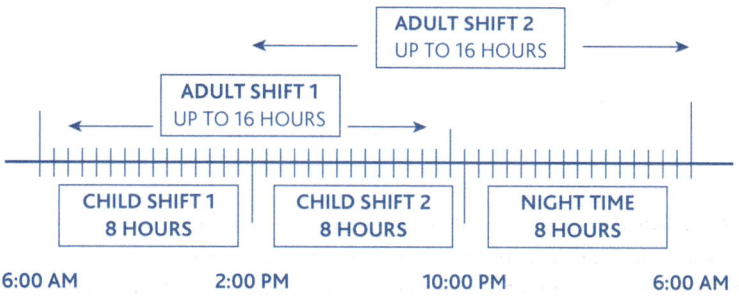

Fig. 3 *A typical shift system in a textile factory*

> **ACTIVITY**
>
> Working in pairs, draw up a list of points that support and oppose the view of this statement: 'The 1833 Factory Act showed a genuine concern by the Whig Government for the need to improve conditions in factories.' Look at your collective evidence and draw a conclusion.

Although attention was paid to the **vested interests** of the manufacturers, the 1833 Factory Act was more effective than previous legislation because of the system of regulation through inspectors. Adult hours were untouched, but the principle of state intervention in working hours had been established. It did not satisfy Ashley, and his campaign for shorter working hours continued. The inclusion in the legislation for some provision of education (if only two hours a day) for child factory workers was the first indication of any government policy introducing an element of compulsory education.

> **KEY TERM**
>
> **vested interest:** a particular interest in maintaining an existing system, for example slavery, because you own a sugar plantation using slaves as your workforce, and usually for financial reasons

SECTION 3 | Political change and social reform, 1832–1846

> **KEY QUESTION**
> - How important was the role of individuals and groups and how were they affected by developments?
> - How important were ideas and ideology?
> - What pressures did governments face and how did they respond to these?

Abolition of slavery

> **SOURCE 2**
>
> This notice went out to the Electors of Cambridgeshire in 1832, warning them not to support the pro-slavery candidate. The abolitionists wanted those sympathetic to their cause to be elected, and to reduce the pro-slavery lobby in the commons:
>
> Captain Yorke in his speech at Wisbech on Saturday last, asserted that the West India Planters have the same right of property in their slaves as the farmers of Cambridgeshire have in their ploughs and wagons. Captain Yorke also asserted that the West India Slaves were better off than the free English Labourers.
>
> It is true that many of the Labourers of this Country have been reduced to poverty through heavy taxes. But, thank God, English Labourers do not work in chains – English Labourers cannot be bought or sold; nor can any Englishman be flogged, or tortured at will of an inhuman taskmaster.
>
> ELECTORS! As ENGLISHMEN, as CHRISTAINS, your duty is to your country. God calls upon you to reject a man who can give utterance to such brutal sentiments as those avowed by Captain Yorke, and Vote only for those Candidates who will support an effectual abolition of the system of Slavery, which is a disgrace to the Colonies, to England, and to Mankind.

> **A CLOSER LOOK**
>
> ### Influence of abolitionists
>
> The influence of long-term campaigners such as William Wilberforce (1759–1833), Granville Sharp (1735–1813) and Thomas Clarkson (1760–1846) should not be overlooked in the achievement of bringing an end to slavery in the British Empire.

In the immediate aftermath of the 1832 Reform Act, its supporters believed the country would benefit from a 'rapid progress of knowledge' and a 'spirit of liberty and independence'. There was disappointment among the **abolitionists** that the abolition of slavery was not included in the government programme. Immediately, Parliament was flooded with petitions against the continuance of slavery in the British Empire, led by humanitarian and evangelical groups. A major change in attitude to the concept of slavery had already taken place years earlier. To the literate, Nonconformist, more democratically-minded urban society, the notion of slavery had become abhorrent.

To the plantation owners in the British Colonies, who depended on slave labour for their workforce, there was reluctance to accept abolition, but according to McCord and Purdue, 'Vested interests might impede or slow down the process of change; they were never able to frustrate it entirely.' Slave revolts were not unusual, but the level of violence of the uprising in Jamaica in 1831–32 caused shock waves in government circles and fear among plantation owners for their lives and their profits. A parliamentary inquiry followed, the result of which was the passing of the Slavery Abolition Act 1833.

Slavery was officially to end on 1 August 1834, but in practice slaves were reclassified as apprentices, with planned release dates set as far ahead as 1840. Peaceful protests brought this forward to 1838. The large amount of compensation (£20,000,000) paid out by the Government to all owners of slaves reflected both the Government's recognition that slavery was no longer morally acceptable and the vested interests of a considerable number of families among the political classes.

> **ACTIVITY**
>
> ### Group discussion
>
> The idea of slavery was abhorrent to many people by the early nineteenth century, but not to everyone. Split into small groups to discuss whether those that argued for keeping slaves were, in the context of the early nineteenth century, behaving in a totally unreasonable and irrational way.

> **A CLOSER LOOK**
>
> ### Compensation for slave owners
>
> 'The Sum of Twenty Million Pounds Sterling', the equivalent of 40 per cent of Government annual expenditure, was paid out in 40,000 separate awards, each sum dependent on the number of slaves owned. The extent

of involvement in slavery and social position of those involved may be surprising to us. Henry Phillpotts, the Bishop of Exeter, received compensation of £12,700 in respect of 665 slaves.

To satisfy plantation owners further and help replace the lost workforce in the British West Indies, a system of **indentured labour** was introduced, by bringing workers from India. Regulations were put in place to safeguard the immigrant workers, who were contracted to stay for a period of five years, but there were many abuses of the system and it could be regarded as a form of forced labour.

The abolitionists did not retreat and a new Anti-Slavery Society was formed in 1839, with the ambitious objective of getting rid of slavery worldwide. That organisation still operates today.

The Poor Law Amendment Act 1834

The system of Poor Relief had become almost impossible to maintain. It was still based on the old **Speenhamland System** of outdoor relief which had persisted since the Napoleonic Wars. It suppressed wages, particularly in rural areas, as farmers depended on workers receiving a wage supplement when prices rose. During the 1820s and 30s price fluctuations and recession caused periods of high unemployment. The wages of those who remained in work were inadequate as food prices remained high, partly as a result of the Corn Laws limiting imports of cheap grain. However, much of the pressure to reform the system came from the middle classes who were seeking a 'magic wand' solution to get rid of 'poverty and unemployment' and the high level of rates that they paid towards poor relief. A Royal Commission, in which Edwin Chadwick played a key role, looked into the existing system. Chadwick's approach chimed with the middle-class objective to cut costs, as he regarded the current system as wasteful and inefficient. The solution was radical and according to historian Chris Freeman was introduced at the poorest people's expense.

Terms of the Poor Law Amendment Act

Outdoor relief for the able-bodied was to be abolished as it was thought to encourage idleness, and in its place a system of indoor relief was to be established. A central authority, the Poor Law Commission (comprising three members) was set up to oversee the implementation of the new law. Parishes were grouped together into Unions and each Union was responsible for maintaining a workhouse, to be managed by a locally elected (by ratepayers) Board of Guardians. The '**principle of less eligibility**' was to be applied to anyone claiming poor relief, in the belief that only the most desperate would submit themselves and their families to the degradations of the workhouse, where conditions were made deliberately harsh.

A CLOSER LOOK

Outdoor relief and indoor relief

Outdoor relief was a payment made from the poor rates to subsidise low wages or unemployment. It was believed that withdrawing outdoor relief would force up wages and end poverty. The intention was to replace it with 'indoor relief', which was only available in a workhouse.

KEY TERM

indentured labour: an indenture is a legal contract between two parties; in this context Indian labourers agreed to work for a specific period, usually five years, in British Colonies, for agreed wages and specified conditions.

CROSS-REFERENCE

The **Speenhamland system** is outlined in Chapter 4, page 33.

A CLOSER LOOK

The '**principle of less eligibility**' stated that the conditions of a person receiving poor relief should be less 'eligible' (meaning less favourable) than the conditions of the poorest labourer who was not. This was to ensure that labourers were discouraged from feeling out-done by the poor on relief and those receiving relief were still encouraged to find work.

Fig. 5 *Paupers breaking stones in a British workhouse in the 1850s*

The workhouse system was designed to act as a deterrent to the 'idle and profligate', as the almost inhuman conditions would stop any but the most desperate from entering. The new system was seen by its creators as a social policy that encouraged the work ethic. It was to ensure that those who were able-bodied found employment, rather than scrounge off the parish, but failed to comprehend the helplessness of many decent hard-working people who were unable to find either a job or one that would pay enough to meet the basic needs of their families. The historian Peter Mathias has pointed out that the new system assumed that unemployment was a chosen option for the worker when in fact it was involuntary, caused by economic, technological and structural changes.

The intention of the new Poor Law was to end the existing arbitrary local provision for poor relief, and to cut the cost to ratepayers. In this it was successful as it deterred all but the most desperate. There was a drop in the average annual poor rates from £6.75 million in 1830–34 to £4.5 million in 1835–39. Parts of the country, however, particularly the industrial north, were resistant to the new measures. Applying indoor relief in industrial towns with large expanding populations was totally impractical, as during any period of recession, when unemployment was high and wages low, it was impossible to accommodate all the needy. As a result an inadequate system of outdoor relief continued in the north and few workhouses were built there.

Poverty was not solved by the Act and the imposition of the grim workhouse conditions angered the labouring poor in the rural south and in 1839 edged them towards **Chartism** – a working class movement for political reform.

In terms of administrative intervention, the Poor Law Amendment Act broke new boundaries. It established a 'standardised administrative structure' (McCord). The Poor Law Commission was an early example of a central

> **CROSS-REFERENCE**
>
> **Chartism** is examined in Chapter 15, pages 143–6.

government institution, with paid officials, which had overall control of locally managed institutions – in this case workhouses. The structure could be applied to other institutions and pre-empted the introduction of departments of State.

ACTIVITY

Thinking point

Why was there opposition to the 1834 Poor Law Amendment Act? Do you think the opposition was justified?

EXTRACT 3

The Poor Law Commission of 1834 saw its task as organising 'a measure of social policy' that would encourage the development of a free market for labour, but it did not want to go as far as Malthus and abolish the Poor Laws altogether. It believed that in 'certain circumstances relief may be afforded safely and even beneficially', but it was careful to specify what those conditions were. Broadly speaking the two guiding principles of the commission that were enshrined in the Act of 1834 were the workhouse test and 'less eligibility', in other words the abolition of outdoor relief and the threat of the workhouse were magic wands to abolish poverty and unemployment. These two simple principles were the theoretical foundation on which the administrative structure of the new Poor Law was built. They were deceptively simple even in relation to the society of their day. They were designed to deal with agricultural rather than industrial pauperism. The introduction of the new Poor Law was approved by Peel as much as by Melbourne.

Adapted from Asa Briggs, *The Age of Improvement*, 1967

ACTIVITY

Evaluating historical extracts

What does Extract 3 suggest are the reasons behind the introduction of a new Poor Law? To what extent was it designed to ease the discomfort of the poor and unemployed?

PRACTICE QUESTION (A Level)

Evaluating historical extracts

Using your understanding of the historical context, assess how convincing the arguments in Extracts 1, 2 and 3 are in relation to understanding the motives behind the Whig social reforms of the 1830s.

STUDY TIP

You must evaluate the arguments in each extract, commenting on the author's interpretation. To demonstrate your understanding of the historical context it could help to use the information on the Whig governments in Chapter 13.

KEY QUESTION

How was Britain governed and how did democracy and political organisations change and develop?

The Municipal Corporations Act 1835

Pressure for reform of municipal corporations came as a by-product of parliamentary reform. Before 1832 corporations played a key role in controlling the election of MPs. A Commission of Inquiry set up in 1833 to look into the state of municipal corporations found that corruption and abuse of the system existed in many boroughs. On the basis of the Commission's report, the Whig government legislated for a complete overhaul of local government. The secretary of the Commission was Radical Joseph Parkes, whose influence can be seen in the clean sweep of the legislation. Over 200 old corporations were dissolved and 179 municipal boroughs were set up to replace them. They were to be run by councils elected by local ratepayers and although this produced a wider franchise than the 1832 reform, the bulk were exempted. A system was set in place to end misuse of borough funds, which were to be held in a clearly defined account, any surplus of which was to be used for 'public benefit of the inhabitants and the improvement of the borough'. New borough boundaries were defined and the first municipal elections were held in 1838.

The Act gave the new councils powers to carry out certain improvements, but in reality they were held back by financial constraints, a desire to cap the rates bill, narrow-mindedness and the lack of vision of some of their members. In some instances, the former Improvement Commissioners retained their old powers to instigate change and this continued for several years. There was no central body, like the Poor Law Commission, to achieve uniform standards, with the result that essential improvements like drainage, cleansing and paving were non-existent in many towns. The rapid growth of towns meant that many councils were trying to operate beyond their level of competence. London was excluded from the reform because of its size and towns like Birmingham and Manchester were not incorporated until later. The Act defined the form of local authorities but did not ensure efficiency and professionalism.

Evaluation of Whig reforms

The Whig reforms were carried through with the cooperation and involvement of the liberal-minded aristocracy, commercial and manufacturing interests and leading middle-class professionals. These groups believed that they could afford to allow a measured amount of reform, yet maintain the integrity of the *status quo*, and that they could also be perceived as responding to pressure for change. The Whig reforms of the 1830s laid the foundations for further reforms in the key areas of education, factory reform, and welfare of the poor. They helped to confirm a held belief that slavery was abhorrent and to establish the idea that all individuals have human rights and a right to be treated decently.

ACTIVITY

Summary

Working in pairs create a *brief* summary chart of the Whig social and administrative reforms. Take each reform separately – which groups would regard the reforms as a success and which as a failure? Explain why. Your groups should include some the following: the Whig Government, the Tory opposition, the Radicals (remember some of them were factory owners), humanitarians and evangelicals, the working classes, the poor, the middle classes.

STUDY TIP

You will need to consider what the problems of industrial society from c1800 were and should evaluate how far the Whigs dealt with these problems. You should comment on and explain why some problems were not tackled and also assess the success of the measures that were introduced.

PRACTICE QUESTION

To what extent did the Whig reforms of the 1830s address the problems faced by society as a result of industrialisation since c1800?

15 Pressure for change

Chartism

EXTRACT 1

But what was Chartism in the first place? It had a loose definition that would sweep in all forms of popular protest – the anti-Poor Law movement, demonstrations against the new police forces, the revolutionary nationalism of the Newport Rising in South Wales (1839) and action by small tenant farmers against improving landlords in the Rebecca Riots 1839–42. The nature of Chartism varied from place to place and there were well over 1000 places showing at least some taint of it, as well as more than 120 local newspapers aligned to the cause. It would be unfair to blame the leaders for failing to unite a movement defined as broadly as this (even supposing a popular movement could be led like a political party anyway), yet alleged leadership failures have dominated historical interpretations. Feargus O'Connor's should be considered in a positive light.

Adapted from Boyd Hilton, *A Mad, Bad, and Dangerous People? England 1783–1846*, 2006

LEARNING OBJECTIVES

In this chapter you will learn about:

- Chartism
- Irish Radicalism
- the Anti-Poor Law League
- the Anti-Corn Law League
- social reform campaigners, including Shaftesbury and Chadwick.

KEY QUESTION

As you read this chapter, consider the following Key Questions:
- How was Britain governed and how did democracy and political organisations develop in Britain?
- How important were ideas and ideologies?
- How and with what results did society and social policy develop?
- How important was the role of individuals and groups and how were they affected by developments?

ACTIVITY

Evaluating historical extracts

What reasons are suggested in Extract 1 for the failure of the Chartist movement?

Causes of Chartism

The Chartist movement was an organisation formed in 1838 to support working-class political activity and to agitate for political reform that would extend the franchise to working men, involve them in government and give them a platform from which their grievances could be heard.

KEY CHRONOLOGY

1836	Formation of London Working Men's Association
1838	William Lovett's six-point People's Charter launched
1839	Chartists' first national petition rejected
1839	Newport Rising
1842	Second Chartist petition rejected and Plug Plot riots

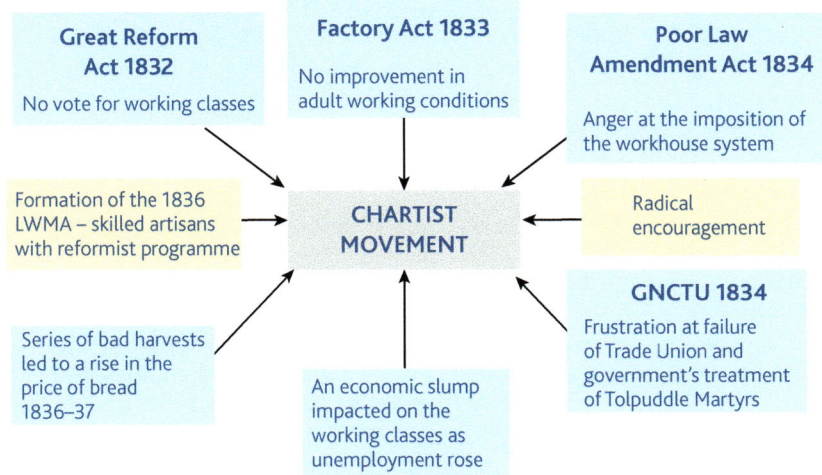

Fig. 1 *The working-class disappointments that led to the rise of the Chartist movement*

Chartist agitation arose out of the disillusionment of the working classes over government reforms that failed to improve their living conditions, working conditions or their political status. Their keenest disappointment was over the 1832 Reform Bill, which excluded them from the franchise. Secondly they felt resentment towards the new Poor Law, which humiliated them and increased their hardships. When the Poor Law Amendment Act finally began to operate in the northern industrial areas in around 1839, it became apparent to the

143

SECTION 3 | Political change and social reform, 1832–1846

CROSS-REFERENCE

The **Grand National Consolidated Trades Union (GNCTU)** is discussed in Chapter 18.

Richard Oastler's Key Profile is in Chapter 14, page 136.

A key profile of **Francis Place** (1771–1854) appears on page 66 and he is referenced in Chapter 12.

Thomas Attwood was instrumental in pressuring the Government to introduce the 1832 Reform Act (see Chapter 12, page 114).

KEY PROFILE

William Lovett (1800–1877), a London cabinet maker, represented the moderate face of Chartism. He resented the influence of the high-profile Chartist Fergus O'Connor. Lovett encouraged members towards self-improvement as a way of gaining official support for an extension of the franchise, but was sidelined within the movement. He believed in collaboration with middle-class supporters, who were alienated by Chartist extremists.

ACTIVITY

Working in pairs, make a note of the six points of the People's Charter and for each point explain why you think it was important to the un-enfranchised working classes.

---

working classes how politically powerless they were to improve their conditions. They were frustrated by the failure of Robert Owen's **Grand National Consolidated Trades Union**, in 1835, which ended hopes of labouring men organising themselves legally to negotiate better working conditions. The Factory Act had released their children from intolerable working hours, but had led to an increase in adult working hours. There were the usual economic downturns, coinciding with poor harvests in 1836–37, which fuelled further discontent. They were encouraged by middle-class supporters like John Fielden, **Richard Oastler** and other Radicals disenchanted with the limited nature of government reform, to organise themselves to fight for their political rights.

The London Working Men's Association was established in June 1836 with a reformist political programme. Two key figures were William Lovett, the secretary, and **Francis Place**. They listed their demands under six main headings – universal male suffrage, equal electoral districts, annual parliaments, payment of MPs, secret ballots in elections and no property qualifications for candidates. In 1838, **William Lovett** called the six points the 'People's Charter', and at a meeting in Birmingham endorsed by **Thomas Attwood**'s Birmingham Political Union, the Chartist Movement was established.

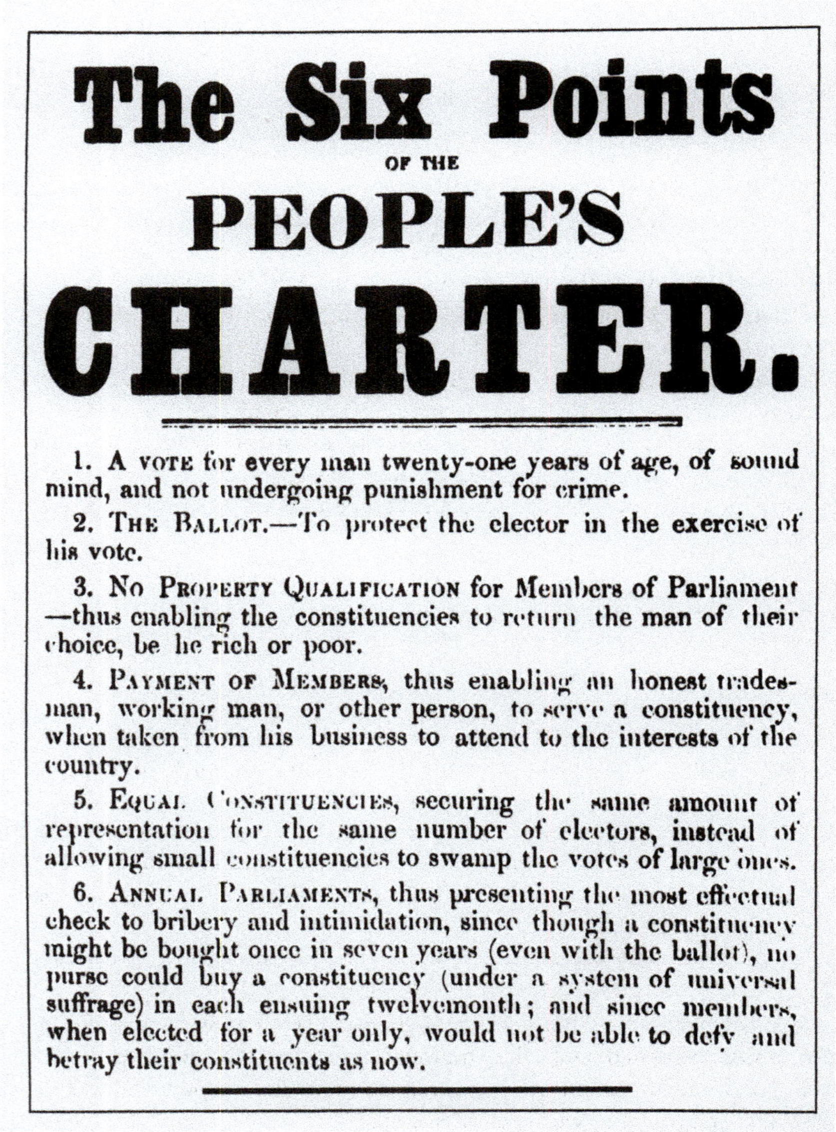

Fig. 2 *A Chartist handbill with a detailed description of the six points of the People's Charter*

Leadership issues and strategy

The composition of the Chartist movement was varied from the very beginning and drew support from several protest groups. It has been suggested that for a movement encompassing a variety of groups and aims, to have a single strong leadership was virtually impossible. There were considerable differences of opinion on how the Charter was to be achieved. Lovett represented the moderate view and advocated persuasion rather than force. He believed that education was vital in order to deal effectively with social and political problems. Thomas Attwood also followed the moderate line and advocated a strategy of petitioning Parliament as the likely method of success. In contrast to the moderates were the more extreme Chartists, who operated mainly in the smaller northern industrial towns that had suffered from miserable conditions since the end of the Napoleonic Wars. **Fergus O'Connor**, Editor of *Northern Star*, an influential Chartist newssheet published in Leeds, threatened to use physical force to achieve the Chartist demands.

The 1839 petition was the first unifying event of the Chartist movement. A Chartist Convention of 39 delegates met in London and drew up this People's Charter, articulating the six main demands. The petition, with its 1,280,000 signatures, was presented to Parliament in July but was overwhelmingly rejected by both Whigs and Tories.

The failure of the first petition

The rejection of the petition brought about the first real clash between the moderates and the so-called 'physical force' Chartists. O'Connor wanted to respond with threats of intimidation and violence, which disturbed the moderates. The Newport Rising in November 1839 confirmed middle-class fears about the movement. It was the moderate William Lovett who was singled out by the authorities and imprisoned for sedition and disorder, and this gave O'Connor an opportunity to promote his own aims and methods. By the beginning of 1840, however, there was an economic revival that sapped the movement's vitality. The working men who had been so vociferous in their support faded into the background once economic conditions improved and they had work, wages and food.

> **A CLOSER LOOK**
>
> ### The Newport Rising, 3 November 1839
>
> The rising at Newport, Monmouthshire in South Wales, stemmed from the discontent of the appalling working conditions in the coal mines and iron foundries there. The outcome was a disaster for the Chartists in the face of the Whig government's show of force. Hundreds of 'armed' Chartist supporters were beaten down by 30 armed soldiers and 24 Chartists were killed. Chartist leaders were imprisoned and the movement seemed to lose impetus.

By 1842, William Lovett had lost ground as leader of the movement and Feargus O'Connor had established himself as the popular leader. There was a slump in trade, wages fell and there was widespread unemployment and distress, which reignited working-class agitation.

> **ACTIVITY**
>
> ### Thinking point
>
> Can you suggest flaws in both the moderate and extreme Chartist approaches to achieving their aims? For example how would most MPs regard peaceful petitions for electoral change? How would they react to violence?

> **KEY PROFILE**
>
> **Feargus O'Connor (1796–1855)** came from an Irish protestant landed family. He had extraordinary talent and energy. He was a member of O'Connell's repeal party, but left Ireland and became involved in Radical campaigns in London. He roused support for Chartism in northern England and raised the profile of the movement to a national level through his newssheet, the Northern Star.

Fig. 3   *An attack by the Chartists on the Westgate Hotel, Newport*

CROSS-REFERENCE

There was a brief **Chartist revival** in 1847–48, stimulated by an economic downturn in 1847. This final episode in the Chartist movement, the causes of its decline and its legacy are addressed in Chapter 21.

ACTIVITY

Draw a flow chart to show the emergence of and developments in Chartism 1836–46.

The second petition

A new petition, supposedly signed by three million people, was ridiculed in Parliament and dismissed. A strike at Ashton-under-Lyne spread rapidly to other industrial towns, where the boiler plugs of steam engines were knocked out to prevent factories and other works from operating. The action, nicknamed the Plug Plot, was regarded by the authorities as subversive and conspiratorial, but it acted as a rallying call for the Chartist supporters. The Peel government, using the newly operational local police forces, dealt firmly and quickly with the unrest. O'Connor was said to have lost his nerve and denounced the strike in his *Northern Star*. There were many arrests and harsh sentences handed out, with the result that the Chartist activity faded.

Between 1842 and 1846 there was a period of economic recovery, a reduction in unemployment and a subsequent lessening of support for the Chartist movement. The circulation of the *Northern Star* fell as O'Connor's influence waned. Other organisations gained ground at the expense of the Chartists, particularly the Anti-Corn Law League and the trade unions. There was often apathy among the working class who did not see the connection between political reform and their conditions. Chartism was never again as strong as it had been in the 1830s. The Chartists seemed to lose a sense of direction and became involved in economic rather than political issues, such as O'Connor's National Land Cooperative Society, which ended in failure. The real problem for the Chartist movement was that the depression of the early 1840s was gradually giving way to a long period of prosperity. As a result, the working-class supporters again lost interest in the Chartist demands for political reform.

Irish Radicalism

Peel's problems with Ireland

The dissatisfaction felt by the Irish centred round the Church, the land (the economy was land-based and couldn't support a growing population) and their national identity and had rumbled on since the Act of Union in 1800. Attempts by successive governments to deal with Irish issues made matters worse, as British politicians lacked a basic understanding of the problems and lacked sympathy for the sufferings of the Irish people caused by famine. In 1842, Peel had indicated that he would pursue impartial policies in Ireland, in an attempt to get the Catholic population on side and to diffuse **Daniel O'Connell's** campaign for repeal. O'Connell was arrested at one of his **'monster' anti-Union meetings** at Clontarf in 1843. But he was a spent force and new young blood was taking up the cause of repeal.

Young Ireland

During the 1840s a new radical group 'Young Ireland' was formed with the aim of repealing the Union with Britain. There were sporadic outbreaks of violence culminating in a rising in 1848, which coincided with disturbances across Europe and with renewed Chartist agitation in Britain. The abortive rising was swiftly put down by the police and the deployment to Ireland of extra troops from mainland Britain. Yet this rising, although inept and idealistic, was **nationalist** in character and to some extent marks the start of a new era of troubles for the British government in Ireland and increasing demands from several sections of Irish society for political independence and **home rule** for Ireland.

The Anti-Poor Law League

In the aftermath of the passing of the Poor Law Amendment Act in 1834, there was a backlash of protest against the proposal to end outdoor relief and replace this with a uniform system of indoor relief, accessible through the workhouses. The tough conditions proposed for workhouse inmates – such as splitting up of families and hard labour – provoked an outcry from many sections of society and prompted an Anti-Poor Law movement. The principle of treating **'undeserving' poor** in this way was seen as unjust and immoral and the operation of the new law was regarded as oppressive and unequal. It gave the poor little chance to better their condition.

KEY CHRONOLOGY

1843 O'Connell arrested at monster meeting at Clontarf

1844 Young Ireland founded

1848 Abortive Young Ireland Rising

A CLOSER LOOK

Daniel O'Connell's meetings were referred to as 'monster' because of the number of attendees present: each was attended by around 100,000 people.

CROSS-REFERENCE

Daniel O'Connell and his influence within Parliament as leader of the Irish MPs is covered in Chapter 13. The content of the 1830s is examined in Chapter 8.

KEY TERM

nationalist: a person who strives for (in this case) the independence of their country from the domination of another

home rule: a desire held by many Irish to repeal the terms of the Act of Union passed in 1800, to establish a parliament in Dublin, from which they could control and be responsible for domestic affairs

KEY TERM

'undeserving' poor: nineteenth-century attitudes to the poor are reflected in the language used to describe them; the 'deserving' poor were those who found themselves enduring hardship through no fault of their own, while the 'undeserving' poor caused their poverty through laziness, wickedness or carelessness

Fig. 4 *The poor in a dust-yard, sifting through the dust; an illustration which featured in* London Labour and the London Poor *by Henry Mayhew, published in 1850*

Protests and rioting, however, immediately after the Act was passed, had little serious impact; they were mostly spontaneous and lacked direction and leadership.

It took a couple of years for parishes to organise themselves into unions with a single workhouse, as stipulated by the Act. In the intervening period the harvests had been good and there was a raised level of employment, with jobs available on the new railways. The numbers resorting to poor relief remained steady and in any case outdoor relief was still available, particularly in the industrial north. Most importantly there was a noticeable drop in the rates bill and this silenced some of the new Poor Law critics.

A recession in 1837 breathed new life into the Anti-Poor Law campaigners. The South Lancashire Anti-Poor Law Association was well-organised and worked closely with Radical reformer John Fielden, to support his motion for the immediate repeal of the Act. Public meetings were called in which claims were made about the abuses of the system. But within a short period the movement fizzled out. It faced competition from other protest groups, especially the Chartists, who had a stronger claim on a broader spectrum of the population. The Anti-Poor Law movement failed to monopolise public attention and support, but in any case the solid opposition to the Act in the northern towns and the impossibility of imposing a workhouse system in an area of dense population during recession led to a more flexible application of the Act. In 1842, Peel extended the 1834 Poor Law Amendment Act, with the unpopular 'less eligibility' clause still part of the strategy.

ACTIVITY

In spite of outrage against the new Poor Law, the Anti-Poor Law movement enjoyed little success. Discuss the reasons for its failure.

EXTRACT 2

The rise of Chartism did not begin to weaken resistance to the New Poor Law until the very end of 1838, but it had posed a serious challenge to the movement since the May of that year, when the Charter and the National Petition were published. Even before this there were signs of a revival of public interest in radical political reform. The Anti-Poor Law League, in common with other popular movements was unable even at its height to monopolise public attention and support. Of the issues kept alive during 1837 by far the most vital and popular was electoral reform. In the autumn, quite suddenly, there was a great increase in radical political activity in the north. Two separate and competing influences were involved. One was the arrival of representatives from the London Working Men's Association and the other was Feargus O'Connor's drive to establish himself firmly in a position of leadership in the north. All this could not have come at a worse time for the Anti-Poor Law movement.

Adapted from Nicholas C. Edsall, *The Anti-Poor Law Movement, 1834–44*, 1971

ACTIVITY

Evaluating historical extracts

According to Extract 2 why did the Anti-Poor Law League experience difficulty in establishing itself?

The Anti-Corn Law League

The Anti-Corn Law League, a nation-wide pressure group formed to persuade the Government to repeal the 1815 Corn Laws, was founded in 1838. Its leaders were **Richard Cobden** and **John Bright**, both owners of large northern textile factories. They were strongly supported by the manufacturing class who were able to finance the movement. It was a key point in their success that the finances were well-organised in order to create the steady income that was needed to pay for the type of campaign the League wanted to run. One of the objectives was to avoid the pitfalls of other pressure groups and so the leaders – respectable, middle-class, god-fearing men – chose to work through Parliament. In this way they avoided riots, strikes or any form of violence and they worked on gaining the support of the churches. They planned a tightly-orchestrated publicity campaign, so that every voter in Britain would receive pamphlets from the League through the new postal service. Maximising the new railway system, the League's key speakers were sent all over the country. They sought the support of the press to publicise and report on their activities. The campaign went as far as putting forward parliamentary candidates for election so that the League's case could be heard in Parliament.

The League put forward a range of arguments in its attempt to persuade the Government to repeal the Corn Laws. Its members argued that it was a myth that the Corn Laws protected the farmers – in fact they protected inefficient farmers. They also argued that cheaper bread would remove the argument for wage increases and this would help keep other prices steady. Free Traders, like Bright, argued that the Corn Laws went against Government policy of laissez faire.

There were plenty of counter-arguments from landowners and farmers. Agriculture was still the biggest employer in the country, in spite of industrialisation, and repeal would damage the farming economy and cause widespread unemployment.

EXTRACT 3

Nothing which the League did in its first years from 1838 to 1840 proved effective. However, in early 1841, it turned to active involvement in electoral politics. The League's financial backing, much of it coming directly from industrialists, was much greater than that of the Chartists. In addition the League had much more effective parliamentary spokesmen than the Chartists ever had, especially after Richard Cobden's election for Stockport in 1841. Even so the actual power of the League in the context of early Victorian Britain remained meagre, although like the Chartists it was capable of making a great deal of noise. The number of constituencies amenable to the League's manipulation remained small in relation to the massed ranks of Conservatives and Whig MPs. Neither of the great radical agitations, the Chartists and the Anti-Corn Law League, came even reasonably close to the exercise of effective power.

Adapted from Norman McCord & Bill Purdue, *British History, 1815–1914*, 2007

ACTIVITY

Evaluating historical extracts

According to Extract 3 in what respects was the Anti-Corn Law League more successful than the Chartists? What conclusions can you draw about both movements?

KEY PROFILE

Richard Cobden (1804–1865), son of a Sussex yeoman, built up a successful calico-printing business in Manchester. He was a great believer in Free Trade and was an early member of the Anti-Corn Law Association formed in Manchester in 1838. He persuaded the League to pursue a single policy. He and John Bright campaigned across the country travelling by train. His great organisational skills contributed to the League's success.

John Bright (1811–1889), a Rochdale factory owner who met Cobden over their shared interest in improving educational provision, teamed up to organise the campaign for the repeal of the Corn Laws. Bright argued that rural labourers were worse off than factory workers. After his wife's premature death in 1841, he threw himself into raising the profile of the Anti-Corn Law League to a national level. He was an inspirational orator.

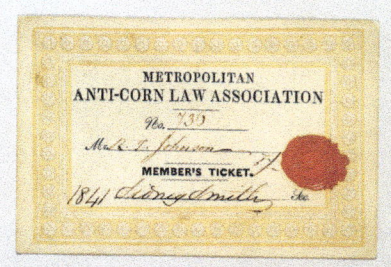
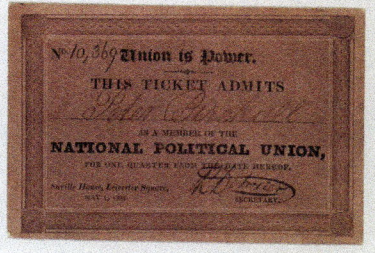

Fig. 5 *A member's ticket for the Anti-Corn Law Association, 1841*

CROSS-REFERENCE

The passing of the **Corn Law** in 1815 is the subject of Chapter 7; it raised the price of bread – the staple diet of the labouring poor – and remained an unpopular policy.

> **ACTIVITY**
>
> The arguments of the Anti-Corn Law League were designed to appeal to a range of groups and individuals. Which of their arguments might appeal to each of the following:
> - the poor
> - the factory owners
> - the farmers
> - the Government?
>
> Explain your answers.

> **CROSS-REFERENCE**
>
> There is more about the **Irish famine** in Chapter 17.

The success of the Anti-Corn Law League

The Anti-Corn Law League distinguished itself from the Chartists by sticking to one simple demand, which it could demonstrate had support from a variety of political and social groups. Although the Anti-Corn Law League was a well-organised and a well-financed body with widespread support, the fight to repeal the Corn Laws seemed an uphill struggle. The Conservative Government, with Peel as Prime Minister, had been elected in 1841 on a mandate to keep the Corn Laws. Peel had compromised and reduced the sliding-scale on imported wheat, but was not prepared to go further. In the end it was the overwhelming disaster of the Irish famine that convinced Peel that the Corn Laws had to be repealed.

Social reform campaigners, including Shaftesbury and Chadwick

Philanthropic activity increased during the second quarter of the nineteenth century. It was partly a response to the extraordinary level of economic and social change brought about by industrialisation, the growth in population and the spread of new urban centres, all of which brought untested social problems. It was also an indication of changing social attitudes. It was not, however, regarded as the official role of the state to accept responsibility for the welfare of its people and in the absence of government commitment to deal with social problems, individuals and groups came forward to offer possible solutions. The result was a growing philanthropic movement. Within this movement there were a number of outstanding individuals committed to social reform, among them Lord Shaftesbury, who made it their life's work to fight for social justice and more humane living and working conditions for the labouring poor.

The real impetus to tackle social problems came after the first Parliamentary Reform of 1832, although the leading social reformers of the day, like Ashley and Edwin Chadwick, opposed political reform. Parliament was still predominantly run by men of substantial wealth, although after 1832 these included a small intake of middle-class men, among them Radicals like John Fielden, a social reformer and benefactor.

The dominant spirit that lay behind much of the impetus for social reform was that of **Jeremy Bentham**, who died in 1832 but whose influence continued throughout the nineteenth century. The Benthamite mindset was that clinging on to the old ways of doing things just because it was the tradition was not a valid justification; institutions must be useful and have a purpose.

> **CROSS-REFERENCE**
>
> **Bentham's** influence is discussed in Chapters 6, 12 and 13.

> **CROSS-REFERENCE**
>
> **Edwin Chadwick** is mentioned in more detail in connection with Poor Law Reform in Chapter 14 and Public Health in Chapters 16, 18 and 21.

Edwin Chadwick (1800–1890)

Bentham's ideas guided Edwin Chadwick in advising on Poor Law reform and although Chadwick had a genuine concern for the welfare of the poor, his application of the 'usefulness test' did not take into account the feelings of individuals. As a member of the Commission of Inquiry into factory conditions, it was his innovative thinking that led to the recommendation of an eight-hour working day for children, as a compromise to appease factory owners and reformers (and perhaps his own social conscience). In 1842, his *Report on the Sanitary Condition of the Labouring Population of Great Britain* exposed the squalid, unhygienic conditions in Britain's towns and cities and it became the blueprint for improved sanitation and eventually a proper drainage system in every community.

The Earl of Shaftesbury (1801–1885)

Lord Shaftesbury, styled Lord Ashley in his father's lifetime, was the foremost social reformer of the nineteenth century. As a young man he was ambitious for a career in politics, but early on developed a keen sense of philanthropy. At this time the introduction of any social measures depended upon the initiative of philanthropists and experts. Ashley entered Parliament in 1826 as a Tory, but, in 1833, after he took over as leader of the parliamentary campaign for the Ten Hour Movement, his focus rested on achieving measures of social reform rather than political advancement. He had a strong social conscience and was determined to bring to public attention the social evils of the day. A Commission on the Employment of Children in Mines recommended an end to the employment underground of women and children. It was Ashley's persistence that got the reform through Parliament. Ashley argued passionately for a Ten Hour Bill and would have succeeded but for the Government's sleight of hand over the subsequent 1844 Factory Act, which established the maximum working hours for women of 12 hours. It was, however, a major step forward as it established the precedent of government intervention in the working hours of adults. Ashley finally got his Ten Hour Bill in 1847 with support from Whigs and Tory Protectionists, who were angry with Peel over the repeal of the Corn Laws.

Shaftesbury was an evangelical and public duty was part of his religious belief. Running parallel to this was a growing conviction among the middle and upper classes that it was their Christian duty to help those less fortunate than themselves. There were, however, moral judgements made. Charity did not stretch to the 'undeserving poor' and help was always more readily given to those who were prepared to help themselves.

> **CROSS-REFERENCE**
>
> A Key Profile of **Anthony Ashley Cooper**, later known as **Lord Shaftesbury**, can be found in Chapter 14.

A CLOSER LOOK

Children in mines

The Mines Act 1842 made it illegal for boys under 10 and all women and girls to work underground, and made provision for government inspectors. The Factory Act 1844 set a maximum 6.5 hour working day for children between 9 and 13, and 12 hours a day for women. The Registration of Births, Deaths and Marriages Act (1836) could be applied to verify a child's age.

Fig. 6 *Two boys in a pit, one pushing a truck loaded with coal, in the mid-1800s*

ACTIVITY

Extension

The literature of the early Victorian period reflects the attitudes of contemporaries to the gulf between rich and poor. Try to read some of the works of Charles Dickens, Mrs Gaskell or Charles Kingsley, all of whom wrote novels incorporating the social problems of the day.

John Fielden (1784–1849)

Fielden's contribution to social reform is often overshadowed by more prominent figures like Ashley. Fielden was born into a respectable, Lancashire Quaker family, with a hard-work ethic. As an adult he took over his father's small cotton mill and made it into one of the largest cotton manufacturing businesses in the country. His success did not compromise his principles. He was deeply religious and became a Unitarian and used his wealth to benefit the poor. He supported several social, egalitarian causes: he argued for male suffrage and early on supported the Chartist movement; he was hostile to the Poor Law reform, believing it would depress the manufacturing industry, and supported resistance to its introduction in the industrial north. His foremost interest was factory reform and he argued for shorter working hours on the basis that it would benefit owners and workers. He admired and supported Ashley, assisting the passage of the Ten Hour Act in 1847.

ACTIVITY

Summary

As a member of Peel's government how would you justify your response to the demands of each of the pressure groups? Groups should prepare a response for different organisations.

 PRACTICE QUESTION

To what extent were those who pressed for political and social change more successful in the years 1832 to 1846 than they had been in the years 1812 to 1832?

STUDY TIP

Look back at Chapter 11 and make notes on groups and individuals who sought political and social change between 1812 and 1832. Think about the political atmosphere at that time and how and why the Government responded to political pressure.

STUDY TIP

You will need to read each extract carefully and give the overall argument of each author, as well as considering any subsidiary arguments. You should assess 'how convincing' these arguments are by applying your own knowledge of the historical context.

 PRACTICE QUESTION

Evaluating historical extracts

Using your understanding of the historical context, assess how convincing the arguments in Extracts 1, 2 and 3 are in explaining the difficulties experienced by groups pressing for change.

16 The Conservative response to change

EXTRACT 1

Looking back on the years from 1841 to 1846, **William Gladstone** told Peel that Peel had exercised more personal authority than any Prime Minister since Pitt. There was much truth in this. Peel introduced the eventful budgets of 1842 and 1845, not his Chancellor, Henry Goulburn. It was Peel who single-handedly determined strategy in Ireland. Such sense of purpose and mastery of business could be intimidating. The key to Peel's dominance was his clarity of vision, and the key to that was an increasingly determined approach to policy-making. If he appeared to change his mind it was because he had avoided making his intentions clear for tactical reasons. Thus almost immediately on taking office in 1841 he wrote to his Cabinet colleagues on issues such as taxation, the Corn Laws and Ireland. These letters put forward the possibilities and invited responses, so that Peel appeared to be seeking advice, but their tone was deceptive. He knew exactly what needed to be done, and was actually seeking to persuade men rather than wanting their opinions.

Adapted from Boyd Hilton, *A Mad, Bad, and Dangerous People? England 1783–1846*, 2006

Finance, administration and the economy

There is some debate over Peel's motivation during his ministry of 1841–46 and particularly in his last Act during that ministry – the repeal of the Corn Laws. There is, however, little doubt that an impressive range of Peelite legislation helped respond to economic and social changes, paving the way for the period of mid-Victorian stability and prosperity.

Fig. 1 *Sir Robert Peel, in the House of Commons, 1845*

LEARNING OBJECTIVES

In this chapter you will learn about:

- finance, administration and the economy
- the Bank Charter Act
- trade and business reform.

KEY QUESTION

As you read this chapter, consider the following Key Questions:

- What pressures did governments face and how did they respond to these?
- How and with what results did the economy develop and change?
- How important was the role of individuals and groups and how were they affected by developments?

ACTIVITY

Evaluating historical extracts

What view of Peel is articulated by Boyd Hilton in Extract 1? What evidence does he offer to support his view? When you have worked through this chapter you should be able to make a comment on the extent to which you agree or disagree with Hilton's assessment of Peel.

KEY PROFILE

William Ewart Gladstone (1809–98), the son of a wealthy Liverpool shipping merchant, was incredibly clever. He became Tory MP for Newark in 1832. Peel offered Gladstone the Board of Trade when he wanted Ireland, but he served Peel well in that capacity. An admirer of Peel he called him, 'my great teacher and master in public affairs'. When the Conservative Party split in 1846, he stayed with the Peelites. He became Liberal Prime Minister in 1868 and served four terms in office.

KEY CHRONOLOGY

1841 Conservatives win general election, with Peel as Prime Minister

1842 Budget introduces peacetime income tax

1842 Mines Act prohibits underground employment for women and children

1843 The Devon Commission

1844 Factory Act shortens working hours in textile factories

1844 Bank Charter Act

1844 The Joint Stock Companies Act

1845 Budget abolishes duties on raw materials

1845 Maynooth Grant increased

1845 Start of Irish Famine

1846 Repeal of Corn Laws

CROSS-REFERENCE

William Gladstone's Key Profile is on page 153.

Read about **Lord Stanley's** and **Sir James Graham's** earlier careers with the Whigs in Chapter 13, pages 125 and 129.

Peel and the Conservatives in government 1841–1846

The Conservatives under Peel won a majority of 76 seats in the 1841 general election. The country was in the midst of an economic slump. The previous Whig government had failed to balance the books and had left a budget deficit. The Conservatives were deeply divided over their attitude towards change and reform, but entered government when there was considerable dissatisfaction among the population with living and working conditions, referred to as the Condition of England question. The election results show that the Conservatives were least successful in winning seats in the large industrial boroughs and that most of their support still came from the small English market towns and the counties. Most Conservative MPs retained a traditional outlook and a satisfaction with the *status quo*. They were Anglican and Protectionist and did not want change. For Peel, the answer to the country's problems lay in reviving the economy and achieving national prosperity. His main focus was to stabilise government finances, stimulate trade and industry and thus lower the cost of living, unemployment and ultimately discontent and distress.

The cabinet

Peel's Cabinet had a fair assortment of talent. It included **William Gladstone**, **Lord Stanley** and Lord Aberdeen, all of whom were future prime ministers. Henry Goulburn, who could be relied on to carry out Pitt's policies, was Chancellor of the Exchequer; **Sir James Graham**, a competent administrator and close ally of Peel, was at the Home Office. The Duke of Buckingham, an old-fashioned protectionist Tory, was made Lord Privy Seal, but his main purpose was probably to satisfy the agricultural interest. Peel appointed Gladstone as President of the Board of Trade in 1843. There was a great deal of mutual respect between Peel and Gladstone, who said of Peel that he was 'the best man of business who was ever Prime Minister'. Gladstone and a group of other young Tories saw Peel as helpful and sympathetic towards them and not cold and aloof as he is most often portrayed. Stanley (a former Whig) quarrelled with Peel over the repeal of the Corn Laws and resigned in 1845.

Reaction to the new government

After the election, the political diarist Charles Greville wrote in his journal 'there was a general feeling of satisfaction by the substitution of a real working government for the last batch [the Whigs]'. Peel's priorities were to improve on the way in which the Whigs had conducted government, to carry through practical reforms and to create a strong government.

Peel's objectives

Peel made clear his intention of exercising his 'personal authority' from the start of his ministry: 'If I exercise power it shall be upon my view – perhaps imperfect, perhaps mistaken – but my sincere view of public duty'. In the same speech he also acknowledged that his position placed on him 'obligations', 'duties' and if necessary 'sacrifices' that he must have to make in the national interest. Peel expected his party to do the same. His interest was in efficiency and progress. Peel's first objective was to concentrate on economic and fiscal reforms.

Financial reform

EXTRACT 2

> At the heart of Peel's policy was the conviction that the only way to overcome both the human misery and the social threat was to increase the purchasing power of the masses. Poor Law, charity, schemes for encouraging emigration, were of only limited use. Steady employment and cheap food were the only

permanent remedies. They were remedies moreover that would benefit all classes. In Peel's words, 'We must make this a cheap country for living.' In this he was, ironically enough, on common ground with some of the more intelligent Chartists. For Peel, there were more ways of helping the poor than Ashley or Oastler were prepared to consider. Peel's obsession with tariffs and finance had its human and social side. Indeed among all the remedies for the Condition of England problem, the broad economic road along which he was leading the country offered perhaps the most immediate, practical and comprehensive way out from the country's miseries which any government in 1842 could have.

Adapted from Norman Gash, *Sir Robert Peel, The Life of Sir Robert Peel after 1830*, 1972

ACTIVITY

According to Extract 2 what were remedies for 'human misery and the social threat'? Why?

In the 1842 budget Peel 'knew exactly what needed to be done'. Pressure was coming at the Government from all sides. There was misery and hardship because of the most recent economic downturn in 1841; exports had fallen, causing a slump in the market, and poor harvests made bread prices unsteady. In response the Chartists revitalised their campaign inciting further unrest and violence. Peel introduced income tax, cut tariffs and lowered the 1828 Corn Law 'sliding scale'. It was the first time income tax had been raised in peacetime and although it was presented as a 'temporary measure', to deal with the inherited debt from the Whigs, it was here to stay. Boyd Hilton points out that Peel had acknowledged as early as 1830 that it was a means of tapping the wealth of 'great capitalists' to reconcile class antagonism and to commute 'taxes bearing on the industry and comforts of the labouring poor'.

People earning more than £150 a year had to pay 7 pence on each £1 they earned, which at about 3 per cent was a very small portion of their income, but was designed to exclude any of the working class. Peel calculated that income tax would raise £4 million which would clear the deficit of £2.5 million and leave a surplus of £1.5 million. He also reckoned that his policy of cutting tariffs would stimulate the economy to such an extent that it would cancel out any fall in government revenue.

The reduction of import duties was in line with the free trade policies earlier adopted by Pitt and Huskisson, but ignored by the Whigs after 1832. It would mean lower prices for finished goods and, as Peel anticipated an increased demand for those cheaper goods, it would bring about a higher level of employment because more people were required to make the goods, therefore giving an overall boost to the economy.

In 1845, a confident Peel introduced further free trade measures. Income tax was renewed for a further three years and was responsible for bringing in about ten per cent of government income. Duties on raw cotton and most other raw materials were abolished. Duties on imported sugar, much of it from the British colonies, was reduced. After the 1845 budget only a ten per cent duty on manufactured goods remained and Britain was almost a free-trading country.

The success of Peel's budgets was due in some considerable measure to 'his clarity of vision' and his 'doctrinaire approach' which ensured that he formulated and introduced his own budgets.

ACTIVITY

1. Use the information on Peel's financial reform to create a chart showing the key dates and changes.
2. Look at the diagram in Fig. 2. Do you agree that Peel's 'vision for economic policy' released the pressure on his government? Explain your answer.
3. What social benefits might occur as a result of Peel's policy of cutting import duties?

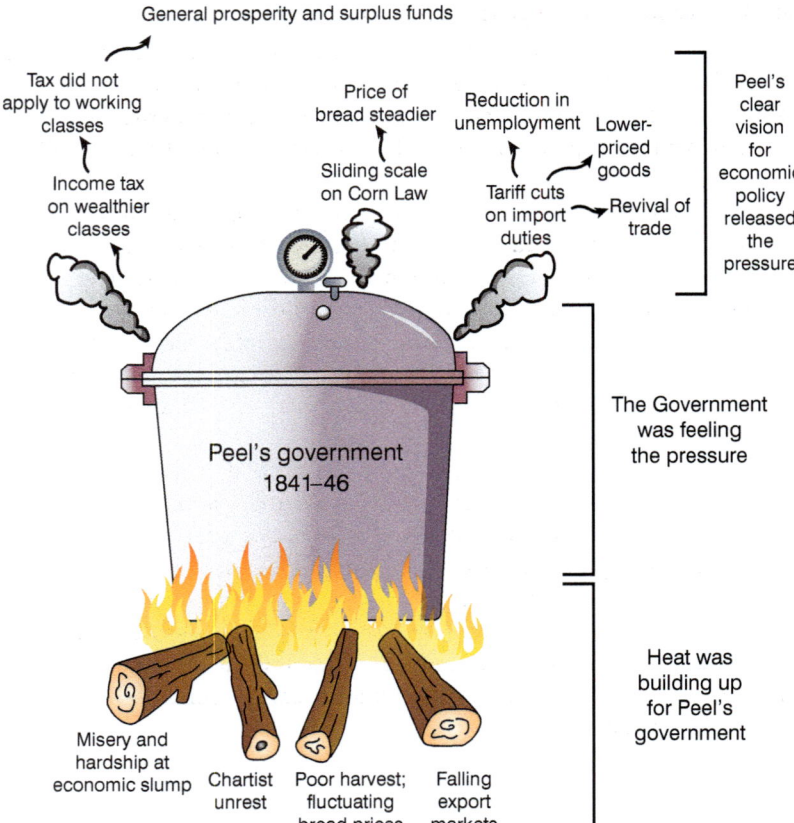

Fig. 2 *The causes and effects of Peel's economic policy*

Administration and legislation

Sir James Graham at the Home Office and William Gladstone at the Board of Trade set a new tone for meticulous attention to detail in administering their respective departments and brought a new level of efficiency into government. Royal Commissions of Inquiry reported on social and economic issues of the day. An impressive amount of legislation was drawn up and passed by Parliament. The Poor Law Amendment Act of 1834 was extended for five years. It prompted **Chadwick**'s report on the *Sanitary Conditions of the Labouring Classes* in 1842, although public health reform was not introduced until after Peel in 1848. The Government responded in part to calls for reforms in the coal mining industry and the textile factories. The acts addressed the worst abuses of children's working hours and of women and children working underground as well as extending state intervention in the labour market. The attempt in 1843 by Graham to introduce compulsory education for two hours a day for factory children was rejected over arguments as to which religious denomination would provide the schooling.

Economic reforms were passed to 'regulate the legal and institutional framework of business without controlling or supervising it' (Briggs). District bankruptcy courts were established to deal with local cases and imprisonment for small debtors was ended. A uniform system of district county courts was established. These and other minor changes increased the efficiency of the administration of justice. As administrative procedures were improved across a number of key institutions more salaried positions were created to carry them out. They were no longer comfortable positions for sons of the upper classes.

CROSS-REFERENCE

See pages 136 and 150 for information on **Edwin Chadwick**.

Peel and the Conservative response to Irish problems

Daniel O'Connell's final bid to achieve the repeal of the Act of Union was met with a firm response from Peel and ended in O'Connell's arrest and imprisonment. It allowed Peel to adopt a policy of concession in the hope that he would win the support of at least the educated section of the Catholic population.

He proposed to increase an annual grant to Maynooth, the Catholic College where priests received their training, believing this would gain the loyalty from the Catholic Church and some of the peasantry, who were under their influence. It was fiercely opposed by Anglicans, Nonconformists and a large number of Conservative MPs, all outraged at the implication of support for the Catholic Church over the Established Church in Ireland. The measure divided the Conservatives and was passed with Whig support.

Peel's policy created divisions within his own Party and made further reform difficult. The few concessions he did make failed to address Ireland's serious economic problems and the ongoing poverty of a large percentage of the population. The report of the Devon Commission, instigated in 1843 to look into the problems of land tenure, reported in 1845, too late for Peel to act on its recommendations. In autumn 1845, the potato crop – the staple diet of the Irish peasant – was destroyed by blight. Within weeks the people were starving. Peel felt he had little alternative but to repeal the Corn Law and allow cheap grain into Ireland.

> **CROSS-REFERENCE**
>
> The economic impact of the **Irish Famine** is considered in the next chapter.

The Bank Charter Act, 1844

Peel's objective in securing the Bank Charter Act was 'to inspire just confidence in the medium of exchange' and to ensure that the issuing of bank notes related to the volume of gold reserves held by the Bank of England, in other words to curb the over-issue of bank notes, which were the cause of 'continuing financial instability' (Mathias). The reform was passed against a background of years of discussion and argument among politicians, financiers and 'experts' into how to make the banking system stable, secure and dependable. The Act confirmed that the Bank of England was able to issue notes with a face value in place of cash, but any notes issue over £14 million had to be supported by gold bullion reserves. The rights of other banks to issue notes was strictly limited in an attempt to give the Bank of England a monopoly of issue, though there were several banks in Scotland that retained the right, such as the Bank of Scotland and the Royal Bank of Scotland. The Act divided the operations of the bank into two – one to issue notes and one to deal with day-to-day banking issues. There was to be weekly publication of accounts.

The Act was partly to meet the requirements of expanding industry, in which larger businesses required larger loans that small banks could not provide. Many amalgamated and then by the terms of the Bank Charter Act lost their right to issue notes. Gradually the Bank of England notes became the normal currency (apart from Scottish bank notes, which are still current). During the period of readjustment, a cheque system developed, enabling business to be carried on without exchange of either notes or cash.

The Bank Charter Act was one of Peel's most important pieces of legislation and remained in place until the First World War. It also had wider significance in that it marked the beginning of the Bank of England's role as administrator of the Government's monetary policy and injected a greater degree of confidence into the economy.

Fig. 3 *The Bank of England and Royal Exchange, City of London, c1845*

The success of Peel's Bank Charter Act was crucial to the rest of his economic policy. The powerful economic interests in Britain – and cotton was probably the most important – depended on a sound currency and a successful international trade. If stakeholders knew that the currency was backed up by gold, which formed the foundations of credit, they would be confident that bank notes issued would be worth their face value as they were supported by a valuable commodity. Investors could be reassured that the new system would deter reckless speculators and boost industry.

Trade and Business Reform

In 1844, the Report of the Select Committee on **Joint Stock Companies** commented that 'for years the world had been at the mercy of anyone who chose to publish an advertisement, call himself a company, and receive money for assurances and annuities'. There were few controls in place to limit fraudulent practice or to curb risky speculation of investors' money. There was an absence of proper accounting. The Joint Stock Companies Act of 1844 introduced measures to regulate company finance. A salaried Registrar of Companies was appointed and it became obligatory for any company with more than 25 members and transferable shares to be on the new Companies' Register. Every registered company had to produce regularly audited balance sheets. The Act could not wipe out all malpractice but it was an important step in the right direction.

Companies formed by a special Act of Parliament were exempted from this legislation, for example the railway companies, who were experiencing a boom at this time and whose directors were making huge fortunes. Determined attempts by Gladstone, at the Board of Trade, to bring in legislation to control these companies were rebuffed because of the strong vested interests in Parliament. The majority of MPs held shares in railway companies and around 90 of them were company directors.

Gladstone had already had a hand in strengthening legislation that regulated the day to day management and running of the railways. An

> **ACTIVITY**
>
> **Thinking point**
>
> What was the importance of Peel's Bank Charter Act and why was it crucial to the rest of his economic policy?

> **KEY TERM**
>
> **Joint Stock Company:** a company or business enterprise with a stated purpose (usually to make money); capital is raised and divided into a number of units, held by different owners/shareholders

> **CROSS-REFERENCE**
>
> The development of the railways forms part of Chapter 17.

Act of Parliament in 1840, which set up the Board of Trade Railway Department, was extended and allowed for the inspection of railways by paid officials.

Fig. 4 *Bristol Railway Station, 1840*

One of the serious economic problems facing Peel when he came to power was the slump in trade. Exports had fallen sharply, causing a recession in industry. Peel's financial reforms detailed above were successful in reviving trade and industry. The removal of duties from raw materials gave factories and businesses a 'kick start' and the reduction of export duties got trade moving again. As unemployment fell and food (except for bread) was cheaper, Britain was on the road to a better standard of living for many of the population.

EXTRACT 3

In essence, Peel was an expert who devoted his political career to developing professional expertise in discharging efficient executive government. The benefits of this are clear. Like Pitt half a century earlier, he got things done. His legislative record is second to none in nineteenth-century politics. He dominated the House of Commons not by natural oratory and certainly not by flattery. He just knew more about the subject under discussion than almost anybody else in the House. He invariably mastered his brief. The negative aspects of 'expertism', however, are worth stressing. They include intolerance, aloofness and arrogance. Peel was consistently criticised for all three vices during a long career which was for much of its span extremely controversial. He was also surprisingly sensitive to criticism and too readily looked for personal rather than political or intellectual reasons to explain it. Like many experts, also, Peel lacked political sensitivity.

Adapted from Eric J. Evans, *Sir Robert Peel, Statesmanship, Power and Party*, 2006

ACTIVITY

Evaluating historical extracts

From reading Extract 3 what impression do you form of Peel (a) as a character and (b) as a politician? of Peel:

a) as a character?
b) as a politician?

SECTION 3 | Political change and social reform, 1832–1846

ACTIVITY

Summary

Peel was concerned with solving Britain's problems through reviving the economy and achieving national prosperity. His main focus was to stabilise government finances, stimulate trade and industry and thus lower the cost of living, unemployment and ultimately discontent and distress.

Working in groups of three, each take a heading: the working classes; industrialists and merchants; farmers and landowners. Summarise how each of these groups benefited from Peel's reforms. Share your findings. Which group benefited most? Explain your answer.

STUDY TIP

In preparation for the Practice Question or extracts, it would be a good idea to note the line of argument in each extract as a preliminary to answering the question.

PRACTICE QUESTION

Evaluating historical extracts

Using your understanding of the historical context, assess how convincing the arguments in Extracts 1, 2 and 3 are in relation to Sir Robert Peel.

STUDY TIP

Quotation questions are asking you to weigh up the evidence for and against the statement – did he or did he not respond to 'the challenges of his age by adapting his policies'? This poses the question, what *were* the challenges of his age? First identify these, then look at his policies. Try to find evidence that he adapted his policies.

PRACTICE QUESTION

Peel responded to the challenges of his age 'by adapting his policies in the light of reasoned argument and practical necessity' (Gaunt).
Assess the validity of this view of Peel's term as Prime Minister of a Conservative government from 1841 to 1846.

17 Economic developments

EXTRACT 1

The economic impact of the railways as a stimulus to the economy cannot be measured by their direct effects only in creating demands for coal, iron and construction materials, and in generating flows of wages. Coal used in every day consumption by railways for **steam raising**, for example, was less than two per cent of national production. Higher demands were made indirectly through the use of coal in metal production and brick production destined for railway contracts. Less directly still, the railways were instrumental in encouraging urban growth and industrial expansion that did not necessarily have direct links with inputs to railway construction, through their effects as a service to the economy generally. They enabled economic activity in all other sectors of the economy to expand. They were also one of the main breeding grounds for the variety of new engineering skills that modernisation of the economy required on an ever-increasing scale. The capital market was also helped.

Peter Mathias, *The First Industrial Nation, an Economic History of Britain, 1700–1914*, 1972

The railway 'revolution' and associated economic growth

The railways had become one of the most important industries in Britain by the 1840s. There was a whole range of fast-growing industries, services and technologies associated with the development of the railway. As well as creating an extra demand for coal and iron to build and run the trains, there were many more indirect 'spin-offs' of railway development that boosted the economy.

Fig. 1 *The inauguration of the Canterbury to Whitstable line, 1830*

The opening of the Liverpool to Manchester line in September 1830 marked the start of rapid railway building in Britain. Its immediate success encouraged other entrepreneurs. There was a vision that a railway system would work on a large, national scale and that it would endure for the longer term. It demonstrates an underlying confidence in the stability of the economy, as it required a huge commitment from investors. Railway development improved the country's infrastructure and dramatically altered the landscape. The feats of engineering required to mould the landscapes to enable the railways to be built still seem impressive today.

LEARNING OBJECTIVES

In this chapter you will learn about:

- the railway 'revolution' and associated economic growth
- agricultural developments
- the repeal of the Corn Laws.

KEY QUESTION

As you read this chapter, consider the following Key Questions:
- How and with what results did the economy develop and change?
- How important was the role of individuals and groups and how were they affected by developments?

KEY TERM

steam raising: the expression used when an engine boiler is stoked up sufficiently to raise a head of steam to make the locomotive run

ACTIVITY

Evaluating historical extracts

In Extract 1 what importance does Peter Mathias give to the development of the railways in economic terms? What examples does he give to back up his argument?

A CLOSER LOOK

The early growth of the railway is the subject of Chapter 9. The opening of the Stockton to Darlington line in 1825 was an important milestone in the early growth of the railway industry. It was the practice run for what was to be known as 'the Railway Age'. The main development of the railway system took place between 1830 and 1850 and was of paramount importance in speeding up the rate of the industrialisation of Britain.

Fig. 2 *Clifton Suspension Bridge in Bristol, designed by Isambard Kingdom Brunel*

Exceptional engineering

There were several outstanding engineers involved in the design and construction of the railway network. George and **Robert Stephenson** and **Isambard Kingdom Brunel** are probably the best known. Robert Stephenson helped his father, George, design the *Rocket*, the first locomotive on the Liverpool to Manchester line, and in 1837 he was appointed Chief Engineer of the London to Birmingham railway. Brunel's career mirrored that of Stephenson's, his equal in genius; he became Chief Engineer of the Great Western Railway and designed the highly-acclaimed London to Bristol line, with its mile-long Box Tunnel.

The early nineteenth century saw the development of professions. Engineering developed hand-in-hand with industrial progress. Engineers applied new technology in the building of railway lines, tunnels, bridges, cuttings, viaducts, locomotives and engines. In 1818 the Institute of Civil Engineers was formed and this helped to shape the development of the profession of engineering. The railway engineers like Stephenson and Brunel, in turn, brought prestige and wealth to the Institute.

Railway development meant there was an increased use of powered machinery and new opportunities for mechanical engineers, and this had a positive effect on the economy.

The Railway Mania of the 1840s

Much of the planning for the railway network took place during the 1830s, but there was always a 'time lag' (McCord) before the railways were actually built – there were investors such as **George Hudson** to be found, subscriptions to be raised, surveys of the proposed route to be carried out, public meetings to be held for affected parties to air their views, and Acts of Parliament to be passed. For example in 1836, 1000 miles of track were planned, but they were not completed until 1841. The initial financial outlay was considerable. By the 1840s, however, many of the lines were operating at a profit and this sparked a mad scramble to construct railways in every corner of the land. This uncontrolled speculation was a boost to the economy, but was a disaster for many investors. McCord and Purdue sum it up as follows: 'It illustrates one of the cycles that mark modern economies: a new invention, far-sighted pioneers, over-optimistic speculators,

KEY PROFILE

Robert Stephenson (1801–1859) was an engineering genius, especially with locomotives. Part of his success was due to the hard work ethic gleaned from his father and his attention to detail. He apparently walked the length of the route on the London to Birmingham line fifteen times while it was under construction. He constructed some magnificent railway bridges, the high-level bridge across the Tyne at Newcastle and the Royal Border Bridge at Berwick-upon-Tweed being among his best.

Isambard Kingdom Brunel (1806–1859) was an engineering pioneer. He epitomised the energy and achievements of the early Victorians in that he was exceptionally gifted, but also worked hard. He designed the Clifton Suspension Bridge in Bristol and the Albert Bridge across the Tamar in Devon. He turned his attention seawards and designed *The Great Western,* the first steam ship purpose-built for crossing the Atlantic.

devious entrepreneurs like **George Hudson** (whose railway companies were based on very creative accounting), a crash, [but] in the long term tangible gains.'

The volume of traffic on the railways rose with the development of new lines. By the early 1840s there were 200 different railway companies. This created a situation where a passenger or a consignment of goods could use the facilities of several companies in the course of a single journey. As a result the allocation of revenues to the different companies became very complicated. In 1842 the Railway Clearing House was set up and managed a system of revenue distribution among the separate railway companies.

Railways and the economy

> **KEY PROFILE**
>
> **George Hudson (1800–1871)**, 'The Railway King', was instrumental in financing and building the line between York, Leeds and the Midlands. His ambition was to link York to London and Edinburgh. He tried to outdo any competitors by offering unrealistically high returns for money invested. In 1842 he formed the Midland Railway, by amalgamating several smaller companies. Financial irregularities were uncovered in his business activities and he was disgraced.

Fig. 3   The extent of the railway network in Britain by 1846

> **A CLOSER LOOK**
>
> ### The Railway Clearing House, 1842
>
> If a passenger bought a ticket at a station owned by one company and travelled on a train owned by another, then during the journey travelled along two stretches of line each owned by a different company and ended the journey at a station owned by yet another company, the Clearing House ensured that each company received a fair proportion of each fare paid.

Rail coverage went from scarcely more than 100 miles in 1832 to nearly 2000 miles by 1843 and this had risen to over 4000 miles in 1846. The railway revolution 'stimulated the wider economy'. The coal industry continued to expand to provide fuel for the increasing number of locomotives; the iron industry expanded to meet the ever-increasing demands for rail tracks and rolling stock. Other industries benefited by being able to transport their goods quickly and more cheaply than by other forms of transport and this gave them a wider distribution. This resulted in cheaper goods. The railways boosted agriculture, although many farmers had objected to railway development, fearing adverse effects on cattle and crops of trains rushing at 30mph past their fields. Fresh produce, especially milk, could be delivered to large centres of population and could be shared by many. Railways extended to ports and harbours and export trade increased. Railway design and construction became an exportable commodity as France, other parts of Europe and South America invested in the British railway model. All this expanding economic activity created many new jobs at a time when there was much unemployment. Developments could take place on a national instead of a local scale – national newspapers flourished and the postal system was sped up. Unexpected outcomes were the new possibilities the railways brought to party politics and to the development of trade unions, improving people's ability to organise gatherings and facilitating communication.

Table 1 *The rapid increase in production and output of iron and coal, before and during the years of railway expansion*

Iron production		Coal output	
1820	450,000 tons	1820	17.4 million tons
1850	2,000,000 tons	1830	22.4 million tons
		1840	33.7 million tons
		1850	49.4 million tons

The social effects of railway development were intrinsically bound to economic developments. McCord and Purdue comment that it is 'impossible to separate economic from social effects of railways' and the 'improvements in passenger transport were themselves an economic stimulant'. Although there was great opposition to the railways and an element of public hysteria about the adverse effects on the human body of travelling at speed, very quickly the general public embraced the idea of travel. It brought the possibility of mobility (to search for a new job) and freedom to explore new horizons beyond the immediate community – taking a cheap day excursion to the coast became a new social activity for the masses.

It is interesting to note that Robert Peel realised the importance of the railway system and its value to the economy, but also its value to the people. Peel's minister at the **Board of Trade**, William Gladstone, was responsible for the 1844 Railway Act which stipulated that every railway company had to provide a carriage for third-class passengers at least once a day and that the fare should be capped at not more than one penny a mile. It was nicknamed the 'parliamentary train' – slow and satirised – but was an important advance towards a less elitist society.

Canals and coaching companies did not hail the arrival of the railway as it stole their business. People deserted coach travel and coaching inns were also casualties. Toll roads that depended on regular traffic to pay for their upkeep also suffered.

CROSS-REFERENCE

Gladstone's other work at the **Board of Trade** is examined on pages 156–8.

ACTIVITY

Pair discussion

1. 'The social effects of railway development were intrinsically bound to economic developments.' List the effects of railway development and identify any that are purely economic, or purely social, or a mixture of both. What conclusion can you draw?
2. There were many easily identified advantages in the development of the railways. Can you identify the possible disadvantages or perceived disadvantages?

EXTRACT 2

What the economic effects of railways were has been much debated. For long it seemed self-evident to historians that railways not only stimulated the wider economy but had profound effects in lowering the cost of transport. In fact, the early railways seem to have had more effect on the transport of people than goods and it was not until after mid-century that passenger train receipts were exceeded by those of freight transport. There were other means to transport freight and the efficiency of the pre-rail transport system has been underestimated, but for passenger journeys over a dozen miles or so the superiority of the rail was quickly demonstrated. It was only in the late 1850s, when freight overtook passengers as the slightly larger earner, that railways became profitable. It is impossible to quantify the economic contribution of railways and impossible to separate economic from social or psychological effects. Improvements in passenger transport were themselves an economic stimulant, while railways made the country effectively smaller, more centralised and more uniform.

Adapted from McCord and Purdue, *British History, 1815–1914*, 2007

CHAPTER 17 | Economic developments

A LEVEL PRACTICE QUESTION

Evaluating historical extracts

Using your understanding of the historical context, assess how convincing the arguments in Extracts 1 and 2 are in relation to the economic effects of the railways between 1825 and 1846.

Agriculture and the repeal of the Corn Laws

Agricultural developments 1832–1846

The late 1830s saw an improvement in conditions for farmers, who had experienced difficulties in the early years of the century. Advances in farming progressed steadily as **enclosure** continued. Enclosure made soil improvement easier and increased grain for an urban population. The Enclosure Acts of 1836 and 1845 brought a rapid scramble among landowners for enclosure, with few open fields left to enclose; a provision in the 1845 Act ensured that the open land in the immediate vicinity of a village or town was preserved in perpetuity. By 1850 the process of enclosure was virtually complete.

Fig. 4 *A meeting of the English Royal Agricultural Society at Bristol, 1842*

There was more money available for investment in farming through the success of enclosure. In addition the price of wheat, which held its price at over sixty shillings a quarter for a few years after 1838, stimulated new capital expenditure. The cost of the poor rates had fallen by almost half, particularly in rural areas, after the introduction of the new Poor Law, which freed up more income for the farmers to invest.

Improvements in drainage techniques had an impact on the type of crop sown and the quality of the crop when harvested. Steam drainage began to replace windmill-drainage wheels and this enabled the land to dry out sufficiently to take wheat instead of the less profitable oats. Drainage was cheap and efficient, and one engine could maintain the drainage of 6000 acres. The drainage of heavy clay soils were dealt with by the manufacture of clay tiles. This process was given a boost by Peel's Agricultural Drainage Act in 1846, which set up loans for farmers to improve field drainage.

The greater use of fertilisers was encouraged – from animal dung, to **guano**, to treated crushed bones – and this generally contributed to increased crop yields. The development of light iron implements, which could be draw by one

STUDY TIP

The starting point as always is explaining what the extracts say and then identifying the way in which they differ. In this instance both mention the importance of the economic effects of railways, but then discuss different aspects. You must identify these differences. Your answer must always take the process one step further and make a judgement between them. The way to do this is by supporting your judgement with a reference to your knowledge of the historical context.

KEY CHRONOLOGY

1836	Enclosure Act
1845	Enclosure Act
1846	Agricultural Drainage Act
1846	Repeal of the Corn Laws

CROSS-REFERENCE

Refresh your memory on the **enclosures** in Chapter 3, pages 27–8 and Chapter 9, pages 85–6.

A CLOSER LOOK

Some effects of improvements

A tenant farmer in East Lothian, Scotland, George Hope, wrote to his brother in April 1846: 'A good many farms have been let this spring and every one at large additional rents. Farms are letting, not at what they are worth at present, but at what they are capable of being made worth by draining and artificial manures.'

KEY TERM

guano: the droppings of seabirds, one of the richest natural sources of fertiliser; it was imported from Peru in huge quantities in the mid-nineteenth century, before it was replaced by chemical fertilisers

or two horses, lowered labour costs and increased efficiency and there was a wider use of steam-powered machines on farms, especially the steam thresher. Apart from the invention of McCormick's steam reaper, however, there was little advance in this area before 1850 and most jobs were still tackled by hand.

Supporting and encouraging the improvements were a large number of agricultural societies. Clubs, farming journals, newspapers and books appeared in the 1830s and 40s all offering the latest advice and of course advertising products for better farming. The most influential was probably the Royal Agricultural Society, which was formed in 1842, and its Journal was an excellent source of farming knowledge.

Over one third of all families still lived off the land during the 1830s and 40s. In spite of the increasing prosperity of farmers, the landless agricultural labourers were still among the poorest paid. Wages and housing, however, varied according to different regions and also depended on the attitude of the farmer and his relationship with his workers. McCord quotes the variation between farm labourers in Dorset who were paid half as much as those in Lancashire. In the south and east of Scotland, the land was fertile, there was a culture of improvement, farms were prosperous and farming families were relatively well-housed. The poorest agricultural labourers were in the south and west of Ireland and their already poverty-stricken existence was challenged beyond endurance in autumn 1845.

Famine in Ireland

> **ACTIVITY**
>
> Draw a spider diagram to show the influences on British farming between 1832 and 1846.

> **A CLOSER LOOK**
>
> **The percentage of people applying for rations** in different parts of Ireland from 1845 to 1849 shows the varying impact of the famine. Western areas were most affected due to the almost total reliance on the potato crop there. These were already the most impoverished parts of Ireland.

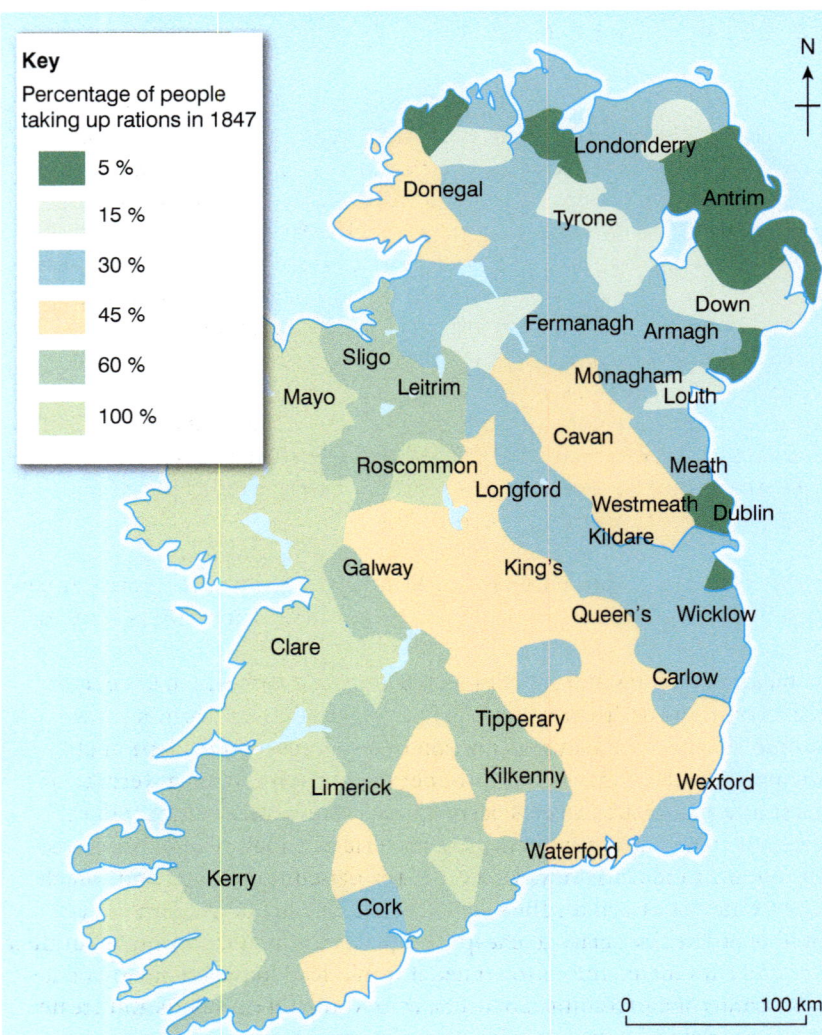

Fig. 5 *Severity of the Great Famine in Ireland, 1845–1849*

The 1841 census recorded the population of Ireland at around nine million. Almost half of them lived in small one- or two-roomed hovels in the countryside, renting out small parcels of land from absentee landlords trying to eke out a living. Most were abjectly poor. Their main crop was the potato. They sold a proportion of the crop to pay the rent and the remainder formed their staple diet – the potato was said to be the exclusive food of nine out of ten of the inhabitants of Ireland. In 1845 a fungus attacked the autumn crop and virtually wiped it out. It was a major disaster for the Irish peasants, most of whom had nothing to fall back on. When they were unable to keep up with their rent, they faced eviction. Within a short time, many were destitute and starving to death. When there were calls from the **Anti-Corn Law League**, Whigs and free traders for the Government to allow unrestricted importation of all foods to prevent a humanitarian disaster, the protectionists ridiculed the suggestion that there was a crisis. They suggested the extent of the potato blight had been exaggerated in a 'plot' to persuade the Government to repeal the Corn Laws. In theory this would bring down the price of bread, which in the short term could replace the blighted potato and provide food for the starving population. Views differed among Peel's contemporaries as to whether the event of the Irish famine finally pushed Peel into repeal of the Corn Laws, or whether the famine was, as Richard Gaunt suggests, 'a convenient pretext for Peel's conversion'. In any event, the **famine** increased the feelings of bitterness against the British and stored up problems for the future.

> **CROSS-REFERENCE**
>
> The **Anti-Corn Law League** is the subject of Chapter 15.
>
> The subject of the **Irish Famine** is raised in Chapter 16.

The repeal of the Corn Laws

> **EXTRACT 3**
>
> The climax of Peel's economic strategy was Corn Law repeal in 1846. He had undoubtedly supported **Huskisson's** project for eventual Free Trade in grain, at least so long as population continued to rocket upwards, and though it cannot be proved that his own determination went back as far as the 1820s, it certainly went back a long way. He could hardly speak out about his intentions before the 1841 election, but his speeches were sufficiently vague to leave the door open.
>
> If Peel was searching for a pretext to undertake repeal of the Corn Laws, a compelling one occurred in October 1845, when reports came through of a catastrophic failure of the Irish potato crop. That it brought such a spontaneous reaction from Peel in favour of repeal suggests he had been waiting for the opportunity. Yet Peel cannot really have thought repeal would alleviate the famine. If he *had* thought so he should have suspended the Corn Laws immediately, not phased them out over three years.
>
> Adapted from Boyd Hilton, *A Mad, Bad, and Dangerous People? England 1783–1846*, 2006

> **KEY QUESTION**
>
> What pressures did governments face and how did they respond to these?

> **CROSS-REFERENCE**
>
> **William Huskisson's** activities in pushing for the amendment of the Corn Laws and introducing a sliding scale in 1828 are referenced in Chapter 8, page 76.

> **ACTIVITY**
>
> **Evaluating historical extracts**
>
> What interpretation of Peel's decision to repeal the Corn Laws in 1846 does Boyd Hilton put forward in Extract 3?

The majority of Conservative MPs held county seats or were members for small market towns. Their main focus was agriculture and farming. The 1841 election had been fought and won in the shires on the question of agricultural protection, which was under threat from a Whig government. This substantial group in Peel's party opposed Peel's interference with the Corn Laws when he extended the sliding scale of duties in 1842 and feared that repealing the Corn Laws would destroy agricultural protection, which they saw almost as a right. They believed that removal of the Corn Laws would open the floodgates to cheap foreign corn, which would undercut their price and ruin them. They also argued it would lead to the unemployment of thousands of agricultural labourers, who would fill the towns and create further problems. They argued it was against the interests of national security to be dependent on foreign corn, in case of war. They attempted

A CLOSER LOOK

Impact of the famine on Ireland

The population of Ireland fell from almost 9 million in 1841 to 6.5 million in 1851. It is estimated over 1 million Irish died as a result of starvation. A cholera outbreak in 1849 brought a high death toll to a population already weakened by malnutrition. Probably about 1.5 million Irish emigrated, mostly to the USA and Canada, by 1851. Politically, the famine had lasting repercussions: an increasing resentment against British dominance, a divided, sectarian Irish society and by the 1860s, the emergence of a new nationalist movement.

to undermine the middle-class manufacturers whom they claimed were in favour of repeal in order to keep their workers' wages low. Not all farmers, however, were against Corn Law repeal. Tenant farmer George Hope of Fenton Barns, in East Lothian, commented in a letter to his brother on 31 January 1846: 'Well I have now seen Peel's plan. He diminishes the amount of all protecting duties and does away with many of them altogether; in three years the Corn Laws to be totally abolished. The Protectionists in Haddington market yesterday were furious at Peel.' And again a few weeks later: 'The progress of free-trade principles is most astonishing. Peel's liberal measure is almost all that we could wish.'

George Hope's correspondence makes no mention of the Irish potato famine, but concentrates on the significance of the pressure applied by the Anti-Corn Law League. However, as soon as news filtered through of the blighted potato crop in Ireland, Peel responded by telling his Cabinet that the Corn Laws had to be repealed immediately. Faced with fierce opposition, Peel resigned in December 1845. When Whig Lord John Russell failed to form a government, Peel returned and after months of bitter argument with his party, the Repeal of the Corn Laws passed through the Commons in May 1846, with the support of the Whigs, and with the loyalty of Wellington passed through the Lords.

Fig. 6 *A destitute family during The Great Famine; one million people died from starvation and disease, while another million fled as emigrants to Britain and North America*

The effects of the repeal of the Corn Laws

The repeal was to be phased in over three years and so brought little relief to Ireland (see Hilton above). In fact, the potato blight continued into the 1846 crop, bringing even more misery. It wasn't until 1850 that there was some economic recovery on the land, in line with the agricultural boom in the rest of Britain.

There was no sudden fall in the price of corn, British farmers did not face ruin and the price of bread did not fall. The repeal did prevent the price of bread from rising and therefore was of some benefit to the poor. Indeed many of the agricultural improvements that were in progress during the 1840s began to be financially successful and the growing urban population further stimulated agriculture by demanding more food. The 1850s turned out to be a period of great prosperity for farming.

The repeal was undoubtedly a great victory for Free Trade. The manufacturers' argument had held up against that of the landowners and had challenged their continuing influence and dominance at the heart of British politics.

Peel's action split the Conservative Party and after 1846 it did not win a majority in Parliament for over 30 years. Boyd Hilton points out that there was already a fundamental division in the Conservative Party and that in 1841 it was elected on a lie, as Peel failed to 'come clean about his intentions' regarding the Corn Laws, although Peel could not have foreseen the Irish famine. It would seem that Sir Robert Peel, the man who reconstructed the Tories into the new Conservative party at Tamworth in 1834, also caused its downfall in 1846 by his inability to free himself from free trade ideology and policies.

> **EXTRACT 4**
>
> In Peel's mind it was not the adequacy or inadequacy of the 1842 Corn Law, but his understanding of the economic impact of the Corn Laws, and the impossibility of pursuing political principles against their logic, which transformed the situation in much the same way as O'Connell's election for County Clare had transformed Peel's understanding of Catholic Emancipation. His ripening in respect of Ireland, the success of his tariff reform policy and the ready availability of income tax as a means of generating a secure stream of government revenue, were the necessary precursors to this change of heart. Consequently the change in Peel's thinking can be dated, in the medium term, to 1843. This interpretation was echoed by Gladstone (in later life) and reflected Peel's own sentiments as expressed in introducing repeal to Parliament. Peel confined the events which had caused the change in his thinking to the three last years. He had already helped to create the economic circumstances in which repeal could occur through his tariff reforms and the re-introduction of the Income Tax.
>
> Adapted from Richard Gaunt, *Sir Robert Peel, The Life and Legacy*, 2010

ACTIVITY

Evaluating historical extracts

1. What do you think is meant by the phrase 'pursuing political principles against their logic'? Can you explain this in the context of Peel's decision to repeal the Corn Laws in 1846?
2. In what ways do Extracts 3 and 4 agree and disagree?

ACTIVITY

Summary

Hold a discussion on what might be the perceptions of the following groups of people living through the 1840s about the economic developments:
- a railway entrepreneur
- an Irish smallholder
- an English landowner with strong views on Corn Law Repeal (bear in mind that he could sell some of his land for railway development, although he may have disliked the idea)
- a tenant farmer like George Hope (Scottish), who was enjoying the benefit of agricultural improvements.

Would there be many common threads between them? Think about how they would know about what was happening in other parts of the country.

STUDY TIP

The essay is not just about the famine. You will need to consider other reasons why Peel might have been accused of 'betrayal'.

PRACTICE QUESTION

'Peel: the great betrayer!'
Assess the validity of this view of Sir Robert Peel.

18 Social developments (1832–1846)

LEARNING OBJECTIVES

In this chapter you will learn about:

- conditions in urban Britain
- changes in the lives of workers and the poor
- unions and other working-class movements.

EXTRACT 1

The new urban environment of the 1830s and 1840s, affecting a steadily rising proportion of the nation, brought problems of discipline in living (of social controls), just as much as factory employment brought problems of discipline and regularity in work. Industrialists solved their problems more efficiently than local government, police and public administrations solved theirs. Money wages were higher in urban manufacturing industry than in agriculture, but the pattern was broken by short periods of intense **cyclical** unemployment. At the same time very little public provision was made for loss of earnings as a result of accident, sickness or old age. Spending habits appropriate to the old style of rural life, as well as other inherited social habits and conventions, increased social problems when translated into the new environment. The weekly wage was the family's only protection against distress; in the rising industrial towns there were seldom gardens, smallholdings or **payments in kind**. Everything needed to be purchased in shops and rent paid, from wages.

Adapted from Peter Mathias, *The First Industrial Nation, An Economic History of Britain, 1700–1914*, 1972

KEY QUESTION

As you read this chapter, consider the following Key Questions:
- How was Britain governed and how did democracy and political organisations develop?
- How important were ideas and ideologies?
- How and with what results did society and social policy develop?
- How important was the role of individuals and groups and how were they affected by developments?

ACTIVITY

Evaluating historical extracts

1. Identify the problems of urbanisation given in Extract 1.
2. What is the social significance of the lack of 'gardens, smallholdings or payments in kind' for the new working-class urban dwellers?

Conditions in urban Britain

Urban growth

Between 1801 and 1851 the population of Britain (excluding Ireland) had risen from 10.5 million to 20.8 million. (There was no official census for Ireland in 1801 and the population there was estimated to be 5.2 million in 1801 but it had declined between 1841 and 1851 due to famine.) Most of the increase can be accounted for in the rapidly expanding urban areas. **Urban growth** and **urbanisation** were major factors in social change.

By 1831, the populations of Glasgow, Liverpool, Birmingham and Manchester each stood at about 200,000 and were rising. By 1851, there were approximately 60 towns and cities in Britain of that size. The effect of such large and rapid increases in population put immense strains on existing urban structures that for the most part failed to cope. By 1846, almost half of Britain's population lived in urban rather than rural areas. Therefore whatever conditions existed in those urban areas affected a large percentage of the population.

KEY TERM

cyclical: ocurring in cycles

payments in kind: the payment for things in lieu of money, in which case what is offered is deemed to be equal to the value of the goods or services required

urban growth: towns and cities becoming larger

urbanisation: an increasing percentage of the population becoming town-dwellers

CROSS-REFERENCE

Population growth during this period is discussed in Chapter 3, page 22.

A CLOSER LOOK

Migration to the towns: Liverpool

Liverpool grew by 46 per cent between 1821 and 1831, an increase of 338,000, of whom 222,000 were migrants from rural areas of Britain. That pattern was repeated across the most rapidly growing urban centres.

A CLOSER LOOK

Tenement housing was overcrowded, draughty and lacked basic hygiene facilities; there would be a single privy (basic toilet) erected for each tenement block.

A CLOSER LOOK

Sanitation in the towns

The lack of proper sanitation was possibly the biggest threat to health in urban areas. One earth privy (a soil pit, i.e. a lavatory without water running through it) would be shared by several families. Even when water closets were installed in middle class areas, for example in Birmingham, they drained into open gutters at the side of the road.

Living conditions in the towns

Population growth and rapid urbanisation meant the crowding together of large numbers of people in towns and cities. The wealthy middle classes segregated themselves from the rest in large houses in leafy suburbs, and the respectable middling ranks, such as trades and crafts people, lived in neat terraced houses, not too far from the town centre. However, the rest – the vast majority – lived in hastily-built, overcrowded and cramped back-to-back terraces or **tenement** dwellings, close to the smoky, smelly industrial centre, with an entire family in one room. They had few basic facilities, a limited water supply and primitive sanitation.

Fig. 1 *Crowded housing in Salt market in Glasgow*

The inadequate housing and crowded, dirty streets caused significant health problems, creating conditions ripe for the rapid spread of diseases. Incidence of disease was often worst in the old districts of towns like Glasgow and York. In Exeter in 1832, out of a population of 28,000, there were 1200 cases of cholera. Endemic infectious diseases such as typhus, whooping cough, dysentery and measles caused 40 per cent of deaths in industrial towns. Life expectancy among urban dwellers was short and approximately half of all children died before their fifth birthday. Mortality rates, which had been falling steadily from about 1750, rose again during the 1830s and 40s. The high death rates and infant mortality among the labouring poor caused problems with burials. The belief that Christian burials must take place in holy ground led to church graveyards overflowing and people being buried in unhygienic conditions. This stimulated the development of specially designated cemeteries, which were constructed through private investment or municipal authorities on the edge of the towns.

Conditions in urban Britain were not all determined by filth, disease and overcrowding. During this period many towns and cities developed into great cultural centres. The 'city fathers' commissioned magnificent public buildings, such as the Town Hall in Birmingham in 1834; commercial businesses and professional institutions established 'state of the art' headquarters in city centres, such as the Liverpool Medical Institution in 1837 and the Royal Institution in Edinburgh in 1836; wealthy benefactors built museums and laid out beautiful public parks. These structural and cultural improvements were not to ease the lot of the workers and the poor, but rather for the social and political aggrandisement of the new elite, the wealthy middle classes who inhabited the grand houses in the smart residential areas of urban Britain. In spite of the splendour of the city centres, however, there was an absence of an infrastructure to cater for the needs of the population as a whole.

Glasgow provides a good example of the two sides of urban life often represented in Britain's major towns and cities during this period. While on the one hand Glasgow was referred to as the 'second City of the (British) Empire' with its vibrant culture and great commercial and industrial wealth, yet in the 1840s it had some of the worst housing conditions in Europe, with its 'foul **housing backlands**' and squalid lodging houses for its labouring poor. The filthy, unhealthy living conditions brought diseases such as cholera, typhus and typhoid, which killed thousands every year.

Fig. 2 Woodside Crescent, Glasgow, 1839, showing the elegant houses of the wealthy middle classes

ACTIVITY

Compare Figs 1 and 2, showing two faces of Glasgow. To what extent do they make a statement about the way in which society was developing during this period?

Urban transport developments

It could be supposed that the development of the railways and the introduction of the '**parliamentary train**', in 1844, could be seen as improving lives of workers if not the poor. Although there was a development of passenger rail services, this didn't have any significant impact on the lives of the majority of workers until later in the century, when it was used by them to seek work further afield.

A CLOSER LOOK

The effects of immigration and internal migration

Apart from the natural rate of growth in the population over the preceding decades, by the 1830s the effects of immigration from Ireland to the industrial towns, and internal migration from the Scottish Highlands, were being felt. The flow of people from the English countryside continued steadily. The highlanders left behind miserable crofts, where either there were too many people tilling the same piece of infertile soil to make a living, or they were evicted by the laird (landowner) to make way for his sheep (a period known as the Highland Clearances). People poured into Glasgow and Edinburgh, where they found themselves in overcrowded slums. The Irish tended to come over to escape hard times at home and so the numbers rose dramatically after the famine in 1845. Of those that came to Britain most settled in London, Manchester, Liverpool and Glasgow. They swelled the ranks of the working classes as textile operatives and railway navvies (navigators or labourers), providing much-needed labour. A contemporary observer noted that the flax mills of Leeds were kept working thanks to the influx of the Irish. But his influx brought about a great amount of squalor in early Victorian England. Some of the problems that developed in the towns stemmed from the fact that, although their location had changed, the migrants transferred the standards of their poverty-stricken rural existence to the towns.

KEY TERM

housing backlands: backlands can mean wasteland; this is a reference to the fact that the housing area of the labouring poor was built away from the fine city centre, lacked amenities and was a slum

SECTION 3 | Political change and social reform, 1832–1846

> **CROSS-REFERENCE**
>
> More information about the '**parliamentary train**' can be found in Chapter 17, page 164.

> **KEY TERM**
>
> **omnibus:** a road vehicle (horse-drawn in the Victorian era) used for carrying a number of passengers; the shortened form of 'bus' is now in general use
>
> **blue-collar workers:** manual workers
>
> **white-collar workers:** other workers not engaged in manual work, e.g. clerks and office workers

> **CROSS-REFERENCE**
>
> It might be a good idea to refresh your memory by reading over the section on standards of living in Chapter 4 before you read this section.

> **ACTIVITY**
>
> **Pair discussion**
>
> In what ways could the development of transport change and improve the lives of working people? Do you think it could have any benefits for the poor?

> **KEY TERM**
>
> **tied housing:** housing in which occupancy depends on continuing to work for the employer who supplied the house; it was (and still is) a common practice for farm workers to have accommodation provided with a job

> **A CLOSER LOOK**
>
> **Agricultural wages**
>
> The wages of agricultural workers had fallen to between seven shillings and nine shillings a week. It meant that families often had to rely on poor relief to make up the shortfall to a basic subsistence level. After the new Poor Law was introduced, the poorest labourers and their families ended up in the workhouse (see pages 139–40).

Otherwise there were very limited possibilities of transport for working people, most of whom walked to whatever was their destination. This posed problems for the industrial workforce: such were the long hours of work and the inflexibility of the shift system, that it was imperative to live close to the factory. This determined the positioning of the rows of cramped back-to-back houses, tenement blocks or lodging houses to accommodate the working population. They had to be close to the urban industrial centre, with all its attendant smoky atmosphere, smells and noises, and so they formed new working-class areas spreading out on one side of the town.

Transport facilities within towns were privately owned and catered for the well-to-do. In Glasgow, in 1845, the first horse-drawn **omnibuses** went into service, but in reality they were used by clerical workers and other non-labouring workers (usually described as **blue/white-collar workers**) to travel to and from work.

Changes in the lives of workers

Urbanisation had changed the way of life for approximately half the working population of this country by the 1830s and 40s and not always for the better. Enclosure and agricultural improvement had changed the way of life for most of the other half. The deterioration of conditions for workers and the poor in many urban areas (see above) at a time when the urban population was rising, suggests a decline in living standards for many people. It is impossible to settle on an overall view because any view is subject to regional and occupational variations. In rural areas, the incomes of agricultural labourers fell by about 30 per cent over the early decades of the nineteenth century. It could be argued, however, that their situation was offset by easier access to fresh food than their cousins in the towns, the health benefits of working in the fresh air and for some the provision of **tied housing** (although that could have a downside).

Although wages were higher in manufacturing than they were in agriculture, these wages for industrial workers were not always reliable and were broken up by periods of unemployment. In the new urban sprawl, the traditional close-knit communities of rural living had been broken up and dispersed. The family ties and friendships that had acted as a support mechanism in troubled times could no longer operate. When wages were stopped because of factory lay-offs, or 'for any cause of dependence – accident, sickness or old age,' workers could no longer rely on kinship ties to see them through bad patches and there was 'negligible public provision' for loss of earnings. The provisions of the new Poor Law of 1834 meant that they could no longer depend on relief from the parish and in any case they had moved from the parish of their birth, where they had been entitled to claim relief. Although outdoor relief did continue in the towns after 1834, the system was chaotic and overstretched, leaving many desperate for hand-outs from charitable organisations to keep them from starvation.

For town-dwellers, the 'periods of intense cyclical unemployment' and the consequent poverty and distress among so many encouraged crime and social disorder and ultimately affected the way society functioned. There was a rise in crime levels, and crime was easier to commit in a large overcrowded city, where you could pass unnoticed. The problem of improving the quality of living in towns and cities became a constant problem for successive governments. The Municipal Reform Act of 1835 was an attempt to improve the administration of towns and the services they offered. The extension of the Metropolitan Police Force to other major towns beyond London was an attempt to deal with spiralling crime rates and disorder. However, the development of an efficient, trustworthy police force came slowly, even though it was an obligation in the 1835 Act, and was another reason why crime often went undetected.

Edwin Chadwick's report, '*The Sanitary Conditions of the Labouring Population*' published in 1842, alerted the Government to the urgent need to improve the living conditions of the poor, although Peel's Conservative government rejected the report as too expensive to initiate.

The Factory Acts, designed to alleviate the worst abuses of labour by outlawing employment of children under nine (in 1833) and by curtailing women's working hours (in 1844), may have slightly improved the quality of life for factory workers' families, but would have meant a drop in the total wages coming into the household. For that reason, not all workers supported the idea of **Lord Shaftesbury**'s campaign for a maximum ten hour working day for all adults.

In the 1830s and 40s it has been estimated that about three quarters of the weekly wage of a worker was spent on food and most of that on bread. Wage rates for workers varied enormously between occupations, regions and different factories and so it is difficult to paint an accurate picture. According to economic historians Deane & Cole, the level of wages (that is money wages) fell slightly overall between 1832 and 1846, although other sources indicate a slight overall rise. When set alongside prices over the period, the difficulties for many workers to maintain any stability in living standards becomes apparent. According to the Price Index shown in Table 1, prices were at the same level in 1846 as they had been in 1832, but problems for workers and the poor during this period were the price fluctuations that occurred between those dates, reaching a peak in 1839 and 1840. The constant variation in the price of bread caused particular hardship.

> **CROSS-REFERENCE**
>
> **Edwin Chadwick**'s social campaigning and contribution to improved public health are the subject of Chapters 15 and 21.
>
> **Lord Shaftesbury**'s social campaigning for better working conditions is the subject of Chapter 15.

Table 1 *Price index of total agricultural and principal industrial products (where the year 1830 = 100)*

Date	Price index
1832	109
1833	107
1834	112
1835	112
1836	123
1837	118
1838	119
1839	130
1840	128
1841	121
1842	111
1843	105
1844	108
1845	110
1846	109

Changes in the lives of the poor

The plight of the hand-loom weavers

While the quality of life for factory workers was tough, the higher wages compensated for the monotony of daily life (six days a week) as machine operatives. For the tens of thousands of traditionally highly-paid skilled hand-loom weavers, their inability to compete with machines and their subsequent fall in status and living standards was a tragedy. Boyd Hilton quotes the example of weavers in the West Riding of Yorkshire, whose earnings dropped to **4s 6d** a week during the 1830s. Put into context it meant that meat was never affordable. Earlier in the century some hand-loom weavers were earning as much as 25 shillings a week and so loss of self-esteem as well as a decent

> **A CLOSER LOOK**
>
> **4s 6d**
>
> This was the short form of writing monetary values – in this case four shillings and sixpence. There were 20 shillings in the pound in old money. In today's values, 4s 6d would equate to about 22p. This amount would hardly feed a family for a week.

livelihood would be an issue. A *Report from the Select Committee on Hand-loom Weavers' Petitions*, 1835, suggested hand-loom workers seek a different means of living.

Improving standards of living

Some workers in the rapidly expanding sectors of industry like the railways would be better off than most of their urban contemporaries. They could rely on a steady wage, and even casual work on the railways, of which there was plenty during this period, was well paid.

The question becomes not just about wages and prices, but about the quality of life or, as historian Edward Royle puts it: 'Were people any happier in the early nineteenth century than they had been 50 or 100 years earlier?' Of course it is impossible to answer without evidence. Though Royle suspects that the 'question would have been meaningless to the very poor'!

> **ACTIVITY**
>
> Working in pairs, identify the changes in the lives of workers and the poor. Divide them into positive changes and negative changes. From your findings write a summary paragraph and draw a conclusion as to whether the changes were for the better or the worse.

EXTRACT 2

Certainly English society was much changed even by 1830, as a result of industrialisation. There is a view that the Industrial Revolution benefited the workers, not only in the long run, but also in the short run. Since in the first half of the nineteenth century average *per capita* real income increased, since there was no trend in the distribution of income against the workers, since after 1815 prices fell while wages remained constant, since *per capita* consumption of food and other consumer goods increased, and since Government intervened increasingly in economic and social life to protect and raise living and working conditions, then the real wages of the majority of English workers were rising throughout the Industrial Revolution. This is not to say the standard of living was high, nor that it was rising fast at any time before 1850, nor that there was no dire poverty, or no cyclical and technological unemployment. But to admit the existence of distress is not to deny the upward trend in living standards, nor the opportunities created by industrialisation.

Adapted from R.M. Hartwell, *The Industrial Revolution in England,* 1965

> **ACTIVITY**
>
> ### Evaluating historical extracts
>
> Read Extract 2. What view does Hartwell put forward of the trend in living standards in the first half of the nineteenth century? How does he support this view?

Unions and other working-class movements

EXTRACT 3

It may at first sight seem surprising that the years after the collapse of general unionism saw a steady growth in unionism of a cautious town-by-town and craft-by-craft type. For these were also the years of Chartism — a political movement which, confused though it was, nevertheless had ambitious national aims based upon a belief in the identity of interests of the entire working class. While Chartism increasingly drew its support from the casualties of the industrial changes of the period, trade unionism developed either among craftsmen who were little affected by such changes, or among workers who actually benefited from the change, as in the case of the new engineering tradesmen, the boilermakers and so on. There was also a certain alternation of interest by the main body of miners and factory workers, depending upon whether or not they were regularly employed. In times of slump, such as 1838–42 and 1847–48, they tended to join political agitation; but when they got their jobs back they gave new impetus to trade unionism.

Adapted from Henry Pelling (Ed.), *A History of British Trade Unionism,* 1967

> **ACTIVITY**
>
> ### Evaluating historical extracts
>
> 1. Why does Extract 3 suggest that the 'steady growth of unionism' was surprising at this time? Among which group of workers is trade unionism developing? Can you think of an explanation for this?
> 2. What 'problem' for urban workers do Extracts 1, 2 and 3 all raise? How does Extract 3 suggest that this 'problem' impacts on the development of trade unions? How convincing is Pelling's argument?

Robert Owen and the GNCTU

After the repeal of the Combination Acts in 1824, there was an upsurge in the formation of small trade unions. As separate entities they had little influence and were easily quashed in the face of threats of job loss from employers. As a response to this, the idea formed that national unions, each representing a particular trade, would have more resources to demand better wages and conditions. Taking this idea a step further forward, Robert Owen attempted to unite all individual unions under the banner of a central organisation called the Grand National Consolidated Trades Union. The aim of the GNCTU was to fight against recurrent economic crises and unemployment and work towards Owen's vision of a cooperative commonwealth. Within a few weeks it had a membership of over half a million, each member paying one shilling. In each district each trade would be represented by a local branch, and link in to a local umbrella branch, which in turn would report to a centrally run Grand Council. It had the potential of a large, strong labour movement, but Owen's vision of a society which replaced private ownership with workers' control terrified the Government. Owen was in fact apprehensive about calling a general strike as he believed, unrealistically, that he could strike a deal with the capitalist factory owners.

On paper the organisation looked good, but communication between the local branches was poor. Some of the bigger unions of mainly skilled workers, e.g. spinners and potters, withdrew, not wishing to submerge their identity with a largely unskilled rabble. There were widely differing opinions among the leaders as to whether or not to go ahead with a general strike. There was an acute shortage of funds. The employers acted swiftly and drew up 'The Document', which required their workers to swear they were not members of the GNCTU. Refusal to sign meant instant dismissal. Outbreaks of machine-breaking and **rick-burning** in the south, not necessarily connected with the GNCTU, and strikes across the country, decided the Government on immediate firm action to break the organisation and suppress unionism. Members of any trade union could find themselves before a magistrate on the slightest pretext. Knowledge of the conviction of a group of agricultural labourers seeking union membership convinced many to withdraw support from the GNCTU. Within months the scheme had collapsed. A deep trade recession set in in 1837; in such times many workers could not afford even the smallest union subscription and membership fell away. Instead trade union members – 'casualties of industrial change' – turned to political Chartism and joined the calls for universal male suffrage.

> **CROSS-REFERENCE**
>
> **Robert Owen**'s career as a socialist, industrialist and reformer is detailed in Chapter 11.

> **ACTIVITY**
>
> **Thinking point**
>
> Do you think Owen's GNCTU had any chance of success? Explain your answer.

> **KEY TERM**
>
> **rick-burning:** deliberately setting haystacks on fire

> **ACTIVITY**
>
> **Class debate**
>
> Was there any justification for the Government's 'knee-jerk' reaction to the GNCTU? Either defend or criticise the Government's heavy-handed response. Listen to each argument and take a vote on which you find most compelling.

The Tolpuddle Martyrs (1834)

An example was made of a group of agricultural workers, from Tolpuddle in Dorset, who had set up a branch of the Friendly Society of Agricultural Workers. The Tolpuddle Martyrs were convicted on the rather spurious grounds that they had taken oaths in secret, and this was interpreted as subversion. Six of the group were prosecuted and transported to Australia for seven years. The unreasonably harsh punishment handed out to the Tolpuddle Martyrs inspired a well-coordinated campaign led by William Lovett, and they were pardoned and allowed to return to Britain.

SECTION 3 | Political change and social reform, 1832–1846

Fig. 3 A demonstration in Copenhagen Fields, London, 21 April 1834, organised by the Central Committee of the Metropolitan Trade Union, protesting against the deportation of the Tolpuddle Martyrs

Other working class movements

The Rochdale Pioneers and the Cooperative Movement, 1844

The inspiration to set up a Cooperative Movement came partly from Owen's ideas, but was also about the social and economic values projected by many of the skilled tradesmen, who saw themselves as a cut above unskilled labourers. They believed that if they applied the currently popular virtues of thrift and self-help in their daily lives, they could continue to enjoy a decent standard of living even during economic downturns. In 1844, a group of Rochdale weavers set up a cooperative store, by each contributing investments of £1. They bought goods at wholesale and sold them at a profit. The quality of the food was reliable and reasonably priced. The members received a share of the profits (a dividend) in proportion to their purchases every year. By 1850 there were over 100 stores and they formed the Cooperative Wholesale Society in 1863, which continues today.

Fig. 4 *Group portrait of the Rochdale Pioneers; founders of the first retail cooperative movement*

The emergence of Friendly Societies

Friendly Societies, maintained by regularly paid subscriptions, had long been a feature of English life. After an Act of Parliament in 1793, Friendly Societies were granted legal status on the basis that they were non-political. It was an important distinction for their members, who aspired to ideals of self-improvement and self-help. The members were mainly skilled artisans and regarded themselves as God-fearing, respectable and working-class people. The Industrial Revolution had taught them to be prepared for periodic variations in the economy and other misfortunes of life.

The societies existed to provide basic welfare benefits when they were required. If the main earner, the husband, died, there would be sufficient provision to protect his widow and children from entering the workhouse. Membership of Friendly Societies continued to grow in both rural and urban areas and numbers soared to about 1.5 million by 1846. They were far more numerous than trade unions, whose popularity had dwindled after the collapse of the GNCTU. In 1842, Peel's government improved their status by appointing a paid Registrar to administrate on behalf of all registered Societies. The Friendly Societies became a symbol of Victorian working-class respectability and emphasised their distance from the poorer labouring classes who were often out of work, could never afford the regular subscription and had no security when times were hard.

SECTION 3 | Political change and social reform, 1832–1846

ACTIVITY

Summary

What was needed to improve urban conditions in Britain and to improve the lives of workers and the poor? Discuss the issues in small groups and try to provide ten to twelve suggestions. What obstacles were in the way of implementing these suggestions?

STUDY TIP

Remember you can come to the conclusion that the argument in an extract is unconvincing as long as you back up your answer with evidence.

 PRACTICE QUESTION

Evaluating historical extracts

Using your understanding of the historical context, assess how convincing the arguments in Extracts 1, 2 and 3 are in relation to conditions for urban workers in the 1830s and 1840s.

STUDY TIP

Your answer should not simply focus on the GNCTU, but also on the other working-class movements that were developing at the time and to an extent competing for membership numbers.

 PRACTICE QUESTION

'The working classes suffered greatly in the years 1832–1846 as a result of industrialisation.'
Assess the validity of this view.

4 Economy, society and politics 1846–1885

19 Government and developing political organisation

The development of the political system and party realignment

EXTRACT 1

For some years after **Bentinck**'s death in 1848, **Disraeli** was regarded by Stanley (Lord Derby) as a stop-gap leader, pending the hoped-for reunion with the Peelites. But this reunion never occurred, although for a long time it seemed to be just round the corner. That uncertainty together with the ultimate perpetuation, indeed widening, of the gulf between the two sections of the old Conservative Party is the key to the confused and shifting politics of the 1850s. The importance of the Peelites was not simply numerical. The rank and file fell, through conversion, retirement, and a few defeats from 89 to only 45 after the election of 1852, and to 26 after 1857. Their importance lay in their talents. They were what Gladstone called the 'Official Corps' – and this is just what the '**Who? Who? Ministry**' lacked. Why did the obvious not occur? Why did the Peelites remain a separate group – a head without a tail? There could be no chance of a reunion as long as the Protectionists refused to drop protection – and Derby was unwilling to press the matter.

Adapted from Robert Blake, *The Conservative Party from Peel to Thatcher*, 1985

ACTIVITY

Evaluating historical extracts

1. According to Extract 1 what is the explanation for the 'confused and shifting politics of the 1850s'?
2. What was the political importance of the Peelites? What evidence is put forward in Extract 1 to support this view?

The damage sustained by the Conservative Party over the repeal of the Corn Laws in 1846 brought about a significant **realignment** of the two main political parties, the Whigs and the Conservatives. This meant there were five different political groups in Parliament: Protectionist Conservatives, Peelites, the Whigs, the Radicals and the Irish MPs. The support of the Irish MPs was split between whichever party they believed would concede to their demands. The Radicals generally supported the Whigs, but on certain issues could be their most bitter critics. The Peelites seemed uncertain whether to finalise their break with Conservatism and support the Whigs or whether to find a compromise and return to their Conservative roots. As Blake suggests, it was that 'uncertainty together with the widening of the gulf between the two sections of the old Conservative Party [which] is the key to the confused and shifting politics of the 1850s'. The fact that there were nine ministries over 20 years suggests a period of political instability and a clear two-party system seemed unlikely to emerge. It could be seen, however, as a formative phase out of which emerged new robust political alignments and the beginnings of a modern party system.

LEARNING OBJECTIVES

In this chapter you will learn about:
- the development of the political system
- party realignment
- the emergence of the Liberal Party.

KEY QUESTION

As you read this chapter, consider the following Key Questions:
- How was Britain governed and how did democracy and political organisations change and develop?
- How important were ideas and ideologies?

KEY CHRONOLOGY

1846	Repeal of the Corn Laws
	Resignation of Peel after defeat in the Commons
	Conservative Party splits into Protectionists and Peelites
1849	Abolition of the Navigation acts
1850	Death of Sir Robert Peel
1859	Formation of the Liberal Party
1865	Death of Palmerston
1867	The Second Reform Act

A CLOSER LOOK

The '**Who? Who? Ministry**' was a derisive reference to Lord Derby's Conservative government, which survived only a few months in 1852. In the absence of the 'Official Corps' Peelites, its ministers were relatively unknown and inexperienced.

KEY TERM

realignment: grouping or dividing on a new basis

SECTION 4 | Economy, society and politics 1846–1885

Fig. 1 *Disraeli's first speech in the House of Commons*

KEY PROFILE

Henry John Temple, Viscount Palmerston (1784–1865) started his political life as a Tory MP in 1807, in a career that spanned 58 years. He was a flamboyant character and as Foreign Secretary he championed the independence of small nations and developed a high-handed patriotic approach in his diplomatic actions. He was Prime Minister twice and always more interested in foreign affairs and liberalism abroad, rather than promoting political reform at home.

A CLOSER LOOK

The Navigation Acts 1849

The Navigation Laws, first introduced in the late seventeenth century, aimed to protect British trade from any foreign competition, by stating that all goods shipped from any part of the world to Britain, or to British colonies, had to be carried in British or colonial ships. This would ensure that profits from trade with colonies would be brought into the British economy. The Navigation Laws were relaxed in the 1820s by William Huskisson (see Chapter 9).

KEY PROFILE

Lord George Bentinck (1802–48) (whose grandfather, the third Duke of Portland, had briefly held office as Prime Minister 1807–1809), became a Tory MP in 1828, but was more at home with horse racing than with political involvement. This changed over the issue of Corn Law repeal. Working with Disraeli, he led the Protectionist opposition to the repeal, but failed. From 1846 to 1848, he led the Protectionist Conservatives in opposition.

Benjamin Disraeli (1804–81) was born into an Italian Jewish immigrant family, but brought up an Anglican. He entered Parliament in 1837 as a Tory and although a gifted politician, he was scorned and distrusted by traditional Conservatives because of his Jewish background. He helped to bring down Peel in 1846, siding with the Protectionists against the Free Traders. During Derby's ministries he was Chancellor and later became Prime Minister. He and Gladstone were political arch-rivals.

A CLOSER LOOK

The five political groups after 1846

1. Protectionist Conservatives had been anti-Corn Law repeal. They were led, first by **Stanley (Lord Derby)** followed by Bentinck and then Disraeli.
2. Peelites, firstly led by Peel until his death in 1850, followed by **Aberdeen** and Gladstone.
3. The Whigs were led by Russell and **Palmerston**.
4. The Radicals were led by Cobden and Bright.
5. The other group comprised the 105 Irish MPs.

KEY PROFILE

Edward Stanley (1799–1869), 14th Earl of Derby, was a Whig MP from 1820 to 1835 and a member of the Whig government that passed the 1832 Reform Act. He introduced the proposals to end slavery in 1833. He became unhappy with the direction of the Whigs and switched to the Conservatives under Sir Robert Peel. He disagreed with Peel over the reform of the Corn Laws and became Prime Minister after the Peelites split from the party.

George Gordon, Earl of Aberdeen (1784–1860), a classical scholar and diplomat, served as Foreign Secretary under Conservative Sir Robert Peel from 1841 to 1846. He supported the repeal of the Corn Laws in 1846 and after Peel's death in 1850 led the Peelites (free-traders) who had split from the Conservative Party. Prime Minister from 1852 to 1855, he was blamed for his inefficient management of the Crimean War and forced to resign.

Lord John Russell's Whig government survived six years with support from the Peelites and achieved the furtherance of Free Trade by the abolition of the **Navigation Acts** in 1849. The Conservatives realised, by the 1850s, that in order to rebuild the party, they would have to abandon Protection and attract industry and commerce, if they were ever again going to enjoy political success. The Conservative showing in the elections of 1852 and 1857 was not convincing and led to ineffective minority governments, although valuable work was being done behind the scenes on Conservative Party reorganisation. Governments followed in quick succession. Palmerston concentrated on foreign affairs, patriotism and promoting British interests abroad and won popular support for a time. It was, however, Lord Derby's minority Conservative government in 1858 that progressed democracy by abolishing the property qualification to stand as an MP, one of the six demands of the Chartists, and in theory opened the way for men of few means to stand for Parliament. It also allowed practising Jews to sit in Parliament.

After more than a decade of shifting political power, various Radical/Liberal groups came to an agreement to work together to achieve a stable government in 1859. It was led by Palmerston, then in his seventies, whose chief interest remained in foreign affairs. In spite of the 'Liberal' label beginning to attach itself to this political group, Palmerston persisted obstinately in refusing to contemplate reform. Gladstone as Chancellor tidied up the loose ends on Free Trade. On Palmerston's death, aged 81, on the eve of winning an election, Russell formed a government and immediately introduced a bill for the reform of Parliament, but failed to convince enough of his own party and was defeated.

Lord Russell's First Ministry, 1846–52	Whig	Seen as weak and ineffective, a conviction politician, unable to inspire his followers, but survived with Peelite support
Lord Derby's First Ministry, 1852	Conservative	No workable majority
Lord Aberdeen, 1852–55	Whig–Peelite coalition	Defeated by stress of Crimean war
Lord Palmerston's First Ministry, 1855–58	Whig	'An impostor, utterly exhausted' according to Disraeli, but at 71 surprised all with his energy, which was directed at foreign affairs
Lord Derby's Second Ministry, 1858–59	Conservative	Assisted by Disraeli; lacked a majority
Lord Palmerston's Second Ministry 1859–65	Whig–Peelite and Liberals	More cohesive government, bridge between group politics of 1850s and party politics, but chief concern foreign affairs; little legislation; Palmerston blocked all reform and died in office
Lord Russell's Second Ministry 1865–66	Whigs, Peelites, Liberals and Radicals	Moving towards unity as Liberals; Russell retired and handed over to Gladstone
Lord Derby's Third Ministry 1866–68	Conservative	Politically powerless, but passed the Second Reform Act, 1867; Derby retired, leaving Disraeli as leader
Disraeli, 1868	Conservative	Politically powerless, no majority, but Disraeli was determined and ambitious for his Party

ACTIVITY

1. Write a profile of a 'typical' supporter of each of the five main groups in Parliament – Whigs, Protectionists, Peelites, Radicals and Irish.
2. Can you put forward any reasons why politicians might begin to see an advantage in aligning themselves to the broader Liberal (Whig)/Conservative division in the 1850s?

ACTIVITY

Evaluating historical extracts

1. What view of the Peelites is put forward in Extract 2?
2. To what extent do Extracts 1 and 2 agree on the significance of the Peelites in the realignment of the political parties?

A brief Conservative government (1866–68) led by Derby introduced one of the most important pieces of legislation of the era, the Second Reform Act. Ill health forced his resignation and he nominated Disraeli as his successor. Although he was supported by the Monarch, Queen Victoria, Disraeli lost the 1868 election after 278 days in office and resigned. Eric Evans sums up this period as one of political uncertainty, but also one that marks an advance in the process of party realignment. 'It is appropriate,' that in 1868, the Monarch is 'forced by the choice of the electorate to part with a prime minister [Disraeli] whom she admired and to accept as his successor a man, William Gladstone, whom she disliked intensely. By his actions in 1868, Disraeli publicly acknowledged the effective sovereignty of the electorate. It was also a symbolic recognition that the modern political system was in being.'

EXTRACT 2

The extent to which the Peelite/Protectionist split affected the two-party allegiances can easily be exaggerated. Only in the election of 1847 were the Peelites a numerous body in Parliament. By 1857 the informed political diarist Greville estimated that 'not a dozen Peelites' remained in splendid isolation from the two-party system. In fact, they had fewer than 50 supporters in 1852 since most of the less prominent Peelites quietly rejoined the Conservatives. This process was aided by the Derby government of 1852 and by its commitment not to reintroduce Protection. One ex-Peelite, Sir John Pakington, accepted a Cabinet post in this administration. Fortunately for future Conservative fortunes, the Protection issue became far less contentious after 1852. It became obvious that the repeal of the Corn Laws had not destroyed the agricultural interest, as had been gloomily prophesied in 1846. The way was thus open for ordinary Peelites, their leader now dead and their cause triumphant, to return to the Conservative fold. Most did.

Adapted from Eric J. Evans, *Political Parties in Britain, 1783–1867*, 1985

Fig. 2 *A young Queen Victoria in 1840*

The development of the political system

The 1832 Reform Act had strengthened the concept of representative government and made the political system more democratic (although at this stage progress was small and slow) and thus it had the effect of weakening the political power of the Monarch. The continuing creation of wealth and growth of prosperity in Britain through industrialisation was gradually increasing the size of the electorate, as more men met the property requirements of the 1832 Act to qualify for the franchise.

There was a question mark over whether or not the monarchy would survive. When Queen Victoria came to the throne in 1837, the British monarchy was unpopular, and members of the royal family were lampooned mercilessly in the press for their vulgarity, low morals, extravagance and stupidity. In fact the monarchy survived and indeed flourished under Queen Victoria, who through her personal integrity restored some of its dignity and popular appeal, although at the same time there were subtle changes in its political function.

The position of the monarchy was based on established traditions and political habits, rather than its power being clearly defined in a written constitution. Although every piece of legislation still required the consent of the Monarch, and the Government was carried on by ministers in the name of the Monarch, the business of government continued, for the most part, without royal interference. It had become accepted that the Monarch would not interfere in elections and this reduced her influence in the Commons. Queen Victoria's clash with Peel over the political affiliation of her Ladies of the Bedchamber in 1839 raised the question of the boundaries of royal power. Historians McCord and Purdue point out that the constitution hadn't changed, but the context within which it worked had. Royal authority was in decline. Victoria, however, was never politically neutral and did not accept her position as being 'merely titular'. She took a great interest in government and wielded influence in the appointment of bishops and high-ranking army officers. She was often humoured by her ministers, but in reality she did not get her way.

> **KEY QUESTION**
>
> How important was the role of individuals and groups and how were they affected by developments?

A CLOSER LOOK

The Bedchamber Crisis

In 1839, Melbourne was defeated in the Commons and Peel was called to form a government. When he asked a young and inexperienced Victoria to replace some of her Ladies of the Bedchamber with the wives of some of his Conservative supporters, to demonstrate her faith in his appointment, the Queen not only refused but took Melbourne into her confidence over the issue. Peel was unable to form a government and Melbourne returned to office to the delight of Victoria.

Walter Bagehot, the political philosopher, in his study of the parliamentary system, *The English Constitution* (1867), defined the Monarch's rights as 'the right to be consulted, the right to encourage and the right to warn'. He was in effect giving an opinion on what he believed to be the appropriate political boundaries within which Queen Victoria should operate.

Although political reform moved at a snail's pace, as it progressed it ensured that the political party in power was the choice of the people and the Prime Minister was the leader of the largest party in Parliament, which could gain the confidence of the House of Commons. As the political parties continued to develop, the power of the monarchy continued to decline.

> **ACTIVITY**
>
> **Thinking point**
>
> Explain in your own words the position of the monarchy in the political system by the middle of the nineteenth century. Did Queen Victoria operate within the boundaries suggested by Bagehot?

The emergence of the Liberal Party

EXTRACT 3

This new party was at first sight a curious alliance. On the one hand there were the parliamentary Radicals. They had led the charge against the outdated pre-industrial system, particularly 'land monopoly' – the special legal, financial and political privileges given to landowners – and the Church of England. Although they were a small **cabal** within the Commons, and even within this new political union, the Radicals provided much of the flavour and individuality of the Liberal message. Most of their leading figures, such as Cobden and Bright, were rich businessmen who wanted to modernise the nation's political practices in line with its economic and trading base. They masked this capitalist purpose behind the language of promoting the interests of 'the people' against 'privilege'. Yet their politics came down to redefining the place of industrialists in a modern society. 'They cannot endure', wrote constitutionalist Walter Bagehot, 'that a rich, able manufacturer should be a less man than a stupid, small squire'. The Whigs might have seemed strange bedfellows for these Radical capitalists.

Adapted from Richard Aldous, *The Lion and the Unicorn*, 2007

> **KEY TERM**
>
> **cabal:** a small group that comes together for a secret purpose, very often political intrigue

> **ACTIVITY**
>
> 1. From your knowledge of the Whig Party, why do you think that an alliance between the Whigs and the Radicals would seem 'at first sight a curious alliance'?
> 2. According to Extract 3 what was the real agenda of the leading Radicals in joining forces with the Whigs?

The Liberal Party was formed in 1859 from the combining of several political groups in Parliament – Whigs, Liberals, Radicals and Peelites. Although personal differences and political backgrounds divided them, by 1859 they increasingly pursued similar aims, the most pressing of which at this time was to remove the minority Conservative administration led by Lord Derby. It made sense to unite into one political party and mount a stronger challenge against the Conservatives. A meeting was held by the key members of the four groups in Willis's Rooms near St James's Palace in London and a motion was passed to come together under the banner of the Liberal Party to achieve this aim. A few days later on 10 June 1859, after a vote of no confidence in the Conservatives in the House of Commons, the first true Liberal government took office, with Lord Palmerston as Prime Minister and William Gladstone as Chancellor of the Exchequer. It was not however until the death of Palmerston, in office in 1865, that Liberalism became firmly established as a political creed and people began to talk about a Liberal Party. The Liberal Party dominated the political scene for the next 20 years under the forceful and inspiring leadership of Gladstone.

The term 'Liberal Party' had first been used during the 1830s and by the late 1840s some 'Whigs' referred to themselves as 'Liberals', although there appeared to be little party loyalty as we know it today. Little remained of the old system of **political patronage** and so, in the absence of any central party organisation, there was little control over the various groups. In addition, there was no compunction to contest seats at elections, particularly where a man held a safe seat. This situation enabled MPs to act independently of any party constraints and contributed to regular government defeats and political instability.

By the 1860s, party organisation was beginning to be regarded as essential in order to pass the increasing amounts of legislation with which governments were dealing. The role of MP was gradually becoming more professional with Parliament meeting more often and MPs taking more of an interest in the concerns of their constituents. These developments would remain insignificant until the electorate was extended. The Second Reform Act in 1867 transformed party politics.

> **CROSS-REFERENCE**
>
> **Political patronage** is explained in Chapters 1 and 7.

Fig. 3 *William Gladstone giving a speech to Liberal Party members in Leeds*

The composition of the Liberal Party

The disparate character of the Liberal Party stems from the 1832 Reform Act. One of its effects was to bring changes to the composition of the two traditional political parties, the Whigs and the Tories. A number of middle-class business and professional men with liberal and radical views were elected to Parliament to represent the newly-enfranchised industrial boroughs. Most of this new entry voted with the Whigs and this enabled them to form majority governments for most of the following three decades.

Table 1 *Occupations of the 456 Liberal MPs sitting between 1859 and 1874 for English constituencies*

Large landowners (aristocrats)	198
Gentlemen of leisure	49
Lawyers	84
Radicals	20
Big businessmen	74
Local businessmen	43
Radical businessmen	34

(Note: Total adds up to 502 as some landowners were also practising lawyers, etc.)

The Whigs belonged to powerful aristocratic landowning families. They had been instrumental in passing the First Parliamentary Reform Act in 1832 and were in favour of a further extension of the franchise, as long as it was controlled. The Whigs were generally supportive of the Nonconformists, yet also included in their number the Roman Catholic peerage. The leading Whigs sat in the House of Lords while the junior branches of their families sat in the House of Commons.

Some of the junior Whigs began to disassociate themselves from their more aristocratic and politically cautious kinsmen and call themselves Liberals. But most Liberals were from middle-class business and commercial backgrounds or were lawyers and professional men and had come into Parliament after 1832. They believed in individual liberty, Free Trade, freedom of the press and religious freedom. Many of them were Dissenters or Nonconformists, who believed that the Church should be separate and free from the state patronage and control.

The Peelites had followed Sir Robert Peel in his repeal of the Corn Laws in 1846, which split the Conservative Party into Protectionists and Peelite free traders and ensured that the Conservatives did not have a majority in the Commons for a long time to come. The Peelites at first held a balance of power in Parliament but they increasingly voted with the Whigs. Gradually their numbers fell away and the remainder were content to fuse with the Liberals by 1859. The Peelites came from wealthy industrial and commercial backgrounds. Gladstone was regarded as one of the leading Peelites.

The Radicals in Parliament were free-thinking middle-class individuals, most of whom adopted the Benthamite doctrine of Utilitarianism – a belief in taking actions that would be of greatest benefit to the greatest number of people. Generally speaking the Radicals wanted change in the social order. They opposed the political and economic dominance of the landowning classes and the privileged position of the Church of England as the established Church. They wanted an extension of the franchise, the removal of government restrictions and Free Trade. Perhaps the most influential Radical in the Liberal Party was John Bright.

Half the parliamentary Liberal Party drew their wealth from land ownership. Historian John Vincent asserts that Gladstone's Liberal Party was 'widely tied to the land, the Church and the Services, which were the informal and real basis of the aristocratic constitution and the object of Radical attack'. On this evidence it is not surprising that division and disagreement dogged the Liberal Party during this period. The other half of the Liberal Party had no aristocratic or landed connections, but had gained recent wealth through industry and commerce and associated themselves with the aristocracy, through public school education and social habits. Vincent characterises the middle-class Liberal MPs as 'middle-class intruders [who] blended into the aristocratic landscape, or wished to!' It was the small group of Radicals in the party who consistently supported change and reform and who acted 'spasmodically, in conjunction with the people, public opinion and the front bench, to achieve progress'.

The Liberal Party supported the principle of laissez faire and the doctrine of **self-help**. The Liberals were influenced by the great political philosophers of the day, **John Stuart Mill**, Jeremy Bentham and Walter Bagehot. They believed in the liberty and freedom of the individual and religious toleration. They supported Free Trade and saw it as a means of creating prosperity for all. They upheld the principle of parliamentary government, within a limited democracy. But they accepted that an overhaul of the parliamentary

> **CROSS-REFERENCE**
>
> **Self-help** was a popular ideology in the mid nineteenth century. It was promoted by the middle classes who believed that thrift and hard work would be rewarded, and espoused by skilled workers as a virtue to be strived for. See Chapter 23 for more detail on this.

> **KEY PROFILE**
>
> **John Stuart Mill (1806–73)** was a philosopher and political economist, son of political writer James Mill and married to Harriet Taylor, an early advocate of women's rights. Mill was influenced by Bentham's political and social theories. He believed in the political domination of the middle class, supporting the extension of the franchise to those who contributed to the country's economy, even women, but feared giving the vote to the uneducated masses.

system was necessary to reflect the changes in the distribution and wealth of the population which had occurred after the Industrial Revolution. The development of Britain into an urban nonconformist and perhaps more secular society was reflected politically in the growth of Liberalism and the Liberal Party.

> **ACTIVITY**
>
> ### Pair discussion
>
> Can you identify any common threads that united the different voices in the Liberal Party? Where do you think there would be discord?

Summary

- In 1846 the Conservative Party split into Protectionists and Peelites.
- Over the next two decades there were nine different governments, which suggests an element of political instability.
- There was a realignment of the two main political parties, the Conservatives and the Whigs, and the beginnings of a modern two-party system.
- With the strengthening of the concept of representative government, through reform, the political system was becoming more democratic and the power of the Monarch was weakening.
- Walter Bagehot defined the Monarch's rights as 'the right to be consulted, the right to encourage and the right to warn', in his view the appropriate political boundaries within which Queen Victoria should operate.
- The Monarch could no longer dictate who should lead the Government. The political party in power was the choice of the people and the Prime Minister was the leader of the party that gained the confidence of the House of Commons.
- The Liberal Party emerged from the combining of several political groups in Parliament. By 1865, Liberalism became firmly established as a political creed and people began to talk about a Liberal Party. The Liberal Party dominated the political scene for the next 20 years under the forceful and inspiring leadership of Gladstone.

> **EXTRACT 4**
>
> The position of the Protectionists, Peel's old opponents in 1846, was as difficult in the mid-Victorian years as that of the Whigs. Although many of the Peelites had returned to the fold between 1846 and 1852, the name Conservative had been adopted again in 1848 and Protection was abandoned as a party cry in 1852, the Conservatives were doomed to be a parliamentary minority. There were times when the Conservative Party seemed in serious danger of breaking up. That it did not disintegrate was of the utmost long-term importance – as was the fact that it remained flexible in practice. It may be reasonably argued that its flexibility and resilience, which disgruntled Conservative critics continued to condemn as treachery and weakness, were valuable long-term. Derby and Disraeli between them – one relying on social standing and representing a genuine aristocratic element in politics, the other depending on ambition and brains – guaranteed the future of the Conservative Party.
>
> Adapted from Asa Briggs, *The Age of Improvement*, 1967

SECTION 4 | Economy, society and politics 1846–1885

STUDY TIP

It would be a good idea to read over the chapter carefully before tackling this question and make sure you understand what happened to the Conservative Party as a result of the repeal of the Corn Laws. Use your own knowledge to support your comments on the arguments of these three extracts.

PRACTICE QUESTION

Evaluating historical extracts

Using your understanding of the historical context assess how convincing the arguments in Extracts 1, 2 and 4 are in relation to the realignment of the political parties in the years 1846–68.

STUDY TIP

Identify the 'several different political groups' and make sure you understand what each group represented, before starting to write your essay. You need to consider what made the party seem 'unlikely' to survive and what would or might ensure its continuance.

PRACTICE QUESTION

'The Liberal Party was a "curious alliance" of several different political groups, which appeared unlikely to survive.'
Assess the validity of this view of the emergence of the Liberal Party in the 1850s and 1860s.

20 Government and democracy

EXTRACT 1

By 1874, the middle classes began to be frightened by Gladstonian Liberalism, as Gladstone's first ministry approached its end. This may seem surprising in view of the number of measures that he carried out in their interest – reforms of the judicature, the universities, the **civil service** and the army. But gratitude is not a characteristic of voters. Having got much of what they wanted from the Liberals, the middle class began to be alarmed at working-class militancy, Radicalism and republicanism that a Conservative government under Disraeli seemed more likely to check than Gladstone, however much he personally disapproved. Disraeli knew what he was doing when he revived the traditional Conservative slogans about the monarchy, Church and constitution. It was vital to avoid doing anything which would frighten away these new allies. A quiet, low temperature election is better for the Conservatives than their opponents. Gladstone was able to raise the temperature high in 1868 and to fever pitch in 1880, but he could not do it in 1874.

Adapted from Robert Blake, *The Conservative Party from Peel to Thatcher*, 1985

ACTIVITY

Evaluating historical extracts

1. What explanation for the desertion of the middle classes from the Liberal Party is suggested in the extract?
2. According to the extract how did Disraeli win over middle-class voters?

By 1866, Gladstone had become leader of the Liberal Party and Benjamin Disraeli leader of the Conservative Party in the House of Commons. Both men represented the powerful prosperous middle class of Victorian Britain. Over the following years, as each in turn led their party to electoral victory, they vied with each other to introduce political and social reforms and to uphold Britain's interests abroad.

Gladstone as Prime Minister; his ministries, ideas and policies

KEY QUESTION

- How important were ideas and ideology?
- How important was the role of individuals and groups and how were they affected by developments?

'Gladstonian Liberalism'

When Gladstone began to take an interest in politics as a young man, at the time of the debate on the 1832 Reform Act, it appeared that his political career would be as a staunch member of the Tory Party. At this stage he was opposed to reform and was described by historian Macaulay as 'the rising hope of the stern unbending Tories'. He was an ardent supporter and admirer of Robert Peel and acknowledged him as his political guiding light when he came to formulating his own policies. After Peel's death, Gladstone was regarded as one

LEARNING OBJECTIVES

In this chapter you will learn about:

- Gladstone, his ministries, ideas and policies
- Disraeli, his ministries, ideas and policies
- increasing democracy
- legislation.

KEY CHRONOLOGY

Ministries up to 1885

1868	Disraeli
1868–1874	Gladstone
1874–1880	Disraeli
1880–1885	Gladstone

KEY QUESTION

As you read this chapter, consider the following Key Question:
How was Britain governed and how did democracy and political organisations change and develop?

KEY TERM

civil service: the body that is responsible for the public administration of the state

Fig. 1 *A cartoon portrait of Gladstone from* Vanity Fair *magazine*

of the leading Peelites – Chancellor under Aberdeen from 1852 to 1855 and again in Palmerston's and Russell's Liberal governments, eventually taking over the mantle of Liberal leader from Russell. As party leader such was his force of character and influence, Liberalism became synonymous with Gladstone and was referred to as 'Gladstonian Liberalism'.

The emergence of the Liberal Party coincided with the emergence of Gladstone to national prominence. Gladstone was renowned for his strong moral principles and religious convictions. He believed in individual liberty and equality of opportunity. Gladstone's personal and firmly held principles gave weight to the wider Liberal beliefs of peace, retrenchment and reform. They centred round his religious devotion and his admiration for Peel. Sometimes Liberals found Gladstone's deeper motivating forces difficult to understand or agree with.

'Peace, **retrenchment** and reform' became Gladstone's catchphrase and that of the Liberal Party. Gladstone believed that if peace could be maintained with other nations, this would enable trade and industry to develop unhindered by the disruptions of war. It would also mean that taxation could be more easily kept under control. As one of Gladstone's aims was to abolish income tax, a policy of cutting back on government spending (retrenchment) would also reduce the necessity of raising taxes. Taxation was seen by the Liberals as depriving people of their freedom to spend their money as they wished. By reform, they were concerned with bringing about changes in laws and institutions which prevented people from acting freely.

These three aspects of Gladstonian Liberalism tie in with the doctrine of laissez faire – that the state would not interfere in the workings of the market economy – and was a basic principle of all nineteenth-century Liberal governments. It was closely associated with Gladstone's belief in Free Trade and his earlier actions as Chancellor when he abolished all duties on goods. The doctrine of self-help was also dear to Gladstone's heart – a belief in reward through hard work and effort. Gladstone lacked any real interest in social reform.

> **KEY TERM**
>
> **retrenchment:** economising or cutting expenditure

Gladstone's ministries

As a result of the 1868 general election, Gladstone became Prime Minister on the first of four occasions, in a high-profile political career which spanned over 60 years. A good majority gave the Liberals a clear mandate to implement policies based on the principles of 'Gladstonian Liberalism'. Gladstone's legislative programme was extensive and the reforms introduced reflected the principles of administrative efficiency, cutting back on government spending, pursuing Free Trade and promoting the freedom of the individual.

The make-up of Gladstone's Cabinet revealed the different political groupings that made up the Liberal Party – Peelites, Liberals, Radicals and Whigs – but that, according to McCord, had a 'strong Whiggish tinge'. At the centre of the administration was the highly principled and deeply religious Gladstone. For him, politics and religion seemed to go hand in hand and his policies were often guided by what he believed to be morally right. According to historian Anthony Wood, 'his opponents often complained of Gladstone's tendency to confuse his own policy with the will of God, but he may well have felt that this particular moment [1868] was to be one of the turning points both in his own career and in the life of the country.' Martin Pugh in his book *The Making of Modern British Politics* appears to subscribe to this view. Pugh remarks upon Gladstone's capacity to maintain a sense of morality in politics – lifting the views of men beyond the merely materialistic – for which he was unrivalled. Historian John Vincent, however, contends that expediency guided his political decisions rather than his belief in God.

His reforms, vast in number, addressed important social and political issues of the period. The extent to which they satisfied the various interests within the party and the pressure groups outside is a matter for debate. At the outset of his first ministry, Gladstone insisted on unity within the party and held it together at least on the surface for five years, but in the end, he was unable to retain the support of the middle-class voters who had put him in power.

A CLOSER LOOK

There were other problems with Gladstone's election campaign, suggested by historian Philip Magnus:

'In framing his appeal to the country, Gladstone wore the spectacles of a Chancellor of the Exchequer instead of those of a prime minister. He reflected at the end of his life that the electorate had been no more interested in his promise to repeal the income-tax, which then stood at threepence [in the £1], than it had been in his call for economy. The country was bored and Gladstone's rigid financial doctrine made no appeal to it. It wanted a measure of social reform at home, rather than in Ireland.'

The general election result of 1874 brought a firm victory for the Conservative Party. The Liberal policies introduced through Gladstone's tireless legislation of the previous six years had alienated most of the support that had brought him to power in 1868. In 1874, the old Whigs, the merchants and industrialists, were disappointed at what they saw as Gladstone's wooing of the working class, or as Blake suggests, were alarmed 'at working-class militancy, radicalism and republicanism'. They turned to the Conservative Party and together with the numerically influential vote of the newly enfranchised artisan class (see below), brought the Conservatives to power under the leadership of Benjamin Disraeli.

Gladstone returned to power with a majority in the 1880 election. Much of this ministry was taken up with problems relating to Ireland. However he was responsible for some far-reaching **political reforms** that moved Britain towards greater democracy.

ACTIVITY

1. What were the uniting factors for Gladstone's Liberal Party? What were the areas of potential conflict?
2. Read the quote in A Closer Look, on this page. Why, according to Philip Magnus, did Gladstone lose the 1874 election? Do you think there were any other reasons?

CROSS-REFERENCE

Gladstone's **political reforms** and the Irish problems are discussed in Chapter 21.

KEY CHRONOLOGY

Gladstone and Disraeli's social legislation

1869	Women ratepayers able to vote in local elections
1870	Forster's Education Act
	Civil Service Act
	Married Women's Property Act
1871	Cardwell's Army Reforms
1871	Trade Union Act
1871	Criminal Law Amendment Act
1872	Public Health Act
1872	Licensing Act
1873	Judicature Act
1875	Artisans' Dwelling Act
1875	Public Health Act
1875	Conspiracy and Protection of Property Act
1874 & 1878	Factory legislation sets code of regulations for conditions in factories

Gladstone's social reforms

An improvement in the provision of education had become increasingly important. After the extension of the franchise in 1867 it was in the Government's interest to have an articulate electorate. In an age of increasing technological and scientific advance and the inevitable challenges to Britain's global industrial supremacy, it was essential to have a better-educated workforce. There were obvious benefits to society as a whole, but in Gladstonian terms, a national system would be efficient and contribute to the development of a meritocracy. It would bring economic advantage in the longer term by creating workers with technical and vocational skills and, therefore, assist Britain in international competitiveness.

- **Forster's Education Act of 1870** made provision for elementary schools to be set up across the country. The Act was important in that it indicated a move away from laissez faire in government social legislation and acknowledged the role of the state in educating its children.
- **Administrative reforms** were carried out in the army and civil service (1870) and the judiciary (1873), which made for greater efficiency, but were controversial as they attempted to establish the principle of advancement by merit rather than connection and created ill-feeling towards the Government from the traditional Whigs. They illustrate Gladstone's adherence to the concept of self-help.

A CLOSER LOOK

Civil service reform

In the reform of the civil service the principle of entry by competitive examination was established. This innovation brought in candidates with intellect and ability and improved professionalism and efficiency at a minimal cost to the Government. The reform allowed bright young men from ordinary backgrounds the chance of a steady career with good prospects and a comfortable standard of living. It won the approval of many middle-class Liberals.

Army reform

The army was riddled with incompetence and inefficiency. Wealthy families bought their sons commissions as officers. The abolition of the system of purchase of commissions presented a difficult challenge to Edward Cardwell, Secretary for war; he was attacking a fundamental belief of society – the right by birth and wealth to privilege. After furious opposition, the Act was finally passed whereby selection and promotion of officers was to be based on merit.

- **The Trade Union Act of 1871** established the legal right of the unions to hold property and funds and have them protected by law. They also had the right to strike. The Criminal Law Amendment Act passed immediately made any form of **picketing** illegal. The trade unions were legalised but almost any action they took to achieve their objectives was illegal. Historians have identified this Act as Gladstone's most serious misjudgement as it cost him working-class support. The skilled artisans who had helped to ensure the Government's success in 1868 were left bitterly disappointed with the lack of any real support for trade union reform.
- **Gladstone's missionary zeal** to improve the moral fibre of the ordinary man probably contributed to his enthusiasm to support the **Licensing Act (1872)**. It was a mild enough measure giving magistrates the power to issue licences to publicans that would fix opening and closing hours. It satisfied neither side: **temperance** groups did not think it went far enough and the

CROSS-REFERENCE

Both Gladstone's and Disraeli's trade union reforms are discussed in detail in Chapter 23.

KEY TERM

picketing: the action taken by strikers to persuade the non-striking workers to join the strike

temperance: moderation or complete abstinince in relation to alcohol

'Beerage' felt it attacked their industry. The Licensing Bill had repercussions beyond the term of Gladstone's first ministry as it alienated brewers and distillers who in future voted Conservative and gave generously to Conservative Party funds.

- Almost unnoticed among this flurry of reforms were measures that involved the first stirrings of a women's rights movement and female emancipation. In 1869, Gladstone agreed to the principle of female emancipation by giving women ratepayers the vote in local elections. A year later, the **Married Women's Property Act** gave married women legal status and allowed a woman to keep a proportion of her own earnings. The Education Act was enlightened as it made provision for girls to attend school. It would possibly be the daughters of that generation who benefited from the introduction of women's suffrage in 1918 and 1928.

> **ACTIVITY**
>
> Study the brief outline of the Liberal government's key reforms and consider the following questions:
> 1. Who would benefit from these reforms?
> 2. Does a pattern emerge?
> 3. Can you explain Gladstonian Liberalism in terms of these reforms?
> 4. Which groups if any would be dissatisfied with the reforms and why?
>
> Present your findings to the class. Have you all reached similar conclusions?

EXTRACT 2

From the standpoint of the twentieth century Gladstone's administrative reforms seem natural and obvious enough, but it is important to stress how revolutionary in implication they were at this time. In the everyday working of society the nineteenth century was an age of patronage and amateurism. A position in government service, a college fellowship, or a commission in the army had been considered a kind of property, and there were many who saw the new doctrine of efficiency as an onslaught on the fundamental principles of society. Efficiency in government had always been the cry of the Radicals and the reorganisation of the administrative departments in 1870 was a natural consequence of the growing complexity of government demanding the greater expertness of the trained professional. Patronage and amateurism were fading fast and the evidence lies in the rise of families of a new intellectual middle class in the upper reaches of the civil service.

Adapted from Anthony Wood, *Nineteenth Century Britain, 1815–1914*, 1982

Disraeli, his ministries, ideas and policies

Disraeli's Conservatism

In the period leading up to the 1874 general election, Disraeli took advantage of Gladstone's increasing discomfort and unpopularity with several sections of traditional Liberal supporters. He began to plant the seeds of the idea of a '**Tory Democracy**', a new brand of Conservatism, in order to revive the fortunes of the Conservative Party.

Disraeli was interested in the new trends towards democracy and the extension of the franchise, but he strongly believed in maintaining tradition and privilege and knew that the Conservative Party was not ready to abandon the old aristocratic hierarchy. He wanted to encourage the working-class voters to place their trust in the Conservatives and persuade them that they could share some of the benefits enjoyed by the more prosperous groups in society.

Disraeli was 70 years old when he became Prime Minister in 1874 in an election in which the Conservatives had a clear majority for the first time in over 20 years. His government (1874–80) was responsible for a number of important social reforms and in a speech to the National Union at the Crystal Palace in 1872 before the election, he appeared to promote a Tory policy of social reform. There is a question mark over Disraeli's sincerity in calling for social reform. It could have been a dig at Gladstone, who had introduced few measures of social reform. It could have been a ploy to pull in the working-class voters. Or was it the case that Disraeli was simply outlining the main principles of his new Conservatism?

> **KEY QUESTION**
>
> - How important were ideas and ideology?
> - How important was the role of individuals and groups and how were they affected by developments?
> - How and with what results did society and social policy develop?

> **KEY TERM**
>
> **Tory Democracy:** a term describing the policies advocated by Disraeli when he became Prime Minister in 1874, namely maintaining Conservative support of established institutions – the constitutional monarchy, the British Empire, the Church of England – but also supporting a degree of social reform

ACTIVITY

What does the cartoon in Fig.2 suggest about Disraeli's and Gladstone's relationship? Do you think this is an accurate portrayal?

Fig. 2 *A Punch cartoon from 1868 depicts Disraeli and Gladstone as rival actors; Disraeli, seen here as Hamlet, is in work while Gladstone awaits his turn*

Disraeli's cabinet contained a new generation of Conservative leaders, although it remained socially exclusive in respect of its landed dominance – only one out of its twelve members was not a peer or a landed gentleman. The loss of the 1868 election had disappointed Disraeli because it was his Reform Act in 1867 that had extended the franchise to the artisan class in the towns. Disraeli had expected thanks by way of support from these new voters, but quickly came to realise that political parties must improve their organisation to reach the new, expanding electorate. He appointed John Gorst to overhaul party organisation and set up a Conservative Central Office in London. The National Union of Conservative Associations, set up in 1867 and the essential link to the constituencies, became the propaganda tool of Central Office. Disraeli used it as his sounding board in 1872 on which to outline his policies and ideas of Tory Democracy.

Whatever the motives behind Disraeli's brand of Conservatism, it is a fact that in the 1874 election, the newly enfranchised 'respectable' working-class voters in the boroughs helped to bring the Conservatives to power. The electorate as a whole was tired of Gladstone's endless legislation and Disraeli was able to present his party as having a 'broad-based appeal' (Blake) to the working class as well as to property owners – land owners in the country and middle-class business men in the towns.

ACTIVITY

Create a political ideology diagram. On one side indicate the influences that created Gladstonian Liberalism; on the other the influences that created Disraeli's brand of 'Tory Democracy'.

> **EXTRACT 3**
>
> Disraeli had a measure of luck, but the test of a political leader is his ability to exploit his luck and on this test Disraeli comes out well. He carried the Reform Act without splitting his party. If Disraeli lost the ensuing election, the reason

was that the cards were so heavily stacked against him. He had the good sense to keep calm after defeat, wait on events and hit back at the right moment. The victory of 1874 owed as much to his prudence and patience as to his capacity to dazzle with new ideas and fresh proposals. The principal Conservative measures did not differ greatly from the type of legislation which a Liberal government might have carried. They added up to a substantial instalment of social reform, but not a major new departure. Disraeli took up the social cry in opposition largely because it was likely to divide the Liberals. In office he was bound to do something about it. But here was no question of a Tory-working class alliance. The working class were kept at arm's length.

Adapted from Robert Blake, *The Conservative Party from Peel to Thatcher*, 1985

ACTIVITY

Evaluating historical extracts

What view of Disraeli is advanced in Extract 2?

Disraeli's social reforms

Disraeli's government of 1874 has gained its reputation on the strength of its social reforms. A broad spectrum of reforms was introduced in quick succession in 1875 and 1876. These measures appear to be consistent with the idea of Tory Democracy. However, there is evidence that Disraeli had no coherent programme of reform and much of the legislation was introduced as a response to pressure from reform groups and from recommendations made by Royal Commissions of Inquiry.

- The major innovation of the **Artisans' Dwelling Act** (1875) lies in the power it gave the local authority to purchase, clear and then redevelop slums. The absence of a compulsory purchase order seriously weakened the Act's effectiveness and many city councils chose to ignore it. However, its longterm importance was that it established the principle of state intervention with regard to private dwelling houses and marked the beginning of local authority housing.
- In 1875 a **Public Health Act** was introduced which pulled together all existing sanitary legislation, which up until then had fallen short of tackling current health problems. It laid down minimum standards of drainage, sewage disposal and refuse. A Medical Officer of Health was charged with the reporting of all infectious diseases. Opposition came from the laissez faire brigade, who saw the measure as involving too much state intervention and interference with personal freedom.
- The **Employers and Workmen Act,** 1875, introduced a contract of service which gave employees terms that were on a par with those of employers. This legislation was a major step in labour law reform and Disraeli was justly proud of his achievement when he said that he had 'satisfactorily settled the position of labour for a generation'.
- The factory legislation passed in 1874 and 1878 was a consolidation of the previous **Factory Acts** and set the code of regulations for conditions in factories and, with the reduction in hours for women and young people, had the effect of indirectly reducing men's working hours. The Acts brought other industries in line with the textile industry and all factories came under the umbrella of a state inspectorate. This was an important reform as it established the principle of the state offering protection to industrial workers.

KEY QUESTION

How and with what results did society and social policy develop?

Fig. 3 *A cartoon portrait of Disraeli from* Vanity Fair *magazine*

Evaluation of reforms

It could be argued that Disraeli established the idea of Tory Democracy through his social reforms. The reforms certainly indicated an awareness of the needs of the emergent working class. Their voice was heard more often, and this was as a result of the growing influence and strength of the trade unions and through improved provision of education – both areas of encouragement in the Conservative reforms. The provisions of the Public

Health Act were so practical that they lasted for over 60 years. The reforms gave credence to the idea of a Tory working-class man and the principle of state intervention was cautiously extended in spite of the reactionary interests in the Conservative Party.

Disraeli's greatest social achievement was in trade union legislation and labour laws. This did much to make trade unions respectable and encouraged their growth. Disraeli's motive was to 'gain and retain for the Tories the lasting affection of the working classes'. But the working class were fickle and by 1880 excitement at what Disraeli did for them was fading fast. In any case there appeared to be an element of cynicism in Disraeli's support of some measures and not of others. The 1880 election returned Gladstone and the Liberals to power.

Much of the legislation of this period was **permissive** rather than compulsory, in that it facilitated change and improvement rather than insisted on it. It was an indication that Victorian attitudes of laissez faire and self-help prevailed among the upper and middle classes and there was still a reluctance to accept a too rapid extension of the state's responsibility for the welfare of its people, although the principle of limited state intervention was accepted.

> **KEY TERM**
>
> **permissive legislation:** a law that allows organisations or individuals at whom it is directed the choice of whether or not to carry out its requirements; it reflects the laissez faire attitudes of the period

> **ACTIVITY**
>
> Study the brief outline of Disraeli's key reforms and consider the following questions:
> 1. Who would benefit from these reforms?
> 2. Does a pattern emerge?
> 3. Can you explain Tory Democracy in terms of these reforms?
> 4. Which groups if any would be dissatisfied with the reforms and why?
>
> Present your findings to the class. Have you all reached similar conclusions?

> **ACTIVITY**
>
> ### Summary
>
> Work in groups. Each group should draw up a table entitled either 'Gladstone's social reforms' or 'Disraeli's social reforms' with the following headings:
>
> | Date | Reform | Strengths | Weaknesses/Limitations |
> |---|---|---|---|
> | | | | |
> | | | | |
> | | | | |
> | | | | |
>
> Share your table with another group so you have one table on Gladstone and another on Disraeli. Using the information collected in the tables, assess the extent to which the reforms of Gladstone, and Disraeli, were successful. As a group can you come to a consensus as to which politician you feel was the more successful?

> **KEY CHRONOLOGY**
>
> 1867 Second Reform Act
> 1872 Secret Ballot Act
> 1883 Corrupt Practices Act
> 1884 Third Reform Act (Franchise Act)
> 1885 Redistribution Act

Increasing democracy

In 1850 few of the principles of what is generally accepted as representative government had been achieved. The population of Great Britain was standing at approximately 21 million, of whom only a tiny fraction were involved in the political process. The Great Reform Act of 1832 could be said to have heralded the beginning of a more popular and democratic form of politics in Britain. However, since that initial extension of the franchise to middle-class men in 1832, there had been little further progress made towards democracy. Although the increasing prosperity of the mid-Victorian economic boom meant that more men held property of the value that qualified them to vote (£10 householders), there were still fewer than a million voters. Working-class men could not vote, not because they belonged to the working class *per se*, but because the voting qualification was set too high to include them. The rapid increase of the population and continuing urbanisation made some redistribution of seats vital to achieve fair representation.

Political reforms

Gladstone's 1866 Reform Bill

In response to the renewed interest and pressure for parliamentary reform, Gladstone and Lord John Russell, the Liberal Prime Minister, drew up a Reform Bill. It proposed a relaxation of the voting qualification to give the vote to skilled workers – who lived mainly in the industrial towns – and to smallholders in the counties.

The Bill was thrown out, not by Conservative opposition, but from a group within the Liberal Party, who claimed reform would give political power to the 'ignorant'. It was a humiliating defeat for the Liberals, who resigned office. The Reform League responded by organising demonstrations across the country. The message to the new Conservative government was clear. The protesters were not going to give up until they had obtained 'registered, residential male suffrage, as the only just basis of representation and the secret ballot to protect them from undue influence and intimidation in elections'.

The 1867 Reform Act

The 1867 Reform Act increased the total number of voters from 1.2 million to approximately 2.5 million, which was roughly one third of the male adult population. No women could vote. The greatest increase in voters occurred in the boroughs, where skilled workers were given the vote for the first time. An elitist perception continued among the political classes that fitness to vote was based not just on income, but on wise use of income – that is, using it to secure a stable home. The poorer, generally unskilled and largely uneducated, working class, who had no ability to save nor security of tenure, were still excluded.

The impact of this landmark victory for the artisan class was reduced because of the limited nature of the redistribution. For example, Birmingham, Liverpool and Manchester, with their huge populations, were given only one extra seat in addition to the two they already had. Overall, the distribution of seats did not correspond to the size of the population in any given area. Rural areas remained over-represented and the industrial Midlands, North and Scotland remained under-represented. Boroughs with a population of just over 10,000 had the same representation (i.e. two MPs) as boroughs with a population of almost 400,000.

The distinction between county and borough franchise was maintained. There was a smaller increase in the electorate in the counties, where the voting qualification was extended to include smallholders and small tenant farmers, but completely excluded agricultural workers.

The increase in the electorate led to both parties improving their party organisations in order to capture the new voters at elections. The Reform Act led indirectly to the 1870 Education Act, as many politicians thought it appropriate to educate the new voters.

A CLOSER LOOK

Features of democracy

We have a system of representative government in Britain today. It is based on the following basic principles which took over 150 years to achieve and are still evolving: universal suffrage, unhindered use of the vote, the right to participate in the political process (e.g. stand as an MP), government by elected representatives, government based on majority support, regular free elections, freedoms of speech, assembly and worship.

CROSS-REFERENCE:

See page 207 in Chapter 21 for more on the pressure for Parliamentary reform.

ACTIVITY

What impact did the Second Reform Act have on:
a) the electorate
b) the distribution of seats?
Which section of the electorate gained most from the changes? Explain your answer.

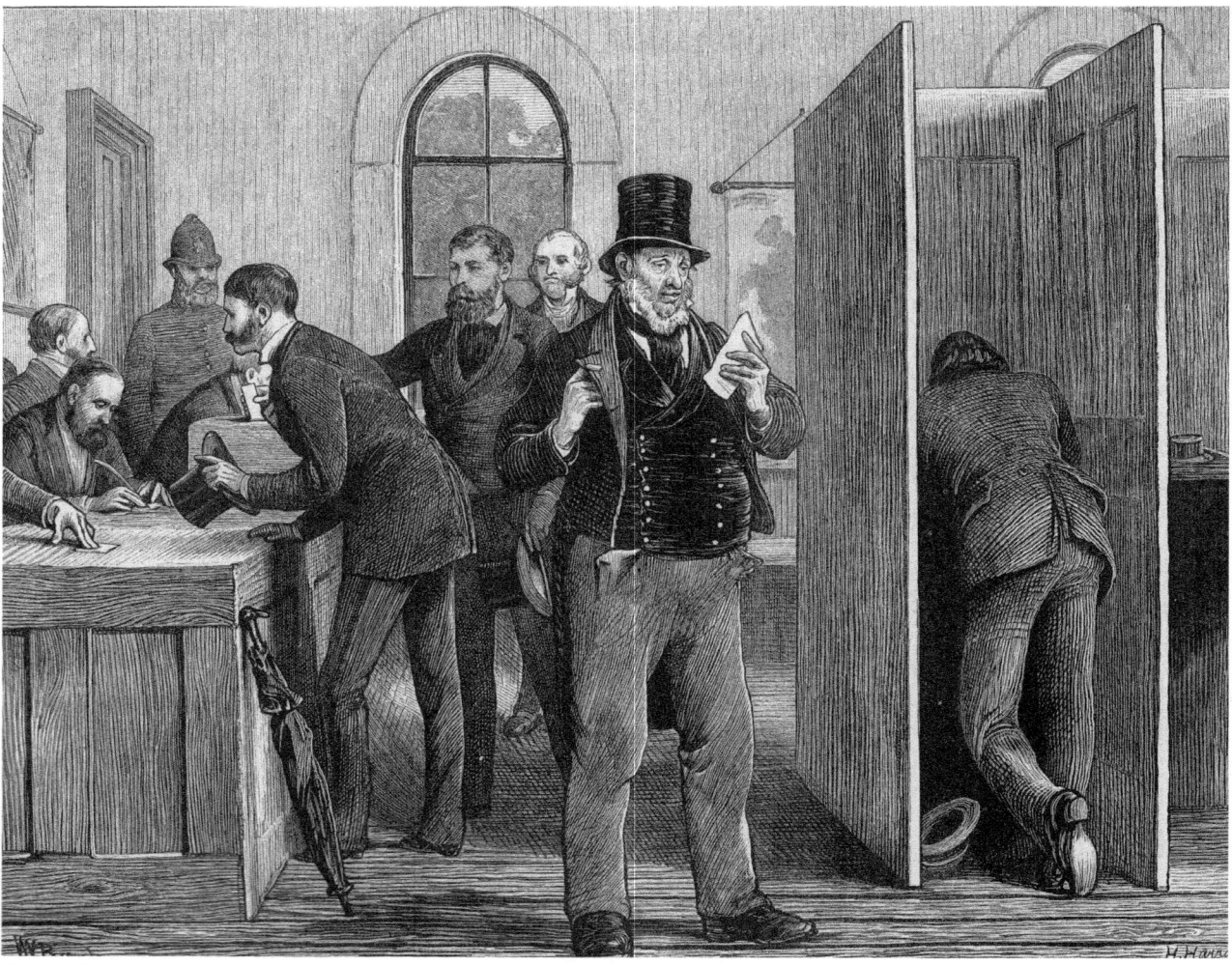

Fig. 4 Men voting by secret ballot as a result of the Secret Ballot Act of 1872

1872 Secret Ballot Act

Although the Second Reform Act was effective in moving the British people closer to a democratic state, bribery, corruption and intimidation remained a common feature of elections. Voting was still carried out in public by a show of hands and allowed landlords and employers to put pressure on tenants and employees to vote for a particular candidate or party. At worst a man could lose his job for not voting as he was told. Money was often laid out by candidates for free transport and free beer on polling days and there were few eyebrows raised. To many politicians, irrespective of party, the right to vote was a privilege and a responsibility which should be carried out in public and open to scrutiny.

In 1867 a parliamentary inquiry revealed the extent of corrupt practices in many boroughs. As a result of that inquiry the constituency of Lancaster was disenfranchised for spending £14,000 to bribe its 1400 voters in a general election. Gladstone's response was to introduce the Secret Ballot Act (1872). It was a further step towards democracy, and although it reduced intimidation of voters at the polls, it failed to stamp out corruption.

Corrupt Practices Act, Third Reform Act and Redistribution Act

Gladstone's next three pieces of electoral legislation introduced in the 1880s brought Britain much closer to democracy. The Corrupt Practices Act of 1883 closed the loopholes that had allowed corruption to continue virtually unchallenged. It set a specified limit for candidates' election expenses and clarified what campaign money could be spent on. The act clearly defined illegal and corrupt practices and introduced stiff penalties for anyone breaking the law. It meant that politicians now had to win support by promoting better policies. This was reinforced by a growing working-class electorate.

By the 1880s, attitudes were changing and there was no logical argument against extending the franchise further. The Third Reform Act of 1884 removed discrimination over voting – it was no longer tied to property. A uniform franchise for both counties and boroughs now existed. Agricultural labourers and miners in rural areas were brought into the voting system. The electorate (which had increased to three million since 1867, as a result of continuing population growth) doubled in size to approximately six million out of a total population of 35 million. Two out of three men were now enfranchised. The act enfranchised some members of the working class and substantially reduced the influence of the landed classes in government.

The Redistribution Act of 1885 brought an end to over-representation of the rural areas and under-representation of the industrial towns and cities. Most constituencies were now single member and equally sized in terms of population. For the first time this meant fair representation across Britain. The larger electorate encouraged the two main political parties to improve their organisation and the efficiency of their party machines. This brought Radical Liberals into contact with new rural voters (a traditionally Conservative area), while the Conservatives strengthened their support in the boroughs (traditionally Liberal). The Act introduced a recognisably modern system of electoral representation.

There was little sign of the pressure groups, public demonstrations and public unrest which had characterised the earlier campaigns for the extension of the franchise. It was according to a prominent Liberal Radical MP Joseph Chamberlain, 'A revolution which has been peacefully and silently accomplished.' Great steps had been taken towards democracy in Britain.

ACTIVITY

Pair discussion

What do you think was the main purpose of legislation against corruption and intimidation at elections?

CROSS-REFERENCE

The extent of democracy in Britain during this period is the subject of chapter 24.

ACTIVITY

Summary

What elements of democracy had been achieved by 1885? What was still to be done? In pairs, create a table to illustrate your answers. It will be useful to review it when you have reached Chapter 24.

 PRACTICE QUESTION

Evaluating historical extracts

Using your understanding of the historical context, assess how convincing the arguments in Extracts 1, 2 and 3 are in relation to motives for reform in the 1870s and 1880s.

 PRACTICE QUESTION

'Gladstone's and Disraeli's social and political reforms did little to improve life for the working classes.'
Assess the validity of this view.

STUDY TIP

Before you answer the question read through the chapter and note down any reference to motives to broaden your understanding of the historical context.

STUDY TIP

First be clear as to what social and political reforms are. Make a note of the reforms of both Gladstone and Disraeli. Assess the benefit or limit of each one to the working classes. Make a judgement of the extent to which the life of the working classes was improved, or not. What else could have been done?

21 Pressure for change (1846–1885)

LEARNING OBJECTIVES

In this chapter you will learn about:

- social campaigns, public health reform
- Chartism
- pressure for parliamentary reform
- Irish Nationalism.

EXTRACT 1

It is difficult to assess the impact that extra-parliamentary pressure had on central government in the mid-nineteenth century. Many groups highlighted particular issues on which government was prepared eventually to legislate. Contemporaries were confident that pressure groups provided an impetus for social progress, but it was always easier to repeal legislation than to introduce new legislation. Lord Morpeth introduced his health legislation with the support of the Health of Towns Association, but legislation was acceptable to the House of Commons only because of the return of cholera. Pressure groups realised that though they could influence, even intimidate, the legislature, the last word lay with Parliament. It could legislate, but it could also refuse to do so. By 1850, pressure groups were recognised as legitimate channels through which opinion had access to government. Popular protest like Chartism had mixed effects on the lives of the working population. They sought to improve conditions through demands for economic and political change, but the extent to which they succeeded, in the short term, was limited.

Adapted from Richard Brown, *Church and State in Modern Britain,* 1991

KEY QUESTION

As you read this chapter, consider the following Key Question:
What pressures did governments face and how they did they respond to these?

EXTRACT 2

The simple fact was that industrialisation was transforming society and as a result the Government was constantly being forced into action as yet another 'great good' came to the fore. No doubt the administrative momentum played a part in all this although the lead was taken by the dedicated reformers of the time – Shaftesbury, Southwood Smith, Chadwick, Simon and the rest. So however desirable government non-interference might seem in theory, in practice it became increasingly inevitable. Yet even here, before 1870, its scope was still very limited. Poor relief, it is true, was offered by the state on a national scale, but it was in a severely deterrent form. The working classes kept well away, preferring self-help through friendly societies, or the immense range of Victorian charitable societies, often in the latter case at the expense of self-respect.

Adapted from Eric Hopkins, *Industrialisation and Society, A Social History, 1830–1851,* 2000

ACTIVITY

Evaluating historical extracts

According to Extract 1, how much impact did pressure groups have in persuading governments to pass new legislation?

ACTIVITY

Evaluating historical extracts

1. According to Extract 2 what reasons are given for the passing of social reforms?
2. According to Extract 2 why can government intervention in poor relief be criticised?

KEY QUESTION

- How and with what results did society and social policy develop?
- How important was the role of individuals and groups and how were they affected by developments?

Social campaigns

The social problems that had developed as a result of industrialisation and urbanisation earlier in the century were becoming increasingly apparent by the middle of the century. The mid-Victorian boom that brought prosperity to so much of the country did not solve poverty and its associated problems, nor relieve the misery and wretchedness of those at the bottom of the economic ladder. There was still unemployment. For those in work some of the conditions were deplorable. There remained the problem of unregulated employment of young children in small workshops. There was no state system of education and poorer working-class children could not read or write. The most pressing problem was the state of housing in the slum districts in towns and cities and the health hazards caused by overcrowded and insanitary living conditions. Action was required, but there were strongly held laissez faire views that it was not the role of Government to intervene in people's welfare.

Nevertheless, social philanthropists and voluntary groups continued to bring pressure on the Government. They campaigned for change in conditions in factories and other workplaces, in the coal mines, for improvements in the application of the poor law, for a national system of education, for relief of the destitute, for the mentally ill, for orphan children, for better housing conditions and for health provision.

Among the great social reformers and philanthropists, Anthony Ashley Cooper (later **Lord Shaftesbury**) continued his campaigns for social improvement, which he had started in the 1830s. The Ten Hour Act regulating hours in factories had been passed in 1847. When the manufacturers found a loophole, Shaftesbury continued his campaign until in the 1850 Factory Act he succeeded in limiting the hours in which a factory could remain open. Not satisfied, Shaftesbury pressed the Government to set up the Children's Employment Commission to extend legislation regulating conditions of child labour to all workshops, however small. The 1864 Act was extended in 1871 to include brickfields, where children were still employed in intolerable conditions.

> **CROSS-REFERENCE**
>
> The Key Profile on **Lord Shaftesbury** appears on page 136 and there is more on him on pages 151.

Fig. 1 *Children carrying loads of clay in the brickyards of the Midlands, 1871*

Shaftesbury was equally tireless in his efforts to end the abuse of young climbing boys, sent up the soot-filled chimneys of Victorian suburbia. After many rebuffs the Chimney Sweepers Act was passed in 1875 to ban the practice. Shaftesbury worked through societies, such as the Social Science Association dealing with public health, penal reform and education for women, and alongside other social reformers to keep up pressure on Government on a wide range of social issues. He was instrumental with Edwin Chadwick in persuading Russell's government to set up a Board of Health as part of the 1848 Public Health reform.

Charitable activity for the poor was popular among the Victorian middle classes. It eased consciences and perpetuated ideas of self-help, and perhaps relieved pressure on the Government of the need to intervene. This comment from McCord and Purdue highlights the extent of voluntary involvement in social welfare: 'British philanthropic activity was greater than that of any other contemporary society. It was also sufficient to arouse fears that it might not have wholly good effects. The voluntary nature of most activity meant some

> **ACTIVITY**
>
> **Extension**
>
> You may be interested to discover more about the novels that were inspired by some of the appalling social conditions of the mid-Victorian period. Charles Kingsley's 'Water Babies', published in 1863, is a good starting point. It did much to raise public awareness of the abuses of child labour, through its central character Tom, a chimney sweep.

overlapping provision and many gaps. Some feared that excessive kindness might sap the invaluable impulse to self-reliance and self-improvement.' Fears of 'excessive kindness' led to the formation of the Charity Organisation Society in 1869 to provide help only to the 'deserving' after full investigation of their needs, and then to set them up to help themselves. 'We must use charity to create the power of self-help,' was their slogan.

Public health reform

The rapid growth of industrial towns and cities in the preceding decades had created problems in the provision of basic amenities: a constant supply of pure water, proper drainage and sanitation and clean, well-lit streets. In working-class areas many of the houses were of inferior quality, lacking light, ventilation, running water and decent sanitation. Multiple health problems, frequent outbreaks of disease and unacceptably high death rates were the direct result of the dirty and insanitary living conditions.

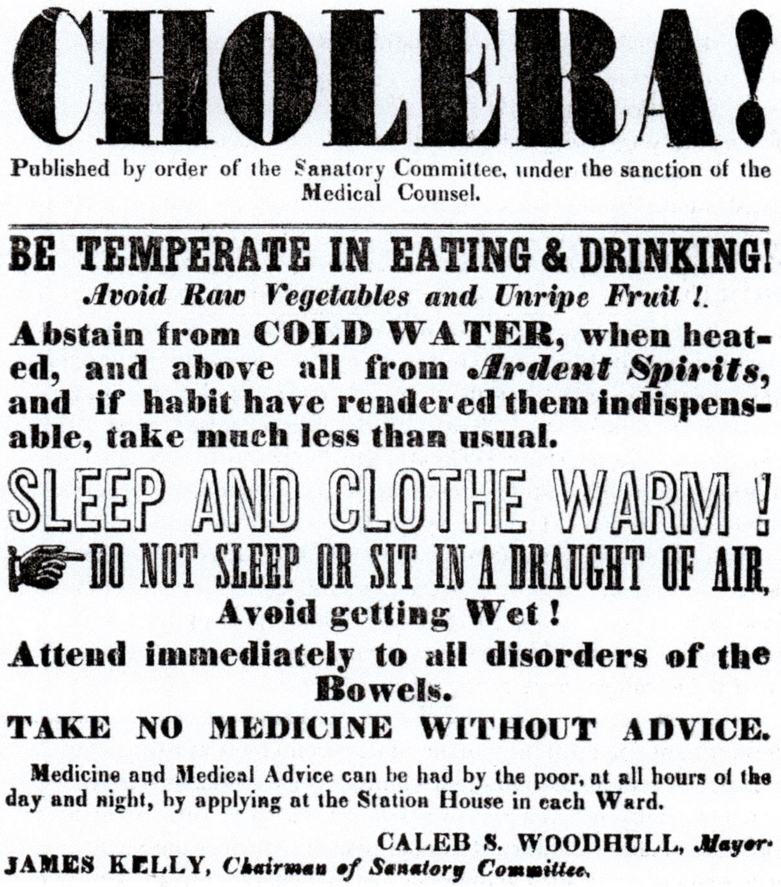

> **A CLOSER LOOK**
>
> ### The cause of cholera
>
> The first outbreak of cholera appeared in Sunderland in 1832. It terrified people as victims succumbed within hours from vomiting and violent diarrhoea and kidney failure, as their skin turned ghastly blue, purple, then black. Thousands died, but the cause was a mystery. Most outbreaks occurred in poor areas, but no one was safe. Dr John Snow suspected that contaminated water was the culprit and in an outbreak in the Soho area of London in 1854, after he isolated a local water pump, the incidence of cholera fell.

CHOLERA!
Published by order of the Sanatory Committee, under the sanction of the Medical Counsel.

BE TEMPERATE IN EATING & DRINKING!
Avoid Raw Vegetables and Unripe Fruit!
Abstain from COLD WATER, when heated, and above all from *Ardent Spirits*, and if habit have rendered them indispensable, take much less than usual.

SLEEP AND CLOTHE WARM!
☞ DO NOT SLEEP OR SIT IN A DRAUGHT OF AIR.
Avoid getting Wet!
Attend immediately to all disorders of the Bowels.
TAKE NO MEDICINE WITHOUT ADVICE.

Medicine and Medical Advice can be had by the poor, at all hours of the day and night, by applying at the Station House in each Ward.

CALEB S. WOODHULL, *Mayor.*
JAMES KELLY, *Chairman of Sanatory Committee.*

Fig. 2 *Advice on how to avoid cholera, issued in 1849*

Edwin Chadwick, whose name is synonymous with public health reform, highlighted the problems of disease and poor living conditions in his *Report on the Sanitary Condition of the Labouring Population of Great Britain (1842)*, which provided a blue-print for the 1848 Public Health Act. Chadwick's argument was economic. He believed if attention was given to improve the health of the poor and particularly to address the problems of infectious diseases, fewer people would need poor relief. Therefore it was sensible economics to spend money on improving public health. Chadwick's arguments met with opposition from vested interests and threatened its effectiveness.

> **A CLOSER LOOK**
>
> **Literary influence**
>
> Prominent writers like Charles Dickens, George Eliot and Charles Kingsley raised public awareness of the need for public health reform through the medium of their novels, as they had done with other pressing social issues of the day.

> **CROSS-REFERENCE**
>
> Details of the legislation concerning public health are given in Chapter 20.

> **ACTIVITY**
>
> Taking the role of a nineteenth-century social campaigner, write a paper to persuade the Government of the necessity of introducing public health reform.

> **KEY QUESTION**
>
> - How was Britain governed and how did democracy and political organisations change and develop?
> - How important were ideas and ideology?
> - How important was the role of individuals and groups and how were they affected by developments?

> **CROSS-REFERENCE**
>
> See Chapter 15, pages 143–5, for more information on **O'Connor** and the beginnings of the Chartist movement.

> **KEY TERM**
>
> **penny post**: a system of pre-paid postage, through the issue of a stamp (one penny was the basic cost for a letter); it was introduced by Rowland Hill in 1840 and was the start of the modern postal system

It needed an outbreak of cholera to get the legislation onto the statute books. The Act set up a General Health Board in London, with three members, Chadwick, Shaftesbury and Lord Morpeth, and Local Boards of Health each run by a medical officer, in areas where the death rate was above the national average. (Twenty-three deaths per thousand was considered unacceptably high.) Once the cholera epidemic was over, there was lingering resentment from those who disliked what they perceived as state interference in their personal lives. Chadwick was dismissed from the Health Board in 1854 and the Board was dissolved in 1858. Its administrative function was placed in the hands of the Home Office and Dr John Simon was appointed Medical Officer of Health. The Act set a precedent for the principle of public health reform that continued into the twentieth century.

Simon oversaw piecemeal improvements, but a strong statutory centralised body was needed to tackle the endemic problems that persisted in the poorer urban areas. In spite of the introduction of the registration of doctors and the passing of a Food Adulteration Act, the problems caused by poor sanitation and lack of fresh water supplies continued. There was no proper central administrative structure and most local authorities were left wanting. Until these problems were addressed any propaganda campaigns were destined to fail.

In 1871, the Royal Commission on sanitary matters recommended that the fragmentary and confused Sanitary Law should be made uniform. As a result the Local Government Board was set up, which reorganised health administration as an office of central government.

Chartism

Renewed pressure for political reform came from the Chartists during a brief period of revival stimulated by the economic depression of 1847 and the influence of the revolutions that were occurring in several European countries at the time. A third Chartist petition was organised. Fired with new enthusiasm for the cause, **O'Connor** drew up a constitution for a British Republic with himself as President. A mass meeting was arranged on Kennington Common in London, before the presentation of the petition (with six million signatures) to Parliament. There was real alarm in government circles and troops were deployed in the capital. O'Connor caved in to advice that the petition be carried to Parliament by a few representatives, as the planned march would be blocked by government forces. The movement was deflated and fell away.

The episodic nature of Chartism was a constant drawback to its success and the intermittent apathy of the working class was a feature of that. The majority were illiterate and unable to organise themselves effectively, especially at local level. It was inevitable that a parliament dominated by landed aristocracy and middle-class wealth would reject the Charter. The divisions among the leading Chartists had done nothing to promote unity and any violence frightened away potential middle-class supporters, who could have helped the funding crisis. Lack of funds made it impossible for the Chartists to make use of the latest means of communication – the railways and the **penny post**. Other better-organised pressure groups drew away Chartist support.

A sustained improvement in economic conditions worked against any future revival of the Chartist movement. Before the next real depression set in around 1873, a section of the working class had been enfranchised, the qualification to stand as an MP had been removed and the Liberal government had passed the Secret Ballot Act, meaning that three out of six of the original Chartist demands had been achieved. It is argued that the legacy of the movement was ultimately the achievement of five of the points by 1918, but it is questionable whether that occurred because of the movement's influence or whether it was a part of the natural process of democratic progress in Britain. Current thinking is that both the Chartist movement and the Anti-Corn Law League have been given more attention by historians than their significance deserves. Indeed, in the context of the period, 'the strong arm of the state' triumphed.

Pressure for parliamentary reform

EXTRACT 3

> The break in economic prosperity in 1866 and 1867 influenced politics directly. There were ripples of economic disorder in all parts of the country and widespread unemployment. In July 1866 there were riots in London. The harvest had been ruined by heavy rains and meat prices were high. To add to the distress, cholera made another of its dramatic reappearances and **Fenian** disturbances created additional alarm. The deteriorating social and economic situation favoured a sharp outburst of political radicalism, and 'the people' were showing as clearly as they could that the reform issue could be trifled with no longer. Establishment threats to trade union organisation drew many skilled artisans, who had previously shown little interest in politics, into the reform movement, and a coalition of extra-parliamentary forces seemed to be massing both in London and in the provinces.
>
> Adapted from Asa Briggs, *The Age of Improvement*, 1967

Historian Asa Briggs maintains that the 'break in economic prosperity' in 1866–67 became the main catalyst for the success of Radical pressure on the Government to introduce reform, which culminated in the passage of the Second Reform Act through Parliament in 1867. Apart from frustration at the lack of progress on the franchise, the working classes were feeling the effects of a bad harvest and a serious outbreak of disease in cattle that raised both bread and meat prices. A financial crisis in the City caused businesses to fail and threatened a rise in unemployment. A flurry of worrying economic and social incidents seemed to awaken a latent interest in reform by 'the people' and their radical leaders.

A LEVEL PRACTICE QUESTION

Evaluating historical extracts

Using your understanding of the historical context, assess how convincing the arguments in Extracts 1, 2 and 3 are in relation to the pressure on Government to introduce reform.

The series of reform bills introduced between 1851 and 1866 appear to have failed because there was little public pressure on the Government. The Chartist movement had collapsed and the middle classes, enfranchised in 1832 and enjoying a period of prosperity, were generally satisfied with the existing parliamentary system.

Changing attitudes from the people

During the 1860s, there was a change in attitude within the political parties and also changes in the make-up of those parties, which helped to bring parliamentary reform to the forefront. The old Whig Party, dominated by landed aristocrats, was transforming into the Liberal Party, in which the

ACTIVITY
Make a spider diagram to illustrate the reasons for the failure of the Chartist movement. Refer back to Chartism in Chapter 15.

KEY QUESTION
- How was Britain governed and how did democracy and political organisations change and develop?
- How important was the role of individuals and groups and how were they affected by developments?

CROSS-REFERENCE
Fenianism is covered later in this chapter, in the section on Irish nationalism on page 210.

ACTIVITY
According to Extract 3, what aspects of the economic situation in 1866–67 were linked to an increase in pressure for reform?

STUDY TIP
In answering this question look at each extract and consider both the overall argument and more specific interpretations. You should make a judgement as to how convincing these are by applying your own contextual knowledge.

commercial and industrial members had growing influence. These successful business men, who lived in the large under-represented towns and cities, sought to extend their political status and power, even if it was only through redistribution of seats. William Gladstone had become convinced of the necessity of reform and began to lead the Liberal Party in this direction. This offered encouragement to Radical reform groups. The Radicals in Parliament who often spoke for the working man were becoming more effective within the Liberal Party. The leading Radical MP **John Bright** increased his influence on Gladstone. The Conservative Party also accepted the need for change, though for Disraeli and the progressive Tories they also saw reform as an opportunity to win the wider support of a larger electorate.

The improvement in the standard of living among the skilled working class, coupled with their improved level of education, made the Liberals more prone to accepting the idea of extending the franchise to include this group. They saved wages in Friendly Societies or the Post Office Savings Bank and in the opinion of leading Liberals like Gladstone, they had proved themselves to be responsible.

The size of constituencies had become very uneven as a result of continuing population growth and movement from the countryside to urban areas. No new constituencies had been formed. This had led to large under-represented populations in the expanding industrial towns and cities. The Liberal middle-class manufacturing MPs had a vested interest in securing an increase in the number of seats in these areas to extend their political influence. In reality the demographic changes were forcing the issue of reform onto the political agenda and they would have to be tackled by whichever party was in power.

The Radicals kept up the pressure for reform both inside and outside Parliament. John Bright, MP for Birmingham, toured the country encouraging ordinary men to demand their democratic rights. Bright put forward convincing arguments on behalf of the skilled workers in favour of extending the franchise. The writings of political philosophers, such as **John Stuart Mill**, elected MP for Westminster in 1865, were influential in raising the interest in the political debates surrounding the extension of the franchise.

Both the American Civil War (1861–65) and the movement for Italian Unification (1859–1861) were seen by many British people as struggles for freedom and democracy, and were instrumental in creating a popular surge of interest in reform. The visit of Giuseppe Garibaldi, the hero of the Italian unification movement, to London in 1864 excited the crowds and spurred on leading Radicals to revive an interest in British politics and reform. Thousands of people flocked to hear Garibaldi speak and when the authorities clamped down on his public meetings, there were angry protests. This repressive response led directly to the setting up of a new political organisation in February 1865 – the Reform League.

The Reform League

The Reform League was a mainly working-class alliance with strong trade union support and a few wealthy middle-class backers. The League's aim was to work towards democracy through universal male suffrage and a programme of radical reform. Local branches sprang up in manufacturing towns and the League was able to mobilise its considerable force of trade union members and make its presence felt. Additional pressure came from leading trade union men in the London Trades Council who met in 1866 and started to organise a campaign for reform.

The Reform Union

The Reform League was more active and more successful than its counterpart the Reform Union, which was created a few months earlier in April 1864.

CROSS-REFERENCE

John Bright is the subject of Chapter 15.

Increasing democracy is examined on pages 198–201.

CROSS-REFERENCE

See Chapter 19, page 188 for more information on **John Stuart Mill**.

This by contrast was a largely middle-class organisation that called for a secret ballot and focused on seeking the redistribution of seats to correct the imbalance caused by the changes and movement in the population. John Bright encouraged the two organisations to work together towards an extension of the franchise for working men, but the class divide created tensions between them.

Fig. 3 *Italian nationalist and politician Giuseppe Garibaldi is received by an enthusiastic crowd at the Crystal Palace during his visit to Britain, 16 April 1864*

The power of public pressure

When Gladstone's Reform Bill of 1866 was rejected by Parliament, the Reform League organised demonstrations across the country. In July 1866 there was considerable alarm at the outbreak of violence near Hyde Park in London, after a Reform League meeting, which had attracted a huge crowd, was prevented from taking place. A similar demonstration took place in May 1867. The resulting pressure from outside Parliament may have been crucial in persuading Disraeli to seize the moment and take the credit for what had generally been regarded as a Liberal reform.

It was paradoxical that it was the Conservative government led by the anti-reform Lord Derby, with the opportunist Disraeli as Leader of the House of Commons, that finally secured the Second Reform Act in August 1867. There may have been an element of giving in to pressure from outside Parliament, but also Disraeli realised that if the Conservatives didn't seize the chance to introduce the reform themselves, then Gladstone would do it as soon as he got back into power.

> **ACTIVITY**
>
> Copy and complete the table below, the answer the following question: What key factors persuaded the Government to pass the Second Reform Act? Explain your answer.
>
> | Pressure from individuals | Pressure from organised groups | Pressure of popular opinion |
> |---|---|---|
> | | | |
> | | | |
> | | | |

> **KEY QUESTION**
>
> - How was Britain governed and how did democracy and political organisations change and develop?
> - How important were ideas and ideology?
> - How important was the role of individuals and groups and how were they affected by developments?

Irish nationalism

The Fenians

> **KEY CHRONOLOGY**
>
> | | |
> |---|---|
> | 1858 | Beginnings of Fenianism in Ireland |
> | 1867 | Fenian disturbances in England and Ireland |
> | 1868 | Foundation of Amnesty Association by Isaac Butt |
> | 1873 | Home Rule League founded by Isaac Butt |
> | 1879 | Land League founded by Michael Davitt |
> | 1879 | Charles Parnell emerges as leader of Irish Nationalists |

> **KEY TERM**
>
> **Fenian:** the generally accepted term at the time to describe all nationalist groups associated with seeking independence for Ireland

> **CROSS-REFERENCE**
>
> See page 147 in Chapter 15 for more details on **Young Ireland**.

The **Fenians** were militant but romantic nationalists whose aim was to achieve an independent Ireland by forcing the British government to repeal the Act of Union. The Fenian movement arose from the remnants of the **Young Ireland** group and can also be seen as the political legacy of the famine, and in this sense it was a response to the increasing suffering of the Irish people. In spite of the idealism of some of the leaders, the Fenians were prepared to use violence to achieve their aim. They wanted an Irish government completely separate from the British government, with their own President, rather than be subjects of the British Monarchy. A secret society was set up in 1858, 'to make Ireland an independent democratic republic'. It became known as the Irish Republican Brotherhood or the IRB. At the same time a parallel organisation was set up in North America and called the Fenian Brotherhood.

There was significant Fenian support in England and Scotland among the Irish immigrant populations of Liverpool, Manchester and Glasgow. The movement rapidly gathered momentum in the 1860s and claimed a membership of 80,000 supporters, but when the rising occurred in 1867, the insurgents were thin on the ground and largely ineffective. A young Fenian, **Thomas Kelly**, organised a simultaneous rising in England that also ended in failure when the small disorganised groups of poorly-armed men were apprehended by police and troops.

A CLOSER LOOK

The attempted rescue of Thomas Kelly from a prison 'van' in Manchester in September 1867 led to the fatal shooting of a police officer and the execution of three of the ringleaders. This time there was no commutation of the death sentence. The three became known as the 'Manchester Martyrs' and became potent symbols of Irish Nationalism.

In many ways the Fenian plot was a disaster. However, the harsh conditions suffered by the prisoners, serving long prison sentences, elicited sympathy from many who had previously opposed the Fenians, and there were calls for an amnesty. This unexpectedly brought a new Irish leader to the fore. **Isaac Butt**, a Dublin lawyer, once a convinced Unionist, was inspired to set up an Amnesty Association, which kept the fate of political prisoners in the public eye.

KEY PROFILE

Isaac Butt (1813–79) was a brilliant Irish lawyer, political economist and Unionist. He saw the poor relationship between landlord and tenant as one of the root causes of Ireland's inefficient economy. He believed the solution to Ireland's problems lay in constitutional nationalism and established the Irish Home Rule Party. When he refused to join in obstructionist tactics in Parliament in 1878, there was an attempt to oust him as party leader.

The Fenian rising proved to be a turning point in Anglo-Irish politics. Anti-Irish feeling in Britain, which had surfaced during Fenian unrest, led to calls from some quarters for tough government measures to be introduced in Ireland to suppress the troublemakers. But in line with the emerging influences of liberalism and a desire for a more equal society in Britain, others were concerned to identify the cause of the violence and introduce some measure of reform to bring peace to Ireland. This latter view was held by Gladstone. He had been shocked by the violence of the movement, but it brought to his attention the urgency of the Irish situation.

ACTIVITY

Copy and complete the table below, then answer the following question: Did the Fenian rising end in failure?

Did the Fenian rising end in failure?	
Points that support that assertion	Points that are contrary to that assertion

From the evidence you present, what conclusion can you draw?

Emergence of the Home Rule for Ireland campaign

Gladstone's Irish policy during his first ministry met with little acknowledged success. He had tackled the problems of lack of equal and fair treatment in religion and land. His reforms were directed at suppressing Fenian demands for the repeal of the Union by satisfying Irish grievances. The majority Catholic population in Ireland, however, remained dissatisfied – they were still poor and still oppressed by their Protestant landlords and were easy prey for violent extremists who tried to whip up anti-English feeling. There was a growing desire among the Irish to manage their own affairs.

By 1873, Isaac Butt had set up the Home Rule League, which had a sufficiently wide-based support among the Irish to be a truly national organisation. In 1874, the general election returned 59 Irish MPs on a Home Rule platform. The group formed the nucleus of a strong Irish nationalist or Home Rule Party, whose actions directed Irish politics for the next decade. Butt was a moderate and believed in achieving political independence for Ireland through peaceful means, but his movement began to give way to a much tougher and less conciliatory group.

Fig. 4 *Irish peasant girl guarding her family's last few possessions after eviction for non-payment of rent*

The Land League and the Irish Nationalist movement

The effects of the agricultural depression were being felt in Ireland by the late 1870s. Tenant farmers who could no longer meet the rent demand were evicted. The agitation of the Irish tenants against eviction and refusal to pay rents was directed by the Land League, founded in 1879 by Michael Davitt, a member of the IRB. It brought considerable pressure to bear on Gladstone's new government to introduce further land reform. It was strengthened by the League's loose alliance with the Home Rule League, now led by Charles Stuart Parnell, after Butt's death in 1879. Parnell agitated in the House for redress for evicted tenants. The pressure contributed to Gladstone's major reform of the Land Act in 1881.

Charles Stewart Parnell emerged on the Irish political scene just at the time the Home Rule movement needed a leader with his strength of purpose and dynamism. His decision, as leader of the Home Rule League, to cooperate with the Land League was inspired and gave great momentum to Home Rule. His skilful management of the Irish MPs led to a strong Irish Nationalist Party, which held the balance of power in Parliament. Parnell became the undisputed leader of Irish Nationalism.

When Gladstone sought to suppress growing disorder in Ireland with a policy of coercion and conciliation, he was challenged by Parnell's Irish Nationalist Party led by Parnell. Gladstone's Reform Acts of 1884 and 1885 extended the franchise in Ireland and the new Irish voters consolidated the position of Parnell and the Irish Nationalist Party and strengthened them for the Home Rule fight.

> **KEY PROFILE**
>
> **Charles Stewart Parnell (1846–91)**, son of an Anglo-Irish landowning father, held a deep dislike of the English. As an MP for the Home Rule Party, he embarked on an obstructionist policy, to bring attention to the cause. President of the Home Rule Confederation, he had a ruthlessness and authority which gave him massive support in Ireland. He condoned the illegal activities of the Land League.

ACTIVITY

Summary

Working in pairs, summarise the main pressures for change faced by governments between 1846 and 1885 and identify any government response. Draw up a table of two columns to record your findings, as follows:

Date	Pressures on government	Date	Government response

From your summary notes, draw a conclusion about how positively governments responded to pressure for social and political reforms in Great Britain and Ireland during this period.

STUDY TIP

You will need to consider the political and social changes in this period and consider the work of the pressure groups in these weighing up their contribution against other factors. What influence, if any, did each of them have on government action to address these problems? Remember that this is a broad period and you should show that you have considered the full time span.

PRACTICE QUESTION

To what extent were the political and social changes of the years 1846 to 1885 brought about by the action of pressure groups?

22 Economic developments

EXTRACT 1

The Great Exhibition of 1851 was celebrated as a symbol of an inter-dependent world economy: it was an international exhibition, with Britain taking most of the prizes for industrial products, and other nations for foodstuffs and raw materials. Never before, nor since, has one country so dominated the world economy. Given the slow means of technology, the first nation to make the jump enjoyed a lead of two or three generations. As Britain assumed this dominant role in the international economy, exploiting the unique advantages of a unique position, the prime **dynamic** in the economy became the industrial sector, and within that the export industries. A 'distorted' industrial structure developed, with the few giant industries — textiles, coal, ship-building, engineering — responding rapidly to the opportunities of this very special position, with the economy becoming dependent on its ability to sell cheap cloth, iron, machinery and coal, and to provide ships to carry the cargoes to the rest of the world.

Adapted from Peter Mathias, *The First Industrial Nation, An economic history of Britain 1700–1914*, 1972

LEARNING OBJECTIVES

In this chapter you will learn about:

- the mid-Victorian boom
- the 'golden age' of agriculture
- industrial and transport developments
- the impact of increased trade
- the Great Depression.

KEY QUESTION

As you read this chapter, consider the following Key Question:
How and with what results did the economy develop and change?

KEY TERM

dynamic: any driving force instrumental in growth or change

ACTIVITY

Evaluating historical extracts

1. In Extract 1, what is Mathias' view of Britain's position in 1851?
2. As you study the chapter, reflect on how convincing the interpretation in Extract 1 is.

The mid-Victorian boom

Britain dominated the world economy in the mid-nineteenth century. It is estimated that Britain produced over 40 per cent of the total traded manufactured goods in the world and that approximately 25 per cent of the world's trade passed through British ports. While Britain was acknowledged as the workshop of the world, other countries (many belonging to the British Empire or dependent on British capital) furnished it with raw materials and foodstuffs for its growing population.

Fig. 1 Queen Victoria and Prince Albert inaugurating the great 1851 exhibition at the Crystal Palace

One of the spin-offs from the Great Exhibition was a rapid increase in export orders, and a growth in overseas markets. One third of all British goods were exported to the British Empire. Coal was exported to Europe. Many goods

SECTION 4 | Economy, society and politics 1846–1885

> **A CLOSER LOOK**
>
> ### The Great Exhibition, 1851
>
> The Great Exhibition took place in London's Hyde Park. The exhibits were housed in a magnificent glass house, which became known as the Crystal Palace. It showcased the variety, inventiveness and skill of Britain's manufacturing industries. Exhibits from competitor countries were included to underline Britain's commitment to Free Trade and to emphasise by comparison the excellence and superiority of British-made goods. The Exhibition was an all-round success. In the five months it was open, it attracted six million visitors. Many of them travelled to the Exhibition on a cheap day ticket via Britain's burgeoning railway network, further proof of Britain's industrial prowess.

> **CROSS-REFERENCE**
>
> The concept of **self-help** and its influence on social development is discussed in Chapter 18, pages 178–9 and Chapter 23, page 234.

> **ACTIVITY**
>
> Create a poster for the 1851 Great Exhibition illustrating Britain's economic success in order to attract British visitors.

> **KEY QUESTION**
>
> How important was the role of individuals and groups and how were they affected by developments?

> **CROSS-REFERENCE**
>
> See Chapter 17 for details of the repeal of the **Corn Laws**.

went to the United States because its own industries were not sufficiently developed to cope with the demands of a rapidly increasing population. This growth in export trade continued almost unchallenged for the next 20 years. It was a period of unprecedented demand for British goods abroad. In every town and city in Britain, producers and manufacturers were working flat out to meet the increasing orders. Britain was justifiably called the 'workshop of the world', importing raw materials, manufacturing the goods and exporting the finished products around the world.

Britain was at the height of its economic and industrial power. Its unparalleled spurt of economic and industrial growth was evident from around the middle of the century and lasted into the early years of the 1870s. It was accompanied by technological developments in Britain's key industries – coal mining, iron and steel, engineering and the textile industry – and a rapid increase in production across the board. New technology and an increase in scientific knowledge boosted British agriculture during this period, generally referred to as the period of High Farming. British manufactured goods were exported around the globe in British ships. Britain's industrial and economic supremacy was unchallenged by any other power. Governments in Britain adhered to the laissez faire principle of limited interference in the workings of the market economy. Taxation was low and Free Trade was encouraged. These were years of peace and prosperity and many, though not all, Victorians shared in the extraordinary wealth created by the industrial boom. Beneath the material success lay the Victorian virtue of '**self-help**' and the belief that good honest hard work brought rewards. The middle classes and the skilled working classes, in particular, enjoyed the rewards of hard work with higher incomes and increased consumption. There was better education and public health. The standard of living rose, but 'the stagnant mass of poverty at the bottom of the social pyramid remained' (Eric Hobsbawm). After 1873 there were signs that, although the economy was still growing, it was at a slower pace. Imports were increasing against exports. Britain was beginning to face competition from newly industrialising nations, such as Germany and the USA. Britain needed to adapt to meet the challenge.

The 'golden age' of agriculture

High Farming

When the **Corn Laws** were repealed in 1846, there was a fear in the farming community that the price of home-grown wheat would collapse against competition from foreign imports, and that farmers would be ruined. That did not occur and by 1853 Britain had entered a 'golden age' of agriculture, during which harvests produced successive high yields, prices were steady, farmers' incomes increased, there was scientific and technological innovation and improvements were carried out.

The expression 'High Farming' has been used to describe the farming practices adopted by many farmers during these years. James Caird, a farmer from Wigtownshire in the south west of Scotland, is often credited with introducing the term, although historian G.E. Mingay in *Land, Labour and Agriculture* suggests the term was used by several agricultural writers of the day and that it probably stemmed from the early nineteenth-century phrase 'to farm high' meaning 'to achieve excellence in farming methods'.

High Farming methods increased productivity. Many farmers moved from purely arable to mixed farming. This meant they hedged their bets by growing wheat and root crops as well as stocking cattle, sheep and pigs. In this way they would be cushioned against a sudden downturn in price of either crops or livestock. The surplus crops fed the animals and the animals' manure fed the crops. There was increasing interest in animal husbandry. Some farmers specialised in specific breeds of cattle such as Herefords and Aberdeen Angus, which produced excellent beef. Much of the profits in farming at this time came from livestock rearing.

Agricultural progress

Fig. 2 *The McCormick reaping machine was displayed at the Great Exhibition in 1851 and over the following decades was widely used and adapted to make it more efficient*

With an increase in scientific knowledge artificial fertilisers, such as superphosphates, were marketed and **guano** was imported in large quantities from Peru. The industry was worth £8 million a year by 1870. There was also a growing market in animal feedstuffs made from linseed and cotton seed. By 1870 this was worth £5 million a year. These two developments eased the pressure on farmers to pursue mixed farming and made it easier for them to specialise in either arable or livestock.

The problems of poor drainage were met by the manufacture of clay pipes. The Government introduced loan schemes for farmers to invest in drainage pipe systems. Improved drainage together with use of fertilisers made substantial improvements in crop yield.

As there was a ready supply of cheap labour – agricultural labourers were among the most poorly paid – the introduction of farm machinery was slow. There was, however, widespread use of the horse-drawn reaper. There were better ploughs, seed drills and stream-driven threshing machines to improve efficiency in crop production.

The steady growth of the population, the rising prosperity and a general rise in wages and prices increased the demand for food and other produce of the land. The demand was met by the agricultural improvements. The development of the railways was beneficial to farming, as food could be transported quickly to the growing towns, where there was a ready and ever-increasing market for fresh produce.

By the early 1870s, British farmers were producing about 50 per cent of the home consumption of wheat and about 90 per cent of meat. Dairy farmers supplied the home market with butter, milk and cheese. Farmers benefited from the rising

A CLOSER LOOK

James Caird and High Farming

In 1849 James Caird produced a pamphlet entitled 'High Farming' advising farmers on how to adapt their methods to cope with the possible fall in wheat prices. He called for more intensive farming, taking account of the new methods and improvements, for example drainage and fertilisation of the land. He also advocated mixed farming. It is difficult to assess the extent of Caird's influence, but High Farming was popular over the next 20 years, coinciding with the 'golden age' of British agriculture.

ACTIVITY

Thinking point

How valid was the fear in the farming community that the price of home-grown wheat would collapse against competition from foreign imports after the repeal of the Corn Laws in 1846? Why do you think this collapse didn't happen?

CROSS-REFERENCE

See Chapter 17, page 165, for an explanation of **guano**.

prices of their produce. With their huge profits, they built themselves solid, spacious farmhouses and enjoyed a comfortable lifestyle. Not all agricultural areas in Britain benefited from this prosperity however. In the remote north and west of Scotland, farming was under-resourced and ploughing and harvesting was still carried out by hand with the old Scots foot plough and the scythe. But for most of the country, the accessibility of plenty of good, cheap, home-produced food helped to improve general health and raise the standard of living in Britain.

Perhaps it was not difficult to achieve success in a market that lacked competitors. In spite of the development of steam ships, many mercantile ships remained under sail. Transporting goods by sea was still comparatively slow. When this changed, then Britain could no longer compete. There was also an element of good luck in the 'golden age' which no one could have predicted. There was an exceptional run of high-yielding harvests between 1850 and 1873, which were attributed to a long cycle of fine dry summers. When the fine dry summers came to an end, the cold winds of competition blew in with a vengeance, the rains fell and the British farmers were faced with a catastrophic fall in prices that was hard to withstand. By 1873 the years of plenty had come to an abrupt end and the farming industry entered a long period of economic downturn.

ACTIVITY

Pair discussion

What verdict can you reach on the overall state of British farming between 1846 and 1873?

Industrial and transport developments

Fig. 3 *The Soho manufactory of steam engines near Birmingham, 1830*

There were several reasons for Britain's exceptional industrial progress. It had been the first industrial nation and by the mid-Victorian years had far outstripped other countries in establishing markets at home and abroad for its vast range of quality goods. As the greatest colonial power, Britain controlled the vital sea routes to and from its colonies and other overseas markets. Britain had a plentiful supply of natural resources, principally coal and iron ore, which it had the technology to exploit, and had been able to forge ahead in design, engineering processes and production. This was against the background of the mid-nineteenth development of laissez faire, which had given British inventors and entrepreneurs the freedom to develop their ideas. Britain's population rose from approximately 27 million in 1851 to 35 million in 1881, providing a large workforce and an expanding home market. Mobility of workforce and carriage of goods was made possible by the extensive railway network across the country, which by 1875 linked every major town and sea port and facilitated industrial development.

The move towards Free Trade, which found practical application in Gladstone's tariff reforms while he was Chancellor of the Exchequer during the 1850s and 60s, encouraged overseas trading and stimulated British industry. The profits from increasing sales and exports of manufactured goods were often ploughed back into existing businesses and used for further enterprises, such as building railways abroad.

The key industries in Britain, which were at the centre of the rapidly growing economy, were **coal and iron**. Textiles, which had spearheaded the Industrial Revolution in Britain at the end of the eighteenth century, still remained a staple and Britain continued to be a major exporter of cotton cloth. Almost all manufactured goods relied to some extent on coal and iron – coal to produce heat or steam and iron to make the machines that manufactured the goods.

Table 1 *The growth of exports from Britain between 1840 and 1879; Textiles included cotton, woollens, silk, hats, haberdashery etc. (but note the additional, separate entry for cotton, as the largest single textile export)*

Date	Textiles (total)	Cottons	Iron and steel	Machinery	Coal
	£m	£m	£m	£m	£m
1840–9	38.2	24.6	8.2	0.8	0.9
1850–9	59.9	35.6	17.9	2.4	2.3
1860–9	98.5	57.6	24.0	4.6	4.5
1870–9	118.6	71.5	35.0	7.7	8.8

> **CROSS-REFERENCE**
>
> For more detail on the importance of **coal and iron** in the process of industrialisation, see Chapter 3.

> **ACTIVITY**
>
> **Statistical analysis**
>
> What evidence is there from the figures in Table 1 that Britain depended on a 'few successful giants of the nineteenth century' to dominate the world economy? (Bear in mind that the exports were carried mainly in British ships.)

Developments in coal mining

The growth of the coal industry during this period was immense. In 1850 the output of coal was almost 50 million tons and 25 years later in 1875 it was approximately 130 million tons and still rising. A drop in the price of coal coupled with an increase in demand helped to stimulate increased production round the middle of the century, after which industry demanded an increasing percentage of the coal produced. The manufacture of iron depended on coke and by 1870 the iron industry was buying one third of the coal produced in Britain.

Coal was required to power steam engines, an integral part of the development of the railways. After 1850 steam power was generally used in most major industries. The development of iron-hulled steam ships demanded coal to fire the ships' engines and iron for their construction. As other countries developed their industries, they imported coal from Britain.

The increasing demand for coal had implications for the organisation and running of the coal mines. Even in this age of rapid industrialisation, the massive quantities of coal were dug out by hand. This surprising absence of mechanical progress at the coal face could be blamed on the lack of a national plan (something unlikely in a climate of laissez faire government) and the continuation of private ownership of the coal mines. There was one serious attempt to develop a coal-cutting machine at Gartsherrie in Scotland in the 1860s, which failed.

Iron and steel

As industry expanded the demand for good quality iron increased. Two important earlier technological developments in the iron industry, John Neilson's hot blast (1827) and James Nasmyth's steam hammer (1844) were responsible for the significant increase of iron output from 1850 onwards. Railways, bridges, iron steam ships, textile machinery and tools – all the great engineering projects of the mid-Victorian era – were entirely dependent on the continuous production of good quality iron. Iron ore production jumped from 9 million tons in 1855 to over 15 million tons by 1875.

The use of steel in manufacturing developed during this period. It is tougher and more versatile than iron. In the 1860s new processes enabled steel to be produced quickly and cheaply and in large quantities, with the result that by 1870, many rail companies had replaced iron tracks with steel ones.

> **A CLOSER LOOK**
>
> **Technical developments in the coal industry**
>
> The introduction of wire rope and steam-driven winding gear at the top of the coal shaft replaced the hemp rope and the system of the horse gin and dealt more efficiently with the 600–800 ton daily haul of coal at some pits.

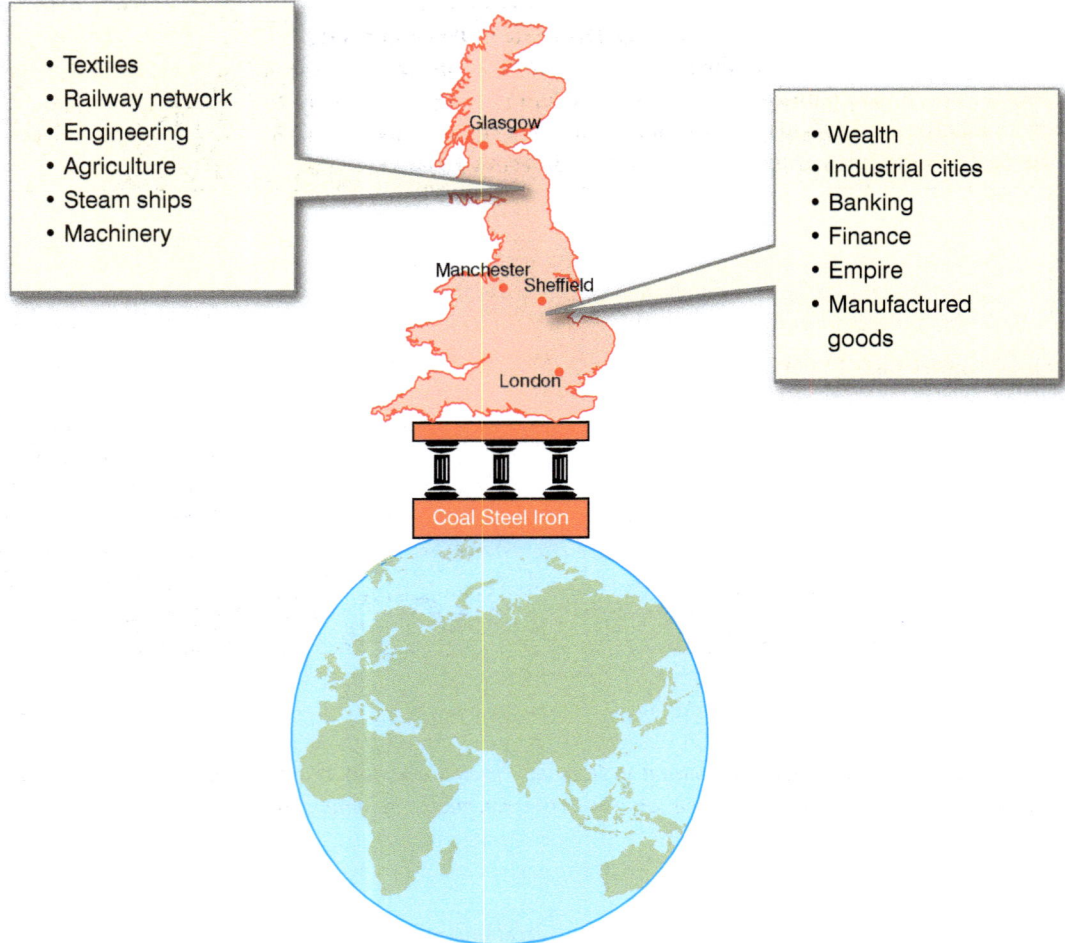

Fig. 4 *Britain's industrial supremacy is shown here, supported by pillars of coal, iron and steel*

Railways and engineering

The railways were already one of the most important industries in Britain by 1850 and this period saw the further expansion of an already established network in England, Wales and the south of Scotland. Laying rail track across the Scottish Highlands was a costly exercise because of the difficult terrain and the sparse population, but it was important in that it linked remote areas of Scotland to the rest of Britain. Most of the new rail track was laid to set up suburban railways or branch lines, often linking seaside resorts to larger towns, and in this way was instrumental in creating an entirely new industry of tourism.

The railway companies became concerned with producing better, faster and more reliable engines and this led to the development of precision engineering. Companies were set up to produce more modern rolling stock and locomotives. This side of the industry led to the development of prosperous railway towns such as Crewe, Doncaster and Derby.

The first London underground line, the Metropolitan line, was opened in 1863. The smoke and fumes from the steam locomotive, together with the sickly smell of oil lamps in the carriages made for a rather unpleasant ride. In spite of this, the Metropolitan line carried ten million passengers in its opening year.

The **Bessemer** steel rails gave a further boost to the railway industry, in that they cut production costs, increased profits and produced more capital for further investment. The profits were often invested in railway building overseas in India, Canada, Argentina and the USA and this export of capital was an indication of a booming economy.

> **KEY TERM**
>
> **Bessemer process:** the first cheap industrial process for the mass production of steel; it was invented by Henry Bessemer (1813–1898)

Fig. 5 *Poster produced for the Midland Railway in 1893, advertising train services to the resort of Blackpool, Lancashire; the poster shows a bird's-eye view of the beach with the pier, paddle-steamers and yachts*

A CLOSER LOOK

Railway statistics

In 1860, 9069 miles of track carried 153 million passengers and 88 million tons of freight, earning £12.2 million from ticket sales and £14.2 million from freight charges.

In 1875 14,510 miles of track carried 490 million passengers and 196 million tons of freight, earning £24.3 million from ticket sales and £32.1 million from freight charges.

Shipping

British shipping dominated the world, but Britain was experiencing fierce competition from American sailing boats especially on the Atlantic route. Sailing ships made up the majority of the mercantile navy. Steam ships had been built earlier in the nineteenth century but were expensive to build and run. The most important stimulus for the increase in ship building after 1850 was the growth in world trade. This coincided with the massive increase in the production of cheap iron and later steel and made it possible for Britain to forge ahead in the development of steam ships and to monopolise the shipping routes. The Suez Canal was opened in 1869 and drastically cut the journey time from the West to India, China and Australia. It was too narrow to allow a large sailing ship to tack through it and this gave a further boost to the British steam ship. Between 1850 and 1880 the tonnage of steam ships registered in Britain rose from approximately 319,000 tons to over three million tons.

ACTIVITY

Working in pairs or small groups, chose one key industry from the following:
- coal
- iron
- steel
- railways
- shipping
- textiles.

Gather evidence from the text and other sources to explain why your chosen industry was vital to the growth of British prosperity. Give an illustrated presentation of your findings to the class.

The cotton industry

The textile industry was centred round the production of cotton and wool and accounted for almost two thirds of Britain's exports in 1851. It remained a major industry but its rate of progress was slower. Its share of the export market began to fall in the 1860s, as the exports of other commodities such as coal, machinery, iron and steel goods rose. However, British manufactured cotton cloth still accounted for two thirds of cotton sold in world markets until 1900.

Impact of increased trade

Fig. 6 SS Great Eastern leaving Liverpool for New York, 1867

Britain was able to build up the staple industries of coal, iron and steel, engineering, shipping and textiles. These industries produced an economic growth rate of about two per cent per year. Their output was far beyond the requirements of home consumption. As a result of growing demand for British goods abroad, they created a boom in Britain's export market and accounted for almost all of Britain's exports. The profits raised provided capital for further investment at home and overseas (for example, railway building overseas – see above).

International trade cemented Britain's relationships with foreign countries, increasing its influence abroad, and the dependence of nation upon nation promoted peace. This chimed with Gladstone's policy of maintaining peace, which further encouraged economic stability, while Britain's potential economic rivals were sidetracked by war – the American Civil War from 1863 to 1866 and the Franco – Prussian War of 1870–71. Britain's economic progress was undoubtedly sustained by its free trade policy. Gladstone's reduction of taxation (a policy made possible because of the vibrant economy) allowed individual entrepreneurs and businessmen to build up their private fortunes as well as the wealth of the nation by investing the large sums of available capital in industrial enterprises at home and abroad.

Wealth creation, however, was not universal and although the aggregation of profits created more wealth, it was not distributed evenly. Therefore,

---

A CLOSER LOOK

The Suez Canal

The Suez Canal was an artificial sea-level waterway in Egypt, connecting the Mediterranean Sea and the Red Sea. It opened in 1869 and significantly reduced sea voyage distance between Europe and India. It was financed by French capital when it was built, but in 1875, British Prime Minister Disraeli purchased a block of shares in the Suez Canal Company with borrowed money. This gave Britain a large interest in the Canal and secured reasonable rates for British ships using it.

although employment in all these industries was substantial there was still unemployment and poverty. Those in work, however, created a demand in the economy, because their wages had risen and their newly-acquired spending power and desire for consumer goods helped to create further prosperity.

The end of Gladstone's first period of office in 1874 coincided with the onset of depression. In simple terms the period of sustained growth was coming to an end but more significantly there was a 'fundamental change' in 'Britain's special position' – Britain's supremacy in world markets was being challenged by foreign competition from a newly united Germany and a rapidly expanding economy in the USA.

The Great Depression

EXTRACT 2

If we mean by depression a failure to sustain previous rates of growth then the description is accurate, but there was no general decline. If unemployment did rise, for those still in work the fall in prices and the growth in real wages produced a continuing sensation of real improvement. We need to bear in mind the absence of comprehensive 'unemployment statistics' and the incompleteness of statistical information on production during these decades. It is worth noting too, that at the time economists and commentators were not unanimous in their interpretation of the data. However, the appointment of Royal Commissions to consider the agricultural depression and also that of trade and industry bears witness to contemporary disquiet about the state of the economy. Anxiety also stemmed from an awareness of the changes taking place in fundamental industrial processes. In 1879 British steelmakers outstripped the European total for the output of steel. In the next decade German production rapidly expanded and it surpassed the British total in 1893.

Adapted from Keith Robbins, *The Eclipse of a Great Power, Modern Britain 1870–1992*, 1994

ACTIVITY

Evaluating historical extracts

What argument does Keith Robbins put forward about the Great Depression in Source 2?

After 1873, the British economy experienced a downturn. Historians are divided as to the cause or causes of the depression and more controversially whether there was a depression at all or whether it was simply a myth. It is, however, generally agreed that there were several significant factors that pointed to the start of a period of decline. Agriculture certainly went through the economic stagnation, but the overall state of the economy is seen by some historians and economists as going through a period of 'readjustment' rather than depression. S. B. Saul argues against it in his book *The Myth of the Great Depression*, but to the Victorians it was a reality. Their confidence was rocked by falling prices, narrowing profit margins and foreign competition in a sphere in which they had been dominant for a century, and they feared national decline.

Depression in industry

Industry was still expanding but at a slower rate, and capital was still being invested abroad. Production continued to increase, but supply was overtaking demand in both home and overseas markets and this led to a fall in prices and a reduction in profit margins. Workers were laid off more frequently, but although there were periods of unemployment during these years, they were not sustained. After 1870, British trade and industry was facing more competition. There was a rising increase in imports over exports, most especially in manufactured goods.

In many manufacturing firms, especially those that were family-owned and run, there was reluctance to consider new science-based industries. Coal and textiles had always made money and many producers believed this would always be the case. They failed to see the necessity for change and began to feel the adverse effects of foreign competition. The British workforce was falling behind that in countries like the newly **united Germany**, where the system of education focused on industrial training for some of its youngsters. Most British working-class children left school at 12, without receiving any training that would encourage innovation. Britain's share of total world manufacture of all types of goods began to decline, as the USA's increased dramatically by the end of the nineteenth century.

By the 1870s both Germany and the USA had potentially stronger home markets than Britain. A comparison of the coal and iron production of the three countries between 1850 and 1880 highlights the problem for Britain of competing in an increasingly crowded market. Another problem for Britain's economy was that Germany introduced trade tariffs in 1879 while Britain clung on to her long-held belief in the policy of laissez faire.

> **A CLOSER LOOK**
>
> **Germany** was not a unified country until 1871; prior to that it had comprised a series of loose confederations of mainly German-speaking states, with the two largest, Austria and Prussia, vying for dominance.

> **ACTIVITY**
>
> **Statistical analysis**
>
> Are there indications of an economic downturn in Britain from the figures in Tables 2 and 3 or could the figures be used to support the theory of the depression as a myth? Consider the rates of growth to help you with your answer.

Table 2 *Coal production (in million tons)*

	1850	1860	1870	1880
Britain	57.0	81.0	112.0	149.0
Germany	6.0	12.0	34.0	59.0
USA	–	3.4	10.0	64.9

Table 3 *Pig-iron production (in million tons)*

	1850	1860	1870	1880
Britain	2.2	3.9	6.0	7.8
Germany	–	–	1.3	2.5
USA	–	0.8	1.7	3.9

It was inevitable that other countries were going to industrialise. Britain had fallen behind the latest technology; her machinery was either old or obsolete and there was a reluctance to invest more capital.

Depression in agriculture

A wet summer and a poor harvest in 1873 signalled the sudden end of the Golden Age of agriculture and the start of a severe depression in farming, particularly in arable. There followed several years of wet summers and disappointing harvests. More damaging to the farming industry was the increasing import of cheaper grain from overseas, particularly from North America, where vast wheat fields were opening up for the first time. Ironically the money that British investors and entrepreneurs had earlier poured into railway building in the USA allowed large quantities of wheat to be brought to the eastern seaboard and taken in steam ships across the Atlantic to compete with the higher-priced British wheat. Prices and profits fell and the results were catastrophic for many arable farmers.

One government remedy could have been to introduce tariffs on imported foodstuffs. By the time the agricultural depression occurred Disraeli was Prime Minister. Although 30 years earlier he had vehemently opposed the repeal of the Corn Laws and supported Protectionism, times had changed. There had been an enormous growth in the wealth and importance of industry, trade and finance, coupled with an increase in the urban population and a decline in the rural population. The influence of the landed interest was weakening, both politically and economically. Disraeli now accepted the policy of Free Trade and took the political decision not to protect British agriculture. If agriculture was to survive it would need to adapt and change.

It was probably a combination of these factors rather than any single cause that accounts for the economic problems after 1873. Of course, it could be argued that Britain simply had come to the end of a long period of economic growth that could not be sustained.

ACTIVITY

Summary

a) Working in pairs, present the factors that were responsible for Britain's great industrial and agricultural progress in diagrammatic form. Indicate which factors you believe were the most important. Explain your choice.

b) Complete a similar exercise in respect of factors that were responsible for Britain's industrial and agricultural decline after 1873.

EXTRACT 3

As regards the 'Great Depression' itself, surely the major outcome of modern research has been to destroy once and for all the idea of the existence of such a period in any unified sense. The last quarter of the nineteenth century was a watershed for Britain as competition developed overseas and the rate of growth markedly slackened. But the process was probably underway before 1870 and most certainly continued after 1900. The downward trend in prices – traditionally the dominant feature of the 'Great Depression' – may have been underway by the 1860s and in several respects had ended its movement by the mid-1880s. However, this is not to ignore the fact that at some time during the last quarter of the nineteenth century Britain (and several other countries) went through unusual and worrying economic experiences that they sometimes characterised as a 'Great Depression'. What is in question is that this was a special feature of the years 1873–96.

Adapted from Samuel B. Saul, *The Myth of the Great Depression*, 1985

PRACTICE QUESTION

Evaluating historical extracts

Using your understanding of the historical context, assess how convincing the arguments in Extracts 1, 2, and 3 are in relation to Britain's economic position in the mid-Victorian era.

STUDY TIP

You need to study the extracts and their arguments carefully and apply your own knowledge to assess these interpretations.

STUDY TIP

This essay requires you to consider the degree of economic prosperity in Britain before 1873 and the degree of depression thereafter. You might want to suggest that the division in 1873 is inappropriate and may wish to advance your own view of Britain's economic position in the years 1846–1885, seeing more continuity than change. Whatever your argument, try to offer some precise evidence, including statistics, in support.

PRACTICE QUESTION

'Britain enjoyed great economic prosperity between 1846 and 1873 and deep economic depression between 1873 and 1885.'
Assess the validity of this view.

23 Social developments 1846–1885

EXTRACT 1

In the mid-nineteenth century the urbanisation of the mass of the population and the decline of the rural areas had profound social consequences for all classes of the population. Most industrial labourers left no memorial save the products of their labour. What we do know suggests complex and varied patterns of life, with regionalism and religion playing an important part. The standard of living of some of the labouring population began to increase quite fast. A significant number began to enjoy leisure time. Some money was available for more than the essentials of food, housing and clothing. Strikingly this surplus coincided not with a rise but with a fall in birth rate. The extra cash was thus not absorbed by extra children. This was a startling and unprecedented development which falsified the predictions of classical political economists that the labouring classes were condemned to subsistence levels of living through the 'iron law of wages' because any surplus would be absorbed by extra children. It opened the way to the relative prosperity of the British working class.

Adapted from H. C. G. Matthew, *the Oxford Illustrated History of Britain*, 1984

LEARNING OBJECTIVES

In this chapter you will learn about:

- prosperity and poverty in towns and countryside including regional divisions
- influences including Evangelicalism and 'self-help'
- trade unions
- education.

KEY CHRONOLOGY

Social developments

- **1859** Publication of Charles Darwin's *On the Origin of the Species*

  Publication of Samuel Smiles' *Self-Help*
- **1867** First Barnardo's Home opens in East London
- **1868** Torrens Act
- **1870** Completion of Bazalgette's sewage system for London
- **1871** Introduction of the Bank Holiday Act
- **1875** Artisans' Dwelling Act
- **1878** William Booth founds the Salvation Army

ACTIVITY

Evaluating historical extracts

1. What views are advanced in Extract 1?
2. As you read through the sections 'Prosperity and poverty in towns and countryside' and 'Regional divisions', find evidence which supports or challenges the views in Extract 1.

KEY QUESTION

As you read this chapter, consider the following Key Questions:
- How and with what results did society and social policy develop?
- How important was the role of individuals and groups and how were they affected by developments?

Prosperity and poverty in towns and countryside

By the mid-nineteenth century, the census returns reveal that about half Britain's population had become town dwellers. In the decades that followed, the escalation of economic progress and the continuing rise in population changed the balance so that by 1871, 65 per cent of the population lived and worked in urban areas. The social consequences were profound. The pace of change was rapid for those whose circumstances led them into the towns, while changes in the countryside occurred at a much slower pace. A large prosperous middle class had developed as a result of industrialisation and economic progress and this helped to create the towns. In the countryside, the social structure consisted of: the landowners and farmers, the tenant farmers and the bulk of the population, agricultural labourers, with a small number of professionals and tradesmen. This continued much as before, but many areas were adversely affected by rural depopulation.

KEY PROFILE

Joseph Bazalgette (1819–91) was Chief Engineer on London's Metropolitan Board of Works and was primarily responsible for the creation of the extensive network of sewers under London's streets. The system was one of the greatest contributions to improving the health of London's poor. Most of it remains in use today. It transformed the appearance of the banks of the River Thames.

In towns

The beneficial impact of the social and political reforms of the preceding decades were beginning to be felt in the town rather than the country, and much remained to be done. For many working-class urban dwellers life could be described as less harsh. The factory reform movement had successfully campaigned for better conditions and limited hours in many major industries by 1870. Simple commodities like soap and matches became more easily available and, more importantly, affordable. Fresh food was quickly brought in from the surrounding countryside by train and food was cheaper. Diets became more varied with more meat, milk and vegetables. Local authorities opened public institutions such as libraries, parks, baths and wash houses in many towns. Visible improvements in town planning and amenities created an impression of prosperity and well-being. Hidden from view, the construction of a sewage system for London, designed by **Joseph Bazalgette** in the 1860s, epitomised the progress and prosperity of the period and the improvement in both living standards and conditions. It cleaned up London's water supply and removed the foul waste along the banks of the Thames. Most importantly it reduced mortality rates.

Fig. 1 *Sir Joseph William Bazalgette (standing top-right) views the Northern Outfall sewer being built below the Abbey Mills pumping station; he constructed London's drainage system and the Thames Embankment*

From 1865, death rates began to show an overall decline, but at the same time, so did birth rates. There are no solid explanations for the trend in birth rates as it was ahead of the development of methods of birth control. The trend was started by the middle classes and mirrored by the working classes a little later. The resulting smaller families ultimately opened the way to greater working-class prosperity.

However, in spite of the higher standards of living, there was little security when workers lost their jobs, possibly through being 'laid off' or through ill health. They might have set money aside in the Post Office savings banks introduced by Gladstone in 1861, or in their Friendly Society. Alternatively they might have resorted to a kind of self-help by relying on family or neighbours, or by accepting charity, but they might also still be in the same predicament. It was the unskilled workers who generally ended up turning to the only state provision available – poor relief and the workhouse, with all the humiliation and stigma that brought to a working man and his family. Economic prosperity could not banish poverty.

Fig. 2 Birmingham City Centre in 1886 looking over Chamberlain Square with the newly-extended Council House and Art Gallery (in the centre), the Town Hall (the building with pillars on the right) and Christ Church between them

The towns were still suffering from problems that made poverty worse. There was a lack of commitment to improve housing and as the demand for housing exceeded supply, rents were beyond the means of most workers. There was little enthusiasm for a programme of slum clearance, as there was not sufficient profit in it for the landowners, who could make more money from rents, and there was no compulsion to comply. In 1866 the Treasury made loans available to local authorities for house-building, but there was little interest. The 1868 Torrens Act bound landlords to keep property in a good state of repair. The evidence seems to point to limited action by central government and local authorities to improve the housing stock except in Birmingham, where Joseph Chamberlain carried out far-reaching improvements in both housing and municipal buildings.

CROSS-REFERENCE

The Artisans' Dwelling Act gave local authorities the ability to purchase, clear and then redevelop slums. It is discussed in Chapter 20.

ACTIVITY

Why was there a shortage of good quality housing for the labouring classes?

In the countryside

The concept of Britain being 'two nations', suggested by Disraeli in his novel *Sybil* published in 1845, which exposed the appalling living conditions of the working classes, still existed by the 1880s. There is another interpretation of two nations – the difference between countryside and town. In the 1870s living conditions for agricultural families on the face of it seemed poor by comparison to those of most industrial workers.

EXTRACT 2

> There were many features of Victorian rural life unconnected with wages, earnings and standard of living that could have led agricultural labourers to perceive themselves as working in an ailing industry and living in times of depression. Their living conditions, especially their housing, remained for the most part poor, rudimentary, or downright squalid; improved communications, increasing literacy, and the spread of information were breaking down rural isolation, and may well have made labourers increasingly aware of their position in the economy and society in relation to other groups, as virtually at the bottom of the heap.

Adapted from F. L. M. Thompson, *An Anatomy of English Agriculture*, 1991

ACTIVITY

Identify the different elements of living conditions, living standards and quality of life of the agricultural labourers in Extract 2. Remember quality of life is very much about perception. What conclusion can you draw about the agricultural labourers' quality of life at this time?

STUDY TIP

Consider Matthew's view in Extract 1 and Thompson's in Extract 2 and note the similarities and differences. Use your own knowledge to decide which is the more convincing.

PRACTICE QUESTION

Evaluating historical extracts

Using your understanding of the historical context assess how convincing the arguments in Extracts 1 and 2 are in relation to the condition of the working classes in the second half of the nineteenth century.

CROSS-REFERENCE

See Chapter 4 for more on the **standard of living** debate.

A CLOSER LOOK

Standard of living

There are difficulties associated with the concept and interpretation of the phrase 'standard of living'. It is really an economic term and refers to real wages or income, which is the income of an individual after taking prices and costs into consideration. It has also come to mean 'quality of life' and is difficult to measure without being subjective. It can include living and working conditions, health, life expectancy, standard of education and amount of leisure time.

The wages of agricultural labourers in the countryside and industrial workers in the towns fluctuated according to the state of the economy. However, an indication of overall rising prosperity was in the increase in workers' wages in both town and country, although rural wages were generally well below those of industrial workers. The wages of industrial workers rose on average by about 50 per cent between 1850 and 1875.

At the same time prices rose on average by 20 per cent, giving workers a rise of about 30 per cent in real wages or spending power. Historian F. L. M. Thompson in his *Anatomy of English Agriculture, 1870–1914*, looks at movements in earnings of farm labourers alongside a cost of living index for the period and concludes that their wages rose in real terms from 1860, dropping to a low point only between 1878 and 1886. He also points out the meagreness of their money wage, which at best rose to about 20 shillings a week. However, comparisons are difficult as agricultural workers received food, housing and fuel from their employer in differing quantities and varying quality. Their dependence on their employer for housing meant living conditions for most were basic and sometimes squalid. Thompson suggests that improved communications, increasing literacy and the spread of information might have made the agricultural workers 'aware of their position in the economy and society in relation to other groups, as virtually at the bottom of the heap'.

The attraction of higher wages and shorter working hours in the towns encouraged rural depopulation and according to Matthew left 'rural society demoralised'. Historian Keith Robbins has made the observation that 'the countryside had to surrender before the advance of urban attitudes and values. Country cousins became ever more conscious of the inferiority of their facilities. Advancement and urban life became virtually synonymous.' For many town dwellers, the countryside became an amenity. With the gradual introduction of a five and a half-day week in the 1870s, urban workers could contemplate a stretch of leisure time, not experienced before, while their country cousins toiled in the fields. With more money in their weekly wage packet they could take their family on a cheap day excursion to a seaside town on the train!

Table 1 *Money wages and real wages in the United Kingdom 1850–1886*

	Money wages	Real wages
1850	100	100
1855	116	94
1860	114	105
1866	132	117
1871	137	125
1874	155	136
1877	152	132
1880	147	132
1883	150	142
1886	148	142

(Note: The wage level in 1850 is taken as the base 100, against which to measure the movement of money wages and the value of wages in terms of purchasing power.)

A CLOSER LOOK

Bank Holiday Act 1871

This legislation provided statutory holidays for workers, many of whom otherwise worked all year round with the exception of Christmas, Easter and other religious and traditional festivals.

Regional divisions

Some counties in England and Wales suffered serious depopulation, particularly those in regions remote from industrial towns, such as Cornwall, Shropshire, Somerset and Westmorland. The local economy stagnated and wages of farm workers, already low, dropped beneath the level of farm workers in other parts of the country. The attraction of higher wages in the towns and easier access because of the railway stimulated a further exodus. Increased mechanisation and other improvements in the farming industry often reduced the need for labour, while at the same time urban industry increased its demand for labour.

ACTIVITY

Working in pairs, draw up a list of ways in which you think the standard of living for the working classes improved between 1850 and 1885. Can you identify any differences between standards of living in the town and the countryside? Produce a diagram to illustrate your findings.

SECTION 4 | Economy, society and politics 1846–1885

> **KEY QUESTION**
> - How and with what results did the economy develop and change?
> - How important was the role of individuals and groups and how were they affected by developments?

When depression hit farming, agricultural workers again headed for the towns. At the same time, counties around London and those containing industrial towns were enjoying an economic boom.

England was the social, economic and political centre of the British Isles. The Acts of Union with Scotland in 1707 and Ireland in 1800 confirmed England's strong central position. Much of Wales had been ruled by England since the thirteenth century and England and Wales became united between 1536 and 1543. England was confident in its national identity. Scotland, Ireland and Wales had to work hard to maintain theirs. Within England, Scotland, Ireland and Wales there were substantial regional differences.

National identity and the maintenance of old traditions and language were important to Scotland, Ireland and Wales, but by about 1870, the national language of each was under threat. According to Marshall the Scottish Education Act of 1872 attempted to Anglicise the Gaelic speakers of Scotland and Ireland and the Welsh speakers of Wales, so that the peasant or agricultural class would be prepared for urban life. In fact school attendance was poor in remote areas of Ireland and Scotland, but steady migration from rural areas to the towns made Gaelic almost obsolete and severely depopulated those areas. Even the railway network failed to connect the north-west Highlands of Scotland to the rest of Britain. Consequently these crofting families were left behind during the golden age of farming, living a hand-to-mouth existence, continuing the use of hand implements like the foot plough and the hand winnower, largely ignorant of new farming methods and financially unable to make any improvements. Their rents became disproportionately high during the depression and in 1882 led to an outbreak of civil disobedience, known as the **Crofters' War.**

> **A CLOSER LOOK**
>
> **The Crofters War**
>
> The Crofters War of civil disobedience forced the Government in London to sit up and take notice. The Napier Commission was appointed to inquire into the problems of poverty and landholding in the Highlands. In 1886 the Crofters Act gave crofting families security of tenure and ended arbitrary eviction by the landlord.

> **ACTIVITY**
>
> **Thinking point**
>
> Many Irish peasants and Highland crofters were illiterate, not out of stupidity but due to lack of opportunity. Can you argue the case for improving their living standards, but preserving their traditions?

Fig. 3 *Crofters on the Isle of Skye planting potatoes using the cashrom foot plough*

> **KEY QUESTION**
> - How important were ideas and ideology?
> - How important was the role of individuals and groups and how were they affected by developments?

Influences shaping social developments, including Evangelicalism

The Evangelical movement, which had its beginnings in the early nineteenth century, had a strong influence on religious and social life during the Victorian era. Its basis was a belief in the importance of faith in salvation. It encouraged thrift, sobriety (being sober), industry and self-sacrifice, all virtues in tune with what we regard today as the standards admired by Victorian society.

It was important in both the established Church (Anglican) and among Nonconformists. Within the Anglican Church it had its firmest support among the upper and middle classes and according to C. P. Hill 'brought a gradual and almost complete transformation of the tone of English upper and middle class life'. One of the leading upper-class Anglican Evangelicals was the social reformer **Lord Shaftesbury**, whose deep faith was said to have inspired his life's work campaigning for social improvement for the less fortunate.

McCord and Purdue, while acknowledging its elitist appeal, comment that 'at all points on the social spectrum there were individuals who shared a belief in the paramount importance of salvation' and cite as evidence 'the converted miners of Bishop Auckland who took to local preaching'.

Evangelicalism was taken up by a section of the Anglican clergy, creating an informal but at times bitter division between what became known as 'Low Church' (Evangelical) and 'High Church', which was more prone to ritual. The heart of 'High Church' Anglicanism was the Oxford Movement (formed in 1833) which criticised the less traditional form of Christian worship of the Evangelicals. Queen Victoria would have classed herself as 'Low Church' and her strong views on moral rectitude, Sunday observance and a strong sense of duty, tied in with this. There was a widespread belief that High Church Anglicans were too close to Roman Catholicism and this idea would be disliked by Victoria. There persisted a lack of religious acceptance and toleration towards Catholics, although most religious discrimination was socially inspired rather than official. McCord and Purdue reference a typical example regarding the newly-enfranchised working-class Salford electors in the 1868 general election, who were asked whether they would have the Pope or the Queen in authority in Britain, in an attempt to discredit a Catholic candidate.

Although their religious outlook seems stern and unbending today and their harshness towards those who 'had sinned' is difficult to understand, their contribution to social reform in the nineteenth century was immense. Apart from Shaftesbury there were other exceptional and inspirational Evangelicals; Dr Thomas Barnardo, who founded the first Barnardo home for orphan children in east London in 1867, and William Booth, who started up the Salvation Army in 1878. Booth's good work among the London poor was incredible, helping many utterly destitute men and women who had lost all hope – supporting them through giving relief and then basic training to make a new start.

For the most part, Evangelicals were keen churchgoers and regular attendance was promoted through the Lord's Day Observance Society, established in 1831, of which Shaftesbury was chairman. In fact church attendance had started to fall as the traditional pattern of churchgoing in small communities was disturbed through population movement to urban areas. The results of the only official religious census, which was conducted in 1851, shocked contemporaries when it revealed that church attendance across the entire population was little more than 50 per cent.

Although the census could not measure belief in God, it was apparent that the influence of the Church and religion was waning during the latter half of the century in spite of Evangelicalism. New ideas and discoveries were beginning to excite the curiosity of a better-educated population. Scientific developments made people question previous assumptions about the workings of the earth and the universe. Charles Darwin's publication in 1859, *On the Origin of the Species*, outlined the process of evolution, contradicting the literal meaning of the Bible story of creation and provoking great turmoil in Christian minds. A group of talented artists known as Pre-Raphaelites, among them Dante Gabriel Rossetti, William Morris and William Holman Hunt, harked back to a purer and more natural

> **CROSS-REFERENCE**
>
> The work of **Lord Shaftesbury** (Lord Ashley until 1851) is discussed in Chapter 14, page 136 and Chapter 15, page 151.

> **CROSS-REFERENCE**
>
> The ideology of **Evangelicalism**, a desire to promote a greater enthusiasm for religious belief that caught on among middle- and upper-class Anglicans, is explained in Chapter 13.

Fig. 4 Day Dream *by Pre-Raphaelite artist Gabriel Rossetti*

expression in art and tried to appeal to the ordinary working man, whose cultural development had been previously ignored. The reality, however, for the Pre-Raphaelites was that patronage of their works of art by aristocrats and wealthy industrialists was more successful than their patronage of the working man.

> **ACTIVITY**
>
> 1. Did the Evangelicals make any lasting contribution to society through their support for social reform? Discuss in pairs or small groups.
> 2. In pairs, prepare class presentations on the individuals and groups who inspired social reform and change. The names of some of them are mentioned in the text, but there are many more for you to explore.

> **KEY QUESTION**
> - How important were ideas and ideology?
> - How important was the role of individuals and groups and how were they affected by developments?

'Self-Help'

As part of the general philosophy of laissez faire, there was an emphasis on the importance of the individual. There was a growing belief that everyone should have the opportunity to fulfil their potential but they must take personal responsibility for their actions and be prepared to work hard to achieve their aim and not blame other circumstances when mishaps occurred. This notion was expressed most clearly in the book entitled *Self-Help*, by **Samuel Smiles**, published in 1859, which came to epitomise the Victorian values of the mid-nineteenth century of constantly striving to improve oneself and change for the better. Smiles' key virtues for success were a sense of duty, strength of character, thrift and helping oneself rather than depending on other people or charitable handouts.

> **A CLOSER LOOK**
>
> **Self-Help by Samuel Smiles**
>
> In his book *Self-Help*, Samuel Smiles created the idea of the modern 'role model' when he featured the activities of high-achieving men to inspire ordinary young people to overcome disadvantage and adversity and work hard to change their lives. His book, which was read and admired by Gladstone, quickly became a bestseller. Since then the book has been translated into more than 40 languages – and it is still in print.

> **KEY PROFILE**
>
> **Samuel Smiles (1812–1904)** is best known as a social reformer and author of *Self-Help*, and he had a successful and varied career. In that respect he practised what he preached! He became interested in franchise reform and campaigned for a national system of education and public libraries. He was well known for his biographies of the great self-made Victorians, such as Stephenson. His most popular book remains *Self-Help, with Illustrations of Character and Conduct, 1859*.

To make progress in both material terms and moral terms was to be admired. There was a clear belief in progress through freedom (laissez faire) and individual effort (self-help). During this period there was progress and improvement in standards of living, in public health, in attention to personal hygiene, and in the provision of education. Great strides forward were made in farming and industry, creating prosperity in town and countryside. This tangible evidence of progress was taking place against a background of improved communications and during a period of increasing prosperity.

There was a reverse side to this coin. The self-help philosophy was not the cure for all ills. Not everyone aspired to or could attain a decent standard of living. Many remained in abject poverty, unable to help themselves. Society looked down on individuals who fell into poverty and they were often regarded as irresponsible, careless and lazy rather than victims of circumstance in need of state support. In Smiles' words, 'When people live in foul dwellings, let them alone. Let wretchedness do its work.' Contemporary thought was that the best way of addressing social

> **ACTIVITY**
>
> Consider Samuel Smiles' key virtues for success – a sense of duty, strength of character, thrift and helping oneself rather than depending on other people or charitable handouts. Draw up a list of examples of the ways in which these values were reflected in Gladstone's reforms, outlined in Chapter 20.

evils was with minimum state interference and a reliance on voluntary activity by middle-class Victorian philanthropists. However, by 1870, the principle and practice of laissez faire and individualism was being questioned. Government, society, and the economic framework of Britain were becoming much more complex and the Government began to accept the necessity of introducing laws to regulate society and to address the most basic needs of its citizens.

Trade unions and education

KEY CHRONOLOGY	
1868	First Trades Union Congress held
1870	Forster' Education Act
1871	Trade Unions Act
1872	Scottish Education Act
1872	Criminal Law Amendment Act
1875	Conspiracy and Protection of Property Act
1876	Sandon's Education Act
1880	Mundella's Education Act

KEY QUESTION

- How was Britain governed and how did democracy and political organisations change and develop?
- What pressures did governments face and how did they respond to these?
- How important was the role of individuals and groups and how were they affected by developments?

Revival of trade unionism – the model unions

There was a revival of trade unionism in the 1850s. It was very different from the Owen leadership of the **GNCTU** that was hampered among other reasons by the illiteracy of the majority of its members. The model or craft unions were small and operated among the skilled workers such as engineers and boilermakers. The leaders were restrained and respectable. They regarded themselves as the elite of the working classes and sought to improve working conditions through self-help, self-improvement and self-education. They functioned as Friendly Societies, setting up benefit schemes for their members in time of hardship. Their subscription rate was relatively high to underline their superiority over unskilled workers. They won the respect of Liberal politicians like Gladstone because of their preference to settle disputes by peaceful bargaining rather than strike action. It was these workers who benefited from the extension of the franchise in 1867. The legal position of the trade unions was not clearly defined and their funds could not be protected by law. By supporting the Liberal Party, they hoped it would in turn strengthen their legal position.

CROSS-REFERENCE

See Chapter 18, page 177, for more on the **GNCTU**.

A CLOSER LOOK

The Trade Union Act of 1871

This Act established the legal right of the unions to hold property and funds and have them protected by law. They also had the right to strike. The Criminal Law Amendment Act passed immediately afterwards made any form of picketing illegal. Therefore the trade unions were legalised but almost any action they took to achieve their objectives was illegal.

Position of Labour and trade union leaders

Regional trades councils, whose importance lay in the opportunities they provided for different unions to exchange ideas, encouraged the setting up of a national organisation for the unions. The first Trades Union Congress (TUC) was held in 1868 to bring pressure to bear on the Government to give trade unions legal recognition. The TUC became an annual event after its London meeting in 1871. From this time it represented the trade union movement as a whole.

ACTIVITY

Thinking point

1. In what ways did trade union development increase the confidence of the working classes?
2. What were the shortcomings of the trade union movement at this time?

Labour laws

Until 1871 the working-class electorate were still firm supporters of the Liberals. In that year the Government passed two pieces of trade union legislation which changed that support to frustration and anger. The leaders of the new model unions, confident that the Second Reform Act had given them bargaining power, pressed the Government for a Royal Commission of Inquiry into trade unionism, to clarify the ill-defined legal position of the unions. During the 1860s, the unions had been weakened by dishonest officials and the violent behaviour of some of its striking members.

Historians have identified the Trade Unions Act as Gladstone's most serious misjudgement as it cost him working-class support at the general election in 1874. They believe the passing of two such contrasting pieces of legislation can be explained by Gladstone's strong religious faith that abhorred violence or the threat of violence. The skilled artisans who had helped to ensure the Government's success in 1868 were left bitterly disappointed with the lack of any real support for trade union reform.

The result of this legislation was to strengthen the position of the trade unions and did much to encourage their growth. Unionism began to spread beyond the crafts and semi-skilled workers to include unskilled workers.

EXTRACT 3

Trade unionism entered a new phase of respectability in the 1850s in which the Government regulation of working conditions was strengthened by trade union action from time to time in defence of their members' interests. Strikes still occurred, but the prosperity of the time allowed both employers and unions to take a more flexible approach in trade disputes. Indeed, the unions themselves were prepared to admit that strikes were not always the best way of resolving labour problems. George Odger, the radical Secretary of the London Trades Council, declared that 'strikes are to the social world what wars are to the political world. They become crimes unless promoted by absolute necessity'. A leader of the Scottish miners spoke on the same theme before a select committee of the House of Commons in 1873: 'I look upon strikes as a barbaric relic of a period of unfortunate relations between capital and labour and the sooner we get rid of it the better.'

Adapted from Eric Hopkins, *Industrialisation and Society, A Social History, 1830–1851*, 2000

A CLOSER LOOK

The 1875 Conspiracy and Protection of Property Act

This Act replaced the unpopular Criminal Law Amendment Act of 1871. The Act altered the conspiracy laws, so that unions could no longer be prosecuted for doing anything collectively that would be legal if done by an individual. An action by a union during a dispute, which could be legally committed by one person, was therefore legal for a trade union. The Act legalised peaceful picketing and, in effect, gave the unions the right to strike.

ACTIVITY

What does Extract 3 suggest are the reasons for the emergence of the 'new phase of respectability' in trade unionism?

The growth of new unionism

The 1880s saw a change in direction in the union movement. It was the beginning of the organisation of unskilled workers, many of whom had endured appalling working conditions for decades and had lacked any real bargaining power with their employers. Their militant approach, with striking as their first line of attack, was in direct contrast to the craft unions. Subscriptions were low to allow for their poor and often fluctuating wage levels, but the large membership gave the unions funds to support some strike action, albeit not for long. Unlike the craft unions their funds did not make provision for welfare payments.

The uncertain economic climate of the late 1870s and 1880s contributed to the growth of new unionism. As manufacturing industries began to experience a downturn in demand for their goods and profits, unskilled workers were the first to be laid off. The high levels of unemployment made wage bargaining difficult and strikes ineffective as there was always plenty of labour to take over from strikers. Those workers lucky enough to be in a job had little choice but to accept the poor rates of pay.

Their confidence was boosted by the spread of education among the labouring classes after 1870, and in 1884 the right for many unskilled labourers to vote. Trade unions had achieved legal status in 1876 and it was inevitable that the unskilled workers would seek the advantages gained by the craft unions, by forming their own unions. It was the start of mass unionism.

Education

The notion persisted among the middle and upper classes that the purpose of extending education to the working classes was to equip people for their station in life (it was even the view of ardent advocate of education reform, James Kay-Shuttleworth). There was also a fear that education would encourage social mobility.

However, attitudes were changing. By the mid-nineteenth century, education was becoming a much more important consideration in government social policy. Utilitarian reformers such as Henry Brougham regarded it as an essential part of a progressive society. The Anglicans and Nonconformists wanted to save the poor from remaining in a state of ignorance, but competed against each other as to which of them could best achieve that. The Radicals who supported the idea of working-class education saw it as the foundation of a democratic society and had begun to see the government as the only effective way of changing education.

In 1846, education still remained the privilege of the middle and upper classes. Educational provision for the working class remained in the hands of the two religious societies, the Anglican National Society and the Nonconformist British and Foreign Society. Even so, many working class families could not take advantage of this opportunity – the schools were not sufficiently widespread, ignorance and prejudice prevented some parents from allowing their children to attend, and in any case many children were still in full-time employment and providing essential economic support to their families. Such schools that existed catered only for children up to the age of 12. Employment was the norm for older working-class children. Factory legislation passed in 1850 sanctioned young people between the ages of 13 and 18 working a 60 hour week.

During the 1850s and 1860s, the National Public Schools' Association and the national Education League promoted the idea of a permissive rather than compulsory education act. The 1870 Forster's Education Act, which made provision for elementary schools to be set up across the country, was an important step forward in acknowledging the role of the state in educating its children. Through the effects of Sandon's Act (1876) and Mundella's Act (1880), education was made compulsory for all children up to the age of ten.

> **CROSS-REFERENCE**
>
> More information on the development of education can be found in Chapters 14 and 20.

> **ACTIVITY**
>
> ### Summary
>
> Working in small groups or pairs, consider the impact on the working classes of the influences highlighted in this chapter, including Evangelicalism, the theory of self-help, the trade unions and education. In your view did these influences improve the lives of the working classes and if so which influences did so? Justify your various suggestions.

> **PRACTICE QUESTION**
>
> To what extent was there a rise in the standard of living for working people in Britain in the period between 1850 and 1885?

> **STUDY TIP**
>
> To answer this question, you should present the evidence for and against the statement, weigh up both sides of the argument, and try to draw a conclusion based on the strength of your findings. You may need to identify 'working people' and what you understand by 'standard of living' at the beginning of your answer.

24 The political, economic and social condition of Britain by 1885

The political condition of Britain – the extent of democracy

EXTRACT 1

By 1885, Britain became more democratic. The steps taken towards democracy had in them a certain bureaucratic logic, a tidying up of such anomalies and discrepancies as the distinction between county and borough seats and franchises. But the steps towards democracy were also driven by popular demand. The implications of the new power of the electorate and in particular its ability to determine who formed a government were considerable; leaders redefined their relationship to MPs and to supporters in the country, and the organisation of that support became a preoccupation. Yet if contemporaries thought of themselves as living in a democracy, it is the limitations of democracy even after the Third Reform Act that are the most striking. It excluded from parliamentary franchise some 70 per cent of adults and the Act operated in a **capricious** way, denying the vote to some men who had every claim to respectability while granting it to those who were without any. Pessimists may have disliked democracy but they could be under few illusions that in due course there would not be more of it.

Adapted from Hugh Cunningham, *The Challenge of Democracy, Britain, 1832–1918*, 2014

LEARNING OBJECTIVES

In this chapter you will learn about:
- the extent of democracy
- Britain's industrial position.

KEY QUESTION

As you read this chapter, consider the following Key Questions:
- How was Britain governed and how did democracy and political organisations change and develop?
- How and with what results did the economy develop and change?
- How and with what results did society and social policy develop?
- What pressures did governments face and how did they respond to these?

KEY TERM

capricious: behaving in unpredictable ways; in this context it means erratic or inconsistent

ACTIVITY

According to Extract 1, had Britain become more democratic by 1885? If so how, according to the extract, had this been achieved? Consider both aspects of the question in your answer.

By 1885, Britain had become more democratic. Since the 1830s, when the first parliamentary reform act was under debate, Britain had moved a long way towards having a democratic system of government. In the 1820s and 30s the argument used by the governing class was that Parliament had functioned efficiently for hundreds of years and therefore there was no need to change it; reform would increase demand for further reform and could lead to a situation of revolution and anarchy. They believed it would be impossible to trust the masses of illiterate workers with political power, and reform of Parliament would lead to demands for reform in other areas. Most of the aristocratic political elite did not wish to share power with the pushy, clever middle-class manufacturers. To abolish rotten and pocket boroughs seemed to them to be confiscation of property without compensation. And worst of all, they believed, the House of Commons would be at the mercy of public opinion. These arguments denied the fact of industrialisation and that it had caused social and economic upheaval on a scale never before experienced. This had made the political system outdated and it needed to adapt.

The anxieties expressed by the anti-reformers in Parliament in 1830 were in some ways accurate predictions of how the political system would develop if a measure of reform was allowed. In the event, there was no revolution or anarchy, but after 1832, the aristocratic elite had no choice but to share power with the 'pushy middle class' to avoid it. They wilted in the face of pressure to abolish decayed and corrupt rotten and pocket boroughs and give seats instead to the burgeoning industrial towns – the hard-working, wealth-producing manufacturers and industrialists insisted on it. After the 1867 Reform Act which extended the franchise to the skilled

A CLOSER LOOK

Terms of the Franchise Act 1884

- In the counties the vote was given to all male householders over 21 and £10 lodgers
- A £10 occupier franchise was created for those living in shops or offices

(This made the franchise the same in counties and boroughs but different regulations added complications to the system, e.g. the older franchise still applied.)

Terms of the Redistribution of Seats Act, 1885

- Boroughs with a population of under 15,000 lost both their MPs
- Boroughs with a population under 50,000 lost one MP
- 142 seats were redistributed

artisan class, the two political parties realised that if they were to win an election on their own merits they needed policies and party organisation to persuade public opinion in their favour. When the franchise was extended in 1884 to include unskilled workers, they would soon no longer be the untrustworthy 'illiterate masses', as their children were now compelled to attend elementary school to learn to read and write and perform basic arithmetic. As Cunningham suggests, the steps to democracy were 'driven by popular demand', at least in part.

Pressure from the National Liberation Federation (formed in 1877), the radical wing of the Liberal Party, to extend the franchise to the working men in the countryside brought about the **1884 Franchise Act**, which ended the discrepancy between county and borough voting qualifications. Agricultural labourers and miners in rural areas were brought into the voting system. The electorate doubled from about 3 million to 6 million out of a total population of 35 million. For the first time in Britain the majority of adult males could vote.

In 1885, the **Redistribution of Seats Act** attempted to equalise the size of constituencies in terms of numbers of population and brought 'a certain bureaucratic logic, a tidying up of such anomalies and discrepancies as the distinction between county and borough seats and franchises' (Cunningham). It brought an end to the over-representation of the rural areas and under-representation of the industrial towns and cities.

Fig. 1 *A cartoon published in the St Stephen's review, 15 November 1884, satirising the Reform Acts; the dress coat of the woman on the left reads 'Franchise', the coat of the woman on the right reads 'Redistribution'*

If in 1885, 'contemporaries thought of themselves as living in a democracy', what was surprising was they were content with the 'limitations of democracy' that still existed. It would seem the new working-class electorate were happy to vote for one of the existing parties, Liberal or Conservative. A general desire for an independent working-class political party had not yet manifested itself, although the situation was changing. In the 1874 election, for the first time two working-class candidates had become MPs. The Secret Ballot Act in 1872 had increased working-class voters' confidence, as they were no longer subject to pressure or intimidation and could vote freely for their candidate. The 1884 Franchise Act strengthened the political status of the working class and it became evident to the Conservative and Liberal parties that they could no longer afford to displease the large working-class electorate with hostile trade union legislation or ignore their social needs.

According to Cunningham, there were still approximately 70 per cent of the adult population without a vote – if women were included in that figure. Up until then, there had been very little debate about female emancipation. Gladstone's Liberal government had passed laws which allowed single female householders to vote in local elections, propertied women to serve on school boards set up in 1870, and, from 1875, women could be Poor Law Guardians.

Although the franchise reform removed much of the class discrimination over voting, it was still linked to complex property-related qualifications and therefore there were significant groups who still didn't qualify for a vote, apart from women. There were adult sons (often from middle-class families and following a profession) living at home, live-in servants, and paupers (who made up approximately 12 per cent of the adult male population). This helps to explain Cunningham's view that the Act operated in a capricious way, denying the vote to some men who had every claim to respectability while granting it to those who were without any. One of the problems was that many men, mainly from among the unskilled workers, who were entitled to vote, couldn't as they had no documentation to prove their qualification and so could not get onto the electoral register.

By 1885, most of the working classes were enfranchised, the influence of the landed classes was substantially reduced and Britain was more democratic than it had been in 1832, but the fact remained that the simple democratic principle of universal suffrage had not yet been achieved.

ACTIVITY

Revision

In Chapter 1 you were asked to 'summarise the main problems with the system of parliamentary representation in Britain in 1783'. Check your answer. Create a two column chart with the left column the problems in 1783 and the right column the extent to which the problems you identified had been addressed by 1885. What problems were still outstanding?

EXTRACT 2

Despite the growing sense that there was a working class and not a number of separate working classes, in 1885 the obstacles to working-class political activity remained enormous. Most obviously, Britain was in no serious sense of the word a democracy, for about one third of all adult men (and all women) did not have the right to vote even after the Third Reform Act of 1884. It is unclear exactly which sections of the community were excluded; the unenfranchised certainly included some middle-class men like sons living with parents and lodgers in transient occupations, but there were also many working-class men excluded. This was partly because of a franchise based generally on the value of property occupied, which naturally most excluded the poorest, but also because the excessive complexity of the registration system itself made it difficult and expensive for the uneducated to *claim* their rights; over time this obstacle became less significant and the class bias in the electorate became less important.

Adapted from Williams and Ramsden, *Ruling Britannia, A Political History of Britannia*, 1990

PRACTICE QUESTION (A LEVEL)

Evaluating historical extracts

Using your understanding of the historical context assess how convincing the arguments in Extracts 1, 2 and 3 are in relation to the political condition of Britain in 1885.

STUDY TIP

Whilst the overall opinion of these two extracts is similar, you should identify how each historian views the stage that democracy had reached by 1885. Consider each interpretation and build up your answer from there.

SECTION 4 | Economy, society and politics 1846–1885

> **KEY QUESTION**
>
> How and with what results did the economy develop and change?

> **ACTIVITY**
>
> In pairs, look back over the sections on the economy. Identify key aspects of economic change and development over the previous century and create a flow chart to illustrate change.

> **ACTIVITY**
>
> **Extension**
>
> Using the information gathered in the previous activity, assess the results of economic change and development in Britain between 1783 and 1885.

> **KEY QUESTION**
>
> How and with what results did society and social policy develop?

Fig. 2 *A studio portrait of a Victorian woman, 1898*

The economic and social condition of Britain by 1885

The economy

Changes were occurring in the British economy during the last decades of the nineteenth century. The contemporary view was that Britain was suffering from a long-term depression, which started in 1873 and appeared to continue into the 1890s. During that time there were periods of marked cyclical downturns, one of which occurred between 1882 and 1886. For years Britain had dominated the export markets, but now it began to face competition from foreign markets and there was a fall in demand for British goods. Prices and profits tumbled in industry and agriculture. By 1885, there was an erosion of confidence in Britain's economic dominance.

In 1885, the Government was sufficiently anxious about the economy to set up a Royal Commission to inquire about the Depression of Industry and Trade. Its remit was to report on 'the extent, nature and probable cause of the depression prevailing in various branches of trade and industry'. The majority report concluded that agricultural prices had been falling since 1873 and that the downward trend continued. It noted an increase in production of most other commodities, but in many instances supply outstripped demand. This led to a reduction in profits, a fall in prices and lower rates of interest on invested capital. There were issues relating to foreign competition. The report, however, commented that there were encouraging signs for the future. The tone of complacency was not shared by everyone.

The social condition of Britain in 1885

By 1885, the Victorians were on the verge of a new, modern society. They were moving into an era of mass politics, mass unionism, mass education, mass production and mass consumption and, according to McCord and Purdue, a 'mass society'. However, the class system was still the dominant feature of Victorian society, although Victorians believed that a person could improve their social position through hard work and self-improvement. While it was possible to move from the working class to the middle class, it was virtually impossible to move into the upper classes, except through exceptional wealth creation or marriage.

In spite of political reform, Britain was still governed largely by the landed aristocracy, although the political power and social influence of men with industrial wealth had made inroads into this elite group. Social differences were developing within the political parties and by 1885, Conservatives tended to come from the landowning classes, while Liberals tended to come from the professions, commerce and industry. However, among supporters there was little difference – the middle-class voters were evenly split between the two parties. Neither the Liberal Party nor the Conservative Party satisfied the needs of the newly-enfranchised working-class voters. Their desire to have their voice heard led to the emergence of the Labour movement in the closing decades of the nineteenth century.

In the century before 1885, there had been a marked development in professions, several of which had become clearly established. Members of the growing urban middle class had to earn their living and many of them did so by providing services – working as doctors, teachers, lawyers, architects, engineers, and so on – to meet the varying needs of their own and other classes.

Regular church-going was a feature of stable, respectable family life and church-building had been a feature of urban development over the previous century, moving in tandem with population growth, until the 1880s.

The position of women was paradoxical in that the monarch was a woman. McCord and Purdue make the point that 'the dominant rhetoric of the day insisted upon distinct and separate roles for the sexes, the exclusion of women from the political sphere and male dominance with regard to divorce and property'. Women's position in the home as wife and mother was regarded as the epitome of stability, respectability and virtuousness. However, many women regarded attitudes towards them as condescending and restrictive and wished to participate in the opportunities of education and employment enjoyed by men. In 1887, the National Union of Women's Suffrage Societies was launched. It was an important step in the movement for female emancipation and democracy.

Poor living standards and miserable living conditions remained the norm for many people. The booming economy did not remove poverty. In 1886, Charles Booth's survey of London was published and shocked the comfortable, confident Victorians with its conclusions that 30 per cent of London's population lived in poverty. The findings drove the political agenda of the future generations.

EXTRACT 3

The coming of mass politics and what has been seen as a 'mass society', preponderantly urban, with efficient transport systems, well-organised spectator sports, the telephone, and newspapers and magazines with large circulations do seem to give the late-Victorian period a new and modern character. Britain was ever more an urban society; religion remained important but was less central to the lives of the majority; there were cultural and moral challenges to the dominant ethics of the mid-Victorian period; a dynamic commercialism and consumerism transformed the lifestyles of all classes; more words and pictures were printed and were read and seen by more people; the views and appetites of the majority of the population became more important, socially, politically and commercially; government intruded more and more; and although Britain remained powerful and confident there were worries about economic competitiveness and military ability in a dangerous world.

Adapted from McCord and Purdue, *British History, 1815–1914*, 2007

Britain's industrial position

EXTRACT 4

On land, while the traffic receipts and operating profits of most of the railway companies steadily grew, the number of new lines constructed dropped sharply. There was, after all, a limit to the number of small seaside towns that could be equipped with a railway for, in effect, two months of the year. The Great Central Railway, establishing a direct Manchester and Sheffield route to London terminating at Marylebone, was the last major railway, and the return on investment was poor. However, the construction of the Forth Bridge and the Severn Tunnel in the 1880s did bring major improvements to the railway system. Some brave spirits wanted even more expansion, but more sombre railwaymen, conscious of the internal combustion engine, feared that their industry was at its peak by the end of the century.

Adapted from Keith Robbins, *The Eclipse of a Great Power*, 1994

By 1885, Britain was experiencing an economic depression, but it followed a period of outstanding economic growth and prosperity. The economy was still growing but at a slower rate. The rate of production in the major industries of coal, cotton and steel was increasing, but more slowly. There was a fall in

ACTIVITY
Evaluating historical extracts

1. According to Extract 3, in what respects does the late Victorian period appear to have taken on a 'new and modern character'? Do you agree with this interpretation of British society? Explain your answer.

2. The extract makes several statements about 'The economic and social condition of Britain around 1885'. Take each one and provide a piece of evidence to support the statement. For example, your first statement will start: 'Britain was ever more an urban society ...' (followed by your evidence).

ACTIVITY
Evaluating historical extracts

What, according to Extract 4, were the problems with the railway industry in the 1880s?

ACTIVITY
Extension

Why was the internal combustion engine seen by some as a threat to the railway industry?

CROSS-REFERENCE

The Bank Charter Act (1844) is the subject of Chapter 16. One of the aims of this Act was to ensure that the issuing of bank notes related to the volume of gold reserves held by the Bank of England.

prices, which meant smaller profit margins for the manufacturers, and workers were laid off more frequently. There were periods of unemployment during these years, but they were not sustained. While the depression in agriculture continued, there was a brief recovery in industry by 1880, but another less severe slump occurred around 1885, during which unemployment rose to a high point of almost 10 per cent of the working population. There had been a steady fall in prices since the early 1870s, possibly as a result of a shortage of gold to support currency, or because Britain had come to the end of a long period of economic growth that could not be sustained.

In contrast with the idea of a continuing depression, there were also signs of increases in Britain's manufacturing output, with the appearance of many new smaller industries, such as the manufacture of boots and shoes, chocolate, soap, tobacco and beer, which all developed successfully at this time.

Fig. 3 *The Forth Railway Bridge under construction in 1887; when completed the 1.5 mile long bridge was the biggest in the world*

Challenges to Britain's supremacy

Britain was dependent on its export trade to maintain its position of economic supremacy in the world markets and had enjoyed almost a monopoly in the production and export of coal, iron and steel – the key industrial commodities. By 1885, Britain was experiencing a serious challenge to its position as a result of the rapid industrialisation of the USA and Germany. The USA was rich in natural resources and in manpower from European immigration, and raced ahead in economic development. By 1890 the USA had overtaken Britain in the production of both iron and steel and Germany was not far behind. Britain was still ahead in the production of coal.

The tariff barriers set up by Britain's new competitors to protect their industries were presenting a problem for Britain's economy. Germany introduced trade tariffs in 1879 and the USA followed in 1890, while Britain clung on to its long-held belief in the policy of laissez faire. The decision by Disraeli (Prime Minister from 1874–80) to continue Gladstone's free trade policy meant there was no tariff protection from foreign competition. The Fair Trade League established in 1881 had pressed the Government for some form of protection against British competitors, without success. It was an indication of the weakening influence of the landed interests in Parliament. It has been suggested by several historians that in the 'scramble for Africa' during the 1880s, one of Britain's underlying motives in securing colonial territories was trade protection. Colonial expansion in Africa would give Britain access to a new supply of raw materials and markets for British goods.

It was inevitable that other countries were going to industrialise. As the first industrial nation, by 1885 Britain was falling behind in the latest technology and its machinery was either old or obsolete. There was a reluctance to invest new capital, especially in the steel industry where the up-to-date British Gilchrist-Thomas method of steel manufacture was adopted by the Germans. There was a perception that the entrepreneurial spirit of earlier industrialists was disappearing as the management of family firms was handed down to less capable or less interested successors. There was little engagement with future development of new industries such as chemicals and electrical engineering. As Robbins comments, the boom in railway-building had ended by 1875, as most major towns and cities already had good rail links. This reduced the demand for iron and steel and led to job losses.

The agricultural industry

By 1885, the depression in agriculture had not lifted. Falling prices forced down rents and the prices of commodities like wool and wheat plummeted. The unpredictability of the weather could always tip the balance between survival and ruin; the summer of 1879 was the wettest on record. Crops rotted in the ground, there was a shortage of animal feed, and there were outbreaks of disease among livestock, such as 'foot and mouth' and swine fever. It was difficult for farmers to get back on track with such unwelcome disasters. With agricultural immunity already low, recovery was made more difficult with the onset of foreign competition.

Advances in farm machinery, particularly the combine harvester in the USA, revolutionised the process of harvesting and was ideal in the vast American wheat lands. The development of the canning process in the 1880s meant that beef from the large cattle ranches in Argentina and Uruguay could be put into tins to preserve it and then exported to Britain. Methods of refrigeration that developed at this time meant that previously perishable goods (mainly lamb) could be transported from as far afield as Australia and New Zealand, and they could compete with British goods in terms of price, if not quality!

The result of these innovations and advances meant fierce competition for the British farmer and a continuing fall in prices. The price of wheat fell from 55 shillings a quarter in 1874 to 31 shillings in 1885. The hardest hit areas were the wheat and cereal counties of the South and East. By 1885 many farmers were bankrupt; many out of work agricultural labourers deserted the countryside and settled in the towns. Life was not much easier for them there as the depression in industry made finding regular work difficult. Some sought a better life by emigrating to the USA and Canada.

A CLOSER LOOK

Lever Brothers and Sunlight Soap

William Lever started up his soap manufacturing business in 1885 in Liverpool, when unemployment was at its height. It was one of the first companies to manufacture soap from vegetable oils, and with Lever's innovative approach and marketing practices the business soon expanded.

A CLOSER LOOK

The Scramble for Africa

'Scramble for Africa' was the term used to describe the competition between several European countries including Britain to take over what was left of the vulnerable underdeveloped territories in the African continent, in order to bring more resources, markets and new outlets for capital investment. Between 1882 and 1900, most of Africa was divided up among European imperialist nations.

SECTION 4 | Economy, society and politics 1846–1885

Fig. 4 A satirical cartoon depicting the Crofter Act of 1886, which was passed to protect the highland croft farmers from the mass clearances and evictions forced upon them by their landlords; a Scottish highlander (left) rolls up his sleeves as John Bull (a national personification of Great Britain) listens to the landlord explain his case

The pattern of British agriculture was changing by 1885, partly as a result of the depression. No region of the country was unaffected and to survive, British farmers had to diversify. Farmers in the south of Scotland, Warwickshire and Lancashire were less badly affected as these areas already concentrated on mixed farming. In some areas there were successful new developments and in others there was less scope for change. Some farmers were slow to spot the need to change. Many farmers moved into dairy farming as milk could not easily be imported and yet it could be quickly transported some distance within Britain by rail. Poultry farming became popular. The development of market gardening as an alternative to farming met with great success, especially in areas like the Vale of Evesham and the Thames Valley where fruit, flowers and vegetables grew well. In Britain as a whole the area under cultivation fell, while the area turned over to pasture increased.

ACTIVITY

Revision

Look back over the earlier sections on agriculture in the book. Consider whether or not conditions had improved over the previous century for farmers and farm workers. Draw up a list of changes that brought advantages and changes that brought disadvantages for each group. What conclusion can you draw?

STUDY TIP

You need to first define your terms, i.e. what makes a country a democracy? It is not just a matter of the proportion of the population who have the right to vote; there are other important issues. Set your criteria. Think about the changes that took place in Britain up until the date of the question. Consider how far these factors brought Britain closer to democracy.

ACTIVITY

Summary

Split into small groups. Create a chart to show the key political, economic and social changes that occurred between c1783 and 1885. What would you consider to be the most important developments that occurred over that century? Note down the key points of your group discussions. As a class can you come to a consensus about your choices?

PRACTICE QUESTION

To what extent had democracy been achieved in Britain by 1885?

Conclusion

In 1885 Britain was still enjoying a position of global supremacy. For most of the nineteenth century it had held the position of the wealthiest, most highly industrialised society in the world. It possessed the largest overseas empire, from which it shipped quantities of raw materials to be manufactured into goods to sell at home to meet ever-increasing consumer demands or to trade abroad. It had reaped the benefits of early industrialisation. It was confident enough to make Free Trade the basis of its commercial policy. In spite of the onset of the Great Depression from 1873, and stiff competition from newly industrialised countries such as Germany and the United States of America, Britain had developed a strong integrated economy that continued to grow, although the pace was slowing. Britain's trade balance remained healthy and the country maintained a dominant position in the world's economy.

Queen Victoria celebrated her Golden Jubilee in 1887, two years after the end of this period. The sudden loss of her husband and consort, Prince Albert, from typhoid in 1861 led to her withdrawal from public life. In spite of this, Victoria retained a strong influence on the social conventions of the nation. The word 'Victorianism' came to suggest a particular attitude. It encouraged self confidence, self-help and thrift. Deference, religious observance and high moral standards were demanded. It also produced an unbending attitude that judged harshly those who fell from grace. It suggested moral authority rather than monarchical power. Queen Victoria often interfered in matters of state and the choice of prime minister, but as the party system developed in the House of Commons, royal influence declined. By 1885 the Monarch was becoming little more than a figurehead.

The Parliamentary Reform Act of 1884 was a great milestone in the move towards universal suffrage, as the electorate was extended to include unskilled working men, which gave the majority of the working classes a political voice for the first time. The Redistribution Act the following year meant that at last, the size of the constituencies corresponded to population distribution. Britain had been regarded as a liberal democracy in Europe, but by today's standards participation was still limited. Although in theory the majority of the adult male population could vote, the detailed residency requirements and unhelpful registration procedures excluded almost one man in three. The fact that women were excluded from the political process was becoming a contentious issue. John Stuart Mill, Radical philosopher and MP, had raised the question of female suffrage in 1867, but by 1885 there had been no compromise to admit any woman to membership of the most exclusive gentlemen's club, the Houses of Parliament. In the years ahead, the number of women's suffrage societies grew, as did the determination to see the franchise widened to include women.

In 1885 there were two main political parties, Liberals and Conservatives, each vying with the other for favour with the new electorate. Gladstone's reforms underlined the principles of equality in a just society but didn't have popular appeal and drew hostility from particular interests, and in the 1874 election he lost many natural supporters. In his second ministry (1880–85), he allowed the problems of Ireland to distract him. Disraeli, who died in 1880, had launched his 'Tory democracy' brand of Conservatism, partly to appeal to the working classes, and his social reforms of the late 1870s, which promised improvements in working conditions, public health and housing, won approval. The mainly adoptive legislation

> **KEY QUESTION**
>
> Throughout the course of your study you have been considering the following Key Questions:
> - How was Britain governed and how did democracy and political organisations change and develop?
> - What pressures did governments face and how did they respond to these?
> - How and with what results did the economy develop and change?
> - How and with what results did society and social policy develop?
> - How important were ideas and ideology?
> - How important was the role of individuals and groups and how were they affected by developments?

of both parties indicated a growing acceptance of the principle of limited state intervention in people's lives. This was in line with the tendency of governments to move away from the principle of laissez faire and to take firmer action to deal with the many social problems thrown up by an urban society.

The extension of the franchise in 1884 to unskilled labourers strengthened the political status of the working classes. Within a few years political reform was stimulating the development of a Labour movement, which was increasingly motivated to form a political party for the working class and which ultimately would pose a threat to both the Conservative and Liberal parties – but that was still in the future.

In 1885 the population of Britain stood at around 35 million. It had more than doubled since the first official census in 1801 and was rising at a rate of just above ten per cent per decade. In general, life expectancy was increasing, partly an effect of medical knowledge and practice, but the death rate was still too high in large towns and cities; the main causes still lay in the incidence of infectious diseases and poor health among urban slum dwellers. Fewer people were in receipt of poor relief: the figure had fallen from 8.8 per cent in 1834, immediately after the passing of the Poor Law Amendment Act, to 3.2 per cent in 1880 – and went against the rise in population. The standard of living for most British families was improving, with better wages and easier access to more plentiful and greater variety of food, and there was a general improvement in the quality of housing for working people. Although wages were keeping ahead of prices, substantial differences remained in wage levels between different skills and different regions, between skilled and unskilled labourers, and between agricultural workers and industrial workers in the towns. Provision of education increased after the 1870 Education Act and levels of literacy had improved by 1885, although in rural areas helping with the harvest was more important than attending school. Higher education institutions were opening in most major cities, some with charitable foundations or generous benefactors, paving the way for more opportunities to be available on the basis of merit rather than family connection.

Over the 100 years of this study, a different social order had developed. In the late eighteenth century levels of society were referred to as lower, middling and upper orders. The landowners and aristocracy comprised the upper orders and they were firmly in control of the organisation of society, the land-based economy and the political system. It was an age of deference in which the lower orders had few expectations in life. By 1885 the language had changed and references were made to class. A large prosperous middle class had emerged and an even larger working class. Life expectations had grown over the previous 100 years, not just for the rich and privileged, but for every man who made a worthwhile contribution to society. Remember Victorian attitudes did not support the 'undeserving poor'. The dominance of the aristocracy was being challenged on several levels and by 1885, they had given up their political monopoly, had been surpassed in economic supremacy and had invited the most successful middle-class entrepreneurs, industrialists and other achievers into their homes, as their social equals. Through industrialisation, the middle class had made the economy more dynamic and that in turn gave them socio-economic power enabling them to press for political, social and economic change. Those changes brought new opportunities for the working classes. The history of Britain beyond 1885 tells the story of the advantages they took of those opportunities.

Conclusion

Fig. 1 *A typical Victorian seaside scene; through industrialisation the middle class achieved political, social and economic change which allowed for the opportunity of leisure time*

Now you have completed this book, think about the questions it raises. What was the impact of industrialisation on Britain and how widespread were its repercussions? How was Britain governed in 1783 and what pressures were put on government by society to bring about the changes necessary for successful economic development and social reform? What contribution did individuals make in encouraging change? Think of the importance of the great social and administrative reforms that stimulated the notion that it is the duty of government to address the needs of all of its people. Reflect on the extent to which political organisations changed with the times and whether or not Britain could be called a democracy by 1885. Your reading of this formative and fascinating period of British history should provide you with some of the answers and encourage you to draw conclusions about the issues raised.

A

agents provocateurs: government spies who went among workers deliberately stirring up trouble to flush out the ring leaders

Alderman: a civic dignitary in the borough, next in rank to the Mayor and elected by fellow councillors

artisan: a skilled manual worker journeyman: a man who has completed his apprenticeship and is competent at his trade

B

Borough member: each borough was represented by two MPs, irrespective of size of population

C

cabal: a small group that comes together for a secret purpose, very often political intrigue

Cabinet: known today as the committee at the centre of the British political system responsible for making decisions in government; in 1783 its role was to offer advice to the King

Civil list: a fixed annual sum, agreed by Parliament to meet the monarch's household expenses

civil service: the body that isresponsible for the public administration of the State

coalition allies: partners of different parties or countries; Britain formed four coalitions with various European countries over the duration of the French wars; the third and fourth coalitions were between Britain Russia and Prussia

combination in restraint of trade: a legal phrase to describe a form of strike action that aims to interfere with the normal course of trade

Continental System: a blockade of Britain inaugurated by Napoleon in the Berlin Decrees issued in November 1806

cottage industry: a business or manufacturing activity carried out in people's homes

County member: each county was represented by two MPs, elected by the men whose freehold land had a rateable value of at least 40 shillings a year

cropper: (cloth-dresser) a well-paid, highly skilled job in the woollen industry; the cropper cut the surface of the cloth, making it smooth, after raising it with special long heavy shears

D

Dissenters: Protestants who broke away from the established Anglican Church and adopted their own practices because they disagreed strongly with Anglican traditions

divine right: concept that a monarch rules by authority of God, not through the consent of the people

E

Enclosure: the new system of dividing agricultural land into compact fields closed in by fences, hedges or walls; it replaced the old open-field system, where the land was divided into strips

Evangelicalism: a spiritual movement within the Anglican Church that encouraged adherence to the message of the Bible, and the seeking of salvation through faith (the idea that you could only be saved from sin through belief in God)

F

factions: small groups of politicians who disagreed with others

farmers' lock-out: a reference to farmers' attitude to the National Agricultural Labourers' Union formed by Joseph Arch in 1873, which resulted in a wage rise; thereafter most farmers imposed a lock-out on any of their workers who remained members of the Union

Fenian: the generally accepted term at the time to describe all nationalist groups associated with seeking independence for Ireland

First Lord of the Treasury: one of the Lords Commissioners of the Treasury and by custom, which continues today, Prime Minister

franchise: the right to vote, which was generally based on a property qualification

free trade: the economic policy that involves a free exchange of commodities (goods) between nations without imposing duties or tariffs

freehold: if land was freehold it meant that the man who held it owned it

free-marketeers: those who believe in an economic system in which prices are allowed to fluctuate in accordance with supply and demand; it is a form of capitalism

G

guano: the droppings of seabirds, one of the richest natural sources of fertiliser; it was imported from Peru in huge quantities in the mid-nineteenth century, before it was replaced by chemical fertilisers

H

habeas corpus: preserves the right of the individual not to be detained illegally; it has occasionally been suspended by the government during social unrest

home rule: a desire held by many Irish to repeal the terms of the Act of Union passed in 1800, to establish a parliament in Dublin, from which they could control and be responsible for domestic affairs

humanitarianism: a belief in the worth of human beings; behaving decently and benevolently to others

husbandry: the care and good practice of a farmer or farming

I

in restraint of trade: a legal phrase to describe strike action

income tax: a form of direct taxation raised on a person's earnings; it has become an integral part of the British taxation system and an important source of government income since being introduced by Pitt over 200 years ago

indentured labour: an indenture is a legal contract between two parties; in this context Indian labourers agreed to work for a specific period, usually five years, in British Colonies, for agreed wages and specified conditions

Industrial Revolution: a rapid development in industry which took place in Britain in the late eighteenth and early nineteenth centuries, chiefly owing to the introduction of new or improved machinery and large scale production methods

insurrectionary: revolutionary

J

Jacobin: a member of a group of more extreme French revolutionaries; the term became used to describe political radicals"

Joint Stock Company: a company or business enterprise with a stated purpose (usually to make money); capital is raised and divided into a number of units, held by different owners/shareholders

joint-stock bank: a limited liability company, engaged in banking as its trade, founded by subscribers or 'shareholders', whose liability is limited to the amount of money they subscribe; if the bank fails, they lose their subscription, but no more

L

laissez faire: the doctrine that the state should not interfere in the workings of the market economy"

M

master: the expression used to describe the owner of a workshop, foundry or factory

mercantilism: the accepted method of trade regulation which involved a complex system of tariffs levied on goods coming into and going out of the country

ministers: politicians who hold significant public office in a national or regional government

mixed constitution: form of government in which a hereditary monarch is head of state, with powers limited by Parliament; it is sometimes referred to as a constitutional monarchy

nationalist: a person who strives for (in this case) the independence of their country from the domination of another

O

Oath of Supremacy: swearing allegiance to the monarch as Supreme Governor of the Church of England; Catholics' allegiance was to the Pope and so their religious beliefs would preclude them from taking the oath

oligarchy: a government of a small elite group, in this context the ruling Whig families who dominated the political scene in the eighteenth century

Orders in Council: orders issued by the British government to blockade France in retaliation

P

parity: equal status

paternalistic: taking on the role of a father; the attitude of a well-meaning boss, whose supervision could be regarded as too interfering

patronage: the right to give privileges or make appointments

penal system: system of law relating to crime and punishment

permissive legislation: a law that allows organisations or individuals at whom it is directed the choice of whether or not to carry out its requirements; it reflects the laissez faire attitudes of the period

philanthropy: a love of mankind, demonstrated by contributing to general welfare

picketing: the action taken by strikers to persuade the non-striking workers to join the strike

Presbyterians: part of a broader group of Dissenters which was widespread in Scotland; there was also a small, strong community in Belfast

Q

quasi: quasi is a Latin word adopted in the English language meaning 'as if it were';

R

Radicals: politicians who argue for political and social change

reactionary: a person who tends to oppose reform or political change

real wages: the spending value of the wage earned

renege: to go back on one's word

republican: supporter of a republic, which is a state in which power is invested in those elected by the people; a republic does not have a monarch

rout: an overwhelming defeat

Royal Commission of Inquiry: a body set up by government to look into a specific issue, e.g. the workings of the Poor Law; it includes 'experts' who make proposals and recommendations to Parliament to help them pass relevant legislation

S

seditious libel: published writings directed against the state that are intended to cause disorder

September massacres: event of 1792 when revolutionary leaders sanctioned the deaths of thousands of French citizens after mock trials, climaxing with the execution of the French King in January 1793

Sinecure office: position with salary, handed out to MPs to gain their support, but that required little or no work; the modern dictionary definition is 'a cushy job'

socialism: the sharing of wealth between all members of the community

speculation: the forming of a theory or conjecture without firm evidence

standard of living: a measure indicating the relative wealth and comfort in which people live"

status quo: the situation as it is; the existing condition

Statute: a written law

Glossary

steam raising: the expression used when an engine boiler is stoked up sufficiently to raise a head of steam to make the locomotive run

T

tariff: a set or list of customs duties on import or export of certain goods

the City: the old centre of London where trading in goods and commodities took place, the home of the Bank of England and the centre of financial activities

The East India Company: the largest and most influential English trading company, formed in 1600; it enjoyed a trade monopoly in India and the Far East until the nineteenth century and large parts of India came under its political control

tied housing: housing in which occupancy depends on continuing to work for the employer who supplied the house; it was (and still is) a common practice for farm workers to have accommodation provided with a job

Tory Democracy: a term describing the policies advocated by Disraeli when he became Prime Minister in 1874, namely maintaining Conservative support of established institutions – the constitutional monarchy, the British Empire, the Church of England – but also supporting a degree of social reform

trade societies: the forerunners of trade unions; they represented the interests of skilled artisans, dealing with employers to ensure a fair wage and also to protect them from unskilled workers taking their jobs

U

undeserving poor: term used by Victorians who believed some poor people caused their poverty through laziness, wickedness or carelessness

urban growth: towns and cities becoming larger

urbanisation: an increasing percentage of the population becoming town-dwellers

V

vested interest: a particular interest in maintaining an existing system, for example slavery, because you own a sugar plantation using slaves as your workforce, and usually for financial reasons

veto: to reject a decision or proposal made by a Parliament

Y

yeoman: freeholder farmers; holding and cultivating a small piece of land

Bibliography

Books for students

Black Jeremy & Macraild Donald, *Nineteenth Century Britain,* Palgrave, 2002

Chapple P., *The Industrialisation of Britain,* Hodder & Stoughton, 1999

Dicken, M., *Disraeli,* Collins Educational, 2004

Evans, Eric J., *Political Parties in Britain 1783–1867,* Methuen, 1985

Evans, Eric J., *William Pitt the Younger,* Routledge, 1999

Evans, Eric J., *Sir Robert Peel, Statesmanship Power and Party,* Routledge, 2006

Fraser, Antonia, *Perilous Question, the drama of the Great Reform Bill, 1832,* W&N, 2013

Goodlad, G., *Gladstone,* Collins Educational, 2004

Leonard, Dick, *Nineteenth Century British Prime Ministers,* Palgrave Macmillan, 2008

Lowe, Joseph, *The Present State of England,* 1822

Lowe, N., *Mastering Modern World History,* Palgrave, 1998

Martin, H., *Britain in the 19th Century,* Nelson Thornes, 2000

Mayer, A., *The Growth of Democracy in Britain,* Hodder & Stoughton, 1999

Morgan, Kenneth O. (editor), *The Oxford Illustrated History of Britain,* Oxford University Press, 2009

Murphy et. al., *Britain 1783–1918,* Collins, 2003

Paterson, D., *Liberalism and Conservatism, 1846–1905,* Heinemann, 2001

Pearce, R. & Stearn R., *Government and reform: Britain 1815–1918,* Hodder & Stoughton, 2000

Plowright, John, *Regency England, The Age of Liverpool,* Routledge, 1996

Pugh, Martin, *Britain Since 1789,* Macmillan, 1999

Rubinstein W., *Britain's Century: A Political and Social History 1815–1905,* Hodder Arnold, 1998

There are several excellent novels written during this period of study which reflect some of the thinking and social and political concerns of the time, for example Charles Dickens, *Our Mutual Friend,* 1865; Elizabeth Gaskell, *North and South,* 1855; George Eliot, *Middlemarch,* 1872

Books for teachers and extension

Aldous, Richard, *The Lion and the Unicorn,* Pimlico, 2007

Blake Robert, *The Conservative Party from Peel to Thatcher,* Fontana Press, 1985

Briggs, Asa, *The Age of Improvement,* Longmans, 1967

Brock, W. R., *Lord Liverpool and Liberal Toryism 1820 to 1827,* Cambridge University Press, 1941

Brown, Richard, *Church and State in Modern Britain 1700–1850,* Routledge, 1991

Gash, Norman, *Sir Robert Peel, the Life of Sir Robert Peel after 1830,* Longman, 1972

Gaunt, Richard A., *Sir Robert Peel, The Life and Legacy,* I. B. Tauris, 2010

Hague, William, *William Pitt the Younger,* Harper Collins, 2004

Hilton, Boyd, *A Mad, Bad, and Dangerous People? England 1783–1846,* Oxford University Press, 2006

Hopkins, Eric, *Industrialisation and Society, 1830–1951* Routledge, 2000

Hoppen, K. T., *The Mid-Victorian Generation, 1846–1886,* Oxford University Press, 2000e, S. J., *Gladstone and Disraeli,* Routledge, 2005

Mathias, Peter, *The First Industrial Nation, an Economic History of Britain 1700–1914,* Routledge, 1972

Matthew, H. C. G., *Gladstone 1809–1898,* Oxford University Press, 1997

McCord, Norman & Purdue, Bill, *British History 1815–1914,* Oxford University Press, 2009

Mitchell, B. R. and Deane, P., *Abstract of British Historical Statistics,* Cambridge University Press, 1962

Newbold, Ian, *Whiggery & Reform 1830–41: the Politics of Government,* Stanford University Press, 1990

Robbins, Keith, *The Eclipse of a Great Power, Modern Britain, 1870–1992,* Longman, 1994

Royle, Edward, *Modern Britain, A Social History 1750–1997,* Arnold, 1997

Stevenson, John, *Popular Disturbances in England, 1700–1832,* Longman, 1992

Williams, G. & Ramsden, J., *Ruling Britannia, a Political History of Britain 1688-1988,* Pearson, 1999

Websites

www.historyhome.co.uk
www.historyofparliamentonline.org
www.parliament.uk
www.visionofbritain.org.uk
www.bbc.co.uk/history/british
http://richardjohnbr.blogspot.com

Acknowledgements

The publisher would like to thank the following for permission to use their photographs:

Cover: Mary Evans Picture Library; **pxii**: SSPL/Science Museum/Getty Images; **pxiii**: AKG-images; **p2**: Private Collection/Bridgeman Art Library; **p3**: North Wind Picture Archives/Alamy; **p8**: Liszt Collection/Alamy; **p12**: (t) Saltram House, Devon, UK/National Trust Photographic Library/Bridgeman Art Library, (b) By kind permission of Viscount Coke and the Trustees of Holkham Estate, Norfolk/Bridgeman Art Library; **p13**: Liszt Collection/Alamy; **p14**: The Samuel Courtauld Trust, The Courtauld Gallery, London/Courtauld Institute of Art; **p16**: Private Collection/Bridgeman Art Library; **p24**: Image Asset Management/Age Fotostock; **p27**: Universal History Archive/UIG/Bridgeman Art Library; **p32**: Mary Evans Picture Library; **p34**: Private Collection/Bridgeman Art Library; **p35**: New Lanark Trust/SCRAN; **p37**: Bibliotheque Nationale, Paris, France/Archives Charmet/Bridgeman Art Library; **p41**: Courtesy of the Warden and Scholars of New College, Oxford/Bridgeman Art Library; **p42**: Private Collection/Bridgeman Art Library; **p47**: akg-images/Alamy; **p51**: Château de Versailles, France/Bridgeman Art Library; **p53**: Liszt Collection/Alamy; **p54**: National Museum of the Royal Navy/Zooid Pictures; **p56**: Private Collection/Look and Learn/Bernard Platman Antiquarian Collection/Bridgeman Art Library; **p61**: Ickworth House, Suffolk, UK/National Trust Photographic Library/Bridgeman Art Library; **p63**: Classic Image/Alamy; **p64**: The Trustees of the British Museum; **p68**: Look and Learn/Peter Jackson Collection/Bridgeman Art Library; **p72**: (l) Georgios Kollidas/123RF, (r) Apsley House, The Wellington Museum, London, UK/Bridgeman Art Library; **p74**: Private Collection/Look and Learn/Bridgeman Art Library; **p76**: Private Collection/Peter Newark Pictures/Bridgeman Art Library; **p77**: Private Collection/Bridgeman Art Library; **p83**: Hulton Archive/Getty Images; **p84**: National Museum Wales/Bridgeman Art Library; **p85**: Private Collection/Bridgeman Art Library; **p87**: M&N/Alamy; **p91**: Private Collection/The Stapleton Collection/Bridgeman Art Library; **p94**: Private Collection/Look and Learn/Illustrated Papers Collection/Bridgeman Art Library; **p98**: Manchester Art Gallery, UK/Bridgeman Art Library; **p102**: Private Collection/The Stapleton Collection/Bridgeman Art Library; **p104**: 2013 Culture Club/Getty Images; **p106**: Everett Historical/Shutterstock; **p107**: National Portrait Gallery, London, UK/Bridgeman Art Library; **p112**: Laing Art Gallery, Newcastle-upon-Tyne, UK/Tyne & Wear Archives & Museums/Bridgeman Art Library; **p114**: National Gallery Budapest/Dagli Orti/Art Archive; **p115**: Birmingham Museums and Art Gallery/Bridgeman Art Library; **p116**: Private Collection/Look and Learn/Bridgeman Art Library; **p124**: The Print Collector/Age Fotostock; **p126**: The Print Collector/Heritage-Images/Getty Images; **p130**: GL Archive/Alamy; **p134**: Rischgitz/Getty Images; **p136**: Classic Image/Alamy; **p137**: Mary Evans Picture Library; **p140**: Pictorial Press Ltd./Alamy; **p144**: Private Collection/Bridgeman Art Library; **p146**: Newport Museum and Art Gallery, South Wales/Bridgeman Art Library; **p147**: Private Collection/Bridgeman Art Library; **p149**: Museum of London, UK/Bridgeman Art Library; **p151**: The Print Collector/Alamy; **p153**: Hulton Archive/Getty Images; **p158**: Guildhall Library & Art Gallery/Heritage Images/Getty Images; **p159**: 2013 Culture Club/Getty Images; **p161**: De Agostini/G. Nimatallah/Getty Images; **p162**: Oldtime/Alamy; **p165**: Royal Agricultural Society of England, Stoneleigh, UK/Bridgeman Art Library; **p168**: Hulton Archive/Getty Images; **p172**: MCLA Collection/Alamy; **p173**: Joseph Swan/Zooid Pictures; **p178**: Ann Ronan Picture Library/The Print Collector/Heritage Images/Getty Images; **p179**: Hulton Archive/Getty Images; **p182**: The Print Collector/Getty Images; **p184**: National Galleries Of Scotland/Getty Images; **p187**: The Print Collector/Heritage-Images/Getty Images; **p191**: Mary Evans Picture Library/Alamy; **p196**: Mary Evans Picture Library; **p197**: Mary Evans Picture Library/Alamy; **p200**: Mary Evans Picture Library/Alamy; **p204**: Ann Ronan Picture Library/The Print Collector/Getty Images; **p205**: The Granger Collection/Art Archive; **p209**: Illustrated London News/Hulton Archive/Getty Images; **p212**: Image Asset Management/Age Fotostock; **p215**: Photo12/UIG/Getty Images; **p217**: Image Asset Management/Age Fotostock; **p218**: SSPL/Science Museum/Getty Images; **p221**: Science & Society Picture Library/Getty Images; **p222**: Science & Society Picture Library/Getty Images; **p228**: W. Brown/Otto Herschan/Getty Images; **p229**: Hulton Archive/Getty Images; **p232**: Pictorial Press Ltd./Alamy; **p233**: The Print Collector/Getty Images; **p240**: Ailsa Fortune; **p242**: Jeff Morgan 11/Alamy; **p244**: Science & Society Picture Library/National Media Museum/Getty Images; **p246**: Hulton Archive/Getty Images; **p249**: Mary Evans Picture Library

Artwork by OKS Typesetting.

We are grateful for permission to reprint from the following copyright texts:

 : *The Lion and the Unicorn*, published by Hutchinson. ard Aldous 2006. Reproduced by permission of The oup Ltd.; **Paul Bew**: *Ireland: The Politics of Enmity*, 103w from p.116. By permission of Oxford University Press;

Vernon Bogdanov: *The Monarchy and Constitution* (1995) 131w from pp.10–11. By permission of Oxford University Press; **Asa Briggs**: *The Age of Improvement* Longmans 1967 p.92–93. © Asa Briggs, 1959, 2000. Reproduced by permission from Taylor & Francis; **W. R. Brock**: *Lord Liverpool and Liverpool Toryism 1820 to 1827*, Cambridge Press (1941). Reproduced by permission of Cambridge University Press; **Richard Brown**: *Church and State in Modern Britain, 1700–1850*, Routledge, 1991, p153–4; **Hugh Cunningham**: *The Challenge of Democracy, Britain, 1832–1918*, Routledge © 2001 Taylor & Francis. Reproduced by permission of Taylor & Francis. **F. O. Darvall**: *Popular Disturbances and Public Order in Regency England* (1934) 103w. By permission of Oxford University Press; **P. Deane and W A Cole**: *British Economic Growth, 1688–1959*, Cambridge (1969); **John W. Derry**: *William Pitt* (1962). Reproduced with kind permission of B.T. Batsford, part of Pavilion Books Company Limited; **Nicholas C. Edsall**: *The Anti Poor Law Movement, 1834–44*. I p167–9 Manchester University Press (10 Sept. 1971). © 1971, Nicholas C. Edsall. Reproduced by permission of Manchester University Press; **Eric J. Evans**: *Political Parties in Britain, 1783–1867*, Methuen (1985). © 1985 Eric J. Evans. Reproduced by permission of Taylor & Francis; **Eric J. Evans**: *Sir Robert Peel, Statesmanship, Power and Party* Routledge, (second edition 2006). © 1991, 2006 Eric J. Evans; **Antonia Fraser**: *Perilous Question, the Drama of the Great Reform Bill 1832*, Weidenfeld & Nicolson (2013), © Antonia Frazer 2013. Reproduced by permission of Orion Books Limited; **Richard A. Gaunt**: *Sir Robert Peel The Life and Legacy*, I.B. Tauris (2010) Copyright © 2010 Richard A. Gaunt. Reproduced by permission; **William Hague**: *William Pitt the Younger*. Copyright © Canyon Research Ltd 2004. Reprinted by permission of HarperCollins Publishers Ltd; **R.M. Hartwell**: *The Industrial Revolution in England* © the Historical Association, London, 1965. Reproduced by permission; **Eric Hopkins**: *Industrialisation and Society: A Social History, 1830–1851*, © 2000 Eric Hopkins Routledge. Reproduced by permission of Taylor & Francis; **Peter Kirby**: *The Standard of Living Debate and the Industrial Revolution*, Refresh, issue 25, Autumn 1997; **Dick Leonard**: *Nineteenth Century British Premiers*, Palgrave Macmillan, © Dick Leonard 2008© Dick Leonard 2008. Reproduced with permission of Palgrave Macmillan; **Donald M. MacRaild and David E. Martin**: *Labour in British Society, 1830–1914*, first published in Great Britain, 2000 by MacMillan Press Ltd and in the USA, 2000 by St Martin's Press Inc. © Donald M. MacRaild and David E. Martin 2000. Reproduced with permission of Palgrave Macmillan.; **H. C. G. Matthew** (ed): *The Oxford Illustrated History of Britain* (1989) 181w from p.481. By permission of Oxford University Press; **B. R. Mitchell and P. Deane**: *Abstract of British Historical Statistics*, Cambridge, (1962). © Cambridge University Press 1988. Reproduced by permission of Cambridge University Press; **Norman McCord and Bill Purdue**: *British History 1815–1914*, (2007), pp93–94, 136, 159–161, 170, 198, 235, 237, 361, 373, 487. By permission of Oxford University Press; **Ian Newbould**: *Sir Robert Peel and the Conservative Party, 1832–1841: A Study in Failure? English Historical Review* (1983) XCVIII (CCCLXXXVIII): 529-557 doi:10.1093/ehr/XCVIII.CCCLXXXVIII.529, 153 words. By permission of Oxford University Press on behalf of English Histoarial Review; **J. H. Plumb**: *The Pelican History of England: England in the Eighteenth Century (1714–1815)*, (Penguin Books 1964) Copyright © J. H. Plumb, 1964. Reproduced by permission of The Glenfield Trust on behalf of the author's estate and Penguin Books Ltd; **Keith Robbins**: *The Eclipse of a Great Power Modern Britain 1870–1992*. © Keith Robbins, 1983, 1994. Reproduced by permission of Taylor & Francis; **Edward Royle**: *Modern Britain, a Social History, 1750–1997* Arnold © Edward Royle 1987, 1997. Reproduced by permission of Bloomsbury Publishing Plc.; **S.B. Saul**: *The Myth of the Great Depression*, Macmillan, (1985); **F. L. M. Thompson**: 'An Anatomy of English Agriculture' from *Land, Labour and Agriculture, 1700–1920: Essays for Gordon Mingay* '1991, Hambledon Continuum an imprint of Bloomsbury Publishing Plc. Reproduced by permission of Bloomsbury Publishing Plc.; **John Russell Vincent**: *The Formation of the British Liberal Party 1857–1868*. Barnes and Noble Books. Reproduced by permission of the author; Glyn Williams and John **Ramsden**: *Ruling Britannia A Political History of Britain 1688–1988*, pp134–5, Pearson. Reproduced by permission of Dr Sue Ramsden and Professor Glyn Williams; **Anthony Wood**: *Nineteenth Century Britain 1815–1914*, Prentice Hall Press: London, 1969 Reproduced by permission of Pearson Education Limited.

We have made every effort to trace and contact all copyright holders before publication, but if notified of any errors or omissions, the publisher will be happy to rectify these at the earliest opportunity.

The author would like to thank the following people: Kirsty Taylor, Sally Waller, Becky Ayre, Janice Chan, and David Fortune.

The publisher would like to thank the following people for offering their contribution in the development of this book: Sally Waller and Roy Whittle.

Index

A

Aberdeen, George Gordon, Earl of 154, 182, 183
abolition of slavery 105–7, 127, 138–9
Act of Union 18, 46, 77, 126, 157, 210
Addington, Henry 18, 52, 53, 58, 62
administration of government 17, 156–7
agents provocateurs 44
agriculture
  by 1783 27–8, 33
  1812-1832 85–7
  1832-1846 165–9
  by 1885 245–6
  depression in 224–5
  'golden age' 216–18
aldermen 7
American colonies 4, 15, 16, 105
Anti-Corn Law League 126, 149–50, 167, 207
Anti-Poor Law League 147–8
anti-slavery movement 105–7
appropriation 125, 130
artisans 38, 43, 66, 68, 193
Artisans' Dwelling Act 197, 229
Ashley, Lord Anthony 135, 136–7, 150, 204 *see also* Shaftesbury, Lord
Attwood, Thomas 114, 119, 124, 144, 145

B

Bank Charter Act 157–8
Bazalgette, Joseph 228
Bentham, Jeremy
  as radical 59, 104, 116
  as social reform campaigner 51, 137, 150
  and Utilitarianism 127, 128, 133
Bentinck, Lord George 181, 182
Bessemer process 220
Bonaparte, Napoleon 51, 52–5
borough members 5
Bright, John 148, 149, 188, 208, 209
Brunel, Isambard Kingdom 162
Bunting, Jabez 108
Burdett, Francis 59, 104
Burke, Edmund 42, 43, 48
business reforms 158–9
Butt, Isaac 211, 212
Buxton, Thomas 107

C

cabals 185
Cabinet, role of 4
Caird, James 216, 217
canals 26, 27, 164, 221, 222
Canning, George 61, 62, 71–2, 73, 107, 124
Canningite Tories 72, 73, 112, 124, 125
Cartwright's power loom 36
catechism, Anglican 134
Catholic Emancipation 18, 45–6, 63, 67–8, 73, 77–8
census information 22, 167, 227, 233, 248
Chadwick, Edwin 136, 150, 175, 205, 206
  legislation 135, 137, 156
Chartism 126, 132, 140, 143–6, 148, 206–7
City, the 14, 207
civil lists 2
civil service 191, 194
Clarkson, Thomas 138
class structure, changes in 31–3
coal industry 25, 84, 161, 219
coalition allies 52, 53
coalitions 4, 12, 18, 72, 73, 183
Cobbett, William 51, 105, 113, 116, 124
Cobden, Richard 148, 149, 182, 185
Coercion Act of 1833 125
Combination Acts 38–9, 66–7, 68, 177
combination in restraint of trade 38
Conservative Party 126, 130–2, 153–60, 247 *see also* Tories
constitutional monarchies 1, 2–4, 42, 127, 195
consumerism 33, 82, 121, 243
Continental System 52, 57, 58
Cooper, Lord Anthony Ashley *see* Ashley, Lord Anthony
Corn Laws 64–6, 76, 167–9, 216
Corporation Act 75
Corresponding Societies 39, 43, 44
cotton industry 23–5, 81, 83, 102, 222
countryside 28, 56, 96, 230–1, 248
county members 5
crime 7, 67, 76, 93, 174
Crofters' War 232
croppers 101–2

D

democracy 6–7, 113–21, 198–201, 239–41
depression 223–5

Derby, Edward Stanley, Earl of 181, 182, 183, 184, 189
disabilities placed on Roman Catholics 46, 75
Disraeli, Benjamin 181–2, 184, 193, 195–8, 222, 230
Dissenters 8, 43, 45, 66, 75, 185
divine right 2, 13
domestic system of production 24, 29, 34

E

East India Company 22
economy
  1783–1812 21–8
  1812–1832 76, 81–9, 119–21
  1832–1846 161–9
  1846–1885 215–25, 242
  under Lord Liverpool 68–9
  and railways 161–4
  reforms 156
  and war 53–6
education 134–5, 237–8
election, 1784 4, 13–15
enclosure 27–8, 33, 85–6, 165, 174
endemic poverty 33, 206
entrepreneurs 21, 26, 31, 218, 245
established order 41, 42, 108
Evangelicalism 128, 133, 232–4

F

factions 3, 8
factory legislation 135–7, 197, 237
famine 167, 168
Fenianism 207, 210–11
Fielden, John 144, 148, 152
financial reforms 15–17, 154–5, 159
First Lord of the Treasury 4
Five Towns 23
Fox, Charles James 4, 12, 43, 124
Foxite Whigs 124
franchise, changes to
  1783 5
  1832 Great Reform Act 116, 117–18, 198
  1867 Reform Act 199
  1884 Franchise Act 201, 213, 240–1
free-marketeers 135, 137
Free Trade 15, 87–9, 149, 169, 182, 218
freehold land 5
freemen 6
French Revolution 39, 41–5, 52
Friendly Societies 32, 38, 179, 208, 235

Index

G

George III   2, 4, 11–13, 46
Germany   224
Gladstone, William
   at Board of Trade   153–4, 164
   as leader of Liberal Party   186, 191, 198
   as Prime Minister   182, 183, 191–6, 222–3, 247
   reforms   193, 199, 200–1, 208, 210, 213, 241
   and trade unions   235, 236
'Gladstonian Liberalism'   191–2
GNCTU   143, 177, 235
Goderich, Frederick Robinson, Lord   72
Gordon, George see Aberdeen, George Gordon, Earl of
government
   c1783   1–6
   under Canning   71–2
   and democracy   198–201
   developing political organisation   181–8
   under Disraeli   195–8
   under Gladstone   191–5
   under Goderich   72
   under Grey   112, 124–5
   under Liverpool   61–9
   under Melbourne   125–6
   under Peel   154–7
   under Pitt   11–17
   political pressures on   41–9
   wartime pressures on   51–60
   under Wellington   72
Graham, James   129, 135, 154, 156
Great Depression   223–5
Great Reform Act   116–19, 120, 121, 143, 198
Grenville, William   18, 19, 53
Grey, John, of Dilston   81
Grey, Lord Charles   74, 112, 114, 117, 124–5
guano   165, 217

H

habeas corpus   44, 66
Hardy, Thomas   43, 44
High Farming   216–17
High Tories   63
Horrocks, John   23
housing backlands   173
Hudson, George   162, 163
humanitarianism   128, 133
Hunt, Henry   105
Huskisson, William   61, 63, 73, 74
   at Board of Trade   68, 76, 88, 167

I

18, 55, 66, 155, 192
our   139
f living and wages   36

Industrial Revolution (definition)   21
industrialisation
   1783-1812   21–3
   1812-1832   81–5
   1846-1885   218–19, 223–4, 243
   Great Depression   223–4
   social effects of   32, 91–5
Irish Famine   167, 168
Irish Nationalism   210–13
Irish Radicalism   147
Irish rebellion and union   45–6
iron industry   25, 81, 83, 163, 219

J

Jacobin spies   44
Jenkinson, Robert see Liverpool, Robert Jenkinson, Lord
joint-stock banks   88
Joint Stock Companies   158
journeymen   38, 39

K

Kay-Shuttleworth, James   135, 237
King's prerogative   4, 12

L

lack of political rights   32 see also universal suffrage
laissez faire principles   87, 188, 194, 198, 218
Lamb, William see Melbourne, William Lamb, 2nd Lord
landowners   32–3
leases   86
legislation
   by 1885   247
   under Disraeli   197
   factories   135–7, 197, 237
   under Gladstone   194, 195, 199–200
   under Lord Liverpool   64–7
   permissive   198
   under Wellington   75–6
Liberal Party   6, 185–8, 189, 191–3, 199, 207–8
Liberal Toryism   63, 71
Lichfield House Compact   126, 130
Liverpool, Robert Jenkinson, Lord   58, 61–9, 73, 87
living standards   36–7, 95–7, 172–3, 176–7, 197, 230
local democracy   6–7
Lower House   3
lower orders   3, 7, 47, 66, 248
Ludd, Ned   101
Luddites/Luddism   49, 57, 101–3

M

Mackinnon, William Alexander   56
magnates   23

Malthus, Thomas   **xiii, 22, 96**
masters   39
Meikle, Andrew   87
Melbourne, William Lamb, 2nd Lord   112, 124, 125–6, 185
mercantilism   15, 88, 93
Methodism   107–8
Metropolitan Police Force   76, 93, 174
mid-Victorian economic boom   215–16
middle class   3, 31–2, 117, 188, 204, 242
Mill, James   104, 111, 116
Mill, John Stuart   124, 188, 208, 247
ministers, role of   1
mixed constitutions   1
Monitorial schools   134
Municipal Corporations Act   141–2

N

Napoleon   51, 52–5
Napoleonic Wars   67, 82, 94, 96, 101
National Debt   11, 15, 55, 58
national democracy   6–7, 113–19, 198–201, 239–41
Navigation Acts   182
Neilson, James Beaumont   83
Nelson, Horatio   52
New Lanark Mills   34, 35, 109

O

Oastler, Richard   136, 137, 144, 155
Oath of Supremacy   75, 78
O'Connell, Daniel   72, 77–8, 126, 147, 157, 206
oligarchy   9
omnibuses   174
Orders in Council   54, 55, 56, 58
Owen, Robert   34, 108, 109, 144, 177

P

Paine, Tom   43, 47
Palmerston, Henry John Temple, Viscount   112, 182, 183, 186
parity   39
parliamentary reform   48–9, 113–16, 121, 207–10
Parliamentary representation   5–6, 104, 239–41
parliamentary train   164, 173, 174
parliamentary whips   129
Parnell, Charles Stewart   213
party realignments   181–4
paternalists   34, 109, 136
patrimony   73
patronage   1–2, 8, 14, 62, 187
payments in kind   96, 171
Peel, Robert

Index

and the Conservative Party 63, 123, 130–2, 169
as Home Secretary 67
Metropolitan Police Force 76
as Prime Minister 153–7
and railways 164
penny post 206
Perceval, Spencer 19, 53, 58
permissive legislation 198
philanthropy 128, 133
picketing 194, 235, 236
pig iron 25, 81, 224
Pitt, William
   anti-slavery movement 106
   impact of French Revolution 42, 43–4, 48
   impact of war 37, 52, 55
   Irish union 45–6, 77
   parliamentary reform 48–9, 62
   as Prime Minister 3, 4, 9, 11–19
Place, Francis 66, 111, 115, 144
political impact of war 52–3
political patronage 1–2, 8, 14, 62, 187
political system 1–9, 119–21, 181–5, 239–41
Poor Law Amendment Act 139–41, 143, 147, 148, 156
poor relief 33, 98
Portland, Duke of 19, 48, 53, 55
post-war economic slump 63
poverty, in towns and countryside 227–32
power, sources and uses 26–7
pragmatism 68
prerogative of the King 4, 12
Presbyterians 45, 46
Price, Richard 11, 22, 43, 47
principle of less eligibility 139
prosperity, in towns and countryside 227–32
protectionists 136, 137, 182, 188, 189
Protestant Dissenters 43, 72, 75
public health reforms 205–6

R

radical agitation 44, 104–5, 126
radicalism 8, 32, 46–8, 59, 124, 147
railway 'revolution' and economic growth 161–4
reactionaries 62
real wages 36, 37, 96, 97, 230–1
Redistribution of Seats Act 240
reforms, attitudes to under Liverpool 67–8
regional divisions 231–2
repression, attitudes to 67–8
republicans 44
restrictive legislation 46, 63
retrenchment 192
Ricardo, David 69, 108
Robinson, Frederick see Goderich, Frederick Robinson, Lord
Roebuck, John Arthur 124
Royal Commissions of Inquiry 133, 236
Russell, Lord John 75, 116, 125, 126, 182, 183

S

Sadler, Michael 136
seditious libel 43, 44, 66
self-help 188, 216, 234–5
September Massacres 43, 49
Shaftesbury, Lord 136, 151, 175, 204, 233 see also Ashley, Lord Anthony
Sharp, Granville 138
Shelburne, Lord 12
shipping 221, 222
sinecure offices 17, 62
Sinking Fund 11, 15, 55
Six Acts 66, 105
slavery, abolition of 138–9
Smiles, Samuel 234
Smith, Adam 15, 16
social campaigns 150–2, 203–5
social developments 31–40, 91–9, 119–21, 171–9, 227–37, 242–3
social impact of war 56–7, 105–7, 127
social reforms 133–42, 151–2, 194–5, 197–8
social unrest 63
socialism 108–9
Speenhamland System 33, 98, 139
spies 44, 103, 104
spinning 21, 25, 119
St Peter's Fields 66, 76
standard of living 36–7, 95–7, 172–3, 176–7, 197, 230
Stanley, Edward see Derby, Edward Stanley, Earl of
Stanley, Lord 125, 129, 154
status quo 8, 72, 102
statutes 2
steel industry 219, 245
Stephenson, George 84
Stephenson, Robert 162
strike action 38, 67, 235
Sunday schools 93, 134
Swing Riots 105, 112–13

T

tariffs 15, 88, 155, 224
temperance 194
Temple, Henry John see Palmerston, Henry John Temple, Viscount
tenement housing 172
tenures 86
Test Act 75
tied housing 174
Tories 7–9, 63, 73, 129–32 see also Conservative Party
'Tory Democracy' 195
towns 56, 171–4, 228–9
trade reforms 15–17, 158–9
trade societies 38, 39
trade unions 38, 176–7, 235–6
transport developments 173–4, 220–2
transportation of offenders 47, 67, 98, 102, 113

U

Ultra Tories 63, 72, 73
unemployment, cyclical 171, 174
union, Irish 45–6
unions 38, 176–7, 235–6 see also working-class movements
universal suffrage 112, 199
Upper House 3, 14
urban growth 171–4
urbanisation 171
Utilitarianism 116, 127, 128, 133

V

vested interests 137, 138, 208
vetoes 2
Victoria 247

W

war, impact of 51–60
Watt, James 26
Watt's steam engine 27, 55
weaving 25, 36, 119
Wellington, Arthur Wellesley, Duke of 63, 72, 73, 74, 78, 117
Whig Party 4, 7–9, 48, 111–13, 127–8, 130, 133–42
whips 129
Wilberforce, William 104, 106, 107, 138
Wilkinson, John 25
working-class discontent 97–8
working-class movements 178–9 see also unions
working conditions 33–5, 174–5

Y

yeomen 23
Young, Arthur 22

Topics available from Oxford AQA History for A Level

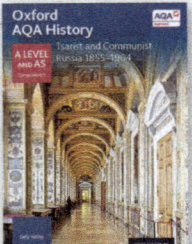  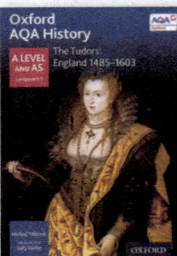 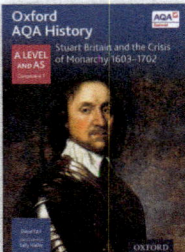   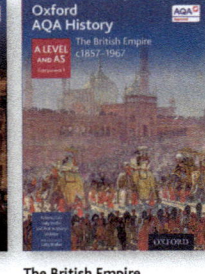

Tsarist and Communist Russia 1855–1964	Challenge and Transformation: Britain c1851–1964	The Tudors: England 1485–1603	Stuart Britain and the Crisis of Monarchy 1603–1702	The Making of a Superpower: USA 1865–1975	The Quest for Political Stability: Germany 1871–1991	The British Empire c1857–1967
978 019 835467 3	978 019 835466 6	978 019 835460 4	978 019 835462 8	978 019 835469 7	978 019 835468 0	978 019 835463 5

Industrialisation and the People: Britain c1783–1885	Wars and Welfare: Britain in Transition 1906–1957	The Cold War c1945–1991	Democracy and Nazism: Germany 1918–1945	Revolution and Dictatorship: Russia 1917–1953	Religious Conflict and the Church in England c1529–c1570	International Relations and Global Conflict c1890–1941
978 019 835453 6	978 019 835459 8	978 019 835461 1	978 019 835457 4	978 019 835458 1	978 019 835471 0	978 019 835454 3

 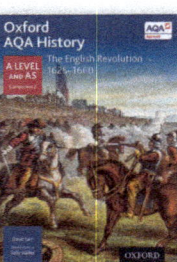   

The American Dream: Reality and Illusion 1945–1980	The Making of Modern Britain 1951–2007	The Crisis of Communism: the USSR and the Soviet Empire 1953–2000	The English Revolution 1625–1660	France in Revolution 1774–1815	The Transformation of China 1936–1997
978 019 835455 0	978 019 835464 2	978 019 835465 9	978 019 835472 7	978 019 835473 4	978 019 835456 7

eBook Available

Student Books and Revision Guides also available in eBook format

---

Revision Guides   RECAP  APPLY   REVIEW  SUCCEED

  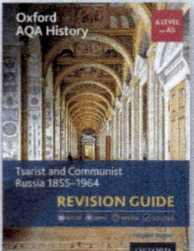   

The Tudors: England 1485–1603 Revision Guide	Democracy and Nazism: Germany 1918–1945 Revision Guide	Tsarist and Communist Russia 1855–1964 Revision Guide	The Making of Modern Britain 1951–2007 Revision Guide	The Cold War 1945–1991 Revision Guide	Revolution and Dictatorship: Russia 1917–1953 Revision Guide
978 019 842140 5	978 019 842142 9	978 019 842144 3	978 019 842146 7	978 019 843253 1	978 019 843252 4

Oxford AQA History for A Level Revision Guides offer step-by-step strategies and the structured revision approach of Recap, Apply and Review to help students achieve exam success.

Order online at www.oxfordsecondary.co.uk/aqahistory   **OXFORD**